Abandoning the Black Hero

ABANDONING THE BLACK HERO

Sympathy and Privacy in the Postwar
African American White-Life Novel

JOHN C. CHARLES

Rutgers University Press
NEW BRUNSWICK, NEW JERSEY, AND LONDON

LIBRARY OF CONGRESS CATALOGING-IN-PUBLICATION DATA

Charles, John C., 1968–
   Abandoning the Black hero : sympathy and privacy in the postwar African American white-life novel / John C. Charles.
     p. cm.
   Includes bibliographical references and index.
   ISBN 978-0-8135-5433-4 (hardcover : alk. paper)
   ISBN 978-0-8135-5432-7 (pbk. : alk. paper)
   ISBN 978-0-8135-5434-1 (e-book)
     1. American fiction—African American authors—History and criticism. 2. American fiction—20th century—History and criticism. 3. African Americans—Intellectual life—20th century. 4. Whites in literature. 5. Race in literature. I. Title.
PS374.N4C47 2012
813'.5409896073—dc23

                                                           2012005168

A British Cataloging-in-Publication record for this book is available from the British Library.

Copyright © 2013 by John C. Charles

All rights reserved

No part of this book may be reproduced or utilized in any form or by any means, electronic or mechanical, or by any information storage and retrieval system, without written permission from the publisher. Please contact Rutgers University Press, 106 Somerset Street, New Brunswick, NJ 08901. The only exception to this prohibition is "fair use" as defined by U.S. copyright law.

Visit our website: http://rutgerspress.rutgers.edu

Manufactured in the United States of America

THE AMERICAN LITERATURES INITIATIVE

A book in the American Literatures Initiative (ALI), a collaborative publishing project of NYU Press, Fordham University Press, Rutgers University Press, Temple University Press, and the University of Virginia Press. The Initiative is supported by The Andrew W. Mellon Foundation. For more information, please visit www.americanliteratures.org.

To my three mothers:
Patricia Ann Williamson Ghannam,
Barbara Lee Williamson, and
Constance Marion Alger

Contents

	Acknowledgments	ix
	Introduction	1
1	"I'm Regarded Fatally as a Negro Writer": Mid-Twentieth-Century Racial Discourse and the Rise of the White-Life Novel	22
2	The Home and the Street: Ann Petry's "Rage for Privacy"	55
3	White Masks and Queer Prisons	86
4	Sympathy for the Master: Reforming Southern White Manhood in Frank Yerby's *The Foxes of Harrow*	130
5	Talk about the South: Unspeakable Things Unspoken in Zora Neale Hurston's *Seraph on the Suwanee*	158
6	The Unfinished Project of Western Modernity: *Savage Holiday*, Moral Slaves, and the Problem of Freedom in Cold War America	182
	Conclusion	202
	Notes	211
	Works Cited	241
	Index	257

Acknowledgments

I want to start by thanking Rita Felski, Caroline Rody, Scott Saul, Lawrie Balfour, and Eric Lott for their invaluable insight, support, and time. I am very lucky to have had such phenomenal mentors and interlocuters. Eric in particular deserves special thanks for being willing to step in as my adviser when he was already overburdened and for helping me far beyond the call of duty when I needed it. Deborah McDowell also provided vitally helpful feedback in the earliest stages of this project.

As the years pass I realize more and more how blessed I was to study as an undergrad with several great professors at the University of Maryland, College Park: John Auchard, Lynn Bolles, Charles Caramello, Sharon Harley, Robert Levine (who also read and commented on the book proposal), Carla Peterson, David Wyatt, and Mary Helen Washington, who directed my undergraduate thesis. Christine R. Gray remains my first and greatest mentor.

This book also owes a great deal to the organizers and faculty of the Dartmouth Futures of American Studies Institute, the closest thing I've known to an intellectual utopia. I especially want to thank the organizers Donald Pease, Elizabeth Maddock Dillon, and Robyn Wiegman, as well as Colleen Boggs, Michael Chaney, Martin Favor, Eric Lott, and Alan Nadel. Over the years I received essential suggestions and encouragement from these faculty, as well as plenary speakers Robert Reid-Pharr, Kenneth Warren, Fred Moton, and Alan Wald. Two Futures faculty generously gave me the opportunity to present my work abroad: Winfried

Fluck at the John F. Kennedy Institute of North American Studies at the Free University of Berlin, and Donatella Izzo at the University of Naples, L'Orientale. I am also grateful to Donatella for opening her beautiful home to me in Rome during that trip.

In addition, this project benefited greatly at different stages from the insights of Rebecka Rutledge Fisher, Jay Garcia, Faith Elizabeth Gray, Daylanne English, Bryan Wagner, Emily Churilla, and Ken Parille. The faculty of the Higher Seminar in English Literature, Lund University, Sweden, were wonderful colleagues and a great audience, and Marianne Thormählen in particular took time out of her duties as dean of research in the humanities and theology to offer not only global feedback and encouragement, but also sentence-level edits that were unfailingly on the mark. Brigitte Shull offered much-appreciated early support for this project. Joanne van der Woude was kind enough to translate a review of the Dutch translation of Richard Wright's *Savage Holiday*—one of the only reviews in existence. Elisabeth Petry graciously provided me copies of her mother's working notes for *Country Place* as well as permission to quote from these notes.

Alex Lubin and Ken Warren read this work in its latest phases; I am profoundly grateful for their suggestions.

My colleagues at North Carolina State University have provided great support and friendship while I was finishing this book: Laura Severin, Sheila Smith McKoy, Sharon Setzer, John Kessel, Tom Lisk, John Morillo, Carmine Prioli, Tim Stinson, Jennifer Nolan-Stinson, Keely Byars-Nichols, Juliana Nfah-Abbenyi, Mary Helen Theunte, and Robin Dodsworth. I want to give special thanks to my department head, Antony Harrison, who has been a great leader in our department and a valued friend for the last several years. The College of Humanities and Social Sciences, and Dean Jeff Braden in particular, provided financial support on multiple occasions—including a Faculty Research and Professional Development Award—that enabled me to reduce my teaching load and to travel to numerous archives for material that was vital to the completion of this study.

I will always owe a great debt to Katie Keeran, my editor at Rutgers University Press, for her professionalism, patience, and especially her confidence in my project.

I want to thank my friends, far and near, old and new: Michael, Veronica, and Maximo Hudlow, Ron Blevins, Patrick "Chewie" Holland, Ken Parille, Finnie Coleman, Sara Håkansson, Marc Dudley, John "Bizzle" Begeny, Rebecca Walsh, Matthew Grady, Bruno, and Jennifer

Ho. So glad that you are my friends. Jen Ho deserves an extra shout-out not only for cooking me so many amazing meals, but also recommending that I read Percival Everett.

Christopher C. Nagle and Dona L. Yarbrough. Thank you for two decades of friendship. You were both there from the beginning.

Finally, I am grateful most of all for my family: Khaled Abu Ghannam, my brothers Thomas Daniel Guinther, Robert Swain Charles, and Michael Patrick Salvatore, and my grandparents James R. Williamson and Barbara Avelar Williamson.

My family has multiplied exponentially in the last year, as I was privileged enough to become part of the de Souza e Silva and Araujo clans. I finished writing this book in Rio de Janeiro and want to thank Nelson de Souza e Silva and Elizabeth Araujo not only for their kindness and generosity, but also for creating my beautiful and brilliant wife, Adriana Araujo de Souza e Silva. Thank you, Adriana, for all of your support, encouragement, and (tough) love; you were essential to the completion of this book.

Postscript: Thank you, Adriana, for bringing my son, Matteo de Souza e Silva Williamson, into this world as I was proofreading the page proofs of this work. A joyous ending and beginning.

Abandoning the Black Hero

Introduction

In 1946, a promising but little-known young black writer named Frank Yerby burst onto the literary scene with *The Foxes of Harrow*, a blockbuster southern historical romance with more than a few resemblances to Margaret Mitchell's *Gone with the Wind* (1936). Yerby's sprawling saga of the rise and fall of Irish immigrant Stephen Fox sold more than a million copies in its first year alone, was made into a feature film starring Maureen O'Hara, and soon made Yerby the best-selling black writer of all time—he would go on to publish thirty-three novels, all but three featuring white protagonists, with sales of more than 55 million copies. Yerby's spectacular success as an author of plantation romances marked a dramatic departure in his career, given that his short stories were still appearing in left-leaning periodicals and expressed a mood and vision that located him squarely within what was then known as the "Richard Wright School of Protest."[1] Yet his mastery of this historically racist literary genre was so convincing that the African American critic Blyden Jackson remarked in his review of *Foxes* that "the wheel is coming full circle. Eighty years after Emancipation, in an area where they have been most sensitive, on the high-voltage subjects of slavery and Reconstruction, *Negroes are finding themselves able to talk like white folks*" (30; emphasis added). Jackson's provocative phrasing begs the question—What does it mean for an African American novelist in midcentury America to "talk like white folks"?

But Yerby was not alone in this shift toward a focus on white life. In 1954, Richard Wright himself published *Savage Holiday*, a novel about a psychotic white insurance executive that bears no resemblance whatsoever to the school of racial protest fiction that he is credited with founding. What can we learn from Wright's decision to, in his words, "[abandon] the black hero proper" (Kinnamon and Fabre, *Conversations* 167)? Yerby's and Wright's novels are part of an extraordinary phase in the history of African American writing—the postwar rise of the "white-life novel,"[2] that is, novels by African Americans with white protagonists. Every major black novelist of the period wrote at least one white-life novel during these years, including Zora Neale Hurston (*Seraph on the Suwanee*, 1947) and James Baldwin (*Giovanni's Room*, 1956), as well as lesser-known yet pivotal figures such as Ann Petry (*Country Place*, 1947), Willard Motley (*Knock on Any Door*, 1947), and Chester Himes (*Cast the First Stone*, 1953).[3] With the exception of *Giovanni's Room*, now considered a foundational work in contemporary gay American literary history, these works have received little attention individually and virtually no discussion collectively, despite the fact that their authors are among the most influential voices in African American literary history. Moreover, these works break new ground in many respects—Yerby is the first black author to publish a southern historical romance (and to become a millionaire from writing); Hurston produced a New South "cracker" romance; and Motley advanced urban naturalist fiction by penning the first queer ghetto pastoral, *Knock on Any Door*, a best seller that was adapted as a film starring Humphrey Bogart in 1949. Chester Himes's powerful prison novel, *Cast the First Stone*, when placed alongside Motley's and Baldwin's white-life novels, reveals a crucial transition in the rise of the black queer novel, a claim that I take up in chapter 3. While these texts warrant study not only for their own individual interest and for their capacity to revise our understanding of the authors' careers, they also deserve attention collectively for what they bring to light about an understudied and undertheorized era in black literary history—the years immediately leading up to, during, and following the Second World War.[4]

These works have remained beneath our critical radar in large part because much of the scholarly apparatus that has developed in recent decades around African American literature presumes an overtly black subject and aims principally to identify various forms of what Henry Louis Gates calls a "signifying black difference."[5] To make matters worse, these novels further frustrate our readerly expectations by providing often sympathetic, and occasionally even sentimental, depictions of their white protagonists, thereby deviating from the unspoken critical dictum that literature by African Americans always registers a fundamentally dissident relation to the dominant culture. Claudia Tate sums it up this way: "[W]e require [black novels] and especially those of canonical status to foreground the injustice of black protagonists' persistent and contested encounters with the material and psychological effects of a racially exploitative distribution of social goods, services, and power" (4). And as Ross Posnock reminds us, "black intellectuals tend to fall outside categories and lose visibility when they are untethered from the race work that typically defines them" (26). Similarly, the expectation that black novels perform a narrowly defined notion of "race work" obscures the many forms of "work"—cultural, political, aesthetic, and racial—that the white-life novels do perform. Instead, the sympathetic orientation of these texts renders them problematic for our dominant critical narratives, even susceptible to suspicions of racial false-consciousness, what Langston Hughes famously termed "the urge to whiteness" within the race.[6] From this perspective, the white-life novel appears to express a racial-cultural *lack* and an acquiescence to and active perpetuation of white hegemony.[7]

However, those qualities that seem to render these works so inassimilable, and thus unserviceable, to our most familiar interpretive protocols may in fact signal alternative critical and creative projects. Rather than dismissing these works for failing to conform to our current preconceptions about black literary production, we could instead ask, how did these novels represent "white life" in mid-twentieth-century America? That is, how did they embody, locate, and historicize the lives of white people, and to what ends? How did they imagine the effects of "whiteness," understood as a racial ideology, on the lives of their characters? What does their appropriation of this privileged discourse enable them to do that they could not do with a focus on "black life"? What are the larger implications of a black author representing white subjectivity *sympathetically*? How might the white-life novel help us think differently about such vexed issues as the politics of racial performance and cross-racial identification and desire? In particular, how does whiteness enable the articulation of a range of otherwise unspeakable desires?[8] How might our attention to cross-racial identification and desire in these works bring to light what is disallowed and disavowed in our *current* critical practice? Finally, how might these African American fictions of white life shed new light on previously overlooked dimensions of racialized subjectivity in the mid-twentieth century?

My answers to these questions begin with an additional inquiry about historical context. Why do so many black authors choose to "abandon the black hero" for white protagonists at this particular historical moment; what is it about this period that makes the white-life novel a compelling option? The first white-life novel was published in 1890, alongside the rise of legal segregation; the subgenre then reappeared intermittently over the next few decades in works by Amelia E. Johnson, Paul Lawrence Dunbar, Charles Chesnutt, and William Attaway.[9] The post–World War II era, however, witnessed a proliferation of the white-life novel, signaling, I contend, the emerging crisis in that same racial regime. The relation between the postwar white-life novel and its larger sociopolitical circumstances has not been readily apparent because the texts do not reproduce those scenes of racial conflict that we typically associate with Jim Crow. Even so, they are nevertheless deeply informed by and intervene in the intense debates (and violent confrontations) taking place at this moment around the meaning of racial identity and the status of the color line.

These conflicts took shape in the literary arena most notably around the politics of representation. The creative and critical work of midcentury African American writers illustrates the extent to which the field of literary production was fundamentally stratified according to race, in many respects a scene of racial production with clear analogues and effects in the national imaginary and political life. As Ralph Ellison wrote in 1946, "perhaps the most insidious and least understood form of segregation is that of the word" (82).[10] The dominant culture's profoundly impoverished and vexed understanding of blackness produced a fictional landscape in which the "American Negro . . . emerges an oversimplified clown, a beast, or an angel." White American authors (as well as editors, publishers, and readers) continuously failed not only to imagine complex black subjectivity, but also to comprehend the degree to which their own identities and imaginations—racial, sexual, and national—were determined by the history of American race relations, and especially fixed and derogatory notions of blackness. In his review of Bucklin Moon's *Primer for White Folks*, Ellison puts it this way:

> For imprisoned in the deepest drives in human society, it is practically impossible for the white American to think of sex, of economics, his children or womenfolk, or of sweeping socio-political changes, without summoning into consciousness fear-flecked images of black men. Indeed, it seems that the Negro has become

identified with those unpleasant aspects of conscience and consciousness which it is part of the American's character to avoid. Thus, when the literary artist attempts to tap the charged springs issuing from his inner world, up float his misshapen and bloated images of the Negro, like the fetid bodies of the drowned, and he turns away, discarding an ambiguous substance which the artists of other cultures would confront boldly and humanize into the stuff of a tragic art. (*The Collected Essays of Ralph Ellison* 149)

Of course, white publishers were equally susceptible to these conscious and unconscious associations, and many black writers resented the extent to which the publishing industry's extremely narrow sense of black life fundamentally restricted the possibilities for black literary expression. "The Negro writer is not to be confined to the specious closed-off entity known as 'Negro literature,'" Richard Gibson argued. "The Negro problem, that is, the question of how to keep the Negro in his place, and Negro literature, which is the same problem removed to a cultural level, are creations of a caste-conscious white society" ("Color of Experience" 123). Hurston's well-known 1950 essay "What White Publishers Won't Print" argues that publishers' racial fixations created "THE AMERICAN MUSEUM OF UNNATURAL HISTORY"—an institution made up of racial and regional stereotypes, including an "American Negro exhibit" peopled with only two figures, both of which have shuffling feet and rolling eyes: "One is seated on a stump picking away on his banjo and singing and laughing. The other is a most amoral character before a sharecropper's shack mumbling about injustice. Doing this makes him out to be a Negro 'intellectual.' It is as simple as all that" (1160; capitalization in original). Black authors who wanted to move beyond these caricatures, either the "conservative" or the "liberal," were all too often met with rejection.[11] Just as African Americans were fighting to achieve new forms of social and political freedom—in terms of jobs, housing, voting rights, etc.—African American writers were searching for greater publishing opportunities and the freedom to express themselves outside preconceived notions about "the Negro" and "the Negro problem." As I describe in detail below, many black novelists responded to the social, political, and literary restraints of the era by drawing on the relative discursive freedom available for narratives focused on white characters—a move that enabled them to circumvent the publishing industry's continuing resistance to representing the full range of African American subjectivity.

But while we might look for these midcentury writers to launch a sustained assault on the wide-ranging, deleterious effects of white supremacy in American society (i.e., "protest"), the reader is disarmed, so to speak, on discovering that the authors are often as sympathetic in their treatment of white characters as they are critical. It is this positive affective relation that poses the greatest interpretive obstacle for a reconsideration of these works. For all their differences, most of these novels devote a significant amount of space to chronicling the suffering of their protagonists. This attention to white suffering should be read not as a naïve or cynical endorsement of white privilege but rather as a revitalization of the discourse of sympathy specifically as a means of resisting Jim Crow aesthetics. *Public* enactments of sympathy, especially in the eighteenth and nineteenth centuries, were performances typically reserved for the socially privileged as a means of symbolically reaching out to those less fortunate, including, in the United States, such socially disfranchised populations as the poor, the insane, Native Americans, and African Americans. As Chris Castiglia has argued, among antebellum reformers the capacity to be sympathetic represented not only evidence of, but even a precondition for, symbolic white citizenship, as the expression of sympathy functioned to establish one's public moral authority. By the mid-twentieth century, sympathy for *white* suffering represents for these authors not necessarily superiority, but certainly a civic equality and "identificational mobility within the national symbolic" that is historically the exclusive domain of the "already-enfranchised white subject."[12] The white-life novel authors were asserting a mobile range of identifications and an expansive moral and cultural authority as part of a critical project that far exceeded what the dominant culture had deemed appropriate or indeed possible for black writers during the segregation era. Contrary to the expectation that African American literary texts maintain a position of critical *exteriority* to whiteness, the at least partly sympathetic rendering of "white life" facilitated a move from what was often referred to as the "ghetto" of public discourse to its center; this move enabled the authors to speak as "insiders" on a range of vital public debates in contemporary American culture, including the legacy of slavery in contemporary battles over segregation, the changing status of racial and ethnic minorities, and the reformulation of gender roles and sexuality—especially in the wake of women entering industrial occupations during the war (e.g., the rise of Rosie the Riveter), the postwar domestication of white masculinity, and the increasing visibility of gay, lesbian, and queer sexualities.[13] Contemporary white reviewers of these works usually did not mention the author's race, and those who did tended to praise the writers for their apparently "neutral" tone and commitment to "Art" over politics—praise typical of the newly ascendant New Critical practice and anti-Stalinist liberal cultural criticism. And yet, however seamless their representations of "white life" may have appeared to contemporary readers, close attention to the figuring of white experience in these texts reveals that in no case did they simply reinstate the discourses of white privilege and authority—for example, white psyches, white families, and white social practices as "universal" loci of virtue, rationality, civilization, and heteronormativity. On the contrary, whether it is Hurston's depiction of the corrosive poverty and ignorance of backwoods Florida, or Motley's attack on unchecked state violence against Chicago's slum dwellers, or even Petry's and Wright's exploration of the moral chaos lurking beneath the bucolic surface of small-town America or behind the authoritative and respectable veneer of the "Organization Man," each of these novels produced non-normative, alternative imaginings of whiteness, or what could be called whiteness with a difference. This "difference" is frequently produced through the suffering of its protagonists, and this suffering ultimately serves a pedagogic function. The resolution of the narrative conflict often depends on the white protagonist, and implicitly the white reader, undergoing a kind of moral reform that frequently includes a symbolic repudiation of his or her possessive investment in whiteness. The white-life novel allows the authors to resist the pressure to endlessly restage "the Negro problem" and instead to offer an interrogation of "white problem(s)"—the authors admonish white America to look inward and "heal thyself."[14]

This shift is effected without overt recourse to what would most readily be recognized as "protest." As I argue in chapter 1, writers like James Baldwin, Zora Neale Hurston, and others believed that white liberal desire for protest was bound up, consciously or otherwise, with a desire for images of black subjection that ultimately functioned to reinstate white authority. Especially following *Native Son* (1940), the growing stream of white-authored, liberal protest novels on "the Negro problem," despite their progressive intent, reproduced racial asymmetries—the authors sacrificed complex black humanity in their attempt to dramatize the plight of Negroes and thereby elicit sympathy from white readers. Moreover, there was a widely shared sense among black writers that the situation was not necessarily remedied when the protest novel was authored by an African American. The racial obligation to protest, rather than expanding black discursive authority, was yet another form of racial imposition that functioned to curtail intellectual freedom by retethering African Americans to the all too familiar position of injured black subject pleading for white sympathy. "Now, as then," Baldwin declared, "we find ourselves bound, first without, then within, by the nature of our categorization [as victims of racial injustice]. And escape is not effected through a bitter railing against the trap; it is as though the very striving were the only motion needed to spring the trap upon us" ("Everybody's Protest Novel" 20). Years ahead of Foucault, Baldwin and his contemporaries asserted that racial protest fiction in particular, and the category "Negro Literature" more generally, operated as regulatory fictions that functioned as "incitements to Jim Crow racial discourse."[15]

White-life novels constituted one way to resist this incitement. They offered a means for black writers to talk back to the nation, and the world, without conforming to hegemonic ideas of what it means to "talk black." They expressed a desire for, and created the possibility of, access to reading publics not overdetermined by white supremacy. In this respect, the white-life novels can be seen to afford their authors a degree of "racial privacy." Racial privacy in this context connotes access to forms of social, political—and, most importantly for this study—authorial autonomy unconstrained by dominant-culture notions of race. In the realm of the literary, white writers had racial privacy insofar as their work was not restricted to "white" material and themes; midcentury black writers, on the other hand, were expected to confine their creative visions to alternately romantic or tragic versions of being "black in a white man's world." We can think of this as an intrusion on the authors' "privacy" insofar as literary texts (and creative acts more generally) are often deemed to be highly personal, even vital, acts of *self-definition, self-expression*, and even *self-realization*. To be expected by the literary establishment, and publishers in particular, to orient their self-expression *a priori* to narrowly defined hegemonic notions of blackness constitutes for these writers a distortion and disruption not only of their literary works, but of their unique personhood and personality, both of which are asserted and extended through their creative work. The category of "Negro Literature," as it was understood at this moment, simultaneously delimited the authors' individuality and bolstered white supremacy by rendering black selfhood little more than an effect of white power.

In lieu of black angels, clowns, jezebels, and monsters, the white-life novels generate authorial racial privacy by shifting the sympathetic gaze of their largely white readership *away* from suffering black "others" and *toward* troubled and troubling white subjects that often unsettle, disturb, and even queer normative understandings of "whiteness," and white heteropatriarchy in particular. Their examinations of white heteropatriarchy typically center on private, domestic spaces, and especially intimate relations—in other words, on signs and scenes of white privacy. At first glance, this focus on white privacy may seem an evasion of political and social critique, evidence of postwar disaffection with the social realism of the previous decade. However, white privacy was structured around hegemonic ideals of white heteropatriarchy, and these same ideals rationalized the violation of black privacy—including the authorial, but also obviously political, familial, and economic forms of privacy.[16]

Prior to the end of legal segregation, the maintenance of the color line was predicated on the systematic violation of black privacy by white-supremacist laws and practices.[17] In the first half of the twentieth century, social scientists legitimated these violations by depicting whiteness as a normative and privileged category in contradistinction to pathologized blackness, especially through theories of "dysfunctional" black domestic and intimate relations. "At the base of sociological arguments about African American cultural inferiority," writes Roderick Ferguson, "lay questions about how well African Americans approximated heteronormative ideas and practices embodied in whiteness and ennobled in American citizenship. For instance, African Americans' fitness for citizenship was measured in terms of how much their sexual, familial, and gender relations deviated from a bourgeois nuclear family model historically embodied by whites" (20). Candice Jenkins has also described the far-ranging repercussions of the "fiercely invasive body of myths that designate the African American community incapable of healthy intimate bonds. Black bodies, understood as sites of sexual excess and domestic ruin in U.S. cultural parlance, are thus doubly vulnerable in the intimate arena—to intimacy itself as well as to the violence of social misperceptions surrounding black intimate character" (44). African American racial protest fiction, such as Wright's *Native Son* and Petry's *The Street* (1946), attempted to counter these beliefs by highlighting black domestic strife specifically as a consequence of white supremacy, rather than as a symptom of racialized moral weakness. However, as I have suggested, these authors resented being expected to retell this narrative of black domestic destruction as their sole source of literary authority. Moreover, as their protest novels demonstrate, no one was more aware than they of the extent to which *white-supremacist* ideals of privacy, especially those pertaining to matters of family and intimacy, fueled systematic assaults on these same ideals in black communities—the need to protect white homes and women, of course, was among the most common justifications for slavery, segregation, and racial terrorism.[18] The authors under study here were perfectly aware that racialized public narratives about intimate relations were key vectors in determining citizenship and national belonging, and thus their fictional interrogation of white privacy functioned as a strategy for critically engaging with a key discursive source of racial (and sexual) oppression without having to reinforce notions of black abjection as a necessary part of that engagement.

Notwithstanding the role that the social sciences played in undergirding white supremacy, the white-life novel authors frequently drew on the work of social scientists in their narratives. It is important to recall that many social scientists were seriously concerned about the decline of white domestic life as well, especially following the Second World War. As I will show, the authors in this study tap into widespread contemporary concerns that the social disruptions of the war had imperiled the authority of white manhood, particularly in the domestic realm. Appropriating these discourses of white domestic crisis, the authors go on to show in varying ways how the ideals that underwrite normative white American identity *actually injure whites themselves*. These discourses enable the authors, therefore, to avoid reproducing "the Negro problem" and instead to problematize white heteropatriarchy. White manhood, traditionally conceived, was a problem, and a more inclusive and egalitarian future necessarily relied on its reconfiguration.

Accordingly, *Abandoning the Black Hero* intends to illuminate the ways in which the postwar white-life novel refuses the narrow boundaries allotted to "Negro literature," and instead voices a range of boundary-crossing identifications and desires that thwart the publishing industry's history of racial proscription and, by extension, enacts the incipient energies of the burgeoning civil rights movement. For these reasons, I submit that the postwar white-life novel should be seen not as a form of racial self-nullification and cultural disavowal, but rather as an overlooked strategy of critical agency and a means of exercising "freedom" and resistance within a deeply constricted social and literary field.

I want to make clear, however, that my grouping of these authors implies neither a racial essence nor a simple unity of politics and perspectives. Even granting the widely differing attitudes toward the meaning of race shared by these authors, each one self-identified as Negro or black, and all in their own way were fully cognizant of and deeply engaged with the effect of the color line on their writing—its potential subjects, themes, and critical and mass reception. Thus however much they wished to refuse its authority, all were acutely aware of the powerful limits attendant on being a "Negro writer" and chose their own strategy of negotiation precisely as authorial black subjects in midcentury America. Ken Warren points out that one of the effects of American racism, particularly during the Jim Crow era, was that black writers knew that their work would be viewed either "instrumentally" or "indexically":

> [N]o writer [during legal segregation] could operate indifferently either to the expectations that African American literature ought to contribute demonstrably to some social end [i.e., as *instruments* in the fight against Jim Crow] or to the belief that novels, poems, or plays constituted proxies for the status or the nature of the race as a whole [i.e., as *indices* of racial progress]. Writers could, and did, insist that their works be judged without regard to their identities and without reference to the political or social status of the black race, but the mere insistence was an acknowledgement of the pressure of these expectations. (*What Was African American Literature?* 13)

When the white-life novel first began to appear in significant numbers, contemporary critics typically applauded their arrival, framing the works indexically as auspicious signs of racial progress and portents of a new era of opportunity for black writers. In a 1950 landmark special issue of *Phylon* on the state of black writing in America, several leading African American authors and critics identified the white-life novel as evidence of the unprecedented "health" and "maturity" of black literature in general, and black fiction in particular.[19]

Langston Hughes singled these works out, stating that "the most heartening thing for me . . . is to see Negroes writing works in the general American field, rather than dwelling on Negro themes solely. Good writing can be done on almost any theme—and I have been pleased to see Motley, Yerby, Petry and Dorothy West presenting in their various ways non-Negro subjects" (Harris 268).[20] Hughes's assessment is all the more striking given that twenty years earlier, in his manifesto "The Negro Artist and the Racial Mountain," he chastised a "Negro poet" for aspiring to be simply a "poet." For these observers, the choice of "non-Negro subjects" implied much more than changing literary fashions. Several contributors went so far as to describe this development in black fiction as signifying a new measure of black liberation—as evidence of "freedom" from cultural, intellectual, and aesthetic "bondage" and thus as registering an important step away from the still onerous legacy of slavery. "In spite of the limiting and crippling effects of racial hypersensitivity and Jim Crow esthetics," the critic Hugh Gloster declared, "the Negro writer has gradually loosened the shackles that have held him in mental bondage for the past two centuries" (Harris 302). Other contributors echoed Gloster's sentiment, including the renowned scholar Alain Locke, who quotes Gloster approvingly in his own piece (Harris 318). Ulysses Lee drew on the discourse of freedom and slavery as well when he wrote: "The Negro artist is viewed as a man knocking at the door of American publishing houses, of American magazines, of American homes and minds. The great hope is that there will be ever widening opportunities for the writer to produce in freedom from racial bonds" (Harris 279). Lee's phrasing is apt. The white-life novelists attempted to create an opportunity to "produce in freedom from racial bonds" and to get their foot in the "door of American publishing houses" precisely by generating narratives centered on white "American homes and minds." And the novelist and critic J. Saunders Redding asserted that the white-life novel emerged from the antiracist principles of Roosevelt's New Deal coalition and the global fight for democracy in World War II: "And so the Negro, but more especially the Negro writer, found himself being liberated from racial chains by the very impulses which he had been reviled for feeling. With his liberation he could begin to see himself as in no fundamental way different and particular. He could begin to explain himself and his motives and his character in terms of conditioning forces common to all humanity.... He began to see that the values were human, not racial. And he began to prove this by testing them in creatures of his own imagination who were not Negro" (Harris 305).[21] A year earlier, in an essay called "The Fall and Rise of Negro Literature," Redding identified Yerby and Motley, along with Margaret Walker and Chester Himes, as evidence that black writers are "creating for themselves a new freedom.... Writing by American Negroes has never before been in such a splendid state of health" (49).[22]

We can better appreciate the kind of indexical work these comments are performing if we consider them in light of Du Bois's lament, in 1913, that the "time has not yet come for the development of American Negro literature" because "economic stress is too great and the racial persecution too bitter to allow the leisure and the poise for which literature calls" (qtd. in Warren, *What Was African American Literature?* 11). In contrast, the postwar white-life novel was welcomed by these critics precisely because of its "poise," demonstrated by the authors' ability to, in Blyden Jackson's phrasing, "talk like white folks." I take Jackson and his fellow critics to mean that the white-life novels evince no signs of racial injury, that the works offer a balanced (not partisan) perspective, and, above all, do not express what Jackson describes as "exaggerated self-consciousness" and what Hugh Gloster calls "racial hypersensitivity." They are taken as signs of authorial self-possession that connote not just increasing distance from slavery in time, but the prospect that African Americans as a race are one step closer to being "free" from slavery's enduring afflictions—psychic, political, and otherwise.

Not all critics were excited about the rise of the white-life novel, though. Black communist intellectuals, for example, held attitudes toward the white-life novel that were decidedly mixed. They denounced Jim Crow in publishing (in terms of form, content, or numbers) and endorsed what Doxey Wilkerson termed the *"right* of Negro artists to master any cultural discipline and to deal with any subject matter, including non-Negro themes" (21; emphasis in original). They vigorously supported representations of progressive interracialism and remained committed to social realism, though they overlapped with figures like Baldwin and Hurston in their critique of what Lloyd Brown called the "Wright-Himes school" of racial protest, which depicts "a narrow range of frenzy, shock, brutality, frustration, in which the Negro character is reduced to an inhuman, helpless victim" ("Which Way for the Negro Writer? II" 52). Wilkerson cautioned, however, that the "Negro artist who aspires to be 'as good as any other' (or even better!) would do well to understand that the high road to his goal lies, *not in self-negation*, but in the full and honest interpretation of his own consciousness—through the expression of those memories, ideas, sentiments and aspirations which constitute the special psychological make-up of the Negro people" (22; emphasis added). Black communists castigated mainstream black critics, such as the contributors to the *Phylon* special issue, for appearing to encourage African American writers to abandon Negro themes (and implicitly their racial identity and history) in favor of "universalism." As Brown put it, "The trouble with Negro literature, far from being the alleged 'preoccupation' with Negro material, is that *it has not been Negro enough*—that is, it has not fully reflected the real life and character of the people" (54; emphasis in original).[23]

The critic Philip Butcher also joined the doubters. He observed that "the trend toward raceless authorship seems a loss to the Negro and to American literature, which would profit most if the skills of our writers were turned on the aspect of American life they know best and which is so much in need of major, artistically mature spokesmen"

(115). Butcher's cautionary remarks anticipate the shift toward increasingly negative and even hostile attitudes expressed by critics toward the white-life novel.

The initial enthusiasm generated by the appearance of these works soon dissipated in the face of shifting political and cultural tides. Julian Mayfield and others cautioned black writers against appropriating "that great-power face" known as whiteness, suspecting that it was leading to "absorption into the mainstream of American life" and thus "oblivion" (75). Probably the best-known evaluation comes from Robert Bone, who, like Butcher, dubbed these works "raceless," an appellation that leaves whiteness unmarked. Bone identifies the motive behind these texts as "an understandable but unsophisticated desire for an 'integrated' art" and a misguided need of the black writer to "demonstrate his cosmopolitanism by writing of the dominant majority" (168). For Bone, the white-life novel emerged from a cultural inferiority complex in which the authors' central objective was to prove their artistic competency to white people by writing about whites.

Bone's damning assessment has echoed throughout the years, intensifying with the arrival of the Black Aesthetic in the 1960s. Although the impulse to exploit literature's privileged public status in the service of producing a redemptive and empowering discourse of blackness has existed in various forms since the beginning of black American literary production, this project was never more urgent than during the Black Arts movement. Artists, activists, and intellectuals called for, in the words of Addison Gayle, a leading Black Arts critic, "a means of helping black people out of the polluted mainstream of Americanism." Gayle argued that "[t]he problem of the de-Americanization of black people lies at the heart of the Black Aesthetic. . . . The question for the black critic today is not how beautiful is a melody, a play, a poem, or a novel, but how much more beautiful has the poem, melody, play, or novel made the life of a single black man? . . . To be an American writer is to be an American, and for black people, there should no longer be honor attached to either position" (1917). This categorical rejection of "American" writers and "American" identity represents in part a response to the tendency of the previous generation of black artists and intellectuals to invoke the "American Creed," its principles of democracy and freedom, as emancipatory discourses. Arthur Davis summed up the attitude of the Black Arts movement toward the white-life novel when he wrote: "[T]he principal tenets of black nationalism, in their very essence, negate the paramount aim of the integrationist writer, which is to *lose* himself in the American literary mainstream" (124; emphasis added).[24] Davis's phrasing suggests that the "self" that would be lost in the mainstream would be one's racial "self," presumably the core of one's identity. For this generation, the white-life novels represented cultural symptoms of internalized oppression and a failure of "race consciousness" (i.e., racial pride).

The generation of scholars that emerged after the Black Arts movement has been far less invested in distinguishing black literature from American literature, but equally invested in identifying specific and "authentic" forms of black particularity. Houston Baker and Henry Louis Gates, influential voices in the efforts during the 1980s to codify a black literary tradition, both identify the "vernacular" as the most authentic site of blackness. Baker proffers a vernacular "blues matrix,"[25] while Gates charges critics of African American literature with the study of "the black vernacular tradition . . . [in order] to isolate the signifying black difference" ("Canon-Formation" 27).[26] To these efforts we can add the continuing proliferation of critical and creative perspectives that aim to identify the multifaceted and intersectional nature of black subjectivity produced in African American literature and culture, including meditations on black masculinity, as well as queer, feminist, postmodern, transnational, and diasporic discourses of blackness.[27] What all of these critical perspectives share in their approach to black literature, however, is the unqualified assumption that black texts focus explicitly on black experience—and this holds for even the most thoroughgoing poststructuralist and anti-essentialist critics. This focus makes sense for a variety of reasons, not the least of which is that the vast majority of novels by black authors have black protagonists. However, the effect of these presumptions is that the white-life novel appears irrelevant to black literary history.[28]

Perhaps more surprising is that the white-life novel has continued to remain obscure even after the rise of critical whiteness studies, a trend that has also led to heightened interest in African American perspectives on whiteness.[29] In 1998, for example, David Roediger edited a collection of fiction and nonfiction entitled *Black on White: Black Writers on What It Means to Be White*, and in 2000, Jane Davis published *The White Image in the Black Mind: A Study of African American Literature*.[30] Virtually absent from these and numerous other studies on whiteness are the postwar white-life novels. It may be that Roediger's and Davis's studies exclude these works because they do not easily accord with their position that when African American authors write about whiteness their central concern is to attack white supremacy, exposing its hypocrisy, self-delusion, and myriad contradictions.

For example, Roediger's introduction pointedly rejects the racist assumption that blacks do not know or see whites, arguing that, on the contrary, blacks of necessity and circumstance often possess a quite intimate knowledge of whites. His approach mirrors that of bell hooks in her influential essay "Representing Whiteness in the Black Imagination"; both authors emphasize those representations of whiteness "[that emerge] as a response to the traumatic pain and anguish that remains a consequence of white racist domination" (hooks 64). Roediger and hooks concur that whiteness functions in the black imagination primarily as terror. Jane Davis's final assessment is even more clear: "According to the tradition of how whites are understood by many black writers, whites are hypocritical, defensive, in denial, arrogant, ignorant, fake, crafty, passive-aggressive, cunning, sneaky, self-satisfied, back-stabbing, silencing, and dishonest" (148). All three of these studies focus exclusively on black critiques of white supremacy, with no consideration of how the texts respond to contemporary historical debates, and with no allowance for the more ambiguous implications of such phenomena as cross-racial identification and sympathy—phenomena that are regularly considered in examinations of white appropriations of blackness.

Conversely, the present study argues that the function of whiteness in postwar white-life novels is highly various, often contradictory, and historically determined. Rather than focusing exclusively on singling out moments of dominant-culture critique in these works, I am equally concerned with exploring moments of sympathy and identification; this double focus allows me to consider how these writers construct their vision of American and Western culture, as Americans and Westerners, while also negotiating and contesting the racial order that attempts to construct them as somehow outside and beyond "normal" national culture.[31] Moreover, attention to sympathy in these works may be helpful in expanding ongoing discussions of social and political *agency* in African American culture beyond familiar, and somewhat limiting, notions of rebellion and resistance. In this respect, careful consideration of the white-life novel may foster a more nuanced understanding of the true complexity of racialized subjectivity, including those dimensions that do not necessarily resolve cleanly with the political desire and orientation of African American studies as it is currently configured.

One final note on a key term. Although I attend to moments of sympathy throughout the course of this study, I do not consider this a work *on* sympathy, per se, and do not intend to present a systematic history of the concept. Rather, I recur intermittently to the notion of sympathy to take advantage of the concept's ability to highlight certain qualities and dimensions of the authors' relation to their subject matter, their audiences, and the publishing industry, among other things. As Tanja Vesala-Varttala notes, the term (Gr. *sympatheia*) originally denoted "suffering with." Over time, however, its meanings have moved gradually toward "feeling with" (31).[32] "Fellow-feeling entails the capacity to enter into or share the other's feelings or suffering," Vesala-Varttala explains, "and the overall attitude involved in such a participatory process is regarded as positive and favourable, consisting of conformity, agreement, approval, and general harmony of disposition." Sympathy is most commonly enacted through *identification* with the other. Identification with and sympathy for suffering others was often considered an altruistic gesture; in Lauren Wispé's phrasing, sympathy was typically seen as "the opposite of ego gratification" (80). Many recent analyses of sympathy, however, tend to focus on illuminating the degree to which acts of sympathy historically have been more self-affirming than selfless. Moreover, though sympathy is avowedly egalitarian in its intention, it may also have the effect of bolstering rather than eliminating hierarchy and difference—a dynamic that is particularly evident in the contexts of slavery and colonialism. Amit Rai has argued that in eighteenth- and nineteenth-century Britain and its colonies, sympathy "was a paradoxical mode of power. The differences of racial, gender, and class inequalities that increasingly divided the object and agent of sympathy were precisely what must be bridged through identification. Yet without such differences, which were differences of power, sympathy itself would be impossible: In a specific sense, sympathy produces the very inequality it decries and seeks to bridge" (xviii–xix). For Rai, sympathy functioned as a mode of what Foucault termed "governmentality," as it not only identified but produced populations in need of benevolence, surveillance, and intervention.[33]

Both the democratic and the disciplinary notions of sympathy are relevant to this study. For example, I will suggest that the sympathetic representations of white life in these novels that indicate a sense of "conformity of feelings, inclinations, and temperaments," as well as the idea of a "community of feeling," can, at times, profitably be seen as a refusal of white-supremacist suppositions of absolute black difference and separation—these attitudes of course rationalized Jim Crow and other forms of state and civil exclusion, not to mention everyday terrorism and violence. Similarly, if "fellow feeling" requires "the fact or capacity of *entering into* or sharing the feelings of another or others," then sympathy in the white-life novels can also be seen as performing a kind of discursive mobility that defies social and cultural boundaries, suspends (momentarily) hegemonic asymmetries, and enacts creative and critical agency. To this end, I attend to the ways in which sympathy connotes more than feelings, highlighting the degree to which it also conveys penetrating insight and boundary-crossing perspicacity, as is suggested in the following observations about James Baldwin by the critic Isaac Rosenfeld in a letter of reference for a Rosenwald fellowship: "I value him as a man, a friend and a writer for his great personal dignity and understanding. . . . He has a sympathy, rare in the rarest of men, that can penetrate outward disorder to the inner meaning, where the fact that men suffer degradation, and the significance for human culture of that degradation, are one. . . . It is an immediate, painful perception. It is this which gives him his right to say 'we,' 'our,' when he speaks for both Negroes and for America; he has instinctively. I know of no one with greater authority to speak both the part and the whole" (qtd. in L. Jackson, *Indignant Generation* 265). Given that "the Negro" and "the Negro writer" were regularly faulted for having too parochial a vision, the stakes regarding a black writer's capacity for sympathy were high indeed. Finally, attention to sympathy has also helped me consider how affect functions within these novels, which in turn illuminates previously overlooked aspects of how these writers work within and at times beyond the racialized spaces of enunciation that were readily available at the time.

* * *

The first chapter describes the interlocking historical, political, intellectual, and cultural phenomena that contributed directly to the rise of the postwar white-life novel. In particular, I describe how the Popular Front (a broad coalition of leftist and centrist groups united against fascism) played a crucial role in the rise of protest fiction, and in the careers of the white-life novelist themselves, both in terms of publishing venues that were part of the Popular Front cultural infrastructure, as well as in terms of key concepts, such as "the people" and critical Americanism. The Popular Front gave rise to the white-life novel in another way too—critical reaction. This chapter concludes with a discussion of critiques by Richard Gibson, Ralph Ellison, Hurston, and Baldwin of the disciplinary effects inherent in the white liberal demand for protest fiction, which they deemed overly reliant on pessimistic and misleading sociological discourses about "the Negro." These critiques voice the widely shared sense of dissatisfaction that contributed to the appeal of the white-life novel as a compelling alternative for critical and creative action beyond the space of the injured other.

Chapter 2 situates Ann Petry's white-life novel *Country Place* within the context of her early career—specifically within the remarkably productive four-year span of 1943 to 1947. By reading this novel alongside her first novel, *The Street* (1946), and two contemporaneous short stories, "In Darkness and Confusion" and "The Bones of Louella Brown," I reveal a unifying dialectic in her "black" and "white" fiction from this moment. I argue that her "black" protest fiction, which is often called "sociological," is deeply engaged with questions of privacy and domesticity and that her white "domestic" novel, which is usually considered more private and less sociological, is fundamentally committed to revising public meanings of race. *Country Place* (1947) in particular enacts a kind of racial privacy both for Petry and the one black character in the novel, Neola, by turning away from a focus on the harmful effects of white oppression on the black community. Instead, *Country Place* sympathetically foregrounds the suffering of its two main characters, the jilted young husband, Johnnie Roane, and the aging matriarch, Mrs. Gramby. Their suffering is redeemed, paradoxically, when the ancestral home, Gramby House, is willed to Neola and the other servants, all of whom are nonwhite minorities. This act symbolically refigures the content of white patriarchal privilege, not only in the Gramby household but in the town and, implicitly, in the nation. Above all, Petry underscores how female sympathy—particularly between white and black women—powerfully disrupts white masculinist exploitation of black female bodies. Hence the desire for racial privacy is also bound up with a desire for sexual privacy.

While Petry's critique foregrounds women's sympathetic ties, Willard Motley, Chester Himes, and James Baldwin insist that love *between men* is a powerful weapon of resistance. Again, racial and sexual privacy are interwoven, though in this instance whiteness affords a symbolic authorial distance from what was considered at the time an unspeakable desire. In chapter 3, Motley's *Knock on Any Door*, Himes's *Cast the First Stone* (1952), and Baldwin's *Giovanni's Room* all tap into the midcentury explosion of discourse around the alleged decline of white American manhood, a decline most alarmingly signaled by the increasing visibility and incidence of male homosexuality. The authors employ these discourses, yet they do so in order to revise, rather than reinstate, the hegemonic stature of straight white manhood. Each work suggests that the masculine ideals of autonomy and self-mastery are achieved not through isolation and the domination of others, but precisely through sympathetic and rebellious connections with those deemed "other," through forms of queer relationality. All three white male protagonists suffer extensively, but their suffering becomes a source of triumph if they are courageous enough to repudiate the state-sponsored violence intended to reinforce white heteropatriarchy. This recasting of same-sexuality as a site of masculine regeneration is unprecedented in the African American literary tradition, and it marks these texts as crucial forerunners of modern black queer fiction.

Chapter 4 explores how Yerby's attempts to master the southern historical romance through a sympathetic and nationalist reformation of southern white manhood are destabilized by a frustrated desire for redeemed black manhood. I describe how Yerby utilizes democratic and nationalist Popular Front discourses to critique the white-supremacist foundations of the genre in general, and Margaret Mitchell's *Gone with the Wind* (1936) in particular. The racially inclusive Popular Front discourses create an alternative frame for Yerby to rethink southern manhood beyond racism, though not beyond patriarchy. In the second half of the chapter, I investigate the subtle yet disruptive effects of Yerby's vexed personal investment in traditional notions of manhood, particularly his sympathetic portrait of the novel's protagonist, Stephen Fox. Yerby indulges hypermasculinist fantasies forbidden him as an African American man by imaginatively inhabiting the role of the white plantation lord, the ultimate embodiment of domestic and erotic privilege. This problematic identification and figurative return to slavery ultimately produces an extremely ambivalent novel, one that expresses both intense longing and resentment—longing for the seemingly unqualified privilege of white masculinity, and veiled resentment of its oppressive effects on black masculinity. *Foxes* illustrates how for Yerby sympathy is a strategy powerful enough to take on a profoundly racist literary tradition, yet insufficient for managing the pain of racialized emasculation.

My fifth chapter reads Hurston's last published novel, *Seraph on the Suwanee*, as a southern romance, though one updated for the New South and set among the "crackers"—that is, among poor whites. Here, too, southern interracial conflict short-circuits the ameliorative capacity of sympathy. I argue that Hurston attempts to reconcile fictively the profound social ills that plague her region while also maintaining a dignified mode of dissent—one not predicated on black suffering. She ends up producing a utopian plantation romance, marked above all by interracial sympathy. The protagonist's husband, Jim Meserve, represents the all-powerful southern white man as the head-of-household who protects and provides for his wife, children, and African American labor force. Hurston's folksy romance is riven with strife, however, due to the "primitive" and ignorant "crackers" who stand in the way of New South progress. In a bid for racial privacy, Hurston displaces the negative qualities usually associated with African Americans onto the poor whites. This move allows her to avoid enrolling in what she derisively referred to as the "sobbing school of Negrohood" and thereby avoid producing black suffering for white liberal consumption. Hurston's contemptuous representation of the "crackers" derails her attempts to deploy southern interracial sympathy, as she obliquely expresses the rage that she steadfastly rejected throughout her career. *Seraph* indirectly yet clearly voices what Hurston most wanted to disavow—that slavery's brutal legacy lives on in the South and continues to determine the lives of African Americans. The real-world failure of southern interracial sympathy poisons Hurston's southern pastoral.

Chapter 6 considers Wright's *Savage Holiday* (1954) in the context of his postexpatriation search for aesthetic and intellectual freedom beyond the reductive labels of mid-twentieth-century American racial and political discourse. Wright wanted to continue his analysis of race in the United States without being remanded to racial protest or to a simplistic political position in the emergent Cold War—either pro–United States or pro–Soviet Union. I argue that *Savage Holiday* should be seen as both an exploration of white (de)privation—the collapse of white racial privacy—and an attempt to protect his own racial privacy as an author. Wright employs a psychoanalytic and existentialist framework to displace "the Negro problem" while simultaneously interrogating white racial privacy (i.e., whiteness as normative, unmarked, and the fount of rationality and self-possession). He frames *Savage Holiday* as an existentialist "family romance" that draws on contemporary theories of white familial disorganization and a critique of what was known as "the organization man." I bring *Savage Holiday*'s previously overlooked existentialist orientation to the fore by juxtaposing it with Wright's second novel, *The Outsider*, published one year earlier. *The Outsider* functions as a key to decoding *Savage Holiday*'s larger racial and political argument, which contends that Western modernity has created the conditions for absolute personal freedom, but that there remain many "moral slaves" who cannot tolerate this freedom and instead cling to "savage" racial, religious, and political practices. Wright advocates embracing modernity's opportunities for authentic self-creation and for building sympathetic "bridge[s] from man to man." Attention to these works reveals Wright as a nonaligned radical American artist generating a space of critique "outside" the disciplinary loci of "Negro Writer" and the polarities of Cold War discourse.

1 / "I'm Regarded Fatally as a Negro Writer": Mid-Twentieth-Century Racial Discourse and the Rise of the White-Life Novel

> *Interviewer:* "Can a Negro ever talk about anything but being a Negro?"
> *James Baldwin:* "I get so tired of black and white, you know, so tired of talking about it, especially when you can't get anything across. What you have to do, I suppose, is invest the vocabulary with something it doesn't contain yet. Don't you see what I'm trying to do? I'm trying to find another word besides Negro to say what I mean, and I can't use tragedy."
> —JAMES BALDWIN, *Disturber of the Peace*

The interwar years were ones of hope and frustration for African American authors. Although figures such as Paul Laurence Dunbar, Charles Chesnutt, Langston Hughes, Zora Neale Hurston, and Jean Toomer, among others, had already achieved minor critical recognition in the American literary establishment, the publication of Richard Wright's *Native Son* constituted a watershed moment in black American writing. As Irving Howe (in)famously declared: "The day *Native Son* appeared, American culture was changed forever. No matter how much qualifying the book might later need, it made impossible a repetition of the old lies. In all its crudeness, melodrama, and claustrophobia of vision, Richard Wright's novel brought out into the open, as no one ever had before, the hatred, fear, and violence that have crippled and may yet destroy our culture" (101). Whatever else one thinks of the accuracy of Howe's analysis, his assertion does speak to the general agreement that *Native Son*, for good or ill, was an extraordinary milestone in black letters. Although the debate over the work's aesthetic merit and representational politics has yet to be resolved, if nothing else, *Native Son* made Wright the first black American writer to actually make a living from creative writing, even though black Americans had been publishing for more than 170 years.[1] Five years later, Wright once again achieved popular and critical acclaim (as well as igniting another round of contentious and ongoing debate) with his autobiography, *Black Boy*, solidifying his status not only as the preeminent African American author, but arguably the most highly regarded black writer in the world. His success was soon followed by works from several promising new voices, including Petry, Himes, and Ellison, among others, which, despite their obvious differences, led critics to proclaim the emergence of a "Richard Wright School of Protest Fiction." Almost as soon as critics named this "school," however, several black writers—including Wright himself—began resisting what they perceived to be its disciplinary presumptions and effects, suggesting that *Native Son* had *not* brought about a change in American culture, but had possibly even reaffirmed the status quo and, in certain respects, rendered a great disservice to the "Negro writer" by narrowing her authorized field of expression. As Lawrence Jackson has argued, "after Richard Wright, black writers could no longer be easily ignored as culturally irrelevant or commercially moribund, but the positing of special categories and automatic racial lineages threatened to continue the confinement of black writers to artistic ghettoes" ("Birth of the Critic" 349). The critical and popular embrace of Wright's work has led many commentators, then and now, to overlook the extent to which Wright himself still felt that dominant-culture attitudes fundamentally delimited his prospects as a writer.[2]

Consider, for example, the following comments made in 1944 by a highly respected and avowedly sympathetic white intellectual, Harry Overstreet, on the proper role of the Negro writer.[3] In the widely read mainstream *Saturday Review of Literature*, Overstreet declared that "The Negro writer of fiction . . . is not free to write what he pleases. Such freedom is reserved for whites" (5). According to Overstreet, the Negro writer has no choice but to function as spokesperson, helping white America to "like" the Negro and learn what the group has to offer what he terms "our culture": "It may be that much of value is to be found beneath the surface appearance of the Negro [which Overstreet earlier defines as "gaiety, devil-may-care, frustration, improvidence"]. Or it may be otherwise. Perhaps the word 'primitive' is the only word that will properly describe him. Perhaps in his very essence he is 'savage' and will so remain. If this is so, we ought to know it, for it will make the course of the Negro problem run more smoothly, even if less hopefully for the Negro." Thus we can see even at such a late date liberal white scholars unself-consciously professing ignorance of anything beneath the plainly unimpressive "surface appearance of the Negro." Overstreet is equally prepared to believe that "the Negro" may be essentially "primitive" and "savage" or, "beneath the surface of what the whites have made of him ... rich in quality and possibility" (5). Clearly the stakes could not be higher for black literary production, at least in the mind of this commentator. Thus far the "chief image" that "anthropologists and historians ... have succeeded in building has been that of a 'primitive' folk. There has been little in these explorations to encourage white Americans to believe that the Negro would be a valuable addition to his culture" (6). Black writers thus must depict the "peculiar promise" of the Negro to "win our admiration and affection." If they fail in this task, then implicitly some sort of social policy decisions will be made regarding "the course of the Negro problem." Overstreet believes that these decisions will make the "problem run more smoothly, even if less hopefully for the Negro," because, implicitly, there will be no more liberal hand-wringing about black equality and civil rights, and social order will be enforced by a rational white-supremacist security state.

These sorts of public displays of avowedly "sympathetic" concern about and support for Negroes and Negro writing not surprisingly rankled many black authors. Six days after this article appeared, Hurston wrote to a friend describing how she had "infuriated at least two editors who are 'friends' of The Negro" by condemning the article: "I told them that their condescension in fixing us in a type and place is a sort of intellectual Jim Crow and is just as insulting as the physical aspects. In fact, it helps to bolster the physical aspect when our 'friends' defend us so disastrously.... The Overstreets insist on seeing us as both moral and mental incompetents and then defending us from our 'enemies.' And they get mad if I don't let them defend me" (Carla Kaplan 502–3).

Overstreet's advice, which may seem shockingly misguided to contemporary readers, was all too familiar to midcentury black authors. In a 1945 diary entry, Richard Wright captured the feelings of many toward this pervasive sense of literary restriction: "This gloomy but sunlit afternoon I've been wondering how I can ditch the literary life and start anew at something else. I've had this yearning many times.... I wish I could make films. Or engage in some sort of government work. I know that as long as I live in the United States, I can never change my profession, for I'm regarded fatally as a Negro writer, that is, as a writer whose ancestors were Negroes and therefore the Negro is my special field" (qtd. in Rowley 307). Wright is painfully aware of the fact that "Negro writer" is a dominant-culture term that is more prescriptive than descriptive; it functions to exclude the author from the rights and privileges of creative autonomy that at least in theory are accorded the unmodified title of "writer." What he lacks, and is yearning for, is the racial privacy available to white writers. Although white authors must also negotiate the compromises demanded by the marketplace, contemporary black writers knew perfectly well that white writers were not restricted *a priori* to addressing the "problems of white America"; the privileged racial privacy available to white writers, particularly men, granted them the epistemological freedom to analyze any cultural group they chose, with only a handful of subjects being off-limits (most notably, graphic, *affirmative*, and nonpathologized depictions of white same-sexuality). One wonders at the sort of "government work" Wright would find more fulfilling than the "literary life," especially following the demise of the Federal Writers' Project, but his sense that being interpellated as a "Negro writer" constitutes a sort of fatality demonstrates forcefully how the category functioned as an extension of hegemonic power, one that enervates black authors' agency and autonomy—a subject that I take up at more length below.

A host of younger and established black writers, including Hurston, Baldwin, Ellison, and Richard Gibson, also chafed against the ways in which contemporary ideas of "the Negro" compromised their authorial privacy. In particular, they all expressed resentment at being constrained by white publishers' desire for more novels as "crude, melodramatic, and claustrophobi[c]" as Howe and others took Wright's novel to be. Given that the prestige of the "protest" tradition continues to this day, however, it might be tempting to write off these critiques much in the same way that some critics have written off the white-life novel—as misguided "integrationist" or "assimilationist" aesthetics and politics.[4] Taken together, however, these black authors' expressions of resistance to white publishers' calls for more racial protest have much to tell us about what it meant to be a "Negro writer" in midcentury America, and, in particular, about the conditions from which the white-life novel emerged. To appreciate the nature and force of these critiques, however, as well as their relation to the white-life novel, it is necessary to provide a brief overview of the interlocking historical, political, intellectual, and cultural phenomena that shaped the terms of racial discourse at this particular moment.

The modern protest novel and, subsequently, the postwar white-life novel emerged from transformations taking place at the global, national, regional, and local level that directly challenged the dominant racial order in the United States. These transformations—economic, political, and geographical—simultaneously ushered many European "ethnics" into tenuous but privileged whiteness, while also slowly creating the conditions for black enfranchisement. Several competing mobilizations were working to reconfigure the color line. For some, the goal was to rethink "race" just enough to broaden the path to whiteness for European immigrants, for others, a minority, the goal was to break down the color line entirely and enable full citizenship rights and privileges for all citizens.

African American civil rights organizations were aided in their struggle by the broad-based social democratic movement known as the Popular Front, which fostered the development of both the modern protest novel and the postwar white-life novel, though in contradictory ways. On the one hand, the Popular Front played a crucial role in launching the careers of several of the white-life novelists, specifically as protest writers—only Hurston and Baldwin did not establish themselves as protest writers. On the other hand, the striking success of the protest novel created two divergent reactions. Given the economic, social, political, and cultural advances African Americans were achieving, racial protest, traditionally conceived, seemed for many black writers, including the protest writers themselves, too limited a field of expression, even another form of Jim Crow. In response, several authors, such as Yerby, Petry, and Motley, claimed a broader discursive field by producing white-life novels that drew on the progressive Americanism and interracialism that were key tropes of the Popular Front. Other authors, such as Baldwin and Hurston, framed their critique of protest precisely as a critique of the Popular Front, arguing that these putatively progressive discourses were in fact deeply complicit with the hegemonic racial order. These authors conflated Popular Front treatments of race with other avowedly liberal racial discourses, particularly those of the social sciences, which they believed still traded in notions of black abjection and thereby contributed to the racial status quo. Whether pro- or anti–Popular Front, the white-life novel constituted an appealing option for negotiating with and at least momentarily containing hegemonic notions of black difference.

* * *

The years prior to, during, and following World War II witnessed a series of profound, if highly uneven, challenges to the public meaning of race—challenges that simultaneously produced the conditions of modern whiteness and bolstered the earliest phases of the civil rights movement. European immigrants and their children became "white" in the first half of the century primarily via joining forces with native whites and the state in excluding people of color, especially blacks, from full citizenship rights, including legal protections, political participation, and a whole host of various forms of economic and social mobility. African Americans struggled against these alliances, achieving great successes alongside enormous setbacks.[5]

The forces that contributed to these changes were varied and complex. The nation moved from recognizing dozens, even scores, of "races" at the turn of the century to as few as three—white, black, yellow—by the end of World War II.[6] One effect of this shift in race thinking—in which biologically based ideas of race were adjusted to include culturally based ethnicities—was the dramatic expansion of whiteness itself. Due to the combined effects of internal migration, imperialism, two world wars, immigration patterns and restrictions, legal precedent, census taking, and social science analyses, whiteness broadened to incorporate a wide array of formerly excluded "nation races"—such as the Celts, the Alpines, Slavs, Mediterraneans, and the Iberians—while continuing to distinguish itself from other "color races"—that is, black and yellow. One crucial twentieth-century milestone in this process was the 1924 Johnson-Reed Act. The legislation utilized racist ideas of genetic difference to dramatically limit immigration from eastern and southern Europe; the subsequent increase in immigrants from western and northern Europe had the effect of easing nativist anxieties about the "hordes" of new immigrants "mongrelizing" the so-called Nordic race. Consequently, native whites and European immigrants redirected their anxiety and hostility to black Americans, who began migrating in increasing numbers to meet the growing demand for labor in northern and midwestern cities. This shift, while reconfiguring earlier notions of race, contributed to the tendency to think of American race relations in terms of a black-white dyad, what Matthew Pratt Guterl calls "bi-racialism" (5). This habit, which culminated in World War II, had the effect of ignoring "yellow," "red," and "brown" peoples, while erasing whiteness as a race and leaving blackness holding the race bag, so to speak.

The 1930s and 1940s witnessed the rise of the New Deal and industrial unionism, two phenomena that appeared to hold great egalitarian promise, but it was the crisis posed by the U.S. entrance into World War II that led to the greatest social changes around the status of whiteness and blackness in America.[7] Try as it may, the United States could not ignore the hypocrisy of fighting fascism abroad while sustaining Jim Crow at home—a glaring contradiction that received significant international coverage. World War II was, in the words of Nikhil Pal Singh, "a war in which a discourse of antifascism, freedom, and democracy was counter-poised with clashes along the color-line—allied colonialism, racial segregation, Japanese internment, white hate strikes, race war in the Pacific theater, and race riots on the home front" (*Black Is a Country* 104–5).

The 1943 Detroit race riot was only one spectacular instance of the race conflict that was erupting with increasing frequency throughout the home front; Roediger points out that this riot was eagerly joined by the still racially ambiguous new immigrants (eastern and southern Europeans) who were attempting to restrict African Americans from moving into "their" neighborhoods and taking "their" jobs. Following the Detroit riots, Fisk University produced a *Monthly Summary of Events and Trends in Race Relations*, where from March to December 1943 alone it reported "'242 major incidents involving Negro-white conflict in 47 cities' (46 percent in the South, 42 percent in the North, and 12 percent in the West). Southern conflict most frequently occurred 'in relation to the armed forces, transportation, civil rights, and racial etiquette'; Northern incidents most often involved housing, labor, and the police" (qtd. in Jacobson 113). This data forcefully belied the notion that "the Negro problem" was merely a southern problem, given that the majority of race conflict was reported *outside* the South. The conditions for this shift stem largely from the historic wartime out-migrations—World War I and World War II—of millions of southern blacks and whites to industrial centers in the North and West. The conflicts reported by Fisk arose both from the southern white migrant's perpetuation of Jim Crow mores, as well as African American competition with immigrants, old and new, for jobs and housing. The overall effect was that, by World War II, "race moved dramatically toward the center of national political discussion" for the first time since Reconstruction. Jacobson identifies the most important political developments as "the debate over Jim Crow military and defense industry policies; the establishment of a Fair Employment Practices Commission; the emergence of 'racial equality' . . . as an issue in the 1944 presidential campaign; and the emergence of lynching, employment practices, and the poll tax as chief congressional issues in 1945. Both the Republicans and Democrats took up civil rights questions and passed civil rights resolutions in their 1948 conventions, and it was race that divided the Democrats, prompting the third-party movement of Strom Thurmond and the Dixiecrats" (115). Although it would take decades before many of the civil rights issues under debate would be resolved, the wartime demand for national unity nevertheless produced the conditions necessary to set the ball rolling on long awaited antiracist state initiatives. Singh has shown that "the early 1940s... gave rise to a profound reconceptualization of the terms of racialized citizenship within the United States":

> The profound irresolution regarding the meaning and substance of universal citizenship, posed again and again through U.S. history, could no longer be sustained, nor upheld. What followed was the beginning of a decade of legislation and reform that would desegregate the military, liberalize naturalization law, prohibit the white primary, restrictive covenants and segregation in interstate travel, integrate Major League baseball, and eventually culminate in the historic public school desegregation decision, Brown v. Board of Education. ("Culture/Wars" 474)

In other words, Jim Crow was under assault at every level of society. This fact was lost on no American, least of all African Americans, many of whom felt increasingly optimistic that America might finally live up to its own democratic promise. This optimism was marked by a sharp increase in black activism, including organizational activities, which grew significantly during World War II. For example, the NAACP went from 300,000 members in 1939 to over 1 million by 1947. Bill Mullen points out that "during the war, black union membership, particularly in the CIO, rose precipitously, as did black worker self-activity in industries like the automotive" (232).

The more progressive, antiracist critique of whiteness during this moment derived from the nationalist wartime mobilization against fascism, and especially the reaction to Hitler's exterminationist policies. The revelations around the Nazi eugenic policies and death camps led liberal scholars such as Julian Huxley, Ashley Montagu, and Ruth Benedict to argue in favor of "eradicat[ing] race altogether as a measure of human capacity and thus as an instrument of state policy" (Jacobson 99).[8] The historian Richard King has shown that the atrocities of the Second World War led to

> a universalist vision in which the different races were understood to be equal in natural capacities and legal-specific rights became a consensus position among intellectual and scientific elites in the West. The vision found expression in the founding documents of the United Nations, especially the Declaration of Human Rights, the 1948 Convention on the Prevention and Punishment of the Crime of Genocide and the UNESCO statement on Race in 1950,

which began as follows: "Scientists have reached general agreement that mankind is one; that all men belong to the same species, *Homo Sapiens*." (2)

But as history has repeatedly shown, significant social advances are always met with a fierce backlash. The historian Gary Gerstle and others have noted that during the years leading up to and following World War II, "the pressures working *for* racialization were as powerful as those working against it. In other words, as the civil rights movement was gathering steam in these years, America's commitment to a racialized society was being reinvigorated" (286). The cessation of global hostilities did not translate into a cessation of hostilities on the home front; the domestic fight against American fascism was far from over. By the end of 1945, the nation witnessed "black workers displaced in rapid numbers by returning white war vets, failure by the Roosevelt administration to persist in application of FEPC policies preventing discrimination in industry, and an increasingly racist tenor in postwar discourse" (Mullen 123). U.S. antiblack mob violence continued unabated after the war, even worsening in some respects, with eleven reported lynchings in 1946 and scores of residential bombings in northern urban neighborhoods in 1947. This intensification of racial violence paralleled that which erupted after the First World War, the infamous "Red Summer" of 1919, in which returning "white" veterans in northern cities not only displaced African Americans from the decreasing numbers of industrial jobs, but also attempted forcefully to repel blacks from moving into formerly "whites only" neighborhoods. In his autobiography, *Long Old Road*, the African American sociologist and author Horace Cayton recalled a powerful sense of deflation and dread at the start of the Cold War: "I felt that the dynamic opportunity which the conflict [World War II] had provided for dark peoples throughout the world had been dissipated. The armed forces were still for the most part segregated; with the closing down of defense industries, employment for Negroes was at a low ebb; left-wing opposition to the status quo had largely disappeared; and the labor unions, with their treasuries bursting, no longer were interested in Negro participation" (254). James Baldwin expressed a very similar mood when he described Harlem in 1948. De facto Jim Crow housing in New York led to overcrowding, which of course meant that "[r]ents are 10 to 58 percent higher than anywhere else in the city; food, expensive everywhere, is more expensive here and of an inferior quality; and now that the war is over and money is dwindling, clothes are carefully shopped for and seldom bought. Negroes, traditionally the last to be hired and the first to be fired, are finding jobs harder to get, and, while prices are rising implacably, wages are going down. All over Harlem now there is felt the same bitter expectancy with which, in my childhood, we awaited winter: it is coming and it will be hard; there is nothing anyone can do about it" (*Notes* 57).

The white-life novel thus arose at a moment when African Americans were experiencing and exercising unprecedented levels of "freedom," politically, culturally, and geographically. Nevertheless, these new levels of freedom were being met with widespread and vicious resistance, often at the hands of those whose status as whites was still somewhat provisional. These socially transformative expansions of racial identity, and the violent attempts to contain them, are inscribed in the white-life novel—though typically in highly displaced forms. The white-life novel obliquely engages these historical pressures, not, as one might expect, by "protesting," but by way of imagining *alternative* fictive spaces that provide symbolic resolutions to what were otherwise intractable forces shaping the lives of African Americans.

* * *

The complex mix of advance and retreat that marked the politics of the moment was also reflected in the state of African American literary production. As I suggested earlier, for many, Wright's success seemed to have inaugurated a new era of aesthetic, ideological, and commercial possibility for black writers. Prior to the publication of Frank Yerby's *The Foxes of Harrow* (1946), Petry's *The Street* (1946), and Motley's *Knock on Any Door* (1947), he was the shining exception that proved the rule—it was nearly impossible to survive as a black writer entirely from the proceeds of one's creative work. Langston Hughes addressed the issue at length in his speech to the 1939 League of American Writers' congress:

> Negro books are considered by editors and publishers as *exotic*. Negro material is placed, like Chinese material or Bali material or East Indian material, into a certain classification. Magazine editors will tell you, "We can use but so many Negro stories a year." (That "so many" meaning very few.) Publishers will say, "We already have one Negro novel on our lists this fall."
>
> The market for Negro writers, then, is definitely limited as long as we write about ourselves. And the more truthfully we write about ourselves, the more limited our market becomes. Those

novels about Negroes that sell best, by Negroes or whites, those novels that make the best-seller lists and receive the leading prizes, are almost always books that touch very lightly upon the facts of Negro life, books that make our black ghettoes in the big cities seem very happy places indeed, and our plantations in the deep south idyllic in their pastoral loveliness.... When we cease to be exotic, we do not sell well. (Stewart, *Fighting Words* 58–59)

Hughes concedes that "very few writers of any race make a living directly from their writing," but he also notes that other opportunities, such as working in publishing houses, publicity firms, radio, and motion pictures are extremely rare for African Americans: "[M]agazine offices, daily newspapers, publisher's offices are as tightly closed to us in America as if we were pure non-Aryans in Berlin" (60). The lecture circuit could provide substantial income to established white authors, but the indignities of travel in Jim Crow America made this option unappealing to most black writers. Fellowships provided an essential, though temporary, means of support, especially the Julius Rosenwald Fund and the Guggenheim; nearly every major black writer of the era benefited from these.[9]

The contemporary black authors Sterling Brown and J. Saunders Redding concur with Hughes's sober assessment of the obstacles facing black authors. Brown writes simply, "Opposition to honest treatment of Negro life in literature is certain and it is strong" (15). Redding adds (four years later in 1945) that "the Negro author who writes primarily for a white audience is up against many long-standing artistic conceptions about the Negro; against numerous conventions and traditions which are more or less binding; against a whole set of stereotypes which are not easily destroyed" ("Negro Author" 1288). Brown and Redding also lament the fact that the market most amenable to sensitive, nonstereotyped portraits of black experience, the black book-buying public, is still far too small for mainstream publishers to concern themselves with; they are in business to make money, and seldom risk bucking the dominant culture's preferences too severely. There were, of course, numerous black newspapers, and even a few established journals that were open to creative work, such as *Phylon*, *Crisis*, and *Opportunity*, but these paid creative writers fairly modest fees, and by midcentury, both *Crisis* and *Opportunity* had fallen on hard times and played nowhere near as important a role in stimulating and supporting black literary production as they had during the New Negro Renaissance. "It is perhaps impossible to overestimate black writers' cultural marginality as a group and their anxiety as individuals about maintaining public prominence during the 1940s," Lawrence Jackson argues. "Their situation was made worse by the dominant culture's practice of appointing lone black representatives" ("The Birth of the Critic" 351).

Attention to the sparseness of opportunities for black writers in mainstream American publishing underscores the significance of the broad-scale egalitarian movement known as the Popular Front. The historical, political, and cultural transformations mentioned earlier in this section occurred at the same time as, and were in many respects central to, the rise of the Popular Front movement, which provided crucial support to radical and progressive artists, musicians, activists, intellectuals, and writers, including black writers, and the white-life novel authors in particular. Nearly all of the white-life novel authors were inspired by and participated in the Popular Front's "cultural front" as an enabling framework, one that offered a progressive ideological alignment, a rich symbolic repertoire, and a network of cultural institutions that in several instances launched and sustained their early careers. Recognition of the Popular Front as an important cultural-ideological matrix out of which several of the white-life novels emerged helps clarify their sources of inspiration, objects of critique, and discursive strategies—from this vantage point, the authors' engagement with white experience is more easily recognized as self-authorizing interracialism rather than race-denying "assimilationism."

During the Cold War, most critics from the Left and Right deplored what they took to be the Popular Front's vitiating affect on culture—centrists and conservatives argued that naïve and deluded faith in the Soviet Union, and Stalin in particular, led to the abandonment of aesthetics in favor of propaganda; critics from the Left argued that the Popular Front abandoned avant-garde leftism for crass commercialism and sentimental nationalism. Post–Cold War scholars have challenged these assumptions, reassessing the Popular Front's complex ideologies and strategies, as well as its influence and effects.[10] Michael Denning defines the Popular Front as "a radical social-democratic movement forged around anti-fascism, anti-lynching, and the industrial unionism of the CIO." Even granting the CIO's limitations in fundamentally altering Jim Crow attitudes and practices at the national and local level, without a doubt the Popular Front, broadly conceived, provided the most committed and legitimately progressive framework for interracial organizing that was available to black intellectuals, activists, and artists. The Popular Front emerged in the wake of the 1929 stock market crash; however, it defined itself in response to both the economic crisis as well as the racial crisis—this was a moment marked by resurgent KKK activity and intense anti-immigrant sentiment in America, as well as the rise of European domestic fascism.[11] Mobilizing against these forces at home and abroad, as well as the forces of capital, the Popular Front "remained the central popular democratic movement over the following three decades" (Denning xviii).

The Communist International (Comintern) officially recognized the period as lasting from 1935 to 1939. The phrase was introduced in 1935, signaling a shift away from far-left "Third Period" policy (1928–34), which advocated a proletarian-led global revolution. The continuing effects of worldwide economic depression and the mounting strength of European domestic fascism prompted Comintern leaders to soften their hard-line positions—which frequently alienated many potential antifascist allies—and to issue a call for a "'Broad People's Front' coalition of liberals, radicals, trade unionists, farmers, socialists, blacks and whites, anticolonialists and colonized. In an effort to unify this broad constituency, the party simultaneously inaugurated a campaign to promote what it came to call a 'people's culture'" (Mullen 3). The first phase of the Comintern's Popular Front ended with the notorious 1939 Stalin-Hitler Nonaggression Pact, which, as Denning says, caused a "near fatal shock" to its antifascism adherents, before resurfacing again as the United States and the USSR joined forces during World War II to defeat the Nazis. This "win the war" front ended up alienating a number of black communists and fellow travelers because of the Communist Party's back-pedaling on its aggressive support of black civil rights—the Communist Party USA (CPUSA) encouraged African Americans to sign a "no-strike pledge," and it choose not to support A. Philip Randolph's powerful March on Washington movement, which led Roosevelt to establish the FEPC.

Even granting these failures and inconsistencies on the part of the CPUSA toward African Americans, several recent scholars have demonstrated the extent to which black activists, intellectuals, and artists, though numerically small, influenced the direction, policy, and cultural formations of the CPUSA and the Left more broadly. As William Maxwell and Bill Mullen have argued, African American writers, including such figures as Claude McKay, Langston Hughes, and Richard Wright, among others, provided leadership, organizing, and key cultural products.[12] The Popular Front can also be shown to have contributed to the earliest phases of the civil rights movement, given that dismantling Jim Crow and ending lynching were among its declared objectives. One of the

CPUSA's many antiracist initiatives was its sponsoring of the National Negro Congress as a companion front to the Popular Front. In addition to civil rights and the empowerment of black labor, the National Negro Congress's goals included "support for the advancement of black 'culture and culture workers,' *particularly in the fight against demeaning and stereotypical images in the public arts.* In the words of James Ford, the party's 1932 and 1936 vice presidential candidate and a keynote speaker there, the congress meant to undertake the fight against the 'retardation of the cultural life of the Negro people by reactionary politics and inferiority doctrines'" (Mullen 3; emphasis added).

At this point, many scholars recognize the Popular Front's "cultural front" as extending into the immediate postwar period, in terms of widespread participation in movement culture, labor victories, and the appearance of powerful "laborist" cultural works. For Denning, the Popular Front's greatest contribution to American literature was that it "enfranchised a generation of writers of ethnic, working-class origins; it allowed them to represent—to speak for and to depict—their families, their neighborhoods, their aspirations, and their nightmares. Even if most of the novels and screenplays are only half-remembered, their cumulative effect transformed American culture, making their ghetto childhoods, their drifters and hobos, their vernacular prose, their gangsters and prostitutes, even their occasional union organizer, part of the mythology of the United States, part of the national-popular imagination" (229). The relationship between the white-life novel and the Popular Front literary movement has been largely overlooked. Several of the white-life novel authors' careers derived crucial support from the Popular Front's cultural infrastructure. Richard Wright is the most obvious example. His adult career as an author began in the Chicago branch of the John Reed Club in 1933, and continued into the League of American Writers and beyond; his publications appeared in a long list of proletarian and Popular Front publications, including *New Masses, Left Front, Partisan Review, International Literature, PM,* and *Negro Story,* among others. He was the Harlem bureau editor of the *Daily Worker* and both a coeditor (along with Dorothy West) and contributor to *New Challenge.* Petry launched her writing career as a journalist for the Popular Front Harlem newspaper *People's Voice,* which helped expose her to a range of experiences and populations on which she drew in her early fiction in one form or another.[13] Moreover, she published several book reviews in the New York daily *PM* and contributed a story to the annual literary anthology *Cross-Section,* which was edited by the former proletarian novelist and critic turned editor and book reviewer Edwin Seaver.[14] Several of Yerby's early poems (1934–35), and nearly all of his short stories were published in Popular Front magazines, including *Challenge*, *Tomorrow*, Jack Conroy's *New Anvil*, and Louis Adamic's *Common Ground*, in which he published two stories. The first, "Roads Going Down," appeared in the 1945 summer issue; the second, "The Homecoming," appeared after *The Foxes of Harrow* had been published in February 1946, a fact that makes more explicit his active participation in the Popular Front literary formation during the early years of his writing career. In addition to the classics and "the slicks," Chester Himes read radical author Dashiell Hammett while in prison; once out, he wrote for the Ohio WPA and participated in a range of communist-sponsored activities while in Los Angeles.[15] The Chicago-based Popular Front journal *Negro Story*—which Bill Mullen maintains "helped foreground the short story as a genre for black radical voicing" (16)—published seven stories by Himes between 1944 and 1946.[16] Willard Motley was encouraged as a young writer by the proletarian authors Alexander Saxton and Jack Conroy. Conroy turned down a short story Motley had submitted to *Anvil*, though only because of its length. He recommended that Motley send the story to more commercial venues and offered to introduce him to some of his publishing contacts (Fleming 31). Alan Wald has discussed Motley's frequent though somewhat informal participation in Chicago Popular Front activities, including a series of vignettes that he published in the short-lived *Hull House Magazine* (1939–40).[17]

The "protest" novels of several white-life novel authors—Wright's *Native Son*, Petry's *The Street*, and Himes's *If He Hollers Let Him Go*—themselves constitute signal achievements of the Popular Front's literary formations. This has often been overlooked primarily because of race, but also because we tend to categorize twentieth-century American literary production according to fairly restrictive, even if at times overlapping, categories—for example, these works may or may not appear as belonging to proletarian literature or naturalism—both of which are usually associated with an earlier period and with European American writers. Nevertheless, their depictions of the urban black working class defy dominant-culture expectations of sentimentality and exoticism; they represent among the most powerful antiracist works the nation had ever seen and introduced a new tenor into not only African American fiction, but radical and progressive American literary treatments of race more generally.[18]

African American protest literature advanced the cause of the Popular Front, and the Popular Front contributed in significant ways to providing a supportive cultural infrastructure and a sympathetic audience for protest literature. However, several of the white-life novels clearly draw on the Popular Front's more moderate, post-1936 coalitionist ideology and progressive metaphors. Because I address these issues in more detail in later chapters, I note them only briefly here. Yerby, Petry, and especially Motley all draw on the key Popular Front tropes of "the people" and Americanism. Both of these expansive tropes are racially and ethnically inclusive, advocating cross-racial recognition of shared struggles and cultural contributions. The identification of common goals and common enemies fosters interracial sympathy and solidarity, which becomes a condition and conduit of social transformation. Langston Hughes, for example, argued that the problems facing the Negro writer should not be a "matter of *mine* and *yours*. It is a matter of *ours*. We are all Americans. We want to create the American dream, a finer and more democratic America. I cannot do it without you. You cannot do it omitting me. Can we march together then? ... Can we not put our heads together and think and plan—not merely dream—the future America?" (62–63; emphasis in original).[19] Denning warns against the commonplace critical tendency of reading these tropes as simple-minded, sentimental, and uncritically patriotic, however. The repeated invocation of America within these texts and the Popular Front movement more generally suggests that it constitutes the "locus for ideological battles over the trajectory of U.S. history, the meaning of race, ethnicity, and region in the U.S., and the relation between ethnic nationalism, Americanism, and internationalism.... [T]he ubiquity of 'America' in the rhetoric of the period is less a sign of deep reverence or harmony, than *a sign of the crisis of Americanism* provoked by the crash" (129; emphasis added). Hughes's gentle and hopeful rhetoric belies the revolutionary content of his gesture; his "American dream" is grounded in interracial activism, which directly contradicts the nation's centuries-long commitment to a white-supremacist racial nationalism, a form of nationalism that a significant portion of the dominant culture was still committed to preserving.

"The people," in contrast, are the sign of and aspiration for a progressive nationalism; their invocation is a performative utterance—they draw on the nation to validate their ethnic and racial difference, and their difference validates the idea of a progressive, inclusive nation. Motley invoked the Popular Front notion of "the people" by way of explaining his decision and capacity to write a novel with an Italian American protagonist: "People in a slum area bear the same burden, regardless of their nationality, their religion, their color. This, above all, I found true when

I lived in a little basement in the slums. I was not alone. The people were not alone. Bread was shared and sympathy was shared. Negroes went to the synagogues with their Jewish friends to celebrate Jewish church days. Jews went to Italian Catholic churches to observe their church days. The whole neighborhood went to the Greek Orthodox Easter. The people in the slums are not alone. They're all together. The people of the slums are a minority driven to the wall. Their search, their strength is undivided" (Cayton, "Literary Expansion" 7). Although Roediger has argued that houses of worship in embattled ethnic urban neighborhoods often functioned as sites of antiblack mobilization (168), in Motley's formulation the slums, however disadvantaged—in fact because of their shared burden—are a united front. This site (and symbolically, Motley's text) articulates the Popular Front aspiration for interethnic, international, and interreligious solidarity. The recognition of, identification with, and sympathy for the suffering of others was a key Popular Front organizing and literary strategy; it was a valorized structure of feeling that was still circulating in the postwar moment, particularly among artists and intellectuals, and one that I contend underwrote the white-life novel strategy of sympathetic cross-racial identification. Moreover, the Popular Front's redeployment of America as a critical, progressive ideological sign helped reform and open up what Chris Castiglia refers to as "the national symbolic" (the signs and symbols that give the national-popular imaginary its coherence). As I will argue, Yerby, Petry, and Motley's white-life novels draw on a critical Americanism, in which the ideological power of "America" lies in its as yet unrealized potential, not in a clearly established tradition. This reformation of "America" and "the people" create the conditions for an emancipatory identificational mobility that far exceeds the limited enunciative authority of injured other—one excluded from the liberatory capacity inherent in the national symbolic. Rather than Jim Crowed "pupils" in the Richard Wright School of Protest, these novelists' voices are authorized by a progressive, antifascist Americanism. Moreover, both the Popular Front critical Americanist discourse and the discourse of "the people" should also be seen as offering racial privacy, insofar as access to and mobilization on behalf of these discourses is equally available to all, regardless of race.

* * *

James Baldwin began his professional writing career in the years immediately following the Second World War by reviewing Popular Front–

oriented books in anti-Stalinist periodicals such as *New Leader, Commentary*, and *Partisan Review*. Looking back, Baldwin dismissed the works he reviewed as feckless products of a moment when "Americans were on one of their monotonous conscience 'trips': be kind to niggers, for Christ sake, be kind to Jews!" (xiv). There were so many "social problem" and "protest" works appearing at this time that, for writers such as Baldwin, they came to represent another incarnation of "the problem." In the "Autobiographical Notes" to *Notes of a Native Son*, he laments that "the Negro problem is written about so widely. The bookshelves groan under the weight of information, and everyone therefore considers himself informed. Of traditional attitudes there are only two—For or Against—and I, personally, find it difficult to say which attitude has caused me the most pain. I am speaking as a writer. . . . From this point of view [that of the writer] the Negro problem is nearly inaccessible. It is not only written about so widely; it is written about so badly" (5–6; emphasis added).[20] A host of black writers seconded Baldwin's assessment, particularly his sense that "protest" and "social problem" novels approached African American life and culture principally as a problem, where the Negro was seen, in the words of philosopher Alain Locke, as the "sick man of democracy" (*The New Negro* 11). Many black writers felt that this sort of discourse inhibited rather than helped black writers, and, moreover, that certain attitudes of white liberals contributed as much if not more than white bigots to the confusion surrounding the debate. Of particular concern was the degree to which writing on "the Negro" appeared to rely on and reproduce mainstream, derogatory social science analyses of the black community. No work on the "problem" made the "bookshelves groan" more than Gunnar Myrdal's massive *An American Dilemma* (1944), which quickly became the most authoritative study on "the Negro" and American race relations for at least the next fifteen years.[21] While *AAD* denounced American racism as a deviation from America's praiseworthy egalitarian principles, it also participated in and even advanced sociology's tendency to depict black cultural institutions as, in the words of Myrdal, "a distorted development, or a pathological condition, of the general American culture" (928).[22]

Several essays appeared in the postwar period challenging the explanatory authority of sociology and bemoaning its effects on the prospects of Negro writers. These essays demonstrate the extent to which many black writers felt that the depictions of blackness found in sociology and protest literature, despite their avowed progressive intent, fundamentally misrepresented the black community and black culture, and indirectly bolstered Jim Crow by lending scientific and cultural legitimacy to white-supremacist suppositions about the debased conditions of black life, and especially black intimate and domestic relations. Protest literature's emphasis on black abjection, in the eyes of these writers, allied it with sociology's rendering of black culture as pathologized, and thus was critiqued for functioning as what the sociologist Roderick Ferguson (following Foucault) refers to as a "technology of racial management" that disciplined rather than liberated the black community. Writers such as Baldwin, Hurston, Gibson, and Ellison came to see the white liberal demand for protest fiction as a kind of incitement to racial discourse, whereby protest literature contributed to *producing* hegemonic discourses of blackness, which in turn also provided key icons and symbols that produced hegemonic discourses of whiteness.

For these writers, sociology and protest literature constitute overlapping discourses that reinforce the larger structures of subordination and exclusion (i.e., the literal and symbolic ghetto) from which black writers were trying to escape. In response, their essays turn mainstream sociological discourse on the Negro—especially that found in *AAD*—on its head, arguing that these discourses betray an enduring and unacknowledged commitment to, and desire for, the black primitive. This investment in the idea of the Negro as primitive is symptomatic, however, of *white* irrationality, perversion, and (to borrow from Myrdal) "a century-long lag of public morals" (24). Thus, it is primitive *white* thought that produces the Negro as primitive. These essays warrant close attention both because they help illuminate the white-life novel authors' rationales for decentering the Negro problem in their works, but also because they help clarify the manner in which these works challenge the assumptions that structure hegemonic whiteness without reinscribing black fixity. As I will argue, not only does the white-life novel deflate the pretense of universal white normativity (particularly as the locus of morality, rationality, and progress), but these works also suggest that white America's deviation from these hegemonic norms is in fact necessary; the white-life novels' representations of "white difference" work to create a space of anti-white-supremacist critical agency that facilitates dissent, enacts progressive change, and produces what we might call, signifying on Myrdal, "a distorted development, [*and thus redemptive*] condition, of the general American culture" (928).

* * *

The recognized "experts" on the Negro problem almost invariably hailed from the social sciences, particularly anthropology, psychology, and, most of all, sociology. From the earliest formations of the discipline in this country, American sociology had been committed to analyzing the meaning of race, particularly as a factor in maintaining or undermining social order. As Thomas Pettigrew contends: "American sociology began as a way to reflect on 'the vast dislocations from extremely rapid urbanization and industrialization. [It] was shaped from the start by a *moral response to immediate national social problems—racial and cultural concerns prominent among them.*'" (xxi; emphasis in original). Daryl Michael Scott has shown that the first generation of social scientists, which emerged in the aftermath of the collapse of Reconstruction, frequently argued that blacks were from "inferior racial stock" and thus incapable of assimilation into modern civilization.[23] These racially conservative Progressive Era social scientists produced knowledge about "the Negro" for the purpose of demonstrating "scientifically" the necessity of Jim Crow legal standing and social policy. From around 1920 on, however, most social scientists who took African Americans as their subject tended to be what Scott refers to as "racial liberals." The most influential of these scholars, white and black, hailed from the Chicago school of sociology. This group made substantial contributions to *An American Dilemma* and included the black sociologists E. Franklin Frazier and Charles Johnson, and the political scientist Ralph Bunche. All of these figures expressly challenged biologically based theories of racial inferiority, arguing instead that whatever group or individual ills were manifest in black communities resulted from social and historical forces, such as slavery; the persistence of white-supremacist attitudes and laws; and the social dislocation and familial disorganization incumbent upon mass migration from close-knit, rural communities to urban centers. This generation hoped to redeem the Negro through an avowed commitment to greater objectivity and science, which they believed would be the most effective approach to dismantling Jim Crow.[24] *An American Dilemma* represented the triumph of environmentalist explanations of social behavior.

However, as Roderick Ferguson makes clear, Myrdal's study "decried African American exclusion as a violation of the American Creed, [yet] the text rationalized it nonetheless by constructing African American culture as the antithesis of that creed" (94). In Myrdal's formulation, the

Creed was believed to endorse "equality before the law, participation in government, and the right to the pursuit of happiness" (Taub 89); it was also presumed to emerge from and represent the highest manifestation of Christian morality and Enlightenment rationality (*AAD* 8). Although the Creed implicitly rejected the long-standing practice of African American exclusion, Myrdal explained the practice as an effect of the "vicious circle": "[W]hite prejudice and discrimination keep the Negro low in standards of living, health, education, manners and morals"; in turn, prejudiced whites point to the debased conditions of black life as the reasons for their prejudice (*AAD* 76). In other words, while claiming that the Negro problem is fundamentally a white problem (which he locates ultimately "in the *heart* of the [white] American" (xlvii; emphasis added), the alleged wretchedness of black life to a certain extent justifies white racism.

An American Dilemma remains in familiar sociological terrain in its assertion that among the most alarming aspects of the Negro's "low standards" is the notorious "disorganization" of the black family. The signs of black familial disorganization include higher rates of "illegitimacy [out-of-wedlock births], divorce, and unattached individuals and 'one-person families'" (*AAD* 934) than were found among whites. Black disorganization, Ferguson argues, was "defined in terms of its distance from heterosexual and nuclear intimate arrangements that are rationalized through American law and cultural norms that valorize heterosexual monogamy and patriarchal domesticity" (93). Black communities, seen through the lens of the family, were considered pathological because of their dissimilarity from the ideal model of the bourgeois heteropatriarchal white family. Consequently, African Americans were cast as gender and sexual deviants, regardless of whether they considered themselves straight or queer. These "moral" questions had high political stakes. They were seen as a significant cause of such ills as poverty, illiteracy, crime, violence, mental illness, and "degeneracy," and they determined the nature of state interventions in the form of social policies from the New Deal to the Great Society.[25] Moreover, black nonheteronormativity implied a kind of civic unfitness, leading Myrdal to argue, for example, that voting rights in the South should be extended initially only to the "higher strata of the Negro population," which were deemed more stable and heteronormative; he then recommended "to push the movement [enfranchisement] down to the lowest groups gradually" (519). It is worth pointing out that although he acknowledges that this "unfitness" is characteristic of poor southern whites too, he doesn't recommend temporarily rescinding this group's voting rights until it achieves middle-class normativity.

Despite its critique of white prejudice and its avowed liberal purpose, *An American Dilemma*, like much sociological work that preceded and followed it, produced African Americans as culturally inferior and pathologized in both body and mind—through no fault of their own, black folk are insufficiently socialized and lacking the benefits of civilization.[26] *AAD* was unique in one respect, though. Singh has argued that *AAD*'s limitations derived partly from its overt nationalist agenda, which was to legitimate the United States' emergent world-ordering authority.[27] Because of his pro-American, liberal-nationalist orientation, Myrdal was unprepared to investigate the extent to which the nation itself, not just white individuals suffering from "prejudice," historically exploited African American subjugation for both material and ideological gain. Instead, as already noted, Myrdal consistently cited the American Creed and implicitly the nation itself as an expression of the achievement of Enlightenment rationality. This supposition led Myrdal to depict African Americans in a manner that many black intellectuals found particularly obnoxious. Myrdal averred that one of racism's tragic effects is that African Americans are excluded from participation in American culture and governance, and thus "Negroes are denied identification with the nation or with national groups to a much larger degree" (782). This exclusion and alienation, according to Myrdal, causes Negro social and political thought to be both irrational and unstable: "To them social speculation . . . moves in a sphere of unreality and futility. Instead of organized popular theories or ideas the observer finds in the Negro world, for the most part, only *a fluid and amorphous mass of all sorts of embryos of thoughts. Negroes seem to be held in a state of eternal preparedness for a great number of contradictory opinions*" (782; emphasis in original). Although he concedes that black intellectuals "usually do not have such a tremendous instability of opinion as the masses," nevertheless, "compared with white intellectuals they show the same difference as Negro masses compared with the white masses" (782).

Black thought is not merely unstable and childlike, but remarkably "provincial" and essentially reactive: "Negro thinking is almost completely determined by white opinions—negatively and positively." Because it is a reaction to white racist beliefs, black social thought is "in this sense . . . a derivative, or secondary, thinking. The Negroes do not formulate the issues to be debated; these are set for them by the dominant group. Negro thinking develops upon the presuppositions of white thinking. In its purest protest form it is a blunt denial and a refutation of white opinions.... Negro thinking seldom moves outside the orbit fixed by the whites' conceptions about the Negroes and about caste" (784). Once again, we also see that Negro provincialism affects not merely the masses, but black intellectuals too: "This vicious circle of caste operates upon the finest brains in the Negro people and gives even the writings of a Du Bois a queer touch of unreality as soon as he left *his* problem, which is the American Negro problem, and made a frustrated effort to view it in a wider setting as an ordinary American and a human being" (784; emphasis in original).[28] In short, despite the contributions of black intellectuals to *AAD* itself, Myrdal deems "the Negro" incapable of rational thought. What thought does occur within the "finest Negro brains" is not merely childlike, "queer," and "unreal," but derivative of white opinions—Myrdal clearly implies that black social thought is in essence nothing more than distorted and substandard white thought.[29]

AAD's analyses of white prejudice and black life permeated American thinking, from the social sciences, to public policy, to the world of letters. Jodi Melamed has argued, for example, that the prestigious Julius Rosenwald Fund self-consciously adopted Myrdalian analyses of American race relations in its rationale for sponsoring creative-writing fellowships—Wright, Himes, Motley, Baldwin, Ellison, and Hurston all received grants. Even so, several black writers authored essays in the years following the publication of *AAD* (Ellison, Baldwin, and Hurston, among others) that either directly or indirectly critiqued its premises, and especially its delimiting effects on the prospects of the Negro writer. Although Hurston doesn't mention *AAD* by name, her 1950 essay "What White Publishers Won't Print" clearly engages and reformulates *AAD*'s conception of African American thought, especially literature, and its relation to the nation. Whereas Myrdal insists that "Negroes are denied identification with the nation," Hurston insists that "for the national welfare, it is urgent to realize that the minorities *do think, and think about something other than the race problem*" (1161; emphasis added). She contends that the belief that minorities can think of nothing but "the problem" actually stems from "the Anglo-Saxon's lack of curiosity about the internal lives and emotions of the Negroes, and for that matter any non-Anglo-Saxon peoples within our borders, above the class of unskilled labor" (1159). The Anglo-Saxon has no sympathy (understood as a "community of feeling") for anyone other than poor, unskilled, and uneducated people of color. Moreover, the sympathy reserved for this abject group is of the most pernicious, dominating sort. Her explanation for why this seemingly trivial matter is, as she says, "much more important than it seems at first glance," is worth quoting in full.

> It is even more important at this time than it was in the past. The internal affairs of the nation have bearings on the international stress and strain, and this gap in the national literature now has tremendous weight in world affairs. National coherence and solidarity is implicit in a thorough understanding of the various groups within a nation, and this lack of knowledge about the internal emotions and behavior of the minorities cannot fail to bar our understanding. Man, like all the other animals, fears and is repelled by that which he does not understand, and mere difference is apt to connote something malign. (1159)

With remarkable economy, Hurston easily moves beyond what *AAD* would call a parochial (and unstable) obsession with the Negro problem to critically engage questions of national identity and international politics—that is, America's Cold War problem. Hurston is obviously alluding to the fact that America's widely publicized racist, antidemocratic practices were fundamentally compromising its claims to moral superiority over the Soviet Union and thus to global leadership. Whereas whites might blame interracial conflict on black "difference," she shifts the terms of the debate by drawing the reader's attention to the seemingly insignificant fact of white indifference to, or skepticism of, African American's capacity for "high and complicated emotions" (1161). The absence within the national literary landscape of works that deal with the internal life of African Americans (and other minorities) beyond "the problem" arises not from black obsession with white racism (as Myrdal might suggest), but from white ignorance and an animal-like (and thus implicitly primitive) fear of difference. She immediately highlights the mutually determining relationship between *individual* white ignorance and fear and the *nation's* ignorance and fear of its own "various [nonwhite] groups within." This widespread ignorance undermines "national coherence and solidarity" and thus she implies that *the nation itself,* not just individual white people, suffers from a destabilizing lack, and is implicitly irrational and primitive. Thus the problem is not that black Americans are incapable of identifying with the nation's exalted, paradigmatically rational, and universal ideals, as Myrdal would have it, but rather that the nation's controlling white elements are unable to identify with and lack true sympathy for its constituent nonwhite elements—the *pluribus* that constitutes the *unum.*

Hurston goes on to argue that American literature, and black literature in particular, can remedy this national lack by demonstrating that for all the surface cultural differences among groups, minorities "react inside" the same way as the dominant culture. The only way to prove this sympathetic "commonality of feeling"—fundamental sameness beneath surface differences—would be to allow black writers to provide representations of complex black subjectivity. In other words, if the dominant culture *allowed* Negro writers to deal with topics other than the race problem (such as "a romance uncomplicated by the race struggle" or stories about the "Negro insurance official, dentist, general practitioner, undertaker" [1161]), the payoff would be that these representations of black humanity (what we might call black presence) would work to remedy the current state of national irrationality and lack, and thereby help produce national coherence, or what we might call national presence.

Unfortunately, however, the midcentury publishing industry amounts to what Hurston calls "THE AMERICAN MUSEUM OF UNNATURAL HISTORY" (1160; capitalization in original). This museum is built on "folk belief" that assumes that "all non-Anglo-Saxons are uncomplicated stereotypes.... They are lay figures mounted in the museum where all may take them in at a glance. They are made of bent wires without insides at all. So how could anybody write a book about the nonexistent?"[30] In addition to figures of American Indians, Orientals, Jews, Yankees, westerners, southerners, and so on, there are two figures in "the American Negro exhibit": "One is seated on a stump picking away on his banjo and singing and laughing. The other is a most amoral character before a sharecropper's shack mumbling about injustice. Doing this makes him out to be a Negro 'intellectual.' It is as simple as all that." Despite the comic imagery and tone, hallmarks of Hurston's racial critique, she makes clear that the "museum" is an effect of the dominant culture's need to believe in stereotypes that evacuate black interiority. The difference between the black stereotypical figure and, say, the "Nordic" stereotype, is that "the public willingly accepts the untypical in Nordics, but feels cheated if the untypical is portrayed in [racial] others." Her point, of course, is that this black absence in fact evinces nothing more than projected, irrational, *white* desire for the black primitive—a desire that bespeaks a white absence.

She argues further that this discursive "blank is NOT filled by the fiction built around upperclass Negroes exploiting the race problem. Rather, it tends to point it up. A college-bred Negro still is not a person like other folks, but an interesting problem, more or less" (1159; capitalization in original). At least in terms of the publishing industry, this problematic is perpetuated less by white conservatives, and more by white liberals whose putatively "sympathetic" attitudes toward African American life are essentially holdovers from the days of slavery. She clarifies her position by relating the story of a slave whose master has taught him algebra and Latin. A neighboring slave owner, skeptical of the African's capacity to learn, submits him to an oral exam. Although the slave answers all of his questions correctly, he declares that the slave's learning is merely an "aping of our culture. All on the outside. You are crazy if you think that it has changed him inside in the least. Turn him loose, and he will revert at once to the jungle. He is still a savage." Although "we have come a long, long way" since slavery, Hurston acknowledges, "there are still too many who refuse to believe in the ingestion and digestion of western culture as yet" (1159). Among the modern-day doubters are the white liberals and leftists who insist "on defeat in a story where upperclass Negroes are portrayed." Hurston contends that this insistence "says something from the subconscious of the majority. Involved in western culture, the [black] hero or heroine, or both must appear frustrated and go down to defeat, somehow." Even if unconscious, the liberal desire for black failure reproduces the slave owner's theory of "reversion to type," which insists that "[n]o matter how high we may *seem* to climb, put us under strain and we revert to type, that is, to the bush. Under a superficial layer of western culture, the jungle drums throb in our veins" (1161; emphasis in original). The white racial liberal's desire for representations of black suffering can be called "sympathetic," but it is a mode of sympathy predicated on pity, and thus it reaffirms hierarchical difference.

Hurston demonstrates that, contra Myrdal and other white liberals, black thought exists, but it is occluded and suppressed by a white ignorance of black humanity, a primitive fear of black equality, and a desire for stories that corroborate the commonplace belief in absolute difference—that is, self-aggrandizing fantasies of the black primitive: "This ridiculous notion makes it possible for the majority who accept it to conceive of even a man like the suave and scholarly Dr. Charles S. Johnson to hide a black cat's bone on his person, and indulge in a midnight voodoo ceremony, complete with leopard skin and drums, if threatened with the loss of the presidency of Fisk University, or the love of his wife" (1161). But this fear and desire is irrational, childlike, and perverse, and ultimately dangerous to the nation.[31] She points out that stories about middle-class, professional black Americans would "destroy many illusions and romantic traditions which America probably likes to have around. But then, we have no record of anybody sinking into a lingering death on finding out that there was no Santa Claus." In a telling phrase, Hurston remarks that the revelation that blacks are just like everyone else "will hardly kill off the population of the nation" (1162). However, America's *primitive need to believe in absolute black difference*, which she broached at the beginning of the essay, will perpetuate national instability and division which, because of the Cold War "international stress and strain," could, in fact, "kill off the nation" (1162).

The author and critic Richard Gibson dispenses with Hurston's wry style, preferring instead a frontal assault on the structure of attitudes restricting the prospects of black writers. The "young Negro writer" must resist the "Professional Liberal . . . the enslaver of his mind and his imagination":

> You are not free yet, he is told. Write about what you know, he is told, and the Professional Liberal will not fail to remind him that he cannot possibly know anything else but Jim Crow, sharecropping, slum-ghettoes, Georgia crackers, and the sting of his humiliation, his unending ordeal, his blackness—that is what the young Negro who wants to write is supposed to know and all his enemies are eager for him to believe the grand lie that no training is possible, no education in this world can add to that bitter knowledge. ("A No to Nothing" 92)

As with Hurston, Gibson pointedly rejects the Myrdalian notion that black thought is wholly consumed with and exhausted by the Negro problem. The "Professional Liberal" cajoles the young writer into affirming this debilitating fantasy because it keeps the liberal installed in a position of authority. For Gibson, the young black writer must be disabused of the idea that the demand for protest is anything other than racist condescension. It is rather a Foucauldian incitement to racial discourse, an operation of power that holds out the promise of release from and transcendence of these abject conditions, but instead violates the black writer's authorial privacy by radically constricting the discursive possibilities of black subjectivity, as well as black cultural and political authority. Social restriction notwithstanding, Gibson declares that the black writer's imagination keeps whatever company it chooses and goes where it lists. The aspiring young black writer must remember that "he lives in the age of Joyce, Proust, Mann, Gide, Kafka and not merely that of Chester B. Himes. The young writer might do well to impress upon himself the fact that he is a contemporary of Eliot, Valery, Pound, Rilke, Auden and not merely of Langston Hughes. And, regardless of what some might wish him to believe, he shares as much as any other literate member of this civilization the traditions that produced those men. His black skin is no iron curtain about his brain; he is not cut off from the main stream" (91).

To put it plainly, an author's race should in no way impinge upon his literary freedom of association. This is a clear violation of his privacy, in that it interferes with deeply personal and self-defining preferences. Gibson declares that his creative and intellectual affinities, affiliations, and influences exceed both racial and national boundaries; he must be free to draw on whichever traditions he chooses—like any white, Western author, the black American writer is heir to them all.[32] The clearly invidious distinction that Gibson draws between these white and black writers anticipates Ellison's famous rebuke of Howe a decade later, in which Ellison points out that "while one can do nothing about choosing one's relatives, one can, as artist, choose one's 'ancestors.' Wright was in this sense, a 'relative,' Hemingway an 'ancestor.' Langston Hughes, whose work I knew in grade school and whom I knew before I knew Wright, was a 'relative'; Eliot, whom I was to meet only many years later, and Malraux and Dostoevsky and Faulkner, were 'ancestors'—if you please or don't please!" ("The World and the Jug" 185). As Ellison says earlier in this piece, "I fear the implications of Howe's ideas concerning the Negro writer's role as actionist more than I do the State of Mississippi. Which is not to deny the degree of viciousness which exists there, but to recognize the degree of freedom which also exists there precisely because the repression is relatively crude . . . and it left the world of literature alone" (181).[33] Ellison rejects Howe's attempt to update Harry Overstreet's earlier claim that "the Negro writer of fiction . . . is not free to write what he pleases. Such freedom is reserved for whites." Ellison and Gibson are acutely aware that, in the words of Etienne Balibar, "Culture can also function like a nature, and it can in particular function as a way of locking individuals and groups *a priori* into a genealogy, into a determination that is immutable and intangible in origin" (22). Refusing the ghettoizing effects of white liberal sympathy, both Ellison and Gibson assert that the artist's cultural genealogy is a private choice, one immune to racialized prescriptions about "Negro literature."

Echoing Hurston, Gibson baldly asserts that the white liberal's preferences for black abjection derive from unresolved psychic conflicts and beliefs that plainly parallel those of the white supremacist: "The Professional Liberal needs the Problem, he needs a cause, a people to defend.

And, in defending, he finds some satisfaction for his own neuroses. He becomes the Great White Father, the 'marse' protecting his darkies. He will not any more than will the ghetto-masters allow a Negro the right to be human, to become a man and walk with his own strength his own way. For the sake of *his* sanity, the Professional Liberal knows the Negro must bear the Problem, must be kept his pet, to be protected at the end of leash" ("A No to Nothing" 90). The Professional Liberal profits both financially and psychologically from black suffering, as it perpetuates the authority he inherited from the days of slavery. The Negro writer should reject any temptation to bolster white liberal agency at the cost of his own freedom, and instead take his place among whomever he feels a sympathetic "harmony of disposition" and intellectual fellow-feeling.

The terms of Gibson's critique bear many similarities to Baldwin's famous attacks on the protest tradition and Richard Wright in "Everybody's Protest Novel" and "Many Thousands Gone," published in the anti-Stalinist liberal magazine *Partisan Review* in 1949 and 1951, respectively.[34] Baldwin also suggests that the white liberal investment in the protest tradition emerges from unresolved dominant-culture neuroses, primarily ones of guilt, though he forcefully demonstrates how these neuroses are often masked in seemingly unrelated discourses: Christian morality and putatively scientific sociological analyses, both of which depict blackness as something to be feared and contained.

Baldwin frames his scathing denunciation of "the modern American protest novel," of which Wright's *Native Son* constitutes an especially perverse example, primarily by asserting that it has not changed since Harriet Beecher Stowe launched the tradition with *Uncle Tom's Cabin*. Despite the fact that nearly one hundred years had passed since the appearance of Stowe's work, Baldwin contends that *Uncle Tom's Cabin* and recent "novels of Negro oppression" deploy the same "medieval morality" and say the same thing about American race relations: "'This is perfectly horrible! You ought to be ashamed of yourselves!'" ("Everybody's Protest Novel" 13, 14). Baldwin argues that their great downfall derives from a shared origin in sympathy, which manifests as a devotion to "Humanity" and a "Cause" (as opposed to human beings, who are "resolutely indefinable, unpredictable" and "complex"); they "lop [the human being] down to the status of a time saving invention [by turning him into] merely a member of Society or a Group or a deplorable conundrum to be explained by Science" (15).[35]

Baldwin goes so far as to insist that *Uncle Tom's Cabin* and modern protest novels are "activated by what might be called a theological terror, the terror of damnation; and the spirit that breathes in this book, hot, self-righteous, fearful is not different from that spirit of medieval times which sought to exorcize evil by burning witches; and is not different from that terror which activates a lynch mob" ("Everybody's Protest Novel" 18). In other words, Stowe, like the lynch mob, is "primitive" (i.e., stuck in the past, incapable of progress), irrational, and driven by an unrecognized, or unacknowledged, guilt that originates in a "sinful" desire for black bodies. This desire manifests as either the racially purifying, dehumanizing, and putatively virtuous symbolic emasculation of Uncle Tom, or the racially purifying, dehumanizing, and putatively virtuous literal emasculation and burning of the lynch victim.

Here we see Baldwin making explicit what Hurston and Gibson only implied, that the sympathetic white liberal demand for discourse on the Negro problem, for images of subjected black bodies, is caught up in what Foucault described as an interlocking and "perpetual spiral of power and pleasure." Foucault's well-known critique of the "repressive hypothesis" recasts conventional understandings of the Victorian era as one marked less by a prohibitive silence on matters sexual, and more by an endless proliferation of discourse in which every aspect of the individual's life (from the subject's body, to her mind, to all her relations, be they familial, religious, medical, or purely social) is "penetrated" by modern power, thereby evacuating the modern subject's capacity for privacy and freedom. The subject is constantly incited to speak about any and all sexual thoughts, sensations, experiences, and in the process her sexuality becomes reified in her person and in discourse as her "truth of self." Foucault insists that whether the inciting mechanism is religious, scientific (e.g., psychological), or educational, each new sexual "confession" creates a "space of intervention" in the subject, which substantiates his thesis that in the modern era the subject experiences unprecedented levels of discipline, and that modern society itself "is in actual fact and directly, perverse" (*History* 47).

Baldwin seems to be anticipating Foucault's critique when he argues that the color line in America operates via the same processes, in which race is disciplined precisely through mechanisms of sexuality. As Ferguson argues, hegemonic notions of blackness, be they scientific, political, or religious, anchor blackness in a sexual truth: these discourses locate (or implant) the "truth" of blackness in the black subject's erotic deviance, as suggested earlier, in her nonheteronormativity (21). But Baldwin makes clear (as do Hurston, Gibson, and Ellison) that this intractable black perversion is really an effect of hegemonic power and thus better understood as evidence of white perversion. One of Baldwin's accomplishments is his illumination of the extent to which these discourses are interlocking. For example, he proclaims that "[t]he aim of the protest novel becomes something very closely resembling the zeal of those alabaster missionaries to Africa to cover the nakedness of the natives, to hurry them into the pallid arms of Jesus and thence into slavery" (20). This analogy suggests that the protest novelist, or the sympathetic white liberal "missionary" publisher, is driven (or, rather, excited) by a certain fantasy of primitive, "naked," and damned blackness that must be redeemed in and by civilization—in the rhetoric of the protest novelist, via liberal-nationalism, Popular Front coalitionism, or Marxism. But this embrace, however thrilling for the protest novelist, represents less a redemption than a conscription. For whatever the African (American) might have represented to herself, "[her] face [is] never scrutinized, [her] voice [is] never heard" (*Notes* xiv–xv), and she enters discourse principally as a projection of white desire and an effect of white power. The protest novel for the young black writer, as discussed earlier in this section, represents a mechanism of "excitation and incitement" (Foucault, *History* 48). For all its promise of imaginative freedom and rebellion, Baldwin insists that protest literature offers the author only ready-made hegemonic versions of reality that violate black privacy rather than empower the aspiring black novelist.

In particular, the protest novelist fails precisely to the extent that he relies on *sociological* analyses of black experience.[36] "Literature and sociology are not one and the same," Baldwin reminds us. And sociology's taxonomies and indices, though representing attempts to find order and possibly solutions to social ills, end up in some respects creating the problems they purport to describe, and thus enacting epistemic violence on the subjects of their analysis. "Our passion for categorization... those categories which were meant to define and control the world for us have boomeranged us into chaos" ("Everybody's Protest Novel" 18). For Baldwin, most literature on the Problem (as well as other social "problems," such as anti-Semitism, homosexuality, etc.) is doomed to fail because it accepts from the beginning the social scientific proposition that black life and consciousness are fully encompassed by the Problem. Most frightening for Baldwin is the degree to which these discourses determine the subject's relation to her self—arguably the greatest violation of privacy possible. In lieu of language suited to voicing her own individual experiences, perceptions, needs and desires, sociology provides language capable of describing only her group's subjugation, deprivation, and deviation. "Now, as then," he warns, "we find ourselves bound, first without, then within, by the nature of our categorization. And escape is not effected through a bitter railing against the trap; it is as though the very striving were the only motion needed to spring the trap upon us" (20). Protest literature, in its reliance on sociological explanations of black experience (rather than, for example, the strategies of individual and communal survival that have sustained Africans Americans for centuries), is an "incitement to [racial-sexual] discourse" that provides additional spaces of intervention and attenuates privacy. It erases evidence of black agency and reinforces the authority of white normativity and white dominance. For this reason, Baldwin argues that "the 'protest' novel, so far from being disturbing, is an accepted and comforting aspect of the American scene, ramifying that framework we believe to be so necessary" (19). Especially if authored by an African American, the protest novel assists in the manufacture of consent that fortifies hegemony. Because of its perceived authenticity, the black protest novel, such as Wright's *Native Son*, validates hegemonic discourses of blackness.

But for all the energy that these authors expended in distinguishing their artistic vision from Wright's, Wright felt the intrusions on his authorial racial privacy as keenly as they did, and he largely agreed with their assessments regarding the role of the white liberal as gatekeeper of contemporary publishing. I discuss Wright's responses to these conditions at length in chapter 6, but for now I will offer one illustration. In his essay "Literature of the Negro in the United States," which appears in *White Man, Listen!* (1957), Wright concluded his survey of black literature with these thoughts on contemporary black writing:

> As Negro literary expression changes, one feels that American liberal thought has sustained a loss. What, then, was the relation of Negro expression to liberal thought in the United States? The Negro was a kind of conscience to that body of liberal opinion. The liberals were ridden with a sense of guilt, and the Negro's wailing served as something that enabled the liberal to define his relationship to the American scene. Today the relationship between liberals and Negroes is hard to define. Indeed, one feels that the liberals kind of resent the new trend of independence which the Negro exhibits. But this is inevitable; the Negro, as he learns to stand on his own feet and express himself not in purely racial, but human terms, will launch criticism upon his native land which made him feel a sense of estrangement that he never wanted. This new attitude could have a healthy effect upon the culture of the United States. At long last, maybe a merging of Negro expression with American expression will take place. (772-73)

Wright, by this time considered the paradigmatic example of a racial protest author, seconds the belief that the white liberal embrace of racial protest, to the exclusion of alternative visions of black experience, reveals the extent to which these narratives may also have supported rather than unsettled racial asymmetries. Each of these authors suspects that the white liberal's excessive investment in protest is ultimately more self-indulgent than selfless. The white liberal "needs" black protest because sympathy for black suffering generates white liberal authority. In short, they argue that white liberal interest in black lack emerges from and compensates for white lack.

The white-life novel, in contrast, evades these structures of white desire by foregrounding white psychological deficits and moral failings, particularly in the domestic realm, sympathetically. The authors train their critical gaze on white privacy not to "protest," but to counter narratives of black domestic pathology while safeguarding their racial privacy. As the following chapters will demonstrate, the white-life novels critique white normativity without reducing whiteness to a series of pathologized stereotypes. The breadth and complexity of these works plainly contradict Myrdal's assertion that black thought is little more than derivative, irrational, and distorted white thought, and that it is incapable of addressing anything beyond the Negro problem. On the contrary, the authors envisage *positive change* principally through modes of identification and forms of sociability that refigure white heteropatriarchy. In effect, they question and reconstitute hegemonic forms of white privacy. This refigured white privacy, however unsettling, or perhaps because it is unsettling, allows for the possibility of a more progressive and inclusive future.

2 / The Home and the Street: Ann Petry's "Rage for Privacy"

> *There is not one writer in a thousand who owns so genuine and generous and undiscriminating a creative sympathy. Ann Petry becomes each character she mentions, grants each one a full, felt intensity of being, the mean and the loving, the white and the black, even when they come and go in only fifty words. Rich sick old ladies, lecherous toads, toddlers, half-animal brutes, the belligerently independent, the loved and unloved, the passion- and obsession-maddened, those who scarcely exist: each one, difficult as it may seem, she enters to become, becomes to create, with a universality of creative sympathy that is honestly Shakespearian. (Or at least Faulknerian; he does it too).*
>
> —DAVID LITTLEJOHN, *Black on White*

One of the central objectives of *Abandoning the Black Hero* is to reconsider a body of works that in African American literary studies have been *devalued* due to interpretive protocols that presume blackness as the privileged object of inquiry. This devaluation of course is in response to a corresponding devaluation of blackness in the United States, culturally, socially, and politically. As Lindon Barrett argues in *Blackness and Value: Seeing Double*, in the United States "value" and "race" are fundamentally intertwined, as "abstract entities [that] keenly reflect one another, even to a point at which they might be considered isomorphic. At its simplest, value is a configuration of privilege, and, at its crudest, race is the same. Insofar as value, as a theoretical dynamic, promotes one form(ation) to the detriment of another (or others), race proves a dramatic instantiation of this principle" (1–2). Barrett is one of innumerable commentators who challenge the underlying rationales and violent effects of white-supremacist values before going on to (re)form "blackness" around alternative logics, infusing this reconfigured notion of blackness with a resistive and inversely privileged *countervalue*. Barrett proffers the African American "singing voice . . . as an esteemed form of countersignificant African American cultural expressivity" (6) in contrast to the "signing" (i.e., writing) voice that is privileged in Eurocentric paradigms of cultural and political value. But what effect does this paradigm have on the value of texts by African American authors that don't "sing" in a "black" voice? Barrett's study itself provides an illustrative answer. He singles out the work of Ann Petry as providing paradigmatic literary examples of the black "singing" voice, organizing entire chapters around careful readings of *The Street* (1946) and *The Narrows* (1953). *Country Place* receives not even a passing mention. Barrett's effort to rescue blackness from what he terms "bla(n)ckness" via recourse to black vernacular expressive "presence," at least within the logic of his argument, produces *Country Place* as "absence."

Barrett's work provides merely one example of this tendency in scholarship on Ann Petry's career. Critics have only recently begun to challenge the idea that Petry's value as an author derives primarily from *The Street* and *The Narrows*. Bernard Bell devotes only one paragraph to *Country Place* in his influential study *The Afro-American Novel and Its Tradition*, with the explanation that "[b]ecause the major characters are white, and because time and place are more important thematically than color and class, it is not as relevant . . . to our theory of a distinctive Afro-American tradition as *The Street* and *The Narrows*" (180). While Hilary Holladay devotes a chapter to *Country Place* in her monograph on Petry, the retrospective collection edited by Hazel Ervin and Holladay, *The Critical Response to Ann Petry*, dedicates only two out of twenty-six critical essays to *Country Place*.[1]

This disparity in critical reception is largely attributable to the fact that *The Street* and, to a lesser extent, *The Narrows* are not only focused on black characters, but are "protest" novels, frequently described as "naturalist," sociological, and political—all of these terms remain valued analytic categories. Despite being denigrated by some both then and now, *Country Place*, in contrast, aside from being focused almost entirely on white characters, appears principally concerned with such "apolitical" subjects as "man" and "his" moral and psychological conflicts. This critical orientation has done more than marginalize *Country Place*; it has also contributed to a lack of attention to themes that were of enormous value to Petry herself—that is, sympathy and, above all, privacy. The reintegration of *Country Place* into her oeuvre sheds light on concerns that persist over the entirety of her career, but especially during the vital first phase—the ten-year span between 1943 and 1953.

I hope to clarify this continuity in Petry's work by proposing that there is a dialectical relation between what might too quickly be termed her black "protest" fiction and her white "domestic" novel. Her writing focused on black characters (work considered more political and sociological and thus more public) is deeply engaged with questions of privacy and the private sphere, and her domestic novel focused on white characters is committed, albeit indirectly, to revising public meanings of race. My reading engages with and destabilizes the series of binarisms that have governed the reception of her work: black/white, protest/domestic,[2] political/apolitical, public/private, street/home. Instead, I examine how Petry employs interracial sympathy (its failures and successes) as a determinant of black privacy. This approach allows me to productively juxtapose works that have heretofore been seen as bearing little relation to each other.

In this chapter, I offer a comparative reading of *Country Place* with two apparently dissimilar works that appeared the same year—"The Bones of Louella Brown" and "In Darkness and Confusion." All three of these works attempt to achieve a kind of provisional racial privacy by symbolically resolving African Americans' overdetermined and exploitative relationship with publicity. Each text in its own way reclaims the public—scene and source of denigration and delegitimation—as a way of projecting a space of private dignity. In *Country Place*, Petry's emphasis on white characters enacts a form of racial privacy for both the character Neola, a black maid, and the author herself; Petry is able to write beyond "protest," and Neola, unlike Lutie Johnson, is not an abject figure destroyed by racism. My reading elucidates the degree to which Petry engages contemporary social science discourses (such as those of Gunnar Myrdal and the debates around "mother-blaming") in order to facilitate a switch from "the Negro problem" (i.e., protest) and its reliance on depictions of black subjection to "white problems"—in this case, white moral and psychological deficits. Over the course of the novel, she renders a powerful refiguring of white male domestic privilege—the very thing that symbolically and materially determines the (im)possibility of black privacy—and in the process imagines an alternative notion of American progress.

Petry's early works that are focused on the lives of African Americans repeatedly figure racial oppression by illustrating how the public construction and maintenance of the color line renders privacy impossible for her black characters. My thinking on race and privacy draws on and extends the treatments of this subject by Phillip Brian Harper, Lauren Berlant, and Alex Lubin.[3] I intend to highlight how, in America, one's capacity for social agency and self-mastery, particularly in the private sphere, is fundamentally determined by public meanings of race.

By "private sphere," I am referring principally to the domestic sphere, intimate relations, and forms of labor, both paid and unpaid—although most paid labor takes place in public, in the United States the market economy is "private" insofar as it is nominally extrapolitical (operating largely independently of the state, and structured around individuals acting as private economic agents and owners of property) (Taylor 101).

A central concern in Petry's early fiction is how America's racialized and sexualized division of labor has had particularly adverse affects on black women's struggle for privacy. Overwhelmingly excluded from white-collar jobs, black women in the 1940s found themselves commodified as either domestics or, at least in terms of dominant culture attitudes, prostitutes.[4] White male sexual exploitation of black women demonstrates forcefully the degree to which the latter historically have been rendered private objects of white male concern—black women are, in the words of Phillip Brian Harper, "not private subjects who can themselves lay claim to and govern their own private domains" (19). Harper explains that these conditions function to solidify the subjectivity of white men "precisely because it emphasizes the degree to which he is master over his own private realm, king in his own castle, while simultaneously voiding the black woman's subjectivity by depriving her of a private realm over which she can hold sovereign sway."[5] More recently, Alex Lubin has demonstrated how the postwar "domestic imperative" (i.e., the national demand for women to give up their wartime participation in public life and devote their energies to the private sphere—to family and home) was rendered largely inoperable for black women, both because of antimiscegenation laws and because of the racialized economy that incorporated black women into the private spaces of white families as domestics.[6] These conditions were powerfully dramatized in *The Street*, and Lubin has shown how "for Lutie Johnson, that which ought to be private (her home and family life) is made public, while that which ought to receive recognition in the public sphere (her labor as mother, civil service worker, and blues singer) is rendered invisible" (129). Lutie is, on the one hand, unable to care for her own home and family because her labor is devoted to reproducing the private life of the Chandlers, while, on the other, the white man who owns her apartment building, Junto, operates a brothel in this same building, and attempts to incorporate her as an object of sexual commerce (128–33). Petry's fiction from this era repeatedly exposes the extent to which the nation's valorization and protection of the domestic sphere—as a locus of private subject formation and a quasi-sanctified zone of noninterference—is, in practice, an *index of white heteropatriarchal privilege* underwritten by the history of whiteness as "usable property, the subject of the law's regard and protection" (Harris 1737). Privacy, understood as a condition of full enfranchisement, is multifaceted—it necessitates the public authority and social agency that allows for the maintenance of the self and family in the private sphere, which includes access to adequate employment, housing, education, health services, police protection (in the case of African Americans, protection from the police), and freedom from unwanted exposure to certain behaviors (e.g., drugs, prostitution, and violent crime). "In Darkness and Confusion" and "The Bones of Louella Brown" in particular narrate incursions into the public sphere on behalf of African American privacy.

"In Darkness and Confusion" provides a fictionalized and highly subjective rendering of one family's participation in the devastating 1943 Harlem riots. The riot was triggered when a black soldier assaulted a white police officer who was arresting a black woman for "disorderly conduct"; the soldier hit the officer with his nightstick, and was then shot by the officer in the shoulder. Reports of the shooting quickly spread, including rumors that the police officer had killed the soldier in front of his mother, who was with him at the time. As Petry's narrative describes in vivid detail, large, angry crowds formed, walking first to the hospital where the solider and police officer were taken, and then to the police station, before turning again toward 125th Street, where the destruction of the businesses and looting began and continued until dawn the next morning. The riot caused an estimated $5 million of property damage, and directly led to six deaths and several hundred injuries and arrests; all those killed were African American, as were nearly all of the injured and arrested.

The explosion in Harlem was of course accompanied by an explosion in publicity. The mainstream press repeatedly insisted that it was not a race riot, but rather, as New York Police Commissioner Lewis Valentine put it, "hoodlumism of the worst kind" ("Valentine Lays Rioting to Hoodlumism"). Some white critics argued that it was the result of racial "agitators," and others argued it was the result of police laxity in law enforcement, especially Mayor Fiorello La Guardia's "irresponsible" policy of police *restraint* ("Trouble in Harlem"). One *Washington Post* editorial denied not only that it was a race riot, but also that it was even a riot at all. Rather, "what seems to have occurred was a complete breakdown of all law and order followed by an outrageous carnival of looting. Certainly it takes something of a *tour de force* of reasoning to translate such an episode into a subtle protest against social injustices" ("Harlem Post-Mortem"). Petry's narrative constitutes just such a *"tour de force* of reasoning." It is at once an intervention in majoritarian public discourses about the riots, as well as a pointed analysis of how the circulation of race in the public sphere destroys black privacy. Although based on a specific historical event, "In Darkness and Confusion" dramatizes a recurring theme in Petry's work: the extent to which African Americans experience their relation to the nation and the state not only as deprivation and violation, but specifically as failed interracial sympathy. In this story, Petry imagines violent protest in the streets not as lawlessness and immorality, but rather as a galvanizing moment of sympathy that allows Harlem's residents to strike out against racist state violence. Her narrative demonstrates forcefully how the state's active role in maintaining white private property and the white private sphere systematically structures and disrupts the possibility of the same for African Americans.

Petry's reading of the event is aligned with other contemporary commentators and more recent historians for whom there is no question that it was in fact a race riot, and specifically a communitywide reaction to racist state violence.[7] Some mainstream leaders, black and white, were concerned about the media's criminalization of the entire community and thus insisted that the rioters were only from the "criminal" element in Harlem ("Race Bias Denied as Rioting Factor"). Petry, however, makes a point of stressing that the riot was enacted by people from throughout the community. As the riot begins to escalate, the protagonist, William Jones, looks around him and exclaims, "'Great God in the morning ... everybody's out here.' There were girls in thin summer dresses, boys in long coats and tight-legged pants, old women dragging kids along by the hand. A man on crutches jerked himself past to the rhythm of the shuffling feet." William also sees bag ladies, numbers runners, and "three sisters of the Heavenly Rest for All movement" (285).[8]

Absent from her depiction of the community are "agitators" and political radicals. Rather, two of the figures responsible for touching off different phases of the riot are the central characters in the story, William and Pink Jones, both of whom appear to be largely apolitical figures. Petry gives no indication that their actions are influenced by involvement with local or national political campaigns and organizations, or even a heightened racial consciousness or resentment due to the outbreaks of white-supremacist mob violence in Detroit and Los Angeles that had captured the nation's attention earlier in the summer. The story is filtered almost entirely through William's consciousness, often utilizing free indirect discourse, and thus the reader learns that his primary preoccupation is his private, domestic life—specifically, his family's well-being. The story makes it painfully clear that it is the state's recent attack on his son, in particular, and the long-term destruction of his private life, more generally, that propels him into public action. Once he has "gone public" by taking to the streets, however, he has new insights about himself, his family, and the state.

The story opens with William sitting alone on a stifling July morning, unable to enjoy his breakfast because "there were too many nagging worries that kept drifting through his mind" (252). The worries all revolve around his family. He hasn't heard from his son, Sam, who was drafted and stationed in Georgia; his wife, Pink, is morbidly obese and has a heart condition, which means that continuing to live on the top floor of his run-down, dark, overcrowded apartment building is jeopardizing her life; and his eighteen-year-old niece seems clearly on the threshold of serious trouble. Although the story seems to revolve around the absent "good" son, the niece Annie May (who at first is presented as the "bad" or "difficult" child) plays a crucial role in the story's development. The first thing we learn about her is that she regularly stays out late and misses work; when William confronts her about her behavior, she dismisses him with disdain, barely containing her rage: "[H]e saw a deep smoldering sullenness in her face that startled him.... Lately every time Annie May looked at him there was open, jeering laughter in her eyes, as though she dared him to say anything to her. Almost as though she thought he was a fool for working so hard" (256). Her late nights, lack of a steady job, and the "cheap, bright-colored dresses she was forever buying" lead William to conclude that she has become a "Jezebel," if not a prostitute (257).

All of these worries coalesce around a long-standing, overarching frustration—his desire to move. His apartment "ain't a fit place to live.... The rooms weren't big enough for a man to move around in without bumping into something. Sometimes he thought that was why Annie May spent so much time away from home. Even at thirteen she couldn't stand being cooped up like that in such a small amount of space" (261). He fears that their living conditions push his children out to the street, and "No matter how you looked at it, it wasn't a good street to live on" (260). William has always been disturbed by the many prostitutes on his block and alarmed by the shadowy, lurking dangers, "disembodied figures" with "stealth[y]" movements "that revealed a dishonest intent that frightened him."

In certain respects, Petry reproduces commonplace images of poor black neighborhoods as zones of immorality. The dominant culture, abetted by conservative social scientists and reformers, attributed the alleged immorality of African Americans to a deep-seated racial non-heteronormativity—black neighborhoods, conflated with black bodies, were inherently pathologized and "broken," as evidenced by high rates of divorce, out-of-wedlock births, female-headed households, etc.[9] This "immorality," however, is exactly what William yearns to protect his family from. He fears it will destroy his children, especially Annie May, if it hasn't already. As the story unfolds, Petry goes on to complicate simplistic and erroneous notions of innate black immorality by situating these black neighborhoods and domestic spaces in relation to larger social forces and power asymmetries.

Two years earlier, William had gone to see Annie May's principal about persuading his niece to stay in school. The principal makes him wait two hours, and then proceeds to "bur[y] [him] under a flow of words, a mountain of words" until he "lost all sense of what she was saying." The only phrase that he fully grasps is her repeated assertion that Annie May is "a slow learner," which he knows is not true. "Confused and embarrassed . . . before he knew it he was out in the street, conscious only that he'd lost a whole afternoon's pay and he never got to say what he'd come for" (265). Instead of finding an ally in his effort to steer Annie May in the right direction, he is silenced and humiliated, implicitly in the same manner that has driven Annie May from school, even though she is "bright as a dollar." William, like Annie May, gets pushed "out on the street." William is also silenced and humiliated by "white" public authority after he and Pink lose a child at birth. Pink's "loud grieving" prompts the nurse to say with "cold contempt . . . 'You people have too many children anyway'" (284). William is stunned "speechless" by the cruelty of her remark, "so he stared at her lean, spare body," "her flat breasts," and her white uniform until he "mumbled, 'It's too bad your eyes ain't white, too'" (284). The nurse's racist remarks stand in for the dominant culture's and the state's attitude toward black domesticity—it is inherently pathological and in need of regulation and intervention. Black families are, clearly, a threat to the state.

The state's crowning assault on William and his family takes place after Sam is drafted into the army. Sam has become the repository for all of their dreams deferred; he is their last hope for a better future. During military training in the South, Sam is shot by a white military police officer "because he wouldn't go to the nigger end of the bus." Sam still manages to shoot the MP in the shoulder with his own gun, an act of resistance that gets him court-martialed and "twenty years at hard labor" (268). This refusal of compromised citizenship (rendered spatially as "the nigger end of the bus") leaves him a criminalized, right-less, and unpaid black laborer for the state. As such, Sam is thrust into a negative form of privacy, understood in the classical sense of the term, as *privation*. Much like the condition of chattel slavery, this notion of privacy indicates complete alienation from publicly guaranteed rights and agency, the absence of self-possession that modern notions of privacy are intended to protect.[10] After William learns about what has happened to Sam from another black soldier who has been stationed at the same base, he feels, once again, incapable of speaking about this injury and avoids telling his wife. The next day, however, when he sees a white police officer shoot a young black soldier, he is so outraged that he ends up leading the crowd into the street.

Before he knows it, he is caught up in a spontaneous but collective act of public resistance. By taking to the streets in protest against police brutality he feels an unprecedented sense of agency and connection with the larger community: "He got the feeling that he had lost his identity as a person with a free will of his own. It frightened him at first. Then he began to feel powerful. He was surrounded by hundreds of people like himself. They were all together, they could do anything. . . . It was as though, standing so close together, so many of them like this—as though they knew each other's thoughts. It was a wonderful thing" (282). For the first time, William is able to speak against racist authority, and when he does, his words are automatically caught up and circulated through the crowd. When he comments that "they moved the black cops out" of the area, "he heard it go back and back through the crowd until it was only a whisper of hate on the still hot air" (283). William and the crowd feel the police's fear, and when the crowd marches to the hospital where the soldier was taken (the same hospital where he encountered the racist nurse), "he saw with satisfaction that frightened faces were appearing at the windows" (284). This time the white state is afraid of him, and "[h]e began to feel that this night was the first time he'd ever really been alive. Tonight everything was going to be changed. There was a growing, swelling sense of power in him. He felt the same thing in the people around him" (284). The rapid circulation of feeling produces a deep sense of intimate communion with his fellow Harlemites. It is a profound moment of sympathy—both for the fallen black soldier and with each other. This moment of sympathy clearly derives from the crowd's collective experience of *failed interracial sympathy* and *violated privacy*, especially by representatives of the state.

Prior to this moment the street has been anything but a scene of sympathy. Rather, it has been an index of his family's unchanging and subordinate relation to the dominant culture. He stopped going to church after the minister sermonized about "the streets of gold up in heaven." The minister's spatial metaphor for salvation in the next life is especially galling, because "[t]his street where he and Pink lived was like the one where his mother had lived. It looked like he and Pink ought to have gotten further than his mother had. She had scrubbed floors, washed and ironed in the white folks' kitchens. They were doing practically the same thing. That was another reason he stopped going to church. He couldn't figure out why these things had to stay the same, and if the Lord didn't intend it like that, why didn't He change it?" (273–74). The preacher's suggestion that the righteous will find a redeemed agency in the next life exacerbates his sense of impotency in secular time. William and Pink resigned themselves to the fact that it was "too late for them" (270) to change their lives, but had held out hope that Sam could have a future with different possibilities.

William had largely given up hope for Annie May, but for the wrong reasons. During the riot he sees Annie May emerge from a storefront and throw a "pinkish" "naked model" into the crowd; she then "stood in the empty window and laughed with the crowd when someone kicked the torso into the street." This act is a revelation for William, as "he felt that now for the first time he understood her. She had never had anything but badly paying jobs—working for young white women who probably despised her. She was like Sam on that bus in Georgia. She didn't want just the nigger end of things, and here in Harlem there wasn't anything else for her. All along she'd been trying the only way she knew how to squeeze out of life a little something for herself" (289–90). Prior to this moment, he perceived her signs of "wildness" exclusively as sexual transgression and moral failure. Now he recognizes that her refusal to go to work *on time* and to keep a "steady" or "regular" job is not laziness, but her means of resisting the deadening regulation of her life, her humiliating incorporation into routines of labor that sustain the domestic sphere and private life of the white family she works for at the expense of her own. Her labor in their private sphere enables them to "progress" while locking her into performing the same tedious acts as countless generations of black women before her. Even so, Petry implies that Annie May's mode of rebellion of "staying out all night" (beyond domesticity and heteronormativity) is not "freedom"; rather, it will likely imprison her within an equally long-standing history of sexual exploitation on the streets. The bleakness of her future is punctuated by the fact that the last time William sees her during the riot she is being arrested with a group of other looters with "a yellow fox jacket dangling from one hand" (291), being punished by the state for taking "a little something for herself."

In the final scene of the story, his wife, Pink—who joined the crowd after it had formed, but was the first to begin destroying property after she learns what happened to Sam—has collapsed in front of William, dying from a heart attack. This explosive moment of sympathy is literally more than her heart can bear. William screams into the night, no longer "strangled by the words that rose in his throat" (295). While "gaining one's voice" is typically associated with personal triumph, William's curses are an expression of agony in the face of the almost total destruction of his private life. However empowering it felt to publicly share his rage and grief sympathetically with other members of the community, and however satisfying it was to know that the "white folks [who] owned these stores . . . [would] lose and lose and lose" (288), while on the streets he also comes face to face with the fact that "There ain't no room for us anywhere. There wasn't no room for Sam in a bus in Georgia. There ain't no room for us here in New York. There ain't no place but top floors. The top-floor black people" (291). This passage elegantly encapsulates the role of the state in the destruction of black privacy. William's inability to control and safeguard his domestic space and intimate sphere—his family's confinement to the top floors of run-down tenements in Harlem—clearly signifies the nation-state's refusal to create "room" for African Americans, a spatial metaphor that highlights a nearly complete lack of political agency and self-possession. The story describes not only dead children and dead parents, but also "surviving" children who are now, like him, *socially dead* subjects of state discipline who must remain trapped in the nation's racist past. Hence we see that the destruction of black privacy derives from the dominant culture's mastery of space *and time*.[11]

"The Bones of Louella Brown" deals with many of the same subjects—death, white supremacy, the quest for a home, spontaneous crowds in the streets, and an engagement with the majoritarian public sphere—though in this case a poor black woman magically speaks truth to power and ends up the master of space and time. It has been almost entirely overlooked by critics, most likely because of its comedic tone and fantastic plotting. It is a farcical tale about a dead black woman who becomes an international celebrity while haunting her way into the house of racial-national privilege. After her remains are wrongfully exhumed from her grave, the spirit of Louella Brown, a poor black washerwoman, returns to dominate the body and mind of powerful white men in order to reclaim her privacy and dignity. It is also a story in which the entire nation, and most of the world, waits in rapt attention to see the resolution of her fate. It is, in short, absurd. Petry's turn to the supernatural and hyperpublicity, however, enables her to express a longing that the world could be otherwise—in particular, to imagine a world where black women have empowered publicity and protected privacy.

At the level of plot, "The Bones of Louella Brown" describes how Louella Brown, a deceased black laundress, secures a place for herself in Bedford Abbey, a newly constructed "private chapel" reserved for the "most distinguished family in Massachusetts" (163). A public scandal ensues after a reporter breaks a story revealing that the exhumed bones of Louella Brown have been mixed up with the remains of an aristocratic Bostonian (the Countess of Castro, "nee Elizabeth Bedford") who was in the process of being reinterred in Bedford Abbey. The problem occurs because an impetuous employee of the undertaking firm, Whiffle and Peabody Incorporated, calls a reporter to document what he believes is "the biggest story of the year"—that the bones of two women occupying such profoundly different social circumstances in life are "indistinguishable" (168). Although the employee is thrilled by the challenge his discovery poses to biological racism, the reporter is more interested in an opportunity for a sensational headline; he poses the employee and the two sets of bones in countless arrangements until the employee finally exclaims in dismay, "you've moved them around so many times I can't tell which is which—nobody could tell—" (170). The story becomes front-page news, featuring a photo of the abbey and a caption posing the question that *"seize[s] the imagination of the whole country*: 'Who will be buried under the marble floor of Bedford Abbey on the twenty-first of June—the white countess or the black laundress?'" (170; emphasis added). Because Bedford Abbey radiates with national power and prestige, which I discuss below, both of the women become, almost overnight, "famous as movie stars. *Crowds gathered outside the mansion in which Governor Bedford lived; still larger and noisier crowds milled in the street in front of the offices of Whiffle and Peabody"* (171; emphasis added). The Associated Press picks up the story and wires it not only around the country, but throughout the world ("New York and London, and Paris and Moscow") (171). The entire Western world (including its new Cold War antagonist) is transfixed for a moment by Louella Brown and the Countess of Castro, excitedly speculating about how America will resolve this symbolic crisis. The hyperpublicity surrounding the mix-up is richly suggestive, particularly in relation to the issue of Louella Brown's privacy.

The original catalyst for the crisis occurs when Louella Brown's privacy was violated by the racist white cemetery owners (referred to in the story as Old Peabody—aged seventy-nine—and Young Whiffle—aged seventy-five); they removed her from her grave in an all-white cemetery in order to remedy the "truly terrible error in judgment" (165) that allowed her to be buried there forty-five years earlier. "It had taken the carefully discriminatory practices of generations of Peabodys, undertakers like himself, to make Yew Tree Cemetery what it was today—*the final home* of Boston's wealthiest and most aristocratic families" (166; emphasis added). "The truly terrible error in judgment" was the result of Peabody's father honoring *his wife's* wishes that Louella Brown, their laundress, be buried there. In other words, Louella Brown's ostensibly permanent place among Boston's most elite white families is the outcome of an act of interracial sympathy between two women. Peabody violates his mother's sympathetic gesture after he notices "with dismay, that due to the enlargement of the cemetery, over the years, [Louella, whose grave 'had been at the very tip edge of the cemetery in 1902, in a very undesirable place'] now lay in one of the choicest spots—in the exact center." When Peabody announces his decision to put her "where she should have been put in the first place" on "the outskirts of the city" (165), he is disconcerted, "for he suddenly saw Louella Brown with an amazing sharpness. It was just as though she had entered the room—a quick-moving little woman, brown of skin and black of hair, and with very erect posture" (166). Her spirit continues to confront Peabody, day and night: "In [a] dream, she came quite close to him, a small brown woman with merry eyes. After one quick look at him, she put her hands on her hips, threw her head back and laughed and laughed" (177–78). After these visitations, "he could not forget the smallest detail of her appearance: how her shoulders shook as she laughed, and that her teeth were very white and evenly spaced" (178).

When Louella was living, Peabody considered her nothing more than "our laundress. Nobody of importance" (165). Consequently he feels free to desecrate the sanctity of her grave, or rather, her "final home," as the narrator refers to Yew Tree Cemetery earlier in the story; both the grave and the home are almost universally considered intensely private, even sacred, spaces that are entitled to protection from the ravages of the marketplace and racial politics. Of course, the history of American race relations demonstrates that the opposite is true—at least for African Americans and other minority populations; the segregation of black neighborhoods and graveyards are the manifest subject of Petry's satire. She highlights this point when Whiffle chastises the careless employee, Stuart Reynolds, by lamenting that "The house... the honor of this house, years of working, of building a reputation, all destroyed" (170). The "honor" of "this house"—the firm of Whiffle and Peabody, Incorporated (163)—is predicated explicitly on the preservation of white racial privacy via the exclusion of black bodies.

Petry undermines this commonplace denigration of black bodies by giving Louella Brown a visibility and mobility she conspicuously lacked in life. Louella enters Peabody's mind in harrowing vividness at the moment he decides to "bereave" her (in the term's archaic sense of forcible dispossession)[12] of her home in Yew Tree Cemetery. Instead of granting her the respect and dignity intended by her original burial, Peabody acts entirely in accordance with his interests as a private agent in the racially structured marketplace—the body of Louella Brown is a valueless object in his possession that threatens the value of his other possessions; it must be stored elsewhere so that he may both protect his investments and extract greater profit from her gravesite, "one of the choicest spots—in the exact center" of his property.[13] Louella's spirit refuses to suffer the invisibility, silence, and immobility that was her former lot, socially and politically. She is now "quick," "very erect," and "merry," with an aristocratic comportment and an irreverent, powerfully unsettling laugh. She responds to Peabody's violation of her privacy by enacting one of the most intimate invasions of privacy imaginable, that is, by claiming unfettered access to his mind. Louella also simultaneously reverses the direction of the interrogating, dominating gaze, which is the historical privilege of the wealthy white man. Peabody's privileged status makes him "quite unaccustomed to being laughed at, even in a dream" (177–78). Nevertheless, he is powerless to return or refuse her gaze, much less punish her for her impudence. Instead, he develops a sort of respect for her. When Young Whiffle continually bemoans that they are "ruined—ruined—ruined" for their role in this fiasco, Old Peabody shouts: "Will you stop that caterwauling? One would think the Loch Ness monster lay in the crypt at Bedford Abbey" (178). As he faces her laughing spirit once again, he observes: "Louella Brown was a neatly built little woman, a fine woman, full of laughter. I remember her well. She was a gentlewoman. Her bones will do no injury to the Governor's damned funeral chapel" (178).

The explosion of publicity surrounding the "Governor's damned funeral chapel" is at the heart of Louella Brown's fight for privacy. The story opens as Peabody and Whiffle read story after story in the Boston newspapers about "this fabulous project," Bedford Abbey, a "private chapel... which would be used solely for the weddings and funerals of the Bedford family" (163). Whiffle and Peabody stand to profit enormously, as the "long-dead Bedfords were to be exhumed [from Yew Tree Cemetery] and reburied" under the abbey chapel floor, and afterward "Bedford Abbey would be officially opened with the most costly and the most elaborate funeral service ever held in Boston" (164). The abbey and the "stupendous funeral service" are both the "brain-child" of Governor Bedford, an aging former governor of Massachusetts (164). The construction of this extravagant "sacred" space intended for the exclusive, private use of the governor and his family—including the deceased "Countess of Castro," who is notably "the nearest approach to royalty in the Bedford family" (167)—demonstrates both the profoundly inegalitarian interweaving of racial, church, and state power, as well as the pathetic attempt of a vain and frightened man to "buy immortality" (176). But the excessiveness of Governor Bedford's actions, including his attempts to generate public attention, may also derive from a more obscure, racialized source of insecurity.

After the newspaper's scandalous revelation about the confused identity of the women's remains, Peabody momentarily tries to minimize the damage done to their reputation:

> "She might have been Irish," said Old Peabody coldly. . . . "And a Catholic. That would have been equally bad. No, it would have been worse. Because the Catholics would have insisted on a mass, in Bedford Abbey, of all places! Or she might have been a foreigner— a—a—Russian. Or, God forbid, a Jew!"
>
> "Nonsense," said Young Whiffle pettishly. "A black washerwoman is infinitely worse than anything you've mentioned. People are saying it's some kind of trick, that we're proving there's no difference between the races." (172)

Hilary Holladay observes that this passage serves to convey a recurring theme in Petry's works, that "blacks are not the only ones who bear the brunt of prejudice" (127). While this may be true, I would add that it also illustrates Petry's awareness of the historically contingent nature of the color line, and whiteness in particular—David Roediger reminds us that all of these ethnic groups were still only "situationally" white in 1947, and remained subject to forms of exclusion, depending on the context. Although during World War II the government celebrated American ethnic pluralism as part of its antifascist mobilization, the process of racial inclusion in the United States occurred in "crazy-quilt patterns" and varied widely across America, depending on such localized factors as the "demographics of particular workplaces and industries, patterns of strikebreaking management strategies, language acquisition, and labor markets" (8).

The significance of these ongoing debates around the exact parameters of whiteness in local, national, and international politics becomes clear when the bones of Louella Brown again disrupt the governor's racial-national theatrics. When he concocted the idea of building a private abbey, he did so believing that he could use his privileged access to the public sphere (especially as an embodiment of state power and prestige) to further enhance his already considerable public stature. The symbolic potency of the abbey would emanate not merely from his private wealth, but especially from his association with the state. The governor is aware that the value of the "privacy" of his abbey is directly related to a maximal amount of (positive) circulation in the public sphere—the more people who know about the privileged privacy of the abbey (i.e., who know about their exclusion from his familial home), the more valuable it becomes—which makes the idea of the "official opening" of the abbey all the more ironic, given that it closes to the public the very moment that it opens. The governor's efforts to exploit publicity end up backfiring, however. After the initial story about Louella and the Countess, Whiffle and Peabody decide to "call in . . . the press" and have their embalmer publicly identify the remains; this gamble at first seems to resolve the question, and the funeral takes place, with the world looking on: "Because of all the stories about Louella Brown and the Countess of Castro, most of the residents of Boston turned out to watch the funeral cortege of the Bedfords on the twenty-first of June. The ceremony that took place at Bedford Abbey was broadcast over a national hook-up, and the news services wired it around the world, complete with pictures" (174).

The next day, however, the same reporter who broke the scandal in the first place runs another story proving that the embalmer's testimony is fraudulent, thereby raising the racial controversy again. The governor "hastily called a press conference [declaring] that he would personally, publicly (in front of the press), identify the countess, if it was the countess" (175). Two days later he returns to "that marble gem," Bedford Abbey, "followed by a veritable hive of newsmen and photographers"

(175). He "forgot the eager-eared newsmen" after he opens the casket, however, and "when he spoke he reverted to the simple speech of his early ancestors. 'Why they be nothing but bones here!' he said. 'Nothing but bones! Nobody could tell who this be'" (176). The governor is undone by the sight of the bones, and tries to assure himself, "I'm alive. I can't die." But at this moment Louella's voice enters his mind, "saying over and over . . . It will. It can. It will. It can. It will" (176).

It is striking that when faced with the bones of his ancestors, and his own imminent death, he loses control of his public, authoritative, and unmarked "white" voice, and speaks instead with an Irish brogue, "the simple speech of his early ancestors." This linguistic reversion brings to light a racial-national subtext that might otherwise be overlooked. The purpose of the press conference is to establish, in front of the nation and the world, absolute difference between the two women—one white and one black—in order to try to manage the crisis that has emerged—the possibility that he has installed a black woman in his family home, making her a permanent part of his public family lineage. When faced with the impossibility of conclusively identifying one woman as white, and the other as black, he becomes *Irish* again, which, depending on your perspective, either undermines the idea of absolute racial difference or significantly qualifies his whiteness and public status authority—that is, if you are sympathetic to Whiffle's and Peabody's attitudes toward the Irish. It seems clear that Governor Bedford's original objective, conscious or not, was to manage the latter possibility: the construction of the abbey can be seen as an elaborate publicity stunt intended to bring all of the "long-dead Bedfords," but most especially the quasi-aristocratic Countess of Castro, into his "home"; it is as though he is trying, through his privileged public status and association with the state, to make his dead Irish (likely Catholic) relatives, and himself, "white" for all time by appealing to national culture and eliminating the historical contingency of race, an act that would whiten his Irish past and future in one great synchronic, dehistoricizing public ritual. To borrow from Lauren Berlant, we could say that his efforts at memorialization were an attempt to make his family's whiteness "dead"—that is, fixed, frozen, and outside history.[14]

He fails spectacularly, though: instead of Irish becoming white, Irish, black, and white become "indistinguishable." As with Peabody's original attempt to remove Louella Brown from Yew Tree Cemetery, Governor Bedford's attempt to solidify the color line ends up directly undermining it. Even more importantly, though, because of the publicity that he summoned, and because of his intentional identification with state power, he, on behalf of the state, unwillingly becomes a powerful antiracist spokesperson. "The Governor's statement ["Nobody could tell who this be"] went around the world, in direct quotes. So did the photographs of him, peering inside the casket, his mouth open, his eyes staring" (176). This statement, the most controversial of all because it comes from the governor and directly implicates the state, ignites a firestorm in the public sphere: "Sermons were preached about the Governor's statement, editorials were written about it, and Congressmen made long-winded speeches over the radio. The Mississippi legislature threatened to declare war on the sovereign state of Massachusetts because Governor Bedford's remarks were an unforgivable insult to believers in white supremacy" (177).

Paradoxically, even as the nation edges toward "civil war" over this apparent assault on America's enduring history of racial nationalism, the half-century-old remains of these women become celebrities: "[M]any radio listeners became completely confused and, believing that both ladies were still alive, sent presents to them" (177). Louella Brown is at least in one sense "alive" in a way she never was before her death. Not only in the confused mind of the public, but also, crucially, in the minds of these powerful white men. Moreover, her contribution to the governor's loss of self-possession at the very moment that he tried to "deaden" his racial identity actually makes it erupt into the realm of the living, or history, once again. In the end, Peabody, in a last-ditch effort to "propitiate" Louella's spirit, is compelled to approach the governor and recommend that her name be inscribed alongside the Countess's name in the abbey, although with the new title of "gentlewoman" supplanting her former public identity of "black laundress." The governor acquiesces "reluctantly" and only because he "had the uneasy feeling that he could already hear Louella's laughter" (180).

The use of the supernatural and hyperpublicity allows Petry to symbolically resolve the exploitative and determinative relation of the majoritarian public sphere and nationality to the violated privacy of black women. It is a fantasy that bears striking parallels to one described by Lauren Berlant, who, feeling overcome with disgust at the abuse of white male public privilege on display in the midst of the Clarence Thomas–Anita Hill hearings, "ache[s] to be an American diva" and to address the nation herself: "The desire for contact sometimes took the phantasmatic form of a private letter to a senator, or one to a newspaper, sometimes a phone encounter, sometimes a fantasy that a reporter from the national news or 'Nightline' would accost me randomly on the street and that my impromptu eloquence would instantly transport me to the televisual realm of a Robert Bork, where my voice and body would be loud, personal, national and valorized" (*Queen of America* 241). She also expresses a more malevolent desire to enter "a senator's body and to dominate it through an orifice he was incapable of fully closing, an ear or an eye. This intimate fantasy communication aimed to provoke sensations in him for which he was unprepared . . . to [make] him so full and so sick with the knowledge of what he has never experienced officially that he would lose, perhaps gratefully, his sensual innocence about, not the power of his own sexuality, but the sexuality of his power, and . . ." (241). She explains that "[t]he desire to go public, to exploit the dispersed media of national life, became my way of approximating the power of official nationality to dominate bodies—a motive which, in a relation of overidentification, I and many others had mapped onto Hill" (241).

"Bones" bears so many structural parallels with Berlant's analyses of black women's national experience and her personal "fantasies"—of exploiting national publicity, of violating white male privacy—that it seems a perfect candidate for inclusion in her archive of national-racial-sexual injury. There is, however, a notable absence of reference to sexual violation in Petry's story. Only echoes remain, especially in the repeated and "shameful" exposure of these women's bones to public scrutiny, and the extraordinary, even otherworldly, lengths to which Louella resorts in order to protect the sanctity of her body. Nevertheless, Petry safeguards Louella's sexual privacy by making no mention of her intimate relations while living, or her sexuality. As a ghost, she has total control of her movements, and her bones are not subject to denigration in the public sphere. It seems impossible to imagine a realist narrative in which a living Louella Brown could persuade a nation to act ethically on behalf of black women. Instead, Petry taps into a fantasy structure readily recognizable to those who experience nationality as private violation—the desire to violate the nationally sanctioned privacy of powerful white men, so much so that they speak publicly against their own racial-national privilege.

Country Place has thus far proven difficult to align with Petry's other work in this period, as it appears to mark a dramatic departure in setting, mood, theme, and even writing style. It takes place in a small, nearly all-white New England resort town, has only one black character, and is not focused principally on racial oppression. Unlike the explosiveness of *The Street* and "In Darkness and Confusion," or the farcical tone and plotting of "The Bones of Louella Brown," Petry says that she "tried to *underwrite* [in *Country Place*] . . . I tried to get into the style something of the surface quiet of a small country town—a slowness of tempo . . . absorbed almost unconsciously ("Great Secret" 217; emphasis in original). Even so, some reviewers faulted the novel precisely for being too melodramatic—presumably because of its frank treatments of sexual desire, infidelity, and attempted murder.[15] One mainstream reviewer compared *Country Place* favorably to *The Street*, however, largely because she believed that the former "waves no flags"; she adds approvingly that "in an age in which we aim to support the thesis of One World, it is wholesome to note that some Negro creative artists are apparently concerned with Art." The reviewer's presumption that *Country Place*, unlike *The Street*, is concerned with "Art" rather than politics derives from the fact that the story's critical gaze is trained primarily on private white spaces: white homes, white families, white "hearts" and minds. Moreover, it appears curiously invested in traditional gender roles, given that the crises in the narrative seem to emerge from bad mothers, promiscuous wives, and weak, perverse men. Finally, *Country Place* has also frustrated more contemporary readerly expectations by providing, with only a few exceptions, *sympathetic* depictions of its white characters—*Country Place*, like "The Bones of Louella Brown," turns on a transformative act of interracial sympathy, one that is also imperiled by a competing failure of interracial sympathy.[16]

Country Place starkly deviates from what Claudia Tate calls the established "protocols of black textuality" (3). However, the same issues that have tended to deter critics represent the most productive points of entry for the novel's reconsideration. My discussion thus far has attended to Petry's enduring interest in the domestic space as a register of power relations and the possibility of African American privacy. In *Country Place*, Petry's use of moral and psychological discourses in her depiction of privileged white domestic space facilitates a two-pronged project: it enables her to simultaneously scrutinize a powerful emblem of American innocence, virtue, and normativity—middle-class, small-town America, which was, notably, often juxtaposed against the supposed immorality of black urban neighborhoods—while also protecting both her, and her character Neola's privacy.

Petry's shift in racial community and discursive strategy allows for several overlapping objectives. In particular, her emphasis on the psychological dynamics of white intimate and family life avoids the reinscription of black suffering that the traditional "protest" narrative typically requires. Petry was well aware that this was a twice-told tale, and one that constrained her choices for imagining the complexity of black experience in particular, and her access to authorial freedom in general. Throughout her career, Petry resisted efforts by critics and publishers to label or, we might say, "name" her, because this naming amounted to a form of racialized or gendered proscription. She was especially sensitive to being categorized as belonging to a particular school, or espousing a particular political position. This sensitivity was a sign not only of her independent spirit, but also the consequence of having her work repeatedly compared to Richard Wright's. These comparisons continue to this day, with Petry often cast as Wright's protégé or, as one critic put it, as having been "fathered" by Wright.[17] Petry's daughter, Elisabeth Petry, says that her mother "found the connection [with Wright] galling" (*At Home Inside* 101). Elisabeth reports that when her mother was asked whether she was a "conscious exponent" of Wright's realism, "she responded that she considered such a comparison to be pigeonholing": "I have never been a 'conscious (or unconscious) exponent' of Richard Wright's 'realism,'" Petry said. "And to describe me as 'a female Richard Wright' is to label me as a copycat female incapable of creating a body of work on my own—it diminishes me as a writer, belittles me." When asked if she saw herself as part of a "Naturalist school" (another way of asking if she was part of the Richard Wright school), she repeated, "I have no interest in writing a series of novels and/or short stories involving characters I've [already] created" (Ervin 95). She also refused more than once to comment on her contribution to the rise of the postwar white-life novel. "I don't know what impelled other black writers to stop writing novels about blacks," Petry said. "I wrote *Country Place* because I happened to have been in a small town in Connecticut during a hurricane—I decided to write about that violent, devastating storm and its effects on the town and the people who lived there." She makes a similar reply in another interview, where she insists that the only reason she focuses on white characters in *Country Place* is because the story is based on a 1938 hurricane that took place in Old Saybrook, Connecticut, "and of course Old Saybrook is mostly white, so the novel has mostly white characters in it. Besides, I have never wanted to write the same kind of book twice. Writing such a different book was a challenge, but one that I welcomed" (99).

In fact, Petry's working notes for *Country Place* reveal that she imagined the characters and themes first, and hit upon the hurricane later as a way to tie them together.[18] Her public responses, however, clearly seem intended to deflect efforts by interviewers to categorize her work racially, or to get *her* to categorize her work this way. The right to draw on one's personal experiences and to experiment with new subject matter and themes is the prerogative of all writers, though at the time it was a right seldom fully available to black authors. Another way to phrase this is that she insists on her right to privacy—although in this case it is her privacy as an author—which means that she will not restrict the range of her creative vision in order to conform to the public's benighted presumptions about "Negro writing." Petry had, in her daughter's words, a "rage for privacy," and on the few occasions in which she granted interviews, she actively cultivated her reputation as an intensely "private person," insisting that "solitude and privacy are essential for a writer" (97). She regularly refused to answer questions, especially ones about the meaning of her writing, politically and otherwise. Complex, open-ended queries were often met with such terse replies as, "No." "I have no idea." "No comment is necessary." As Hillary Holladay observes, these replies had the intended effect of forestalling further questioning along a particular line (22).

Petry's assertion of her right to privacy as a writer can be seen as an attempt to manage her circulation in the majoritarian, always-already racialized public sphere. I've described this strategy at some length because I believe it can help shed light on the racial structure of *Country Place*, especially in relation to her other work of this moment. We've already seen that "protest" fiction demands black suffering, and we've also seen how, in realist works such as *The Street* and "In Darkness and Confusion," black women in particular experience publicity as exposure and violation. Petry wants to critically engage white domesticity, but without also being compelled to renarrate black female injury. In *Country Place*, Petry protects both her own authorial privacy and the personal dignity of her black female character, Neola, by making her a highly private and largely asexual character, which allows her to avoid subjecting Neola to the explicit forms of racial and sexual degradation that destroy Lutie Johnson's life, and have historically delimited the life chances of black women in America. Instead, via the suffering of her morally conscious white characters, she reimagines white male patriarchal authority and in the process transforms the privileged white home from an archetypal site of white-supremacist racial formation into a locus for the production of social justice. As we will see, Petry grants Neola, to paraphrase Virginia Woolf, a "house of her own," but Neola's private, domestic triumph also notably transforms the town's (and, symbolically, the nation's) racial structure.

Country Place provides a snapshot of a small New England community immediately following World War II. The town is depicted as undergoing subtle but powerful change, changes wrought by modernization in American society more broadly but accelerated by the war, and then suddenly exposed by a hurricane—what one character refers to as a great "outrage of weather" (4).[19] The violence of the storm exposes the violence that exists "under the surface quiet" (4), causing a series of revelations among its panicking citizens; the narrative is given over to exploring the effects of these revelations on their interconnected lives. The story opens with the idealistic young veteran Johnnie Roane returning from the war to discover that his beautiful though selfish, frivolous, and fairly racist wife, Glory, is having an affair with Ed Barrell, the town rake. Glory's mother, Lil (who is even more selfish, materialistic, and racist than her daughter), is driven to desperation during the storm, and plots to kill her formidable mother-in-law, Mrs. Gramby, in order to inherit her opulent ancestral home. Lil's plan is to leave the aging, overweight, and diabetic Mrs. Gramby alone in the house with a box of candy and no insulin, but her scheme is thwarted when Mrs. Gramby's maid, Neola, discovers her in a coma and calls a doctor. While Lil's feckless attempt on Mrs. Gramby's life goes unpunished initially, "The Weasel," the town's scandal-loving taxi driver, has passed a stolen love note to Mrs. Gramby's son, Mearns, that reveals that Lil too has had an affair with Ed Barrell. Mearns shows the note to his mother, who, after recovering from her illness, immediately changes her will, leaving her house to her three servants, Neola, Portulacca (the Portuguese gardener), and Cook (Gramby House's Italian immigrant cook). While an omniscient narrator controls seventeen of the twenty-five chapters (Holladay 65), the remainder is told primarily from the perspective of Doc Fraser (a stodgy bachelor pharmacist who "openly admit[s] to having a prejudice against women" [1]). Much of the novel's dramatic action, however, is precipitated by The Weasel, who not only exposes both Lil's and Glory's affairs with Ed, but also orchestrates the lethal encounter that occurs between Ed and Mrs. Gramby. The Weasel selects Ed to help Mrs. Gramby navigate the steep Town Hall steps, and when she realizes that the arms encircling her are the same that embraced both Lil and Glory, she shoves Ed away, causing both of them to fall down the steps to their deaths. Mrs. Gramby's demise in front of town hall is fittingly public, given the ways in which her revised will is intended to restructure the town.

Mrs. Gramby is one of Lennox's most revered citizens, and she functions as something of a moral barometer in the work. Because she is dying, she spends a good deal of time reflecting on the changes she detects in the town, all of them bad. The most visible change is the apparent moral decline of the town's women. After Mrs. Gramby witnesses Glory and Ed together on a tryst she thinks: "It was a changed world.... During the course of the years—not all at once, but slowly and surely—the line between good and evil had been rubbed out" (85). She wonders whether "Gloria was not to be condemned. Instead of a sharp line of demarcation between right and wrong, Gloria and her generation had found only the vague blur made by erasures—it was all that remained of a moral code after the impact of two world wars" (86). Here Petry links Mrs. Gramby's perception that women have become less morally upstanding to the moral ambiguity of national violence—a connection that will reappear later in the novel. Her anxiety about the morality of Glory and her mother, Lil, is personal as well, as they stand to inherit Gramby House when she dies. Mrs. Gramby worries about this possibility "as though it were a *world* which Lillian would inherit" (220; emphasis added).

Gramby House represents nothing less to Glory and Lil. Glory, like her mother, Lil, admits openly that she is eager for Mrs. Gramby to die so that they can inherit Gramby House and thereby "be somebody here in Lennox. I want to live in this house some day and have parties and dances here—in the Gramby House—and be waited on" (66). In her letters to Johnnie when he was away at war, she spoke not of missing him, but rather of her mother marrying Mearns, and of "Gramby House. It seemed to run through her thoughts like a connecting thread" (38). Lil and Glory both come from working-class backgrounds, and they both covet outward signs of wealth and power. In one flashback, Lil recalls "hating" Mearns when he presented her a book for Christmas instead of a diamond bracelet, a "circle of running fire to wear around your wrist; or a ring with a stone so big and so perfect it would be like looking at a hot coal" (166). Lil's desire for "fire" ironically contrasts with her coldness; Mrs. Gramby describes Lil as "a hard, shallow woman with an acquisitive, seeking mouth, a woman who dyed her hair and starved herself in order to stay slender" (83). Glory also appears to have inherited her mother's "hunger": Doc Fraser remarks that she had always stood out among the other town girls because of "the way she looked at things.... It was as though she tried to see all of a thing at once, devouring it, because she was impelled to decide then and there, in that first hungry glance, whether it was something she would want and had to have; or whether it was undesirable, completely worthless, and therefore to be discarded, quickly" (99–100).

The one character flaw all three women share, however, is their "failure" as mothers. We learn that Glory refuses motherhood for fear of losing her figure, while Lil seems almost pathological in her total self-absorption and hostility to mothering. She is an anxious and occasionally vicious woman obsessed with leaving behind her former life of penury and becoming "Mrs. Gramby." She insists that her daughter call her by her first name, and when Glory forgets this dictum, Lil shouts, "Don't call me 'Momma.' I can't bear it!" (66). When angered, she "says the meanest things she can think of," and her first words to Glory after she marries Johnnie are: "You're settled and safe now. I won't have to think about you any more. I can put my mind on myself" (72). Glory thinks to herself that "Momma had perfected the knack of withdrawing from other people's problems" (71).

In contrast to Lil's gift for "withdrawing" from her daughter's needs, Mrs. Gramby represents a classic case of the dominating mother. Mrs. Gramby is an arrogant and aloof old widow. She considers the one "enormous crime" (84) in her life to be her overly intense love for Mearns, which she believes "had made it impossible for him to leave, binding him closer and closer to [me]" (83). She effectively dominated his love life as well, intimidating and harassing the women he brought home for her to meet. We learn that she ruined nearly all of his marriage prospects by "flaunting her jewels and her house in their faces; bullying them by her arrogant manner; staring them out of countenance when he brought them home to dinner. When they had gone . . . she had laughed at them, using her malicious wit to make them ridiculous in his eyes" (83). She acts this way because she "had been terrified lest he marry some cheap impossible young girl," and so naturally Mearns ends up with Lil. Mrs. Gramby reflects that "nothing worse could have happened to him. The name would die out. Lillian was too old to have children" (83). Thus Mearns's experience of mother domination leads him to marry Lil, who is hard, shallow, and barren; these qualities mark Lil as a monstrous woman, where the "ideal" woman would presumably be "soft," "deep," and fertile. Lil's barrenness means that there will be no male heir to carry on the Gramby patronym—after Mrs. Gramby dies, she will become "Mrs. Gramby." Thus we can see that both the Gramby name and the Gramby house—symbols of traditional patriarchal authority—are in a state of crisis; they are dominated by women with "excessive desires" and there's not a (white) man in sight to bring them in line.

Although Petry self-identified as an "ally of feminists" (100), her treatment of gender fits fairly comfortably within the midcentury discourse of "momism," a term coined by Philip Wylie, an author best known for the enormously popular misogynist diatribe *Generation of Vipers* (1942). Wylie proclaimed with alarm and disgust that "[t]he mealy look of men today is the result of momism.'" "Moms," according to Wylie, were (implicitly) white women whose apparent maternal love masked their narcissism and desire for power. Their "policy of protection" led to a "possession of the spirit of a man" akin to "slavery" (Feldstein 41). Many critics associate the proliferation of "momism" with a postwar conservative backlash—white male anxiety about the need to force women back into the home after the relative freedom of World War II. But Ruth Feldstein has demonstrated that this discourse had been around at least since the Depression, and that it was deployed for liberal as well as conservative agendas. By the 1930s a consensus across social science disciplines emerged that mothers "were not only responsible for the physical, educational, and religious well-being of future citizens, but also were responsible for their children's *psychological* well-being" (6; emphasis in original). Psychology became increasingly important among progressive thinkers for assessing social, political, and personal issues. "After World War II, psychological and political analyses increasingly overlapped. Categories like repression, neurosis, paranoia, insecurity, and frustration became vehicles for analyzing both personal and political problems, and for determining who and what was a healthy American citizen" (6).[20] "Bad" women were not just those who wielded power in the public sphere, but also those who "failed" in the private sphere as wives, and especially as mothers.

Feldstein explains that "most liberal narratives equated healthy and strong citizens with healthy and strong men; hence their primary concern was with sons, black and white. In maternal ideologies, women who failed as mothers were objects of concern because they raised men who (for different reasons at different moments) failed to meet the criteria of healthy citizenship" (5). Accordingly, Feldstein argues, the midcentury liberal social scientists' fixation on the psychological health of families, and especially the role of mothering in the production of fit or unfit citizens, despite consistently relying on normative, conservative gender roles, was intended to do progressive political work. Social scientists believed that racism and other antidemocratic sociopolitical ills (such as personal tendencies toward fascism and communism) were frequently caused by "unhealthy" family dynamics, especially bad mothering. For example, it was believed that many racists had failed to adequately resolve their oedipal conflicts with their mothers. The mothers were to blame because they had either been too dominating or too "rejecting." Despite the inherent misogyny of this supposition, this approach was in fact a hopeful one—if "the problem" is properly diagnosed and addressed early enough, it might be changed, and thus American families could instead produce psychologically healthy, antiracist (as well as antifascist and anticommunist) democracy-loving citizens.

Mearns seems to be a case study in the deleterious effects of mother-domination, as bad mothering was alleged to produce "sons who were either insufficiently aggressive, inhibited, and sexually passive and repressed; or sons who were too aggressive, insufficiently cooperative, and violent" (Feldstein 60).[21] Doc Fraser comments disdainfully that Mearns has been a "walking medicine cabinet ever since he was born. [He has a] fussy, old-maid concern about the state of his internal organs" (134). His mother worries that "[t]he name of Gramby had once stood for something.... It was almost gone now, for the name meant nothing—just an old, diabetic woman and a house made of pink brick and a middle-aged man who was addicted to vitamin pills and mouth washes" (83–84). Mrs. Gramby's maternal domination has produced not only a womanish, finicky man, but also something of a sexual deviant. Doc "tattles" on Mearns when he reveals that Mearns has long been a surreptitious, yet avid reader of "The Tattler," "a weekly newspaper which specializes in unpleasant stories of sexual perversion and promiscuity. It is the only paper I have ever seen that prints the detailed verbatim testimony in divorce cases" (231). Based on this evidence, Doc asserts that "I am certain that he expected Lil's lean shanks would offer him the same hot excitement he had found recorded in The Tattler's shabby pages" (231). (We might ask about Doc's intimate knowledge of the newspaper's contents, as well as his habit of looking over his customers' shoulders while they read these "dirty" rags.)[22] Petry had considered making Mearns even more overtly "perverse," as her working notes for *Country Place* have The Weasel discover "where Mearns Gramby goes at night and why—he and Snow White [Crane, an aging bachelor teacher] sit up in Snow White's room." She contemplated having Mearns divorce Lil and then pair up with Snow White, with a final scene in which "Snow White and Mearns talk together over the logs in Old Mrs. Gramby's fireplace, and Petunia [Neola] brings in fragrant tea in thin china cups and small rich fruity cakes."

Petry opts against this queer resolution for Mearns in the published version of the novel. By the end of the narrative, she redeems Mearns's manhood in spectacular and decidedly normative fashion. Notably, this transformation takes place after his mother dies, during the reading of the will. At this time it is revealed that Gramby Pasture has been willed to the Catholic Church, and that Gramby House has been left to Neola and the other servants, both of whom are first-generation southern European immigrants whose accents and swarthy skin mark them, according to contemporary racial attitudes, as ethnic minorities. When the will is read by the Jewish lawyer Mrs. Gramby has hired to make the changes that exclude Lil, she loses all composure, and launches into a tirade of racist epithets, shouting, "I won't have niggers living here—this is my house . . . pigpen Irish . . . everybody in the will but me" (263). Eventually, Mearns "grabbed her by the arm and shook her, 'Keep quiet!' he roared." When she attempts to scream, "he covered her mouth with his hand, pushed her toward the sofa, forced her down on it, held her motionless there." She keeps trying to scream, however, so he slaps her, and again shouts at her to "keep quiet!" Doc remarks, "The sound startled me, for it was so like his father's voice, and it was the first time I had ever heard Mearns speak in that fashion" (264).

Mearns, finally released from his mother's dominating yoke, has become his father—most pointedly through violently disciplining his shrewish wife. The manner in which Mearns becomes his father raises questions about what precisely it means to be "Mr. Gramby." Mearns's father, who died years before the beginning of the narrative, has been a spectral presence in the narrative, primarily as the ghost of a patriarchal authority in decline. At the reading of the will, Lil screams, "All of them are crazy—they talked about Mr. Gramby until I thought he was alive, not dead—I was always expecting to meet him on the stairs, here in this room—everywhere—because that horrible old woman thought he was still alive" (263). But Mearns is not simply Mr. Gramby reincarnated. By participating in the decision to will the house to the servants, he has chosen *not* to perpetuate the tradition of inherited, unearned white male privilege. Instead, he symbolically divests himself of his possessive investment in whiteness by giving up the house, as the house symbolizes white heteropatriarchal authority in the town, just as it does in the nation more generally.[23] In other words, rather than consolidating his patriarchal privilege by becoming "master" of Gramby House, he refuses his "white man's estate" by transferring one of the most powerful signs of his authority to his "ethnic" servants. He has in fact become Mr. Gramby, but he has also changed what it means to be "Mr. Gramby." Once he succeeds in overcoming his mother's domination (and implicitly becomes psychically healed), he puts the meaning of white heteropatriarchy into play—he brings his status as a white man to "life" so to speak, in contrast

THE HOME AND THE STREET / 83

to Governor Bedford, and Lil and Glory, who were using the ancestral home to deaden and fix whiteness.

For Mrs. Gramby, willing the house to the servants is a method of addressing her anxiety about the family "name," which is linked in her thoughts to the nation's future. During the storm, Mrs. Gramby finds herself serving Lil tea, which prompts her to think:

> This is proof of the great advance of our civilization, this pouring tea for a woman I despise, a woman I hate, when what I want to do is turn her out of the house. That is the point of view of a pessimist, and yet, looked at in that fashion, man had come a long and futile way. He had crawled up out of the ooze and the muck only to fall back, to get up and try again, and finally he had walked, stood erect and walked, built cities, left them, gone into a wilderness, founded churches, hunted witches. Was it for this? And then there were the wars, for he fought Indians, the French, the Dutch, the English; and then later fought a Civil War, the Spanish, fought in Europe and in Asia—yes, a long and futile way. All those layers of living between me and the day when man first walked erect keep me pouring tea for this woman instead of driving her out into the storm. (157–58)

I've quoted this passage at length because it provides an interesting sketch of the ambiguity of hegemonic notions of racial, national, and civilizational "progress." Although it goes unspecified, much of Mrs. Gramby's historical narrative has to do with violence, and specifically the violent subjugation of those deemed "other"—the persecution of "witches" in the name of Christianity and patriarchy, and the fighting of colonialist and imperialist wars. At this very late stage in her life, she has just begun to critically reflect on her privileged position in this "civilization," and in the above passage she is finally questioning what she has formerly taken for granted, "man's" triumphant march of progress.

Despite her age, she shares with Johnnie Roane the role of the innocent being initiated into a painful new consciousness. Throughout her adult life she has been fully enfranchised by her husband's property and prestige, and has taken every opportunity to lord her authority over others. But her rapidly declining health and physical suffering cause her to develop a new capacity for self-reflection that translates into a new capacity for *sympathy*. In one instance, after seeing "Rosenberg, the young Jewish lawyer" treated coldly on the street by other residents of the town, she pities what she imagines to be his loneliness; she think to herself, "when the town was younger, when she was growing up, a man was judged solely by his actions; not prejudged because he was born in Russia or Poland" (87).[24] This thought is clearly a symptom of her nostalgia and privileged ignorance of these matters, as the text has already revealed that, for instance, the old Irish Catholic church and graveyard lie on the outskirts of town because of social proscription as old as the town itself (10). Nevertheless, when The Weasel objects to the lawyer having moved into town, Mrs. Gramby reproves him and declares, "[W]hen you get to be as old as I am, you don't have 'feelings' about who buys a house or a piece of land" (87). Regrettably, this comment is far more illustrative of her recently developed capacity for sympathy than a universal truth.

For all her naiveté, she puts her money (and her house) where her mouth is when she changes her will. By revising her will, she authors the next chapter or the next "step" of "man's" progress. This step, however, is predicated on social justice, rather than oppression and war. Even so, Mrs. Gramby and Mearns's decision to integrate the town (and by extension, the nation), though bloodless, is no less of an assault on the racial structure of the town. In her notes, Petry describes the will as "a very strange and disturbing document.... There were so many shocks in it, the town reeled under its blows" ("Working Notes for *Country Place*"). Although there is clearly a selfish motive in her desire to thwart Glory and Lil, she also wishes to prevent them (and people like them) from controlling "the world" in the future. Early in the narrative, Glory fantasizes that when "Mrs. Gramby dies you [Neola] or someone very like you will bring me my breakfast in the morning" (57). Thus the danger of Lil and Glory inheriting the house is precisely that they *won't* change things—they will perpetuate, even worsen, the town's racial and ethnic stratification.[25] They will intentionally stand in the way of progress and make a point of firing Neola and then hiring, say, Lutie Johnson, or Annie May Jones, or Louella Brown—any one of whom will do as interchangeable symbols of black female subjection that consolidate their ascent to white-supremacist authority.

Mrs. Gramby had worried that the patronym "Gramby" now "meant nothing." It does in fact still signify, but now it signifies the change for which William Jones so desperately longed. It is the new American house of progress, with a harmonious, multiethnic, even queer domestic arrangement (Neola and Portulacca are engaged by the novel's end, and they will share the house with Cook, whose Italian ethnicity, mannerisms, and sibilant speech mark him as a queer of color). The family name and home now signify hope for an integrated national future. Myrdal believed that white America was "*free to choose whether the Negro shall remain her liability or become her opportunity*" (1022; emphasis in original). Mearns and Mrs. Gramby in a sense solve their "American Dilemma"—by refusing to will the world to selfish white bigots who would perpetuate social oppression by keeping African Americans trapped in the past. Instead she makes the "Negro" her "opportunity" to change the "world" symbolically by changing the racist social structure of Lennox. This has the effect of restoring moral order in town, even as it reconfigures its social structure. Thus we see that Neola, much like Louella, moves from the margins to the very center of privilege.[26]

Petry asserted her right to authorial privacy by insisting on never being coerced into writing the same story twice. And while I believe she succeeded in this objective, there are, nevertheless, striking continuities in her work from this phase of her career. She repeatedly foregrounds the manner in which the circulation of race in the majoritarian public sphere underwrites white male domestic privilege and destroys the possibility of African American privacy in general, and domesticity in particular. Moreover, we can also see that the loss or achievement of African American privacy frequently revolves around property, which again underscores that whiteness, historically, has instantiated itself through an investment in and mastery of property. Petry's rendering of domestic spaces also exceeds normative contemporary understandings of the home as distinctly separate from the public sphere; on the contrary, the home is precisely a publicly determined site of racial and gender contestation and transformation. Given Petry's sense that black women in particular experience publicity as exposure and violation, she represents their acquisition of private, domestic spaces in these narratives as simultaneously protecting the black female body while also publicly destabilizing, however provisionally, the meaning of white male authority. And while Petry's fictions shine a light on the extent to which access to property seems to determine access to privacy, Petry also presents interracial sympathy, especially (though not exclusively) between women, as the moral force capable of disrupting sedimented histories of race relations. In *The Street* and "In Darkness and Confusion," failures of interracial sympathy ensure that the future is doomed to be an oppressive and traumatic repetition of the past. In "The Bones of Louella Brown" and *Country Place*, interracial sympathy leaves the future tantalizingly unscripted. The dramatic reconfiguration of the racial structure and authority of Bedford Abbey and Gramby House (and Gramby Pasture, which was willed to the Irish Catholic church) simultaneously rewrites and puts into play the future and the past of Lennox, the Bedford family, and, implicitly, the nation.

3 / White Masks and Queer Prisons

> *In a way, if the Negro were not here, we might be forced to deal within ourselves and our own personalities with all those vices, all those conundrums, and all those mysteries with which we have invested the Negro race.*
>
> —JAMES BALDWIN, *Nobody Knows My Name*

James Baldwin's second novel, *Giovanni's Room* (1956), has long been established as a foundational work in modern gay literary history. It has only been within the last fifteen years, however, that the novel has been brought out of African American literary history's closet, so to speak, where it languished as apparently irrelevant to the tradition and to Baldwin's status as a powerful chronicler of black American experience. Critics such as Marlon Ross continue to remind us that not only are questions of sexuality always of uppermost concern in Baldwin's work, but they are also inextricably related to his analyses of American racial attitudes.[1] Baldwin repeated in one context after another his belief that "the sexual question and the racial question have always been entwined. . . . If Americans can mature on the level of racism, then they have to mature on the level of sexuality" ("Go the Way Your Blood Beats" 178). Renewed attention to *Giovanni's Room*'s subtle exploration of this thesis has belatedly granted the work a somewhat privileged position among scholars of black queer literature. Dwight McBride's assessment of the novel is worth quoting at length because it provides a sense of the remarkable breadth of "work" that the text now performs:

> As a novel with no African American characters, written by an African American, gay writer, *Giovanni's Room* itself challenges dominant understandings of what constitutes African American literature, the work that proceeds under the rubric of African

American literary criticism, and the forms of analysis that would come to have congress under the institutional formation of African American studies. Given the novel's unusual status, it seems to me somewhat prophetic in its call for a criticism, a way of thinking, a critical sensibility that would not arrive on the scene until many years after its publication in 1956. In this regard, Baldwin's novel perhaps represents one of the early direct calls for a more textured conceptualization of the kind of complex formulations necessary in artistic production, criticism, and discourse to truly address anything that approximates the richness and complexity of that most politically essential and politically irksome appellation, "the African American community." (53)

I would argue that, to a large extent, McBride's claims for *Giovanni's Room* could be applied to all of the postwar white-life novels under study here, but especially to two other seldom-discussed "queer" white-life novels from this era, Willard Motley's *Knock on Any Door* (1947), and Chester Himes's *Cast the First Stone* (1952). These three works have not previously been read in tandem, largely because of significant differences in style and setting, as well as questions of sexual self-identification on the part of the authors and protagonists, issues that I take up in detail below. I propose reading these novels as a constellation in order to effect a mutual illumination; their juxtaposition casts into relief a series of heretofore unrecognized points of overlap, brings to light underplayed dimensions of the individual works, and clarifies our sense of the conditions and strategies of black queer novelistic discourse at this moment.

All three of these novels are centered on individuals whose relation to hegemonic notions of privacy is deeply problematic. They each aspire to privacy in one form or another, but their gender and sexual deviance seem to render this impossible. Accordingly, their desire for privacy takes shape as an abiding concern with the *content* of modern American manhood. Along the way, they offer a powerful interrogation of the norms that structure white heteropatriarchy, an ideology manifested in social relations through what Marlon Ross has called *homoraciality*. Homoraciality is a term that Ross deploys to revise Eve Sedgwick's influential notion of *homosociality*, "indicating how in United States culture homosociality historically relies on the systematic exclusion of black men, as well as the central targeting of women as sexual objects and homosexual men as scapegoats" (*Manning the Race* 11). Motley's, Himes's, and Baldwin's narratives are all drawn at least partly from "queer" personal experiences that were occluded under a representational order structured by homoraciality. The authors are able to negotiate homoraciality's suppression of the black queer subject by strategically appropriating and refiguring the foundations of white American manhood. In the process, they also imagine alternative notions of privacy's racial, gender, and sexual underpinnings. The use of a white protagonist also offered a modicum of authorial distance from their queer subjects, and thus in addition to racial privacy, the white-life novel functioned to provide sexual privacy for the authors as well.

The need for sexual privacy was particularly urgent at this moment, as all three novels were written and published in a moment when race, gender, and sexuality were increasingly subject to state surveillance and discipline, manifested both juridically as well as through a proliferation of discourse in the social sciences and mass media more generally. Through these discourses, Roderick Ferguson has argued, the dominant order presented "normativity and humanity as gifts of state compliance and heteropatriarchal belonging" (72). We could extend Ferguson's formulation to include privacy as another of those "gifts of state compliance and heteropatriarchal belonging." By design, these particular forms of compliance and belonging were most readily achieved by straight, white men, leaving racial minorities, queers, and women more susceptible to various forms of regulatory state intervention and disenfranchisement (political, economic, and social). Notwithstanding white heteropatriarchy's structural and ideological dominance, many social science "experts" and social critics believed that contemporary white manhood was in a state of perilous decline. White men were perceived as beset by growing demands to submit to a variety of external, often authoritarian forces—most obviously the specter of totalitarianism, but also to the demands of the workplace (factory, bureaucracy, and corporation) and the demands of the domestic space, given that it was believed to be increasingly ruled by domineering wives and mothers, and hopelessly mired in rampant consumerism. As in the past, but to a greater degree, there was serious concern that middle-class white men in particular were becoming increasingly weak, soft, passive, and feminized. Contemporary sociologists such as David Riesman worried that social transformations had rendered men "other-directed"—that is, weak-willed, conformist, and overly reliant on others for approval and decision making. Instead of relying on "his" own inner voice, the other-directed individual (nearly always presumed to be a man) was "molded by schools, peer groups, and mass produced culture, all of which imprinted on him not drive and ambition ... but rather the imperative to get along with others" (Cuordileone 106).² Critics believed they were witnessing an unprecedented "flight from masculinity," with homosexuality representing the most extreme and alarming manifestation.³

The novels under study here tap into these anxieties, not in order to reinstate white heteropatriarchy, traditionally conceived, but to challenge and reshape its underpinnings. Autonomy and inner-direction were considered key facets of manhood; Motley, Himes, and Baldwin all endorse these qualities, but recast them as, paradoxically, the *effect* of being in certain respects *other-directed*—not in the sense of the term popularized by Riesman, but through a conscientious, courageous, and rebellious form of *queer relationality* committed to the recognition of and connection with those deemed other—in other words, committed to active and engaged modes of sympathy. These characters must do more than merely "feel right," as Harriet Beecher Stowe puts it a century earlier in *Uncle Tom's Cabin* (385). These characters must take action. Sympathetic engagement with and commitment to others redeems autonomous manhood, as it actually enables these characters, and by extension, the American man, to *resist* society's demand to conform to the norms of white heteropatriarchy, an ideal predicated on the racist, misogynistic, elitist, and homophobic exclusion and domination of others and otherness. These novels help illustrate the degree to which this oppressive ideal not only injures the disenfranchised, but also radically disciplines and regulates normative white manhood (in terms of permissible relationships, self-stylization, and desires) rather than producing autonomy and individuality. Within these works, the path to white manhood, and by extension white privacy, runs directly through queer sympathy.

* * *

There are several factors that can account for why scholars have not previously offered a comparative analysis of these novels. The notable generic differences among the texts, especially in plot, style, and setting, are the most obvious. *Knock on Any Door* is usually seen as a late installment of the "Chicago school" of naturalist writing; this placement makes sense, as it chronicles in painstaking detail the inexorable fall of (the beautiful) Italian American Nick Romano from altar boy to street thug, gigolo, and finally cop-killer, which leads to his death in the electric chair. Despite its anti-establishment content, *Knock* was marketed as a sensational urban tale of straight sexual conquest, and was soon a best seller. Himes's *Cast the First Stone* is a claustrophobic prison narrative that details white Mississippian Jimmy Monroe's desperate efforts to survive prison life. *Giovanni's Room*, in contrast, is a Jamesian expatriate novel that considers, among other things, the moral and ethical implications of its protagonist's inability to accept the love of another man. What links these works, beyond their use of "white" protagonists, is that each deploys queer desire as a means to articulate its larger social critique of the dominant culture's moral, economic, and political failings. Each of these novels suggests that the only possibility for moral redemption within these worlds exists *within* the space of same-sex desire. This vision, of course, represents a radical intervention in and departure from the increasingly homophobic attitudes of postwar America.

Unlike *Giovanni's Room*, Motley's *Knock* and Himes's *Cast* (which was republished in 1998 in a restored edition as *Yesterday Will Make You Cry*) have received fairly scant critical attention. The latter two novels are seldom mentioned in discussions of midcentury black writing because, as with other white-life novels, they seem to have little to say about "blackness." Their invisibility in black queer literary history more broadly can be accounted for by the fact that neither the authors nor their protagonists self-identify as "queer" or "gay." Motley's sexual identification remained largely unscripted publicly until the recent work of Alan Wald, who through gathering personal accounts has shown that Motley quietly participated in same-sexual communities while in the United States, and eventually lived an openly gay lifestyle after expatriating to Mexico in 1952.[4] Chester Himes's sexuality has in some respects been overscripted; his tumultuous and sometimes violent affairs with white women in particular are frequently mentioned in connection to his treatments of interracial sexuality in his novels.[5] In terms of the novels themselves, a significant amount of the queer content that appeared in the early versions of these texts was edited out before publication; although they were first drafted in the late 1930s and 1940s, they were repeatedly rewritten over the years, and the revisions seem to reflect increasingly rigid, homophobic Cold War sensibilities. The published versions of these novels are much more "hard" and "straight" than they were originally conceived. Even with these concessions to the homophobic mores of the moment, both of the texts are replete with homoerotic desire, and this is true despite the anxiety and even hostility toward homosexuality that surfaces periodically in the narratives. Another reason the "queerness" of these works has failed to attract more notice is that the homoeroticism occurs primarily within the context of prison and prostitution, and thus has not been understood as "true" homosexuality.[6] The authors' appropriation of both whiteness and what was known in midcentury America as "situational homosexuality" enabled them to intervene in the changing public discourse around homo- and heterosexual identity—in particular male same-sexuality. The redeployment of certain "heterotopic spaces," literally places of difference, enables these authors to wrest some kind of redemption out of the pathologizing, moralizing, contemptuous, and at best condescending public discourse on homosexuality that was available to them—a moment twenty years before the Stonewall rebellions. In a sense, the spaces are able to speak even when the characters and their authors are silenced.

In both *Knock* and *Cast*, queerness functions as an oppositional consciousness and mode of relationality—even though both protagonists remain deeply ambivalent about same-sex desire. At different points, both protagonists affirm, participate in, and align themselves with queerness—a socially abject and irredeemable status—especially as a means to resist state violence. In *Giovanni's Room*, by contrast, it is David's flight from the queer privacy available in Giovanni's room, due to his *acquiescence* to dominant-culture norms and biases—including the "law"—that amounts to an identification with the state; Baldwin implies that David's identification with the state, with the "law of the father" in a very broad sense, suggests not merely culpability but even participation in the state violence enacted against Giovanni, and thus also against himself. In these respects, *Knock* and *Cast* clearly anticipate the central argument of *Giovanni's Room*.

These works also share, quite notably, the absence of the black queer subject. And this is in contrast to the relative visibility of black queers in the literature of the New Negro Renaissance, especially in the work of Bruce Nugent, Wallace Thurman, Nella Larsen, Rudolph Fisher, and Claude McKay, to note only fiction.[7] Marlon Ross has argued that same-sexuality in the work of these writers effectively counters mainstream contemporary accounts of sexuality in the black community, particularly those from black and white sociologists, and from white "slummers" in the early twentieth century who regularly visited black urban neighborhoods. The former came to document and analyze conditions of black life under the disruptions of migration and industrialization. Social scientists, working for the state, private foundations, and universities, widely considered black neighborhoods "zones of immorality"; it is important to note that this attitude persisted largely unchallenged well into the post–World War II moment. As I've already shown black families and households were deemed queer due to their deviation from heteropatriarchal norms. Both black and white social "uplift" agencies propagated what Hazel Carby has called a "moral panic" about the "loose" sexual mores endemic to black neighborhoods and manifested by female-headed households and out-of-wedlock children.[8] In the so-called "disorganized" black family, the women were deemed sexually aggressive and overly dominant in the household; the men, though excessively sexual too, were passive and impotent; and the children were doomed to a life of crime and immorality. White slummers visited black districts in search of taboo experiences to be had in the famous rent parties, drag balls, and "black and tan" cabarets, which not only served alcohol during Prohibition, but were also known to tolerate interracial sexuality, and same-sexuality as well. (I revisit this issue at greater length in my discussion of Motley's *Knock on Any Door*.) Ross demonstrates how the black protagonists in New Negro Renaissance novels, while relatively straight themselves, were frequently bonded to erotically queer best pals, who through acts of manly solidarity helped the male protagonists achieve a sort of moderated manhood under the demoralizing conditions of Jim Crow. These minor black queer figures were "heroic" in their commitments to the protagonists, and precisely not deviant urban primitives served up to satisfy the prurient appetites of white slumming spectators.[9]

All of these conditions persisted into midcentury America (minus of course, the euphoric mood that marked the "Jazz Age" and "The New Negro Renaissance"). In some cases, they intensified primarily due to increased black migration and European immigration around World War II. As discussed in chapter 1, the state continued to assert that black communities and households were "pathological," abetted not only by Myrdal's analyses in *An American Dilemma*, but by the influential black sociologist E. Franklin Frazier, who asserted with increasing urgency the charge that black communities and families were ensnared in a "tangle of pathology"; black children in particular were no longer receiving "values" from their parents, and hence were essentially becoming savages, existing outside of civilization (Scott 75). White slummers continued traveling to black districts to indulge their tastes in jazz and forbidden pleasures, though wealthy white slummers from the previous era, such as Carl Van Vechten, were replaced by a less patrician group of bohemians, the most well known being the Beats and figures such as Norman Mailer.

In light of these enduring socioeconomic dynamics, and the precedent of black queer literary representation in the New Negro Renaissance, the absence of central black queer characters in these white-life novels seems all the more noteworthy and strange. The use of a white protagonist may be due to the fact that in these texts the protagonists are erotically involved with other men, rather than simply bonded with queer men, and thus whiteness may help distance the authors from an unspeakable desire. Race functions slightly differently in each of the novels, though, and I will address these differences separately. The missing black queer character may also be attributed to changing definitions of same-sexuality, especially the panic-driven movement in the social sciences and popular discourse toward an increasingly rigid sense of a homosexual/heterosexual binary. The visibility of homosexuality, especially in American cities, had been growing steadily over the first half of the century, notably during the state's "backlash," which culminated in the obscenity trial of Radclyffe Hall, the author of *The Well of Loneliness*. George Chauncey and others have documented how this backlash led to the closing of Broadway shows with gay content and increasing police raids on gay venues, both of which "had the unintended effect of making homosexuality more visible still" (*Gay New York* 331–58). Regina Kunzel reminds us that the increasing presence of queer communities in American cities following the war, along with Alfred C. Kinsey's revelation in 1948 that "perhaps the major portion of the male population has had at least some homosexual experience," "fueled a growing concern about the pervasiveness of perversion and a vigilant commitment to stigmatizing homosexuality and persecuting homosexuals" (258). Of course, antigay sentiment would reach a fever pitch with McCarthy and the hysteria over the invisible threat of infiltrating communists. Numerous historians have shown how in American culture as the Cold War "heated up," ideologues attacked homosexuality as a triple threat—to suburban domestic heteronormativity, to America's self-generated images of tough-guy masculinity, and, relatedly, to national security, because homosexuals were seen as especially susceptible to communist influence and infiltration.[10]

Of particular relevance for *Knock* and *Cast* is what Kunzel has described as midcentury America's "explosion [of interest]" in prison homosexuality and situational homosexuality more generally, including male prostitution. The "criminological, sociological, reform and popular writing on prison homosexuality reflected a new urgency about homosexuality in the culture at large" (258). The increasing discourse around the notion of situational homosexuality signaled changing conceptions of homosexual identity more generally. Chauncey has shown that in the early decades of the century there was extensive sex between so-called "normal" men and "fairies." While the "fairies" conceived of themselves and were conceived of by others as "queer," their masculine partners were able to maintain the status of "normal" men. "Queerness" was constituted by the "fairy's" gender deviance, not by his solicitation of male sexual partners. In other words, fairies were considered "constitutionally different 'not in their sexual object choices but in their gender inversion—i.e., they were physically male but were spiritually and psychically female. The men they had sex with, so-called 'wolves,' conceived of themselves and were conceived of by others as normal so long as they 'abided by masculine gender conventions' and performed the penetrative role in sex" (Chauncey qtd. in Kunzel 257–58). But this distinction was steadily losing its explanatory power, and the historian Allen Drexel in his study of gay life and culture on Chicago's South Side has found that "by the 1930s, this conceptual distinction between the practice of having sex with a 'fairy' and the identity of *being gay* was becoming blurred" (125). As the dominant culture felt an increasing need to identify and control newly emergent and visible gay populations, situational homosexuality as a discourse stepped in to resolve the contradiction of how apparently "normal" men could participate in homosexual activity under certain circumstances, such as in prison or in prostitution—in short, the rhetoric of situational homosexuality aimed principally to *protect* a clearly threatened even though putatively stable binary of homosexual and heterosexual identity.

* * *

Kunzel's observations on how mainstream culture in midcentury America was struggling to contain and stabilize heterosexuality as an identity formation in the face of emergent (or should we say insurgent) queerness are helpful in reconsidering Himes's prison novel, *Cast the First Stone*—helpful in terms of providing a heretofore absent dimension of historical context in the criticism of the novel, and helpful as a means to begin deciphering the text's own deep ambivalence about its queer investments. Society's efforts to contain the disruptive, destabilizing effects of queer desire are reenacted in the efforts of Himes's editors, reviewers, and critics, and at times Himes himself, all of whom struggled with how to manage the disruptive sexual energies of the original manuscript.

Cast the First Stone initially garnered a mixed reception, with most reviewers typically offering moderate praise for what seemed to be its authentic representation of prison life. Several found the work somewhat aesthetically flawed, and *Kirkus Reviews* urged "caution" because of its "raw vernacular." Interestingly, reviewers were split on whether or not they found Jimmy's claims for the "innocence" of his relationship with Dido plausible. Frederic Morton of the *New York Herald Tribune* wrote that "the relationship which develops, though homosexual in origin and intensity, is entirely and believably platonic. Their feeling for one another is a remarkable mixture of fervor, asceticism and selflessness. It is a peculiar passion in which the participants will love, but not touch one another. In this experience, the psychological triumph of the book, Jimmy receives the conclusive impetus to regeneration" (8). The protagonist and the novel's "triumph," in other words, is that Jimmy Monroe masters and purifies his queer desire. Although Morton's assertion that their relationship is "entirely and believably platonic" rings a bit excessive (his need for not one, but two, adverbs), it appears that he reads their relationship in the way in which the editors and Himes seem to have intended it—as an example of romantic friendship or "male love"—what David Halperin identifies as one of four "prehomosexual categories of male sex and gender deviance" (92) that exist both outside and within the more capacious and totalizing modern notion of homosexuality.[11] Romantic friendships were understood as passionate male unions based in a love that is "egalitarian, nonhierarchical, and reciprocal" (101), that is, in sameness—of class, social status, selfhood, etc; the sameness of this union marks it as nonerotic, as most premodern discourses of erotic bonds were structured around hierarchical and gender difference. As I discuss below, although Jimmy draws on this rhetoric of romantic friendship, his relationship with Dido does not fit this classical model, precisely because Dido sees himself as an invert, and Jimmy sees himself as a "man," even if he is plagued with doubts.

W. R. Burnett's review addresses this issue at length, and his vexed, avowedly "prejudiced" comments bear quoting in full:

> [Y]ou begin to feel little by little that the author is overdoing it and that this one item is throwing the whole picture out of focus. Shortly you discover that your feeling is correct. Homosexuality takes over the book in the last hundred pages, and the plain day-to-day recital of prison life turns into a feverish account of a love affair between two young men serving long sentences for armed robbery. Although the author—frank otherwise—insists on calling this business "friendship," it bears no resemblance whatsoever to any sort of friendship I've ever noted or experienced and when these two young criminals began to yearn and humorlessly call each other "Sweet Man" and "Puggy Wuggy" the author almost lost

> me. However, I'll admit I'm prejudiced and that prejudice makes for false judgments. So I will conclude by saying that the account of this love affair is highly original—I've never read anything like it—and for that reason alone is perhaps worth the reader's while. (15)

Even though Burnett admits that his comments exhibit his "prejudice" (and his insistent assertion of ignorance of such matters, in life and fiction), it is noteworthy that, unlike later critics, both reviewers accurately identify the centrality of same-sexuality to the narrative. In other words, *Cast* is no less an account of Jimmy's "love affair" with Dido than it is a realist account of prison life. Moreover, Burnett's remarks also indirectly support my contention that despite having undergone heavy-handed efforts by editors to minimize its queer investments, what takes place between Jimmy and Dido is "highly original" for its time—I would say pathbreaking.

Literary scholars have remained largely silent on the novel, and the treatments that have appeared generally subordinate the romantic and erotic quality of Jimmy's relationship with Dido, and the other men he is involved with, in order to focus on Himes's critique of the prison system. Stephen F. Milliken argues bluntly that "prison is its one and only subject, its unique and exclusive concern" (160). He explains that "prison permits the writer who attempts to describe it with total accuracy no second overriding concern" (161). Although he does briefly acknowledge that the narrative is structured in part around Jimmy's relationships with various men, ultimately, he concludes, *Cast* "demonstrated that human beings can fulfill their potential, for good or evil, can achieve maturity and wholeness in even the most negative and hostile environments" (179). Gilbert Muller opts for a similarly humanist reading, claiming that the novel is "existentialist" and "probes the indomitable universal quality of the human spirit to resist oppression and brutalization—to find ways to transcend the perversities and absurdities of a degenerate culture" (40). H. Bruce Franklin briefly introduces issues of race in his discussion of *Cast* by including Himes's oeuvre within a tradition of American prison writing. He observes that for the authors of prison literature, "America is itself a prison, and the main lines of American literature can be traced from the plantation to the penitentiary" (xxxii). Franklin spends almost no time addressing sexuality in *Cast* because he is more concerned with linking the novel to Himes's treatment of violence and rebellion in his larger body of work. As Himes himself claimed, "Nothing happened in prison that I had not already encountered in outside life" (*Quality of*

Hurt 61). For these critics, the specifics of race, gender, and sexuality are relevant only as they are shaped by the prison experience, and, for Milliken and Muller, finally irrelevant to the novel's larger claims about the human spirit.

These critics are certainly not wrong to locate the novel within the tradition of prison writing. But their narrow emphasis on genre, context, and universal humanism underplays how fundamentally the work is structured by and engaged with dominant culture prohibitions around race, gender, and sexuality. Their approach leads them to largely ignore race, leave gender uninterrogated, and desex sexuality. Queer desire in the work is circumstantial (i.e., "situational") and thus apparently no threat to Jimmy's status as a heterosexual—that is, despite all evidence, his sexuality remains "normative" and thus not deserving of serious consideration. Here we can see that Milliken's and Muller's readings of the novel in universalist terms as a triumph of the human will also implicitly requires that we see Jimmy's triumph as, at least partly, his success in surviving prison with his straight, white manhood intact. Muller attributes the "perversities" represented in *Cast* to a "degenerate culture," thereby protecting Jimmy Monroe and implicitly Himes's normative manhood. By attending to and foregrounding gender, sexuality, and race, however, I intend to read against the silences imposed on the text; with this reorientation, the work may be seen not only as a pointed critique of state violence, but also as a powerful and innovative, even if deeply conflicted, black queer novel. The difficulty, of course, is that for all its queer eroticism, which is more plainly on display in *Yesterday*, the text never relinquishes its stake in normative notions of manhood, and its anxieties around same-sexuality. And so, paradoxically, in order to fully appreciate the work as the important black queer intervention that it is, I must also read through Himes's own resistances.

To some extent, Himes's work encourages readers to not engage fully with the importance of queer relationships to the protagonist's struggle to survive. This is effected through Jimmy repeatedly expressing a deep ambivalence, often disgust, toward homosexuality—especially homosexual acts. Notwithstanding this discomfort, queer desire is not merely present from the book's opening pages to its conclusion, frequently originating with the protagonist himself, but it also sustains him throughout his sentence—seven and a half years for armed robbery in an Ohio penitentiary. There is a consensus among Himes's critics and biographers that the novel is a heavily autobiographical translation of Himes own seven-and-a-half-year prison sentence in the same Ohio prison for the same crime. Jimmy's intensely eroticized relationships with different men plays the greatest role in enabling him to endure the manifold deprivations and injuries of prison life. Thus much of the narrative is given over not merely to chronicling the many forms of state discipline and abuse, but also to Jimmy's incessant struggle to reconcile both his own and the larger culture's pathologization of homosexuality—especially the destabilizing effect of same-sex desire on masculinity—with his own powerful investment in homoerotic relationships.

By the novel's end, when Jimmy is finally paroled, he is a new man, so to speak, having survived and even triumphed over his brutal conditions. Jimmy's relationship with Dido (called Rico in *Yesterday*) precipitates the novel's climax, where Jimmy volunteers to be written up for "sex perversion" after Dido/Rico has been charged with this crime. This act of solidarity initially costs Jimmy his parole, but it also has what is presented as the far more important effect of preserving his sense of self, which he understands primarily in terms of his masculinity. Jimmy declares: "I had done it to be a man. And if I had lost freedom by doing it, I'd never had freedom, anyway, and it couldn't hurt me much. . . . I had done a lot of time and I could do plenty more. But I couldn't be a man later. I couldn't wait. I had to be it, then. For me, though. Just for me" (*Cast* 337). Jimmy's grand act of defiance against the prison system is remarkable on several counts. It was rare indeed in mid-twentieth-century America for a man to reclaim his masculinity by publicly embracing the deeply stigmatized status of "pervert." Within the narrative this gesture is even more surprising given that Jimmy has just repudiated Dido's impassioned request that their relationship become more explicitly sexual. Jimmy's refusal is laced with a somewhat unaccountable disappointment and disgust: "I was afraid to look up. When I looked up I would have to face it. I didn't want to ever face it. I didn't think I could face it." Jimmy's first words are: "'Jesus Christ, I thought we'd gotten above that. Especially that.' I had to swallow. 'You said once you put me in the stars. Remember? And now this puts us in the gutter. . . . Is this all you ever wanted from me?'" Dido replies simply, "What else would I ever want?" (319). In *Yesterday*, Jimmy says that he is horrified to "discover" that "what he thought they had was just the same as all the rest, all over the slimy prison. . . . If that's all it ever meant then I've wasted a hell of a lot of feelings" (345). In his attempt to avoid "facing it" (or, quite plainly, facing some disturbing aspects of himself), Jimmy attempts to reduce Rico's powerful and complex emotional attachment into simple immorality or pathology, or both: "it's all sex with you ... and no kind of sex was ever worth the value you put on it, much less your kind" (346).

Jimmy's expression of disgust seems harsh and highly inconsistent given how much of the second half of the narrative has been given over to detailing precisely the erotic quality of his relationship with Dido/Rico. Their interactions are marked by the exhilaration and sentimentality that typically accompanies young love—Jimmy and Rico are "drunk with each other" (293); Jimmy tells Rico that his lips "look like crushed strawberries" and that his "eyes are filled with stardust"; they also call each other pet names such as "Puggy Wuggy" and "Sweet Babe."[12] The only overtly sexual act that occurs between them, however, is a single kiss, which *Cast* notably attempts to chasten by describing it as "passionless"; *Yesterday*, however, includes no such purifying term.

For the moment, though, I want to point out that Jimmy's seemingly implausible act of disavowal is actually of a piece with the ambivalence he expresses toward same-sex desire throughout the text. His relationship with Dido is his third since entering prison, and each relationship is marked by Jimmy's constant vacillation between attraction, repulsion, and denial. During the chaos of a devastating prison fire, for example, Jimmy kisses his "cousin" Mal and then declares: "I want you for my woman—my old lady. I want you right now. I don't want no more of this goddamned cousin stuff" (*Cast* 156/*Yesterday* 107). Jimmy's proposal is rebuffed. Only a few pages later, however, he expresses visceral horror at the unchecked hedonism that breaks out among the prisoners after a devastating fire is put out: "It was bitchery and abomination, Sodom and Gomorrah in the flower of its vulgarity, stark and putrid and obscene, grotesque and nauseating" (166). After witnessing "an indescribably lewd act of degenerate sex staged by two naked, sex-mad marijuana-jagged convicts," Jimmy runs outside, trying to "get the dirt from his lungs; he wanted to bend over and eat the earth; he wanted to tear his regenerative organs from his body; his senses were outraged" (*Yesterday* 163).

It seems puzzling at first that neither version of the novel ever expresses the slightest awareness of any contradiction inherent in Jimmy's desire to take another prisoner as "his old lady" and his revulsion at "degeneracy." Moreover, the image of him tearing off (or should we say pulling off?) his penis after witnessing these sex acts not only recalls a masturbatory act, but also plainly suggests guilt and anger insofar as he feels a need to rid himself of his penis *precisely because* his disgust is not sufficient to suppress his erotic response (Oedipus preferred to put out his eyes).

The disavowal that occurs at the level of the text gets reproduced publicly by Himes and, as I've suggested, his critics. Himes's biographers have argued persuasively that the character Dido/Rico is based largely on one of Himes's lovers while in prison—in particular a man named, not coincidentally, Prince Rico. According to Himes's biographers, Himes told Carl Van Vechten in a 1952 letter that "the most fulfilling relationship he had ever had was with the man whom he called Dido in *Cast the First Stone*" (34). Moreover, in a June 10, 1946, letter to Van Vechten, Himes informs him that he has written a four-hundred-page manuscript with all white characters focused on the imprisonment of a "juvenile delinquent." He describes it as being structured in three sections, one of which he says directly is a "homo-sexual love story" that takes place during the prison sentence. He says the manuscript elicited a good deal of positive feedback from readers, especially about the writing. However, the queer love story is what kept it from being published.[13] In this letter, Himes explicitly identifies his protagonist's relations with other prisoners as a homosexual love story, rather than simply prison degeneracy. Himes's long-standing friendship with Van Vechten, and his awareness of the latter's queer orientation, may have prompted greater frankness. Himes also wrote in his first memoir, *The Quality of Hurt*, that *Cast* "obviously . . . was the story of my own prison experiences" (117). By the time he'd published the second volume of his memoirs in 1976, however, he'd changed his mind: "My publishers wished to imply that the story in *Cast* was the story of my life and problems and I wanted to state outright that it had nothing to do with me" (*My Life of Absurdity* 125). This sense of repression or flat-out denial also appears in his remark that "I find it necessary to read what I have written in the past about my prison experiences to recall any part of them." Himes's critics have perpetuated this amnesia and disavowal. While the critics mentioned earlier focus on prison and humanism at the expense of the specifics of identity, most critics ignore the work entirely.[14] Nearly every treatment of Himes's career gives this work little more than passing mention beyond referencing his early life and writing career. Moreover, with the exception of the brief but illuminating discussion provided by Marlon Ross in an essay focused principally on *Giovanni's Room*, there has been only one other in-depth queer reading of either *Cast* or *Yesterday*.[15]

While the text's disconnect between same-sex desire and same-sex acts may arise partly from a need on the part of Himes and some of his critics to preserve his avowedly straight sexual identity, Jimmy's struggle around acknowledging his relationship to queer desire nevertheless speaks eloquently to contemporary debates around the changing definitions of homosexual identity. As I discussed earlier, the years leading up to the Cold War witnessed a transition from mainstream understandings of "true" homosexuality as gender style—that is, the notion of homosexuals as gender inverts (e.g., a woman trapped in a man's body)—to homosexuality being defined by same-sex object choice. This distinction at least in theory had previously allowed the "top"—that is, the masculine and "penetrative" role—to retain his "normal" gender identity despite having sex with other men. But this distinction had been steadily eroding, and to engage in any kind of sexual act with another man posed a dire threat not only to one's sexual identity, but also necessarily to one's masculinity—despite the claim of the experts that one's sex acts in prison could easily be kept separate from one's sexual identity. As David Halperin explains, under the modern conception of homosexuality, one's choice of sexual object reveals what Foucault identified as "the truth of self"; this sexual truth assigns the individual to "one or the other of two sexual species," and for the homosexual a denigrated place in the social order (112).

Jimmy tellingly evokes the contemporary public debate around this issue when he observes that in the hospital ward of the prison, "[e]veryone was either a wolf or a fag. *The wolf is the so-called male of the species, a rare and almost obsolete animal. The fag is the female*" (*Cast* 71). He then mentions that "wolverines" were quickly taking the place of the wolf—a figure that was located somewhere between the gendered binary of wolves and fags. According to Jimmy, the wolf, that male figure whose masculinity remained untarnished despite same-sex object choice, was at this point an "endangered species." Jimmy's anxiety about the growing extinction of the wolf position seems to account at least partly for his desperate need to distinguish between his erotic and romantic interest in other men and his avowed loathing for erotic same-sex acts.

Jimmy takes on (or at least aspires to) the more "masculine" role in each of his prison relationships; Dido especially is a classic "invert" figure—at one point, Jimmy thinks, "Poor little kid . . . what a terrible mistake he was not a woman" (323). (Could this also be wishful thinking for Jimmy?) Notwithstanding Jimmy's "male" identification, he is plagued by a fear of his own "effeminacy"—a "soft" mode of masculinity understood generally in premodern (that is, prehomosexual) times as exhibiting a preference for matters of love, pleasure, and sensuality over more austere, presumably unpleasurable pursuits as war, politics, business, sports, etc. (Halperin 92–94). Again, this formation exists in modern times, though the effeminate boy is perpetually at risk of falling into the degraded status of girl-boy. Jimmy expresses a great deal of anxiety about being called "pretty" and "soft"—something he has struggled with his entire life. In *Yesterday*, Jimmy is described as having "clear-cut patrician features and wide blue eyes with lashes as long as any woman's. His hair was crinkly and golden, and his skin was clear white, the kind that bruises easily and blushes easily, too" (149).[16] *Yesterday* also includes a moment in Jimmy's adolescence when his girlfriend catches him staring at a sunset and tells him "he was the prettiest person that she had ever seen. And he blushed." Another time she told him, 'You're not so tough and casual, Jimmy. *Not as much as you try to be. You're soft and sentimental inside as a girl in love.* You have a great, grand mind full of beautiful dreams and ideals" (149; emphasis added). Jimmy's "effeminate" side emerges in prison as well, despite his best efforts to hide it. Rico tells him that "you are full of softnesses [*sic*] all inside, but they come out in rather unexpected ways" (293). Jimmy admits that he turned to delinquency at a young age because he "was different from everybody and didn't know exactly why" and thus felt compelled to prove that "he wasn't a sissy." He hoped that these acts of rebellion "made [him] like other boys" (311). Delinquency, therefore, has functioned throughout Jimmy's life to compensate for his disturbing sense of gender deviance.

In light of Jimmy's lifelong anxiety about his ability to measure up to normative standards of masculinity, we can thus see that while his decision to take the rap of "sex perversion" may appear to compromise his manhood, in fact it affords him an opportunity to shore up his increasingly threatened masculinity. The charge allows Jimmy to rebel against his condition of privation under state authority—as he says, "I had done a lot of time and I could do plenty more. But I couldn't be a man later." In prison, the will of the state supplants that of the self. The state asserts absolute control over the body, especially over its relation to time and space, and thus the prisoner (much like the slave) has no privacy. By publicly claiming this stigmatized status, Jimmy is also publicly declaring that he can "take it [punishment for his transgression] like a man." Jimmy hereby exercises choice, and thereby takes back some authority over his relation to the time and space of the prison system and thereby reclaims a modicum of privacy.

Moreover, given Jimmy's sense of Dido's inverted nature, his decision to stand up for Dido in his mind is tantamount to standing up for his woman. Jimmy's need to recuperate his masculinity and to make a bid for nominal privacy supersedes the penalties of being labeled a "pervert" or losing his "freedom." By the end of *Cast*, Jimmy's overtly queer passion appears to have been displaced entirely onto Dido, who now functions as an abject vessel of homosexuality. After Jimmy's sentence is commuted, Dido hangs himself, and consistent with Kristeva's notion of the abject corpse, is thus expelled from the narrative—an act that clearly serves to reconstitute Jimmy's ambiguous sexual identity and to free him to reintegrate into "straight" white society unencumbered by queer attachments formed in prison (I address the role of race in this transformation shortly). In *Yesterday*, by contrast, Rico does not kill himself, but instead is buoyed by Jimmy's sacrifice and thereafter becomes more emotionally stable and self-reliant. The more homophobic ending of *Cast* seems in keeping with its appearance during the Cold War; Himes's editors believed that death was the most conclusive method of closing down the text's homoeroticism. In the final analysis, the urgent necessity of remasculinization and an absolute closure of the queer story line of course can, and I believe should, be read as the strongest testament to the depth and significance of Jimmy and Dido/Rico's emotional connection.[17]

The text's anxious investment in reinstating normative heteromasculinity ultimately fails, however, to erase the many moments of intense homoeroticism, sympathy, and queer affect that mark the text from its opening pages. Presumably because Jimmy doesn't engage in same-sex intercourse, he appears to have narrowly preserved his straight identification. Accordingly, the work seems to keep intact a psycho-symbolic boundary between his straightness, which usually also functions to signify his masculinity, and his queer desire, which in effect gets displaced into the queerness of the space and the queerness of the others in that space. Himes's seemingly unflinching, documentary portrait of prison life leads on the one hand to the work being classified as "naturalist"; but this documentary, "naturalist" style, with its emphasis on the effect of environment on character, also allows for the representation of alternative modes of sexuality that neither the author nor its protagonist is free to openly endorse.

As I suggested earlier, the queerness of the text may have been overlooked or repressed by critics because the protagonist never self-identifies as queer and never engages in queer sex acts. Rather, the queer material in this work often becomes legible *around*, rather than *within* the protagonist's consciousness. His queer desire is frequently legible to the reader and to other characters in the work, despite Jimmy's inability to acknowledge or recognize this desire himself. For example, long before Jimmy publicly takes on the rap of "sex perversion," he is repeatedly accused by other prisoners and guards of being "fish" (i.e., receptive to queer sexuality). In *Yesterday*, he actually solicits another prisoner sexually by saying, "Sure, I'm fish . . . Kiss your little baby fish" (188). He is told by one sympathetic guard that "three lieutenants have asked me about you and Rico, and last week the deputy called me into his office and showed me a whole stack of notes which convicts up here in the dormitory had written over there about you and him." Jimmy insists, however, that he has "the name without the game." At one point, when he is kidded for his friendliness with Dido, Jimmy "denie[s] everything. 'You guys got me wrong,' I said. 'I'm not making any play. I'm going to get a pardon and I'd be a fool to get involved in something like that.' 'That ain't nothing,' Signifier [another inmate] said. 'That ain't no more than you've always been.'" Jimmy admits to himself, "I didn't like that" (261).

When Jimmy is first accused of sex perversion by the prison officials, he claims that the charge is "a lie." The deputy replies simply, "I believe that you are guilty." Jimmy then thinks to himself, "but you know the deputy, he just sits there and looks at you with his head bobbing and knows more about it than you do yourself" (349). Both here and at several other points in the work, the reader can hardly avoid agreeing with the deputy and the other prisoners and guards who believe that Jimmy is "guilty" as charged. Jimmy's denials seem more and more implausible as the text unfolds, until at a certain point the reader feels that, to paraphrase Jimmy himself, she "knows more about [Jimmy's queer desire] than [he] does [himself]." Jimmy's seemingly willful, even desperate, lack of self-knowledge regarding his sexual desire, which is everywhere evident in the text, brings to mind Eve Sedgwick's notion of textual ignorance, secrecy, and opacity as constitutive signs of the epistemology of the closet. But whereas in Sedgwick's formulation, the text seems to invite the reader to decode its encrypted queerness, the sexual ignorance or opacity in Himes's work seems to be operating at both the level of the protagonist's consciousness, as well as that of the narrative. Due to the narrative's apparent sympathy with the protagonist's perspective, it seems to encourage the reader to join with the protagonist in denying the copious evidence of queer desire that it insistently introduces. It is as though the text remains closeted to itself. There is no arch knowingness, no sense that if one is in on the joke, then its "true" queer investments will be obvious.

But for all of the text's and Jimmy's disavowals, his emotional attachment and commitment to Dido/Rico is ultimately more significant than whether or not they have sex. Michel Foucault has argued in his essay

"Friendship as a Way of Life," that contrary to common belief, it isn't "unnatural" sex acts between men that most outrages people, but rather the threat posed when two men begin to love one another. The image of two men having furtive sex in an alley is, according to Foucault, the "kind of neat image of homosexuality without any possibility of generating unease, and for two reasons: it responds to a comforting canon of beauty, and it cancels everything that can be troubling in affection, tenderness, friendship, fidelity, camaraderie, and companionship, things that our rather sanitized society can't allow a place for without fearing the formation of new alliances and the tying together of unforeseen lines of force" (136).[18] Jimmy and Dido/Rico's sympathetic bond and romantic relationship represents above all a threatening new alliance. It is their refusal to hide their delight in being together that most outrages the other convicts and guards. And, more importantly, it is their romantic intimacy, their eroticized bond that enables Jimmy to not only survive in prison, but to stand up to and resist the state's attempt to discipline and dominate what he considers his most basic sense of self.

Because his gender and sexual identity are perpetually being challenged, they are a constant source of concern and self-reflection, and thus they are manifest aspects of the story line. Jimmy's racial identity—particularly its privileged status—appears never to be challenged, and there is surprisingly little racial conflict among the inmates. Although we could say that his freedom from having to reflect on the manner in which his race secures him privileged access to resources inside and outside the prison is evidence of his whiteness, race, in general, remains fairly opaque in both *Cast* and *Yesterday*. While the black convicts are in segregated units, we never see, for example, how this segregation manifests in black inmates receiving worse treatment than white inmates, and we never encounter a black convict evincing any discontent about racially motivated treatment. The novel was, however, originally written with a black protagonist and is, according to Himes's biographers, essentially the same story—including of course the detailed accounts of his relationships with Prince Rico, who was in this version, as in real life, black.[19] Himes's agent diligently circulated the original version of the novel among the publishing houses, but to no avail. Given that largely the same story was eventually published—though with a white protagonist who was romantically involved exclusively with other *white* convicts—we are forced to conclude that the story of a black man *triumphing* over his victimization at the hands of the state through a love affair with another black man was unpublishable, and in certain respects, unspeakable. At first glance, the publisher's insistence on the use of a white protagonist for such a queer story seems to run counter to the tendency in early twentieth-century America of projecting deviant sexuality onto representations of racial others.[20] However, *Cast* emplots its movement from prison to freedom via moving from queerness to recuperated manhood. With this story in mind, the protagonist had to be white. As already discussed, black manhood was in the popular and scientific imagination inherently "deviant," nonheteropatriarchal, and unfree. In a 1952 letter to Richard Wright about *Cast*, Himes conjectured, "[M]aybe the boys can stand the truth about life in a state prison better than they can stand the truth about life in the prison of being a Negro in America."[21] As Himes's comments suggest, a black protagonist could never fully leave behind queerness, and never fully enter freedom. He would in essence be automatically deemed more "guilty," more unacceptably deviant, and thus more deserving of punishment, and less deserving of freedom. The only way that a black man could in fact gain release from what Himes calls "the prison of being a Negro in America" would be to leave the country, which is precisely what Himes did in April 1953. Thus we can say that the novel went through progressive stages of "straightening" and whitening. The original narrative that celebrated, however ambivalently, black-on-black erotic love was then whitewashed into white-on-white erotic love and sensibility (*Yesterday*), until finally it was published in its more "hard boiled" Cold War incarnation, as *Cast the First Stone*.

Cast/*Yesterday* is bound to frustrate any readerly search for an unambiguous affirmation of queer desire, given that the text frequently reminds us that Himes was in no way immune to the demeaning and pathologizing homophobic discourses of midcentury America. And yet in his engagement with these profound discursive constraints he still manages to tell a very complex story that challenges the dominant culture's fictions around sexuality in important ways, and all without the assistance of a redemptive public discourse about homosexuality. For all its disconcerting repudiations, it remains one of the most sensitive and in-depth treatments of same-sex desire in the African American novelistic tradition prior to Baldwin's *Giovanni's Room*. In a sense you could say that, to borrow from Zora Neale Hurston, he hits a straight lick with a crooked stick. Even in its hardest, straightest, and whitest version, we are left with a radical challenge to the sexual content of normative white manhood. In Himes's narrative, if Jimmy had publicly *repudiated* his erotic intimacy with Dido/Rico, as the state demanded, then he would have forfeited his own sense of manhood and what little access he had to privacy—his capacity to choose his destiny and shape his identity.

Finally, decisions to ignore or downplay the queer content of the work because it represents an instance of "situational homosexuality" rather than "true" homosexuality ultimately miss the point. The so-called situational homosexuality of Himes's text, rather than preserving a stark division between heterosexuality and homosexuality, instead finally highlights how permeable and unstable these boundaries are. Given that sexuality, straight or queer, is always determined in some respects by space and location, Himes's text may have just as much to teach us about situational heterosexuality.

* * *

Knock on Any Door (1947), Willard Motley's first novel, was a huge success among both critics and readers. Chester Himes read *Knock* while writing *Cast*, and wrote to Carl Van Vechten that he considered it "a terrific book, a great book, far greater than anything I expected. [. . .] The guy has done something very wonderful. And frankly he has inspired me to do something just as wonderful with my story." One month later he wrote to Motley himself, "you know, *Knock* reveals a great similarity to my thought processes when I was in and first came out of prison. And Nick rings true as any liberty bell—I was so much like Nick at seventeen it isn't even funny."[22] Unlike *Cast*, though, *Knock* was more than once compared favorably to Theodore Dreiser's *An American Tragedy* and Wright's *Native Son*, and it ultimately sold more than 1.5 million copies by the time of Motley's death in 1965. In addition to being made into a noir-esque courtroom-drama film starring Humphrey Bogart, *Knock* was also made into a comic book series—needless to say the latter two incarnations of the text were almost entirely stripped of the original's anti-establishment and homoerotic investments. *Knock on Any Door* is now typically viewed as a fairly impressive but late installment of urban naturalist writing. The story focuses on the violent and brief life of "Pretty Boy" Nick Romano, whose catchphrase was "live fast, die young, and leave a good-looking corpse." The narrative begins in the Depression era, when innocent young Nick, just beginning adolescence, was still "at the prayer age" (3). Hardships force the Romano family into a slum area of Chicago, and new schools, where Nick has the first of many violent encounters with authority that determine the direction of his life. He takes the blame for a prank in school to keep another student from getting expelled, and is viciously beaten with a ruler by a priest; this is a profound moment of disillusionment, "right then . . . something started *feeling* wrong inside of him" (15; emphasis added). This is the beginning of his shift from being naturally sympathetic to naturally violent. He is later sent to reform school for, once again, keeping another kid from getting in trouble, and here Nick is subjected to scenes of cruel and malignant punishment that harden him forever. These acts of state violence against the weak simultaneously commit him to a life of rebellious antistate criminality, and to solidarity with anyone oppressed by the law, especially the poor, people of color, and eventually "queers." He embarks on a life of crime that includes robbery and prostitution, and he eventually shoots and kills a police officer notorious for torturing and killing suspects. This final act gets him the electric chair. Motley's deployment of naturalism's more familiar thematic and stylistic conventions has led critics to overlook his crucial innovations, especially his critique of the state and his pathbreaking treatment of race and sexuality.

We can begin to appreciate Motley's unique contribution by focusing less on an abstract notion of the effects of "environment" on the individual, and more on the narrative's emphasis on transgressive and progressive intercultural encounters in borderlands of Chicago's slums.[23] Motley addresses his lifelong commitment to intercultural contact in an unpublished essay on the hypocrisy of Jim Crow military training: "I was born a Negro in the City of Chicago twenty-eight years ago. No matter. This is America; this is a democracy. And my way has been the 'American way'—extensive co-mingling and association with all races and religions: as people; as Americans. What has all this traffic back and forth *across borders, without respect for borders*, done for me? I think it has given me a true perspective, a true democratic viewpoint" (1; emphasis added).[24] The essay is entitled, ironically, "I Discover I'm a Negro," and its point is to attack the government's unjust violation of his racial privacy precisely at the moment in which it is asking him to fight for democracy. To Motley, this racialized state interpellation effectively places him "just outside of democracy" (1). This subordination is all the more galling given that Motley claims to have already enjoyed a lifetime of racial privacy, at least through his interpersonal relations: "If I have had a choice of whom I cared to live and play with—if they have been, democratically, all races—why have I not the choice of whom I shall train with—and perhaps fight and die with?" (3). Although liberal national ideology has authorized his racial privacy thus far, the state, despite promises of freedom of association and mobility, is the site and agent of racial exclusion, division, and immobilization.

This essay's celebration of interracial intimacy in a democratic borderland clearly anticipates the racial, spatial, ideological, class, and sexual border-crossings that frame the novel and provide its narrative energy. Most obviously, Motley, as with the other authors in my study, enacts racial privacy through his choice of a "white" protagonist. As mentioned earlier, this decision led critic Robert Bone and others to dub his work "raceless," thereby obscuring the racial effectivity of whiteness and ignoring Motley's concern with questions of racial identity and race relations. As mentioned at the beginning of the chapter, another critical element of transgression in this work that has not received proper attention is the degree to which the work is structured by homoerotic desire. This oversight has been due, as I suggested, to Motley's choice not to speak about his own sexual identity in print, the protagonist's putatively "straight" sexual identity, and the bowdlerization of the original manuscript. *Knock* was rejected thirteen times before being accepted; publishers objected not only to the manuscript's length (1 million words), but especially its blunt treatment of sexuality in general, and homosexuality in particular. Editors at Macmillan also rejected it because they feared that its critique of the Chicago police, public schools, and other institutions would lead to economic reprisals.[25] In short, the earlier version is too threatening on all fronts, and publishers were unwilling to risk being punished for the work's critique of state and civil institutions.

My reading of the work is drawn partly from the original manuscript and takes into account the extensive homoerotic and more politically radical material that was suppressed in the editing process. As with *Cast the First Stone*, homoerotic desire permeates the text. Everyone wants Nick. Men, women, young and old. And Nick takes them all, self-consciously exploiting his extraordinary beauty as hustler, and sometime lover, of both men and women. And the reader is taken too: the text returns repeatedly to Nick's innocent eyes, his curly black hair, his broad shoulders, his tight pants.[26] Given the impossibility of representing fulfilled and nonpathologized same-sex desire within the text at this historical moment, Motley constructs Nick himself as an erotic object, and thereby opens the possibility of queering his male reader's gaze.

Though no critic or reviewer has thus far acknowledged the political implications of the work's racial and sexual border crossings, Motley was deeply committed to his novel doing antiracist, antisegregationist, anticlassist, and (implicitly) antihomophobic work. His challenge was that he also wanted to protect his racial and sexual privacy—he did not want to speak as a "Negro writer," and certainly not as a "Gay (or Queer) writer" (an identification that didn't yet exist in the public's mind), because of what it would mean to occupy those profoundly circumscribed, and in the case of queer identity, pathologized spaces of enunciation.[27] Motley wanted to attack the violence committed by the state on its minority populations—racial, sexual, and economic—without also acquiescing to *ideological* forms of violence in the process—that is, the violent exclusions of homoraciality.[28] Accordingly, Motley evades the strictures against representing *nonpathologized* queer blackness by narrating the suffering of an eroticized, manly, and queer white ethnic man who, though a member of the lumpenproletariat, is committed to resisting state violence against all those deemed socially other.

And it is precisely through these representations of otherness that Motley imagines the possibility of resistance. As Michel de Certeau reminds us, the oppressed regularly exploit the cracks, fissures, and gaps in the grid of social control to create unseen spaces of freedom. As I will argue below, Motley represents the slum, its streets, and public places of leisure as loci where society's oppressive divisions break down—especially those that separate straight from gay, rich from poor, and black from white. These spaces are rife with suffering, but they are full of sympathy. It is in everyday moments of boundary-crossing interpersonal contact that Motley imagines the possibility of interracial, interethnic, and homoerotic solidarity as sites of resistance. Thus, rather than focusing on how Nick is destroyed by his environment (as in the classic naturalist formulation), I want to highlight Motley's sense that state violence *produces* Nick as a criminal, though in this context criminality also functions as a redemptive discourse—an honorific badge of queer nonconformity that is the source of his sense of manhood. Nick becomes rebelliously "other-directed" as an act of manly solidarity with those oppressed by the state. Motley's valorization of subversive contact and sympathy across rigid social boundaries of race, class, and sexuality is what identifies his work as an important forerunner of modern black queer writing.

A queer reading of *Knock* necessitates reading race, sexuality, history, and biography back into the text, beginning with Motley's story of the text's origins. When researching the novel, Motley moved from Englewood, a predominantly white middle-class neighborhood, into the slums on the Near West Side of Chicago, just a block or so away from the famous Hull House. Motley framed this decision precisely as a critique of his neighborhood's increasingly racist and segregationist attitudes: "Feeling that I could not write or learn about man in the narrow boundaries of my neighborhood where a Pole was a 'polack' and an

Italian was a 'dago,' where no new thoughts *were moved in*, I moved to the slums of Chicago.... And here I wandered around at 2 or 3 in the morning 'looking for material.' No knives, no razors were pulled on me. Friends were made" (Cayton, "Literary Expansion" 7; emphasis added). According to Motley, the racial and ethnic minorities who live in the slums possess a clear moral superiority over the middle-class whites who look down on them. As mentioned in chapter 1, Motley even presents the slums as sites of religious tolerance, where "Negroes went to the synagogues with their Jewish friends to celebrate Jewish church days. Jews went to Italian Catholic churches to observe their church days. The whole neighborhood went to the Greek Orthodox Easter." Here and at moments in *Knock on Any Door* Motley suggests that though the slum is a place where the American dream seems most clearly out of reach, it is nevertheless a totally integrated space and thus, paradoxically, is where America's democratic ethos is most fully realized. Thus even though white middle-class neighborhoods do not appear in the novel itself, we see that the homoraciality to which they subscribe is in fact a central object of his critique. For Motley, his former neighbors, and those who share their attitudes, bear direct moral responsibility for the state violence enacted against minorities in their name.

Motley's vision of the slums reminds us that *Knock* can be seen as classic example of what Michael Denning calls a "ghetto pastoral," a Popular Front pan-ethnic "Ballad for Americans" that synthesizes elements of naturalism with that of the pastoral, "yoking ... slum and shepherd, the gangster and Christ in concrete" (251). The Popular Front's interracial, interethnic ethos offered an enfranchising alternative to the reigning Jim Crow ideology of both publishers and the dominant culture more generally. It's worth noting, however, that Motley departs from the proletarian novel's usual commitment to normative gender and sexuality. Though Nick has broad shoulders, he is far from what Robert Corber calls the "muscle-bound male worker who embodied phallic power"; Nick is defined more by the power of his soft, beautiful eyes and curly black hair—these qualities enable him to "make" men and women (sexually) rather than to make things in the factory. In lieu of "the Worker as sacrificial hero" (Denning 250), Motley offers the sex worker as sacrificial ethnic hero. Nick exploits the "exchange value" of his personal appearance, which has the effect of transgressing hegemonic social arrangements.

Motley's personal migration northward in Chicago actually bears a suggestive relationship to the Second Great Migration, where hundreds of thousands of African Americans moved into Chicago in the 1940s in search of greater job opportunities and social freedom. At first glance, Motley appears to be sacrificing his economic privilege for the sake of his art and social vision.[29] However, what remains unspoken is that by moving into a slum, he was also moving into a vice district. The vice districts, what the cultural historian Kevin Mumford has dubbed "interzones," were sites not only of interracial sexuality, but also of queer sexuality. Mumford and others have shown how the relative sexual freedom available in these impoverished neighborhoods played a crucial role in the development of gay communities in America. This aspect of life in the slum was obviously a central concern for Motley, as his original manuscript returns to same-sex activity repeatedly—far more than any other naturalist writer before him.[30] In light of this consideration, we can begin to reread Motley's claim about wandering the streets "at 2 or 3 in the morning 'looking for material'" and making friends. As with other migrants, the slum does in fact offer Motley a vital form of personal freedom, though one that he couldn't claim publicly. I believe that many of Motley's remarks on race and the conditions of "minorities" can and should be mapped onto his concern with sexual oppression. The interethnic slum grants Motley a form racial and sexual privacy.

Motley's experience of racial and sexual freedom on the streets recalls Certeau's notion of walking through the city as an everyday practice of social resistance, or what he calls a "tactic." Certeau tells us that "[t]he space of a tactic is the space of the other. Thus it must play on and with a terrain imposed on it and organized by the law of a foreign power. . . . [It must] make use of the cracks that particular conjunctions open in the surveillance of the proprietary powers" (36–37). Motley's personal and fictionalized narratives of the West Side streets are unquestionably the space of the other; walking the streets at two in the morning affords him chance opportunities to cultivate a whole range of transgressive "friendships" that cross highly policed racial, sexual, and economic boundaries. Friendship operates in Motley's life and in *Knock on Any Door* as a resistive and, in many respects, queer form of public imagination that counters the state's violation of its marginalized citizens' privacy.

This vision of the slums as a locus of profound oppression and liberatory possibility is fully in evidence in *Knock on Any Door*. Nick becomes a street walker, literally and figuratively, after a series of scenes of violent subjection by the state. He is beaten by a priest, a policeman, and a reform school officer, but probably his most formative experience is when he witnesses the savage whipping of a fellow reform school inmate following a failed attempt to escape. After being forced to watch the reform school warden administer scores of lashes against the bare bottom of a thirteen-year old boy, Nick decides: "He'd never be sorry for anything he ever did again.... He'd never try to reform now. He was on Tommy's side. All the way. For good. Forever. He knew how men treated boys. And he knew how they reformed them. He hated the law and everything that had anything to do with it" (60). This scene in many respects recalls Frederick Douglass's famous account in his 1845 *Narrative* of the radical transformation of self that he experiences after witnessing his Aunt Hester being whipped. For both the young Douglass and Nick, it is a moment of profound subjection. For Douglass, it is the moment when he is produced as a slave; for Nick, it is the moment he is produced as a criminal. And in both scenes, the horror is heightened by a sense of sexual violation—both authors represent the state as immoral, perverse, and cruel.

Nick's behavior instantly changes after witnessing Tommy's beating; his sympathy for and horror at Tommy's violation turns him into an antisocial, antistate rebel. His first act of rebellion is to purposely violate the code of racial segregation among the inmates by openly befriending other minorities. He continues this pattern of behavior after leaving reform school, where his closest friends are invariably other ethnic minorities, including Mexicans and African Americans. Once he's back on the streets, Nick begins to engage in sexual transgressions as well. He quickly learns that his good looks can earn him money, and before long Nick is turning tricks with men. He soon develops a relationship with one man in particular, Owen, whom he picks up in an all-night café. The published version of the text significantly downplays the intimacy—physical and emotional—that Nick shares with Owen, which is evident in the following excised quotations. "For Nick, a certain liking and friendship had grown up. Owen was somebody who understood.... Maybe because Owen, in his way, lived outside the law too.... He liked Owen. Damned if he didn't. Even if people wouldn't understand if they knew. People never understood anything anyway. Not the 'good' people. They were too damn good—and too cruel. Owen was the only true friend he had.... And now he stopped fooling around with other men. Just Owen; and all the girls he could get" (770).

Nick identifies with Owen specifically as a fellow "criminal," an identity in opposition to what society deems "good"—despite his youth, Nick has already learned that "good" is an exclusionary and disciplinary category, and those who represent and enforce compliance with these ideals and values are also quite "cruel." Nick's compassionate and sympathetic identification with Owen—his friendship—allows Motley to represent a caring, intimate, and even sexual bond between these men without identifying Nick as gay. Thus we can say that state violence in certain respects ends up queering Nick, that it leads him to relinquish his possessive investment in straight white manhood, to paraphrase George Lipsitz, and to form a range of transgressive alliances. Motley's depiction of the queer bond as a means of resisting state violence may have authorized and inspired Himes's climactic scene of queer masculine redemption in *Cast*. In any event, Motley's reimagining of life on the streets constitutes a nascent kind of "queer counterpublic," which is Lauren Berlant and Michael Warner's phrase for those publicly enacted "criminal intimacies ... [that] bear no necessary relation to domestic space, to kinship, to the couple form, to property, or to the nation," but nevertheless constitute "a public world of belonging and transformation" (555).

What's most remarkable about Motley's queer counterpublic, aside from the fact that it exists at all in 1947, is that it is always already a genuinely open, heterogeneous space. Recent "Queers of Color," to borrow Roderick Ferguson's phrase, have criticized practitioners of queer theory, including founding figures such as Foucault and Sedgwick, for defining queerness as a radically open concept on the one hand, while their primary attention to an unmarked notion of sexuality ends up forfeiting considerations of how race, class, and gender determine sexuality, and vice versa. This focus often has the unfortunate effect of reinscribing elite white male biases.[31] But Motley's political and personal investments demand that race, sex, and class always be thought together. As a black gay man in an increasingly segregationist and homophobic culture, Motley valorizes the crossing of all social borders as a way to resist the manner in which dominant culture notions of identity functioned as a mechanism of social division and control. It is in this respect that his work anticipates a range of contemporary black queer writers, including James Baldwin, Charles Wright, and Samuel Delaney. For example, in *Times Square Red; Times Square Blue*, Delany writes against the urban dictum, "Never speak to strangers," arguing instead that "I propose that in a democratic city it is imperative that we speak to strangers, live next to them, and learn how to relate to them on many levels, including the sexual. ... Tolerance—not assimilation—is the democratic litmus test for social equality" (193–94).

Although Motley is drawing specifically on contemporary Popular Front notions of "critical Americanism," he and Delany are both strategically invoking the discourse of "democracy," a founding national principle, *not* in the name of strengthening the nation-state, but of securing social and economic freedoms theoretically guaranteed for its citizens but regularly denied in practice. Motley's vision can be said to anticipate such scholars as Sharon Holland, Mae Henderson, Phillip Brian Harper, Robert Reid-Pharr, and Marlon Ross, to name only a few, who have all challenged not merely essentialist notions of race and sexuality, but also the idea that blackness and queerness should be seen as competing identities—where an individual and his or her work is either fundamentally "black" *or* "queer." Ross in particular has demonstrated in an essay on *Giovanni's Room* how this needlessly limited mode of inquiry is incapable of allowing that race and sexuality are only two of many radically intertwined dimensions of selfhood. It is Motley's critique of static, univocal, and oppressive notions of identity, be they racial, sexual, or otherwise, that mark him most clearly as a crucial forerunner of contemporary black queer writing.

* * *

The differences between the previous two novels and *Giovanni's Room* extend beyond issues of genre and sexual self-identification. Nick and Jimmy are socially marginalized figures, while David is intentionally depicted as an emblem of middle-class America—Baldwin commented in a letter to Bill Cole, his publicist, that he had chosen a protagonist who was "the most stereotypical of Americans, 'the good white Protestant'" (Leeming 127). Baldwin drives this point home in the text's opening paragraph, where David introduces himself to the reader by observing, "My reflection is tall, perhaps rather like an arrow, my blond hair gleams. My face is like a face you have seen many times" (7). The texts' settings and circumstances also seem to set these works apart—Nick and Jimmy, both the product of working-class American urban neighborhoods, are largely devoid of social agency, a fact most pointedly expressed in their imprisonment and experience of state violence. Conversely, David's wealth and social entitlement enables literal and figurative mobility: his trip to Europe, at least judging by appearances, is part of a long tradition of wealthy white Americans traveling in the Old World as part of their "education." But even if David's social privilege enables this sojourn in Europe, Baldwin immediately makes clear that his trip is not one of leisure and cultivation, but panic and flight, and though he may be able to afford to book passage across the Atlantic, his desperate attempt to get away from his American "home" connotes entrapment, rather than "freedom." Baldwin further undercuts David's privileged mobility by shifting from a description of his appearance as being "perhaps like an arrow" to a revealing admission that "My ancestors conquered a continent, pushing across death-laden plains, until they came to an ocean which faced away from Europe into a darker past." David's straight white male identification directly evokes an authority based on genocidal domination of space. In terms of style, Himes's and Motley's texts are realist, while *Giovanni's Room* is classically modernist—indeed, Baldwin first established his public voice as a writer by lambasting realist, naturalist, and, in particular, Popular Front social realist texts, such as *Knock on Any Door*.

Giovanni's Room blends aspects of the prior two works—it voices *Cast/Yesterday*'s anxieties about balancing same-sexual desire with traditional notions of masculinity, and *Knock*'s argument for the moral necessity of resisting the nation-state's role in policing disruptive border crossing. Baldwin fuses these concerns through appropriating and revising the interrelated concepts of anti-Stalinist liberalism, modernist aesthetics, and contemporary discourse on the "beleaguered male self." This strategy enables him to avoid presenting a narrative foregrounding the dominant culture's victimization of the disenfranchised, and instead to dramatize how normative notions of American white manhood (i.e., heteropatriarchy) injure not only America's "others," but those whose authority the norms appear to underwrite.

Several critics have recently analyzed *Giovanni's Room*'s immanent critique of white American manhood.[32] Thus far, however, no one has fully attended to the manner in which Baldwin's critique actually emerges from his critical *appropriation and redeployment* of Cold War notions of manhood, especially the ideal of the "autonomous male self." Baldwin takes up this ideal strategically, as it seems to open a space for a less compromised mode of resistance, in contrast to "protest" literature, which, as discussed earlier, seems to bolster the status quo by acceding to a set of representational norms and practices that naturalize the power asymmetries already in place—for example, injured, stigmatized, marginalized other railing against a normal, idealized mainstream citizenry. Baldwin's treatment of American ideals of manhood is not purely dissident, nor is it simply assimilationist or chauvinist. Rather, he aspires to reform these ideals. Instead of reproducing what publishers expected, a narrative of damaged black otherness, Baldwin deploys the ubiquitous contemporary discourse about the *damaged white male self*, for which experts found evidence in the pervasive anxiety, self-doubt, indecision, and even anguish among white men over their inability to conform to society's expectations regarding their roles in public and in private.

Baldwin's appropriation of this discourse may seem surprising, given that American ideals of manhood habitually erased or pathologized "queers" and "Negroes." These ideals function at least partly as a point of entry into public discourse. Once on the inside, so to speak, he utilized the popular psychological and moral discourse of the moment for his own purposes, exposing the blind spots, biases, and contradictions embedded in *mainstream* uses of the ideal of white male autonomy. In particular, he reveals the extent to which these putatively universal norms were more often than not put to work in the service of propagating white heteropatriarchy. Mainstream experts and commentators, never doubting the social value of white heteropatriarchy, considered their analyses objective and "realist"; Baldwin countered that these norms were themselves central aspects of the alleged crisis in manhood and needed to be challenged, not preserved. Contemporary discourses on "the Negro" and "the homosexual" were, paradoxically, evidence of this crisis. While commentators worried over how to get modern white men to better conform to normative roles and behaviors, Baldwin countered that the racism, homophobia, and sexism that produced "normal" white manhood, what Ross calls "homoraciality," were what interfered with "the American boy" emerging into "the complexity of manhood."[33] In other words, while experts worried over how to shore up white heteropatriarchy, Baldwin worried over its continued hegemony.

Baldwin's early essays and reviews elaborate in fairly extensive detail both the qualities that constitute his ideal of the "autonomous male self" and the social forces working against that self; it is this conflict that structures *Giovanni's Room*. As Geraldine Murphy and others have shown, Baldwin's particular conception of American manhood clearly bears the impress of the anti-Stalinist intellectuals who gave him his start as a professional writer reviewing books and occasionally authoring essays for publications such as the *New Leader, Commentary*, and especially *Partisan Review*; his pieces reflected the periodicals' valorization of "irony, complexity, ambiguity, and maturity," as well as their denigration of the Popular Front's reputed sentimentality, ideological fatuity, and middlebrow aesthetics (1023). Baldwin also reproduced the "gendered inscriptions" of anti-Stalinist liberalism, Murphy notes, which proffered a manly, strenuous, liberal politics and modernist aesthetics in place of what were considered the "soft" and feminized positions of the radical Left. For example, Baldwin's two best-known essays from this period, "Everybody's Protest Novel" and "Many Thousands Gone," challenge Richard Wright's literary and political authority precisely by, in Murphy's reading, "smearing him as the literary mother. Just as Bigger is Uncle Tom . . . so Wright is Harriet Beecher Stowe." In "Everybody's Protest Novel," Baldwin figures the "contemporary Negro novelist and the dead New England woman . . . locked together in a deadly, timeless battle; the one uttering merciless exhortations, the other shouting curses. And, indeed, within this web of lust and fury, black and white can only thrust and counter-thrust, long for each other's slow exquisite death" (qtd. in Murphy 1028). Murphy understands this parodic scene as Baldwin's anxious attempt to defuse his own gender and sexual vulnerability by preemptively feminizing Wright, "the virile revolutionary," transforming him into "a schoolmarm in bustle and whiteface" (1028–29). But Baldwin is no "dupe of anti-Stalinism," she stresses, pointing out that, for all his belletristic style, he was, unlike the New York Intellectuals, committed to dramatic social transformation: "There's no question that for most anti-Stalinist intellectuals, Cold War liberalism marked a retreat from the left yet provided an illusory iconoclasm in the figure of the heroic, tragic individual at odds with society. In short, the anguished dialectics of saying yes and no inside and out masked accommodation to the warfare-welfare state" (1037). Baldwin most clearly outstrips these figures in his persistent attention to questions of African American subjectivity, American race relations more generally, and what we now might term heteropatriarchy. As Murphy observes, while Baldwin shares the anti-Stalinists' valorization of "freedom," he was far less concerned with protecting the "American way of life" from the threat of communism; on the contrary, he was at pains to illustrate how the "American way of life" was itself, as an incarnation of white heteropatriachy, the greatest obstacle to freedom for African Americans and queers.

Murphy's astute discussion of Baldwin's debt to anti-Stalinist liberal aesthetics, especially his redeployment of many of its "neo-traditionalist" attitudes toward gender, still manages to underplay the extent of his divergence from these thinkers, and the reasons for his divergence. In particular, Baldwin's animus toward "protest" and Popular Front literature, unlike the anti-Stalinists, is first and foremost an attack on the way in which these literary modes participate in hegemonic discourses of race, gender, and sexuality, discourses in which both "blackness" and "queerness" were unmanned, so to speak. As already discussed, Baldwin sees these modes as relying blindly on sociological discourses that depicted blackness and homosexuality in terms of pathology and deviance—renderings that constituted rationales for state surveillance and discipline.

Baldwin's essays on sexuality in particular could be read as not merely diverging from anti-Stalinists' positions, but actually directed against these presumably enlightened, progressive thinkers. Influential figures such as Arthur Schlesinger construct their version of masculine consensus liberalism precisely by attacking forces in society that were believed to be feminizing men and spreading the plague of homosexuality. Schlesinger argued that "America has its quota of lonely and frustrated people, craving social, intellectual, and even sexual fulfillment they cannot obtain in existing society. For these people, party discipline is no obstacle; it is an attraction. The great majority of members in America, as in Europe, *want* to be dominated" (qtd. in Cuordileone 27). He declared that communism "perverts politics into something secret, sweaty, and furtive, like nothing so much...as homosexuality in a boy's school; many practicing it, but all those caught to be caned by the headmaster" (qtd. in Cuordileone 28). Schlesinger was far from alone in his derision of communism as a haven for "sexual perverts." Leslie Fiedler, to take another consensus liberal thinker, chastised left-wing intellectuals for allowing homosexuals to become "the staunchest party of them all" in their apparent rejection of bourgeois society (qtd. in Corber 1). Many, if not most, anti-Stalinist liberals were overtly homophobic, unself-consciously gay-baiting and gay-bashing (rhetorically at least) alongside the most conservative Cold War conservatives.

Baldwin, however, was extremely skeptical of recuperating American manhood by denigrating homosexuals and women. In his 1949 essay "The Preservation of Innocence," he writes: "Matters are not helped if we...decide that men must recapture their status as men and that women must embrace their function as women; not only does the resulting rigidity of attitude put to death any possible communion, but, having once listed the bald physical facts, no one is prepared to go further and decide, of our multiple human attributes, which are masculine and which are feminine" (*Collected* 597). In fact, nearly *everyone* believed themselves prepared to make just these sorts of discriminations: from anti-Stalinist intellectuals, to sociologists, psychologists, and religious leaders, to producers of popular culture, to presidents and congressmen as well as the "man on the street," liberal and conservative alike. If pressed by a thoughtful interlocutor such as Baldwin, however, the certainty of their categorizations and attributions would begin to unravel, revealing instead incoherence and contradiction. Baldwin contends that on some level, even if unconsciously, most Americans suspect this incoherence, which is precisely what fuels the ongoing desperate, futile, and internecine effort to clearly demarcate gender and sexual identities. This is the losing battle to which Baldwin alludes when he observes that "[the homosexual's] present debasement and our obsession with him corresponds to the debasement of the relationship between the sexes; and... his *ambiguous and terrible position in our society reflects the ambiguities and terrors which time has deposited on that relationship* as the sea piles seaweed and wreckage along the shore" (595; emphasis added).

For Baldwin, "the homosexual problem" is first and foremost a gender problem, or, more precisely, a problem with hegemonic notions of manhood. He chooses not to catalogue the ways in which American patriarchy and homophobia "debase" women and homosexuals (a move for Baldwin that would be akin to "protest") but instead focuses the reader's attention on the lack, however unconscious, that compels the debasement—the inherent *ambiguity* of *manhood*. This ambiguity "terrifies" men and leads them to be obsessed with their own possible femininity, which in turn leads them to set about debasing women to manage their own internal sense of gender instability. By extension, because normative notions of manhood and heterosexuality are believed to be intertwined, the same *ambiguity* of *manhood* leads straight men to set about debasing homosexual men. The latter were frequently perceived in common parlance as "inverts," that is, men with female psyches or souls; the possibility of standing in a "female" relation to other men socially (for example, being "passive" or "other-directed") bleeds into an anxiety about standing in a female sexual relation (that is, "passive" or receptive) to other men as well. Baldwin makes clear that the "obsession" of the dominant culture with "the homosexual" functions in much the same way as the obsession of the dominant culture with "the Negro." The discourse of the homosexual and the Negro are, as he says in "Everybody's Protest Novel," "an accepted and *comforting* aspect of the American scene, ramifying that framework we believe to be so necessary"—comforting and necessary because they serve to reinforce queer and black otherness, which solidifies an anxious, ambiguous, and terrified white heteropatriarchy (19; emphasis added). A fundamental rethinking of the content of white American manhood would obviate the need to compulsively denigrate women, homosexuals, and African Americans.

Normative masculinity, for Baldwin, is itself a problem, and thus while he agrees with midcentury experts and intellectuals that idealistic boys need to put away childish things and assume the mantle of manhood, he directly challenges how we habitually recognize, embody, and enact manhood in America. A key element of manhood is the seemingly innocuous notion of "maturity." As Cuordileone points out, the importance of maturity and courage in the face of anxiety were themes that in one form or another reappeared in countless psychiatric and psychological texts. Maturity in particular was promoted as the hallmark of the well-adjusted male, and was often equated with fulfilling a particular life trajectory—landing a respectable job, getting married, maintaining a home, and establishing a family.[34] These milestones and roles—key tenets of privacy—were considered the "reality" that "mature" men had to accept and enact. They are also, quite plainly, structured by normalized gender and sexual binaries and hierarchies. As we have already seen, Baldwin takes great pains to illustrate that these naturalized gender and sexual binaries are precisely not natural and stable, but above all marked by a profound ambiguity and complexity. Accordingly, he argues, the true "signal of maturity" is not the blind embrace of these ideals, but rather "the recognition of [gender and sexual] complexity," a recognition which "marks the death of the child and the birth of the man" (*Collected* 597).

The American notion of manhood, according to Baldwin, is predicated on fleeing this recognition, which necessarily would transform one's self and one's relations to "others": "One may say, with an exaggeration vastly more apparent than real, that it is one of the major American ambitions to shun this metamorphosis. In the truly awesome attempt of the American to at once preserve his innocence and arrive at a man's estate, the mindless monster, the tough guy, has been created and perfected; whose masculinity is found in the most infantile and elementary externals and whose attitude toward women is the wedding of the most abysmal romanticism and the most implacable distrust" (597). The "tough guy's" childish romanticization of and distrust of women is actually a romanticization and distrust of "manhood." This fact necessitates, again, the repudiation of all things associated with the feminine in the male self, as well as the "exploitation of externals, as for example, the breasts of Hollywood glamour girls and the mindless grunting and swaggering of Hollywood he-men" ("The Male Prison," *Collected* 235). The phrase "strident exploitation" conveys Baldwin's sense that American gender and sexual norms are notable less for their stable and secure divisions and more for their telling excess and overcompensation. It is a nagging sense of what Judith Butler would later call "gender trouble" that leads Americans to attempt to stabilize gender meanings (especially their capacity to anchor social arrangements) by fixating on secondary sex characteristics (women are sex objects) and by the excessive performance of normative gender behaviors (men are hard, aggressive, and dominant).

For Baldwin, the seldom-recognized consequence of perpetuating these norms is the harm that it enacts not just on oppressed others, but specifically on presumably straight, white men. What Baldwin calls the American "prison of masculinity" "put[s] to death any possible communion" not only between men and women but also between men and men. This "powerful masculinity" (235) makes real love impossible between men and women, and when this happens men also "cease to love, or respect or trust each other, which makes their isolation complete. Nothing is more dangerous than this isolation, for men will commit any crimes whatever rather than endure it" (235). Baldwin would have us understand that our isolation comes from the internalization of dominant-culture norms regarding race, gender, and sexuality, which prohibit us from seeing ourselves in others, and vice versa, and this isolation leads to desperate acts of violence. Hegemonic manhood, not same-sex desire, leads to "crimes" against others and ourselves. When American men (and women) "debase" women, Jim Crow "the Negro," and imprison "the homosexual," they simultaneously debase, Jim Crow, and imprison themselves. The antidote to these conditions is to be found in "communion" and "experience." Baldwin insists that a defining national characteristic is "that Americans [evade] so far as possible, all genuine experience, [and] have therefore no way of assessing the experience of others and no way of establishing themselves in relation to any way of life which is not their own" ("Many Thousands Gone" 41). "Genuine experience" with others would belie the childishly simplistic "American ideals" of race, gender, and sexuality that organize American society, and lead to "communion" with others, and thus with ourselves.

The term "communion" evokes on the one hand the Eucharistic rites of receiving the spirit of God, but it also denotes deep intimacy, an act of sharing or holding in common, and an interchange of thoughts and feelings.[35] This interchange could be said to facilitate the recognition of what is held in common—in the case of blacks and whites, a shared history and bloodline (42); in the case of men and women, straight and gay, shared strengths and weaknesses (which are usually referred to in gendered terms, but are never the exclusive possession of either gender ["Preservation of Innocence" 597]). Baldwin insists that it is the task of the writer to leave behind misleading labels and stereotypes and instead "reveal how profoundly all things involving human beings interlock" (600). Without this recognition of fundamental interconnectedness among individuals "we may all smother to death, locked in those airless, labeled cells, which isolate us from each other and separate us from ourselves" (600).[36] For Baldwin, the ideals of white American manhood actually generate privation, rather than enfranchised privacy.

When the reader first meets David in *Giovanni's Room*, he is in an abyss of solitude and deprivation; he is smothering to death in an airless, labeled cell, separated not only from others, but first and foremost from himself. He is entirely alone in "this great house" in the south of France, drinking and staring at his reflection in the window "as night falls" (7). The narrative unfolds in the form of David's recollections over the course of one evening, which is leading, as he says, to "the most terrible morning of my life." This morning is terrible, as David eventually reveals, both because his ex-lover, Giovanni, is to be executed for murder, and because he is contemplating his own "ambiguous and terrible" position in society as a middle-class, American white man who is also a "homosexual." As the night passes, and more details of his relationship with Giovanni come to light, David spends more and more time imagining how Giovanni feels sitting in his cell. Before long, David and Giovanni's experiences become insistently fused. David comments, "[N]o matter what I do, anguish is about to overtake me in this house, as naked and silver as that great knife which Giovanni will be facing very soon. My executioners are here with me, walking up and down with me, washing things and packing and drinking from my bottle. They are everywhere I turn" (148). David thinks, "I might call—as Giovanni, at this moment lying in his cell, might call. But no one will hear. I might try to explain. Giovanni tried to explain." He, like Giovanni, is in prison, alone, devoid of friendship, and beyond any hope of mercy. By the text's final pages, he is experiencing everything with Giovanni, the terror, the desperate attempt to pray, and the sense of being trapped in a "dirty body" (222) that "is under sentence of death" (223). David's sympathetic connection with Giovanni at this point has come tragically late. Had he allowed himself to sustain his intimate connection with Giovanni, they could well be in a great house together, reinventing privacy on their own terms, rather than suffering life-destroying privation in separate prisons.

But even in this moment of sympathetic connection with Giovanni, a merger possible because, as he "confess[es]" (148), he loved him, and knew him intimately, he also narrates these scenes from outside

Giovanni, from the perspective of the priest, who "gently lifts the cross away" (222), out of the "cling[ing]" hands of Giovanni, from the perspective of the guards, who "lift [the kneeling] Giovanni," and from the perspective of the executioner who "[throws] him forward on his face in darkness" (223) and releases the knife. By having David imagine all of these scenes (rather than putting us directly in Giovanni's mind, or using an omniscient narrator), Baldwin underscores David's ambivalence, and especially his multiple, competing, and ultimately self-defeating range of identifications.

The central crime (or rather, the great sin) in this text, as many commentators have observed, is David's failure to love. As Baldwin insisted on numerous occasions, *Giovanni's Room* is "not about homosexual love, it's about what happens to you if you're afraid to love anybody" (Leeming 125). What David fears is the cost of love, which, if understood as a fear of vulnerability, might be a "universal" concern. But, for David, loving Giovanni in particular represents a specific threat, principally to his sense of manhood, one produced by his American identity, and his white middle-class frame of reference. As his feelings for Giovanni grow ever more powerful (and, therefore, disruptive), he frequently finds himself longing for scenes of normative domestic contentment, though containment may be the more accurate word: "I wanted children. I wanted to be inside again, with the light and safety, with my manhood unquestioned, watching my woman put my children to bed." The function of "woman" in this equation is to be "a steady ground, like the earth itself, where I could always be renewed" (137–38).

He tries desperately to realize this fantasy with Hella, his fiancée, who appears perfect for him because she too is looking for heteronormative safety and reassurance of her gender adequacy. They meet initially after he sees her in a bar "drinking and watching the men" (one of his favorite pastimes), and he thinks, in tellingly childish phrasing, "she would be fun to have fun with" (9). Hella is educated and thoughtful, but in her words, "I'm not really the emancipated girl I try to be at all. I guess I just want a man to come home to me every night. . . . I want to start having babies. In a way, it's really all I'm good for" (163). Even so, she admits that she finds it "difficult" to "be at the mercy of some gross, unshaven stranger before you can begin to be yourself" (165)—to lose her privacy before she can attempt to reconstruct it within the terms of heteronormative domesticity. In this traditional conception of marriage, the woman is an extension of the man, a function of his privacy. The problem is, as Hella, puts it, that "*you've* got *me*. So now I can be—your obedient and most loving servant" (167; emphasis in original). Although David claims that he doesn't "understand [her] at all" (168), it is precisely this domestic sense of gendered hierarchy and privilege that structures (and restricts) his sense of the possibilities inherent in a domestic relationship.[37]

When splitting with Giovanni, David accuses him of wanting to "go out and be the big laborer and bring home the money, and you want me to stay here and wash the dishes and cook the food and clean this miserable closet of a room and kiss you when you come in through that door and lie with you at night and be your little *girl*" (188; emphasis in original). Giovanni refutes this, saying, "If I wanted a little girl, I would be *with* a little girl." David's domestic dystopia obviously arises from a fear of losing his straight white man's entitlement, what Lauren Berlant terms the white man's "domestic and erotic privilege."[38] He can only imagine domestic arrangements where one person is a man, the other a woman, and the one playing the woman is, as Hella puts it, "the obedient and most loving servant," the supplement that stabilizes the terrible ambiguity of normative manhood. Giovanni, however, is not interested in gender roles, but in relationships. He reminds David that "you are the one who keeps talking about *what* I want. But I have only been talking about *who* I want" (189; emphasis in original). The most powerful symbolization of Giovanni's desires is his attempt to install a recessed bookcase in his tiny room, which requires breaking down the walls; David describes this effort as "hard" and "insane" work (152). But it is clear that Giovanni wants to reconstruct his privacy; by making room for new narratives he hopes to transform his domestic space to accommodate his desires, rather than living within the strictures handed him by others.

David, however, cannot allow for any other domestic arrangement, and thus rejects Giovanni for fear of forfeiting his masculine prerogative, which specifically is a fear of being "feminized." The fear of emasculation, and specifically the fear of becoming a "fairy," has a complex function in the work. The first person who confronts David publicly about his homoerotic desire is a transvestite, a grotesque figure David describes as looking "like a mummy or a zombie . . . something walking after it had been put to death" (54). The "mummy" asks David bluntly, "you like him—the barman?" (55). David refuses to answer, but immediately afterwards begins to recognize, with horror, his "awakening, [his] insistent possibilities" (59). The "mummy" recalls David's dead mother (whom he as a child dreamed about "blind as worms, her hair as dry as metal and brittle as a twig, straining to press me against her body" [17]) and evokes his fear that he will become his mother if he becomes gay—clearly for David both the feminine and homosexuality constitute social death.

The association of deadness and homosexuality evoked by the transvestite is reinforced in the figures of Guillaume, and especially Jacques, two older, wealthy, and effeminate gay men who are widely known for preying on beautiful young men. Immediately after David viciously spurns the "mummy," whom he also refers to contemptuously as "the flaming princess" (59), Jacques directly picks up the conversation and remarks, "everyone in the bar . . . is talking about how beautifully you and the barman have hit it off . . . I trust there has been no confusion?" (56). After David persistently rebuffs Jacques' inquiries, he admonishes David "with vehemence, 'love him and let him love you" (77). He admits that his own relationships are "shameful" because "there is no affection in them, and no joy. It's like putting an electric plug in a *dead* socket" (76; emphasis added). He has become, like the mummy, the undead. There's still hope for David, whose relationship with Giovanni and others will be "dirty" only if "you think of them as dirty, then they *will* be dirty— . . . because you will be giving nothing, you will be despising your flesh and his. But you can make your time together anything but dirty; you can give each other something which will make both of you better—forever—if you will *not* be ashamed. If you will only *not* play it safe . . . [otherwise] you'll end up trapped in your own dirty body, forever and forever and forever—like me" (77). As one of my students put it, this is one of those "ghost of Christmas future" moments, where the protagonist is given a horrifying glimpse of his future courtesy of another character who is an older, wiser, and sadder version of himself. David has all the information he needs to change the course of events, and the opportunity, but he lacks the courage.

Even before meeting Giovanni, David has already been afforded a chance at a transformative connection, however fleeting, in his one night with Joey, a young friend of his with whom he had his first sexual encounter. That night he felt a "great thirsty heat, and trembling, and tenderness so painful I thought my heart would burst. But out of this astounding, intolerable pain came joy; we gave each other joy that night" (14). In the morning, though, he is consumed by panic, and Joey's "brown" "body suddenly seemed the black opening of a cavern in which I would be tortured till madness came, *in which I would lose my manhood*" (15; emphasis added). This cavern is "black, full of rumor, suggestion, of half-heard, half-forgotten, half-understood stories, full of dirty words. I thought I saw my future in that cavern" (15). His act with Joey, because of his age and lack of experience, remains for one fleeting moment innocent and revelatory of new possibilities; almost immediately, though, he recalls the "dirty words" that society ascribes to same-sexuality, and fears that he will be forever banished to a place in the world that will feel like a "black cavern." His fear of the cavern suggests a fear of being trapped in the feminine, specifically, a feminine form of sexuality. The imagery also clearly recalls his dead mother, who in his dreams tries to drag him into her body, which he imagines as "a breach so enormous as to swallow me alive" (17). Baldwin reinforces David's association of homosexuality, female sexuality, and death again when he admits that his experience with Joey "remained... at the bottom of my mind, as still and as awful as a decomposing corpse" (24). To these connections we can also add that David is in flight specifically from Joey's "brown" body, which suggests that he fears not only the social death of becoming "female" identified, but also becoming socially equivalent to despised dark American racial others.

Thus he embarks on his transatlantic flight, and the harder he tries to "protect his manhood," the more inexorably he moves toward losing it. Giovanni even predicts who David will become. When telling David about his baby boy who died in infancy, he proclaims, "[I]t would have been a wonderful, strong man, perhaps even the kind of man *you* and Jacques and Guillaume and all your disgusting band of fairies spend all your days and nights looking for, and dreaming of" (185; emphasis in original). Neither David nor Giovanni is, when they first meet, "a fairy," and the text implies that if he had loved Giovanni, they could have "give[n] each other something which [would] make both of you better." David fails at precisely the moment where Jimmy rises to the challenge in *Cast*, in which he claims the status of "pervert" in order to be a man.

Instead, when David is faced with taking responsibility for his relationship with Giovanni, he retreats to his white American moral and gender codes. As he says to Giovanni, "People have very dirty words for—for this situation.... Besides, it *is* a crime—in my country and, after all, I didn't grow up here, I grew up *there*" (107; emphasis in original). He fails to summon the courage necessary to be "true to himself" and instead conforms to social expectations. Baldwin insists that David's personal struggle, however perverse it may seem to most Americans, is an example of the central conflict facing midcentury American men—learning how to cope with the burden of "freedom." As Arthur Schlesinger argued in *The Vital Center*, "Most men prefer to flee choice, to flee anxiety, to flee freedom... man longs to escape the pressures beating down on his frail individuality" (qtd. in Cuordileone 6). But where Schlesinger and others equated "homosexuality" as evidence of a "flight from masculinity" (Cuordileone 145), an extreme form of the same weakness of manhood that drives "mass man" to totalitarianism, Baldwin depicts David's failure to own his desire for Joey, and especially his love for Giovanni, as the most damning proof of David's lack of manhood. As David discovered soon upon arriving in Europe, "nothing is more unbearable, once one has it, than freedom. I suppose this is why I asked [Hella] to marry me: to give myself something to be moored to.... But people can't, unhappily, invent their mooring posts, their lovers and their friends, any more than they can invent their parents. Life gives these and also takes them away and the great difficulty is saying Yes to life" (10). "Life" in this passage is the "reality" that midcentury intellectuals and experts insisted that "mature" men had to look directly upon as individuals, without "childish" idealism and sentimentality. Real men had to be "inner-directed," which means that they relied on the moral compass of the autonomous "self," not the "safety" of authoritarian compulsion. David's engagement with Hella shortly after he arrives in Europe, and his return to her after living with Giovanni, is proof not of his maturity, that he is ready to "settle down," but rather that he is in desperate flight from himself; it is proof of his immaturity, his commitment to a childish ideal of manhood even when it is contradicted by his experience with Giovanni.

By acceding to the state's idea that what they gave to each other was "dirty" and a "crime," he has, as Jacques prophesied, failed in his efforts to protect his "innocence" and instead criminalized both himself and Giovanni. Not simply as "perverts," however, but as murderers. Giovanni, who strangles Guillaume with the sash of his "theatrical dressing gown" (205), an unambiguous symbol of his "fairy" status, commits the most obvious murder. But it is David who abandons Giovanni with no job and no money, which leads him first to be Jacques' "kept boy," and then to sleep with Guillaume in the hope of getting his bartending job back, the situation that David imagines leading to the murder. But not only did David have a direct hand in creating the circumstances that lead to Giovanni's committing murder, and therefore being "under sentence of death," he rejects Giovanni *because* he aligns himself with the state, and thus indirectly, he contributes to Giovanni's murder, an association that Baldwin reinforces by having David imaginatively participate in the scene. Long before the execution, though, David feels that his doomed relationship with Giovanni is "committing the longer and lesser and more perpetual murder" (157). Giovanni also accuses David of "want[ing] to kill him in the name of all your lying little moralities. And you—you are *immoral*. You are, by far, the most immoral man I have met in all my life. Look, *look* what you have done to me" (187; emphases in original). David's immorality derives not from his same-sexual desire, but from his inability to challenge his native country's dicta regarding gender and sexuality. Baldwin sees this as a peculiarly American weakness:

> It seems to me that the Americans—unluckily for them—always have had a receptacle for their troubles, someone or something to pay their dues for them.... The white American who only became a white American after he crossed the ocean and after some effort—some time and some pain—always had someone else to bear the burden for him: The Indian or the "Nigger." And what might have happened to him, what might have transformed him and made him grow up, happened instead to other people. It happened to Uncle Tom, it happened to Uncas, it didn't happen to him. You know, it would really be quite an extraordinary spectacle, for someone sitting on Mars perhaps, to realize that the most powerful nation on Earth—the viceroy of the Universe—is one of the most astounding examples of retarded adolescence in human history. ("Interview" 49–50)

David, unlike Nick and Jimmy, has resources available to him that enable him to make someone else "pay his dues" (e.g., Joey, Hella, and Giovanni), but in his avoidance of this responsibility, he also fails to "grow up" and stand his ground, and thus fails to redeem his manhood, as Nick and Jimmy do.

David fails as a man because he is not brave enough to suffer the cost associated with rewriting the hegemonic scripts of white male privacy, preferring instead the "safety" and privation in his "father's house." This is the "great house" where we meet David, which, as I've suggested, is also "the big house," both the "master's house" and a "prison of masculinity." Two alternative titles for *Giovanni's Room* were *A Fable for Our Children* and *One for My Baby*. Both titles imply a refigured manhood—one where the father initiates the "son" into the holiness and necessity of communion with others, rather than inculcating prohibitions, self-ignorance, and bigotry. *Giovanni's Room*, as with *Knock* and *Cast*, insists that to blindly submit to the "law of the father," and automatically condemn love between men is fundamentally immoral because it is a condemnation of "man's" greatest hope for transcendence in a fallen, corrupt world. All three novels argue, well in advance of publicly redemptive discourses of same-sexuality, that crossing boundaries in defiance of the state and its disciplinary mechanisms—designed to keep "man" from "man" and to maintain oppressive social hierarchies—is not merely possible, but a moral obligation.

4 / Sympathy for the Master: Reforming Southern White Manhood in Frank Yerby's *The Foxes of Harrow*

Though he's now largely forgotten, Frank Yerby was, for a time, granted greater *indexical* significance—as a sign of racial progress—than nearly any other contemporary black writer. *The Foxes of Harrow*, his 1946 "reconstruction" of Margaret Mitchell's *Gone with the Wind* (1936), sold millions of copies and was one of the best-selling novels of the postwar era.[1] Yerby's unprecedented commercial success was not the principal source of his significance, though. African American critics in particular were struck by the fact that Yerby penned a bona fide southern historical romance, as Blyden Jackson says, "quite comfortably, and with no sense of unbecoming or forbidden ventriloquism" ("Full Circle" 30). For Jackson, the implications of Yerby's accomplishment far exceeded the literary; *Foxes* constituted a major milestone for *all* African Americans in the centuries-old struggle for freedom. Jackson concludes his review of the novel with the portentous assertion that if the "'sacred' treatment of what happened in the Old South is no longer a life-and-death issue to the Negro it means that the Negro is coming into his American heritage of assurance.... It means that now the great passion is spending itself. Not that all passion is already spent, but that we no longer have strong reason to resign ourselves to the terror that it never will be. It means not only that we can look back with greater equanimity. It means also that we can press forward toward the mark of a new world with somewhat fonder hope" (35). Yerby's ability to represent slavery without overt protest suggests to Jackson that African Americans *as a race* are one step closer to mastering the pain of the past, and thus should be that much more hopeful about eventually entering "a new world" of full citizenship rights. The author and critic Arna Bontemps is only slightly more measured, declaring in his review of *Foxes* that "Yerby's success with this type of material, unrelated to the problems that have occupied most of the other Negro writers in the United States in recent years, marks a sort of coming of age for the group. It is a healthy evolution, and it speaks well for the state of mind of the writer as well as his publisher. In the past both have suffered from a certain mental block which has prevented the normal development of Negroes simply as writers and not as 'Negro writers'" (1). Hugh Gloster asserts that Yerby's "chief contribution . . . has been to shake himself *free* of the *shackles* of race . . . signaliz[ing] the emergence of Negro novelists from the circumscriptions of color" (13; emphasis added). And Thomas Jarrett argued in 1954 that "Yerby probably demonstrates more than any other writer the Negro's growing *freedom* in the choice of materials and themes for fiction" (90; emphasis added). Yerby's choice of this genre, and especially his capacity to look on its subject matter "through dispassionate eyes" (Carter 14), constitutes evidence for these commentators that the psychic wounds inflicted by America's tragic history of race relations are beginning to heal. The appearance of *Foxes* also suggests the relaxation of long-standing racial strictures in publishing, itself an indication that the dominant culture has begun to heal and "develop" too.

All of these assessments are predicated on Yerby's "dispassionate" representation of the Old South overall, and especially his *sympathetic* portrait of Stephen Fox, a plantation lord. Yerby's treatment of this topic is considered so extraordinary because the antebellum plantation was the archetypal locus of white supremacy, and the southern historical romance, especially following *Gone with the Wind*, was the literary form most closely associated with valorizing the former regime and arguing for the persistence of black subjection (legally or otherwise) in the New South. Hence, southern historical romances functioned *instrumentally* in the maintenance of white supremacy, in Ken Warren's sense of the term, as cultural tools intended to achieve some larger social end. Yerby's decision to decenter "protest" in his appropriation of the southern historical romance and thus, presumably, to forgo writing instrumentally against Old South legends, is for these critics what makes him so indexically significant.

While *Foxes* is not a protest novel, Yerby does not, of course, endorse white supremacy. The few scholars who have written on Yerby in more recent years, such as Darwin Turner and James Hill, have focused almost exclusively on the subversive elements in Yerby's work.[2] This emphasis, partly an attempt to recuperate the author from charges of literary Uncle Tomism—due to his unsavory complicity with a racist genre—has led these critics to downplay one of the most fascinating aspects of *Foxes*— Yerby's successful reproduction of the genre and his complex investment in certain of its attitudes. Yerby does indeed critique the Old South, particularly the more familiar clichés of aristocratic gentility, but he intends to reach a large readership, and thus he articulates his critique in a manner designed to avoid alienating his chosen audience—middle-class white Americans. To better understand the specific rationales and effects of Yerby's representational strategy, I examine *Foxes* with reference to its production during and after World War II, highlighting Yerby's careful blending of American pluralism, civic nationalism, and Popular Front celebrations of "the people." Attention to the historical context in which the novel was written illuminates the interrelationship of Yerby's treatment of race, gender, class, and genre.[3] These categories of analysis help us see more clearly how Yerby simultaneously preserves the trappings of the genre, while supplanting the white-supremacist ideological project at the core of Mitchell's work with a Popular Front–inflected, nationalist parable of American manhood. Contextualizing Yerby's re-vision of Mitchell's work also throws into relief what the genre offers him beyond a space for critique and financial reward.

In the second half of this chapter, I sharpen my focus on gender in *Foxes* to illuminate the vexed sources and effects of Yerby's sympathy, especially his obscured and deeply conflicted personal investment in the southern historical romance. Yerby often remarked that he turned to writing historical romances because he failed as a protest writer. He decided that he wanted to reach as broad an audience as possible, but in order to do this he also deemed it necessary to mask many of his attitudes about race and gender in America, particularly his feelings about the compromised status of black manhood. My reading highlights how these repressed elements return throughout *Foxes*. They return not simply as "protest," however, but also as *longing* for the plantation lord's seemingly unqualified patriarchal authority. Thus I argue that Yerby not only wanted to correct Mitchell's representation of blacks, he also wanted to put Scarlett back in "her place." Via an improbable *identification* with and appropriation of southern whiteness in its most extreme incarnation—that is, as plantation lord—Yerby metaphorically reestablishes the man as unquestioned head of household. In short, Yerby's sympathetic treatment of Stephen Fox emerges at least partly from admiration for his unchallenged claim on *privacy*, his patriarchal capacity to build, govern, and protect his own private domain. Stephen Fox's creation of and rule over Harrow is, as we will see, at the very center of his identity.

But however satisfying it might have been in the postwar moment to depict a man beyond the circumscriptions of domesticated suburban masculinity, *Foxes* is, nevertheless, a text at war with itself. Yerby's ultimately problematic identification with the plantation lord produces an extremely ambivalent novel, one that expresses both intense longing *and* resentment—longing for the privilege of white masculinity, and veiled resentment of its oppressive effects on black masculinity. The civil rights gains of the World War II era were accompanied by widespread violent resistance, directed particularly against black men claiming citizenship rights. Yerby's censored feelings about suppressed black manhood, ones he expressed explicitly in short fiction from this era, erupt repeatedly in the text, frequently disrupting the manifest narrative. The pain is there, even if his contemporary readers and reviewers missed it or chose to ignore it in favor of signs of racial progress. Yerby's conflicted treatment of race in *Foxes* is not surprising, given that, as Eric Lott has argued in his own work on cross-racial performance, the imaginative inhabitation of the racial other is quite often an expression of both aversion and desire, contempt and longing, hatred and envy.[4] *Foxes* illustrates in the final analysis how for Yerby masculine sympathy is powerful enough to master Scarlett and her literary forebears, yet insufficient for managing the pain of black male subjugation.

* * *

Like many other black writers of this generation, Yerby first established himself within the Popular Front movement. He was a member of the Chicago branch of the League of American Writers,[5] and began making a name for himself as a promising protest writer by publishing stories in such Popular Front periodicals as *New Anvil, Common Ground*, and *Tomorrow*. He garnered early critical recognition with his short story "Health Card," which appeared in *Harper's Magazine* and won the 1944 O. Henry award for best first short story. He was unable, however, to publish his first novel, *This Is My Own*, which he later described as "a social protest novel that had an odor about it. It was pretty shabby stuff" (Carter 14).[6] In a 1959 *Harper's* article entitled "How and Why I Write the Costume Novel," he recalls receiving a "housefull of rejection slips for works about ill-treated factory workers, or people who suffered because of their religion or the color of their skin" (146). He says this chilly response soon led him to the "awesome conclusion that the average reader cares not a snap" about such things as injustice, racism, and sexism. Yerby quickly decided that "an unpublished writer, or even one published but unread, is no writer at all," and that to continue as a protest writer would be "roughly analogous to shouting one's head off in Mammoth Cave" (145).

In order to gain a hearing, he turned to the southern historical romance, a genre that would seem to be as far afield as one could possibly get from social protest fiction. This change in subject matter and perspective is less surprising and yet more complex than it initially appears. In an 1977 interview, he claims to have begun writing historical novels "almost accidentally, because when I started moving out into the world of commercial writing, historicals—I call them hystericals—were what was popular at the time" (217). Southern romance literature had been a mainstay of popular fiction since the nineteenth century, and its currency seemed at an all-time high following the publication of *Gone with the Wind*, book and film.[7] When the film version appeared in 1939, Yerby was living in Chicago, working for the Illinois Writers' Project, and attending University of Chicago's doctoral program in literature. Yerby left Chicago later that year in order to take teaching positions at Florida A&M and Southern University at Baton Rouge, Louisiana, which is where he began researching the historical material for *Foxes*. *Gone with the Wind*, the film, remained in the headlines for the next several years, both because of its extraordinary popularity, and because it provoked small but vociferous opposition throughout the nation in cities such as Chicago, Pittsburgh, and New York.[8] Both the celebration and criticism of the film led Yerby to conclude that the time was right, politically and economically, for an engagement with *Gone with the Wind*. Although he repeatedly tried to distance himself from his origins as a protest writer, he did admit that he was at least partially motivated to write *Foxes* to correct Mitchell's distorted representation of blacks.[9]

Yerby was fully aware that the plantation novel usually functioned as a vehicle for the glorification of white supremacy and a rationale for contemporary segregation, especially in the works of the best-known southern historical romance authors, Thomas Dixon, Thomas Nelson Page, and Margaret Mitchell.[10] The historian Grace Hale argues that the plantation romance "played a specific role in the creation of a New Southern racial order" (53). She demonstrates how novelists, along with academic and amateur historians, antiquarians, Confederate memorialists, and short-story writers, joined "to create a broad historical narrative that ... praised a romanticized past of racial 'integration,'" a past where whites and blacks knew their place and thus could function like a happy family. This revisionist fantasy of antebellum integration facilitated "a national white reunion" that sanitized the horrid violence of the war, "shifting the location of the tragedy for both Southern and Northern whites from the war itself and their sectional animosity to Reconstruction and the setting of blacks over Southern whites" (68). Blacks appeared in these narratives as either simple, loyal slaves, as treacherous and promiscuous slatterns, or as rapists. White men appeared as rulers of these black men, lynching them when necessary to protect white women, the race, and southern honor.

Yerby's published short stories were devoted to critiquing these southern racial myths and mores, especially as they functioned to bolster the regime of segregation. He was particularly interested in exploring the emasculating effects of racial violence against black men—four out of six stories addressed this theme. During the war years, the nation witnessed explosions of racial violence, big and small, virtually on a daily basis, primarily due to wartime migration to cities, increasing federal action on behalf of civil rights, and growing African American activism. Following the 1943 Detroit race riots, Fisk University produced a *Monthly Summary of Events and Trends in Race Relations*, where from March to December 1943 alone it reported "'242 major incidents involving Negro-white conflict in 47 cities' (46 percent in the South, 42 percent in the North, and 12 percent in the West). Southern conflict most frequently occurred 'in relation to the armed forces, transportation, civil rights, and racial etiquette'; Northern incidents most often involved housing, labor, and the police" (qtd. in Jacobson 113). U.S. antiblack mob violence continued unabated after the war, even worsening in some respects, with eleven reported lynchings in 1946, the year of *Foxes*' publication.

Yerby addresses these conditions directly in his short fiction. "The Homecoming," for example (which appeared a few months after *Foxes* in 1946), describes the ill-fated return of a decorated black veteran to his southern hometown. He violates several aspects of racial etiquette the moment he gets off the train (by refusing to say "sir" to a white man and by refusing to wait to be served after a white woman), and then heads directly to the home of his former employer, "Colonel Bob," to declare that "I done fought and been most killed and now I'm a man. Can't be a boy no more. Nobody's boy. Not even yours, Colonel Bob" (44). Colonel Bob asks him to leave, but later saves him from being lynched; he sends out military medics who intervene in the gathering mob and take him away to be committed for "combat fatigue . . . [he's] not responsible for his actions" (44). In "Roads Going Down" (1945), Robert, a black teenager, accidentally comes upon two white teenagers, a boy and a girl, swimming in the nude. The two boys fight, and afterward the white boy tells his father that Robert attacked the girl while they were out walking. The white boy's father comes to see Robert's father, Rafe, the next morning and insists, as an act of mercy, that Rafe punish his son's alleged transgression, rather than the lynch mob. In a powerful and symbolically dense scene, Rafe takes Robert into his dead mother's room (which neither of them has entered since her death), lashes his wrists painfully to her gleaming, "magnificent brass bed," and whips him brutally. Rafe demands that Robert say aloud that he will "never say nothing to no white man! . . . an roun er white gal . . . doan even breathe!" (71). Robert refuses to speak, but is so wracked with pain and undone by "something black and nameless" rising in his throat that he vomits. This is Robert's initiation into black manhood. Given the overdetermined nature of the mother's bedroom and bed, the scene is one of perverse, violated intimacy—simultaneously a moment of birth, death, and sexual violation. His emasculated father must teach him, as a stand-in for white male authority, that Robert has no "voice" and is socially dead (expressed in his father's command that he must not "breathe" around white women). In one sense, this can be read as his father trying to protect his son, in a "maternal" manner, from being lynched in the future. But Rafe is utterly incapable of protecting his son, and, in this instance, he embodies and executes the white man's authority in the black man's bedroom. According to the logic of the scene, Robert becomes (and is doomed to remain) the absent, violated black woman. Indeed, Rafe's name, which bears a striking orthographic similarity to "rape," underscores the tragically overdetermined relationship between race, gender, and sexuality in the region. The private, sacred space of the home has been invaded and violated, confounding and polluting multiple intimacies—familial and sexual. Robert's vomiting also underscores that this is more than a scene of subjection, but one of abjection: as Kristeva reminds us, the abject does more than induce horror; it is that which above all disturbs identity.[11] The "black and nameless thing" rising in Robert's throat is his emerging recognition that, socially, he and his father are black and nameless things. But the violence is even more intimate and disturbing as Robert is forced to recognize that white supremacy also determines his relation to his father and his own sense of gender identification.

The climax of Yerby's prize-winning short story "Health Card" occurs after a black solider is unable to defend his wife from being treated like a prostitute by white MPs (they insist that she must get her "health card," in response to which her husband shouts, "this girl my wife! She ain't no ho!" [552]). His wife then literally drags him to the ground to keep him from "standing up" for her because, as she says, "you be kilt!" (552). The protagonist weeps with shame, his head in her lap, and cries, "I ain't no man!" (553). The one story focused on female characters, "White Magnolias" (1944), describes a young white woman's efforts to resist her family and society's demand that she become a "white magnolia"—that is, a traditional southern white woman who is supposed to be passive, socially ignorant, and bigoted. She invites a black friend of hers, "a graduate of Fisk and vice-president of the International League" (321) to have lunch at her family's home. Her parents (as well as her family's black maid) insult her friend and object to their eating together as equals. The story ends with the white protagonist ripping up a white magnolia as a gesture of solidarity to her black friend who, throughout the story, remains calm and dignified. This brief discussion of Yerby's stories is intended to illustrate how he was in certain respects already engaged in rewriting the southern historical romance, at least in terms of the genre's reliance on certain attitudes toward questions of race, gender, sexuality, class, and region. His vexed feelings about these issues, especially regarding black manhood, resurface in *Foxes*, though in necessarily altered forms. It is also worth noting that although each of these stories is focused primarily on the poisonous effects of racism, they also include classically Popular Front moments of *interracial sympathy*, moments that appear in *Foxes* as well. As we can see, Yerby's switch to the more popular form did not require an abandonment of his primary concerns; *Foxes* evinces far more thematic continuity than either Yerby acknowledged or his critics have recognized.

Yerby's challenge was to redeploy the southern historical romance in such a way that allowed him to speak to the nation's current obsession with the Old South without condoning and capitalizing on its racist dimensions. In order to pull this off, Yerby claims to have set about making a "rather serious study of the elements that go to make up a novel of wide appeal" ("How and Why I Write" 145) before beginning *Foxes*. As the following remarks make clear, Yerby's generic and racial concerns are inextricable from questions of (and anxieties about) gender. The first and most important element of successful popular fiction, he decided, was the creation of a "picaresque protagonist"—specifically, a "charming scoundrel" and "a dominant male" (145).

Yerby learned from his initially unsuccessful efforts to publish a novel that mainstream U.S. audiences weren't interested in a "dominant male" who was black, especially one who openly rebelled against a racist society.[12] He accepted this reality, after concluding that "People want their prejudices, and their beliefs, however unethical, confirmed, not attacked. To confirm them [their prejudices] is, of course, as nearly immoral as anything is in this world. But one can hold one's tongue. And with dignity. Whining about one's lot ill becomes a man" (149). In a subtle rhetorical sleight of hand, Yerby revises his origins as a protest writer into a naïve and unmanly phase of "whining" that was then superseded by his more coldly rational and realistic ascent into his current status as a successful commercial writer.[13] Yerby claims to have eschewed contemporary popular fiction in the search for his successful formula, and instead read the "classics" that were successful in their day and had stood the test of time—works by Fielding, Thackery, Defoe, and the Brontës. His invocation of a highbrow literary genealogy, despite the presence of female authors, masculinizes what he experienced at times as a threatening descent into a female-identified, middlebrow genre.[14] According to his own account, Yerby safeguarded his "dignity" (and, he suggests, his manhood) by "holding his tongue" and creating Stephen Fox, a "blackhearted" Irish scoundrel (*Foxes* 3). Through Stephen Fox, as we will see, Yerby negotiates between his audience's desire for a romantic tale of the Old South and his own refusal to reproduce a white-supremacist hero. Unable or unwilling to openly attack his audience's racial prejudices, Yerby revises the racist conventions of the genre while also "confirming" patriarchal privilege. He ultimately draws on Popular Front rhetoric and the nation's wartime commitment to American ethnic pluralism to transform the genre into a nationalistic parable of American manhood.

* * *

The reviews of *Foxes* that appeared in mainstream publications, though largely favorable, all commented on how faithfully the work reproduced the well-worn, even clichéd features of the southern historical romance—grand passions, plantations, and slavery. The reviewer for the *Christian Science Monitor* remarked that "it could not have been hard to find the material [for *Foxes*]; for, in essence, it is the stock of many a Southern novel" (February 16, 1946). The *New York Times* described *Foxes* as a "good, old-fashioned, obese historical novel of the Old South that seems, more than once, to be haunted by the affluent ghost of Scarlett O'Hara"

(February 10, 1946). Ben Burns, a white reviewer writing for the *Chicago Defender*, a black Popular Front newspaper, found Yerby "following closely in the footsteps of confirmed peddlers of 'corn' ... Kathleen Winsor and Margaret Mitchell.... [T]he young Negro novelist matches the swashbuckling heroes, swooning romantic ladies and jasmine-scented countryside of the best old-timers in this money making field." Burns, however, notes (with approbation) certain important differences: "Where the Peachtree Street tome vilified the Negro with stereotypes, Yerby has turned the tables. He has done a book fully as sweeping and lavish as Miss Mitchell's 'Wind' but his Negroes are an admirable, sympathetic, human, heroic lot rather than the cringing, whining types portrayed by Miss Mitchell" (15).[15]

Yerby's revision of what Burns refers to as "the racial angle," even though ignored by mainstream reviewers, is no small deviation. Mitchell's work, at least racially, was ideologically aligned with that of Thomas Dixon, whose heroes in *The Clansman* establish their manhood by "enact[ing] a drama of fierce revenge" against blacks.[16] Although she rejected Dixon's anxieties about strong women, she fully endorsed his attitudes toward African Americans. Scarlett's self-worth depends in large part on never having to "work like a nigger" again: "[S]he knew she would never feel like a lady again ... until black hands and not white took the cotton from Tara.... [She was] ashamed that she was poor and reduced to galling shifts and penury and work that negroes should do" (506). Racial oppression plays an even more significant role with the identity and self-esteem of her male characters. When Scarlett is startled to learn that Frank Kennedy (her second husband) and Ashley Wilkes (her forbidden love) are in the Klan, India Wilkes shouts, "Of course, Mr. Kennedy is in the Klan and Ashley, too, and all the men we know.... *They are men, aren't they? And white men and Southerners.* You should have been proud of him instead of making him sneak out as though it were something shameful" (665; emphasis added). The violent subjugation of black men even transforms Frank Kennedy, who was usually "so nervous and fussy and old-maidish" (491). When Tony Fontaine arrives at Frank and Scarlett's Atlanta home late one night as a fugitive after killing a "black buck" for accosting a white woman, Scarlett observes: "This was not the meek Frank she knew, the nervous beard clawer who she had learned could be bullied with such ease. There was an air about him that was crisp and cool and he was meeting the emergency with no unnecessary words. He was a man and Tony was a man and *this situation of violence was men's business in which a woman had no part.... She seemed so much on the outside of this affair, this purely masculine affair"* (536–37; emphasis added). In this and other passages, Mitchell uses "this purely masculine affair" of racial violence to not only recuperate her broken southern white men but also to reconstitute the traditional gender roles of women; this reversion even applies to Scarlett, whose most salient character trait has been, until now, her rejection of female passivity. The color line, it seems, constitutes the limits of Mitchell's much-celebrated gender bending. When it comes to lynching, men are men and women are women.

In contrast, Yerby ultimately predicates Stephen's manhood on his adherence to popular American ideals of the mid-1940s, especially American exceptionalism. In the most basic terms, Stephen Fox's story enacts the American dream: the rise of a young, penniless Irish immigrant to extraordinary wealth in the land of opportunity—the world's only meritocracy. This archetypal American myth was especially potent during the Second World War, when the "common man" was promised that his or her wartime sacrifice would be rewarded with material abundance in the postwar era. Also plainly legible are the frequently overlapping domestic wartime discourses of the Popular Front and American pluralism. *Foxes* repeatedly asserts that America is great because it is the only place in the world where men can be men—regardless of ethnicity, race, or class.[17] Many historians have commented on the great lengths to which the American government went in its wartime campaign to downplay the nation's racial, ethnic, and class divisions. United under the aegis of a pluralist democracy, the American home front mobilized against the fascist Germans and Italians. This propaganda took on a particular urgency in light of the heightened racial conflict engendered by wartime changes—the same racial conflicts, as we have seen, Yerby was addressing directly in his short fiction from this same moment.[18] The new national ideal was that all Americans could and should work together "for a common political [goal], unhampered by ethnic, racial, or class differences" (Erenberg and Hirsch 1). Interracialism, egalitarianism, and antifascism had of course been the Popular Front's key organizing principles since the mid-1930s. The Left was redeploying these ideals at this point as part of its "win the war" coalitionist strategy.

This ethnic pluralist ethos manifests in Stephen Fox and is central to Yerby's refiguring of the tradition. Stephen embodies both the realization and the failure of American pluralism. His elevation from poor immigrant pariah to prominent gentleman reproduces the same idealized trajectory of social mobility experienced by Gerald O'Hara. But

Yerby, unlike Mitchell, tests this ethos when he attributes Stephen's fall to his deviation from America's democratic ideals, especially because of his use of slave labor. While Yerby studiously avoids overt "protest," Stephen is brought low by the end of the novel precisely because of his earlier racist and elitist behavior. By the conclusion of *Foxes,* Stephen is a broken, but wiser man; he comes to realize, in stark contrast to the recalcitrant Gerald O'Hara, that it is only through the freedom of all "men" that America will ever live up to its own ideals. This rhetoric enables Yerby to both affirm the ideal of liberal nationalism that was circulating at this moment and to critique the nation's failure to enact these beliefs, all without violating the genre's strictures against protest.

There are several key steps in Stephen's path to manhood, including the acquisition of land, slaves, a wife, and sons. But first and foremost, Yerby suggests, Stephen had to come to America. Stephen waxes patriotic at every turn, contrasting his past in Europe, where he was a "rat in the world's rat holes," with his future in America, "a big land ... for big men to carve out and build and conceive the shape of human destiny." As the narrator explains, Stephen sought "freedom for himself and his sons; mastery over this earth; a dynasty of men who could stride this American soil unafraid, never needing to cheat and lie and steal" (30). For Stephen, America is the only place in the world where a poor boy can grow into true, unqualified manhood.

Initially, Stephen's ideal of manhood is fundamentally elitist; a true man must be a gentleman. Because "a man must be free of labor," Stephen believes, the first step he takes toward realizing his goal of becoming a gentleman is to purchase a personal servant (23). Work, he claims, must be left for "the blacks." After he wins land (New Orleans has "thousands of acres of virgin river land, as yet untouched by ax or plow" [64]), purchases more slaves, and builds his mansion, he then must find a wife. This is his greatest challenge so far, because his future wife, Odalie, is an aristocratic Creole. As one Creole character explains, the Creoles from "old families" "see no reason why Louisiana should not still be a part of France. And perhaps they hate the devil worse than they do an American, but, frankly, I doubt it" (32). The narrative begins in 1825, just twenty years after the Louisiana Purchase. Many of the Creole characters, including Odalie, consider their French culture far superior to that of the Americans, and are especially resentful of its new dominance.

Yerby gives considerable narrative space over to what the narrator calls the "racial quarrel" between Creoles and Americans.[19] Yerby's decision to focus on Creoles and their distaste for Americans may seem like little more than romantic "local color." In fact, it allows Yerby to partially dispel the racist energy of the tradition and avoid making the preservation of Anglo-Saxon white supremacy the driving moral force of the narrative. Instead of a "white knight" crusading for race and region, Yerby depicts the nation in its early stages, struggling to incorporate ethnic, racial, and national otherness. Although Stephen Fox is working toward southern whiteness, his hero remains a noticeably "ethnic" immigrant, one endlessly devoted to America, "the truest republic in the world." This shift allows Yerby to foreground less inflammatory national, ethnic, and class tensions over the genre's usual black-white racial conflict.

Stephen eventually wins Odalie's hand, and when she gets pregnant, Stephen believes his American dream has come to fruition. Upon hearing that his wife is pregnant, Stephen rejoices that he will have "A son for Harrow, . . . not his nor hers, but Harrow's—a son to be shaped by the house into the finely tempered image of a gentleman, who would grow with it until at last he became master of it, until his son came, too, to manhood. . . . This was it. Completion. Fulfillment" (179). Yerby's representation of Stephen's investment in Harrow as the core of his family's identity, both in the present and in the future, clearly echoes Mitchell's treatment of Tara and the land. Scarlett declares, "These were the only things worth fighting for, the red earth which was theirs and would be their sons', the red earth which would bear cotton for their sons and their sons' sons" (362). However, Yerby embeds his sharpest critique of *Gone with the Wind* in Harrow's fate, particularly through its "son," Etienne, who grows up to despise the very American principles that Stephen holds sacred.

Etienne (the French equivalent of Stephen) is obviously his father's foil. He obstinately refuses to call himself American, preferring to identify himself as Creole, and is the most virulent anti-American, elitist, and racist character in the novel. For example, when Etienne is a child, Stephen gives him a birthday party and invites Americans, rich and poor, as well as Creoles. This party is one of the first signs of Stephen's transformation into a spokesperson for "the people" and American pluralism; as the narrator explains, the guest list includes planters, traders, merchants, and "many working men, for Stephen Fox's philosophy of democracy had become a thing very real to him" (238). Etienne, however, wants none of the "rabble" at his party and curses his American guests as "Mericain Cochons!" Stephen responds, "Tis ye who are a pig, my lad." Later in the day Stephen comes upon Etienne mercilessly whipping the pony he received as a birthday gift. Etienne is engaged in more than a temper tantrum. In this context, the pony tied to a tree and "covered all over with stripes" (242) evokes the single-most recognizable image of violation associated with slavery, though Yerby has displaced the violence and cruelty onto a pony. (This is one of several instances of displaced racialized anger evident in the text to which I return later in the chapter.) This act foreshadows Etienne's behavior as an adult, when he will abuse his personal slave, order a free man of color nearly beaten to death, and rape a black woman. All of Stephen's shortcomings are writ large in his son—especially his racism, elitism, and arrogance. Etienne is not only Stephen's greatest frustration in life, but he is directly linked to Stephen's eventual ruin in the Civil War.

As the years pass, the national debate over slavery intensifies, and Etienne and other Creoles begin agitating for secession. At this point, Stephen begins his reformation in earnest. He grows more democratic, less racist, and more patriotic with age. In an argument with Etienne over secession, he states: "I was a man grown when I came to this country. I made comparisons and soon I knew that there was nothing like this land in all the earth.... I don't believe any longer in aristocracy—even self-made aristocracy such as the South has. Ye can't have a land like America unless the people—all the people—have a hand in its shaping. And the South has never dealt fairly with the people. Why, we've treated the Negroes better than we have our own. What of your landless white? Your mountaineer—your swampfolk?" (488). To which Etienne replies, "The people,... that rabble!" Stephen finally admits the hypocrisy of believing in human freedom while owning slaves, declares that his slaves will be freed upon his death, and adds: "When I came to this land, 'twas in my mind to rise in life and everybody else could go hang. But 'tis an old man ... I know that we've all got to rise together or else we fall separately. I want to see this the best land in all the world for the common man, and if we have to rid ourselves of the aristocracy to do it, then we're best rid of them and quickly I say" (490). Stephen is voicing the classic Popular Front argument for a unified front: the nation's well-being depends on recognizing not only the rights and needs of disenfranchised blacks, but of poor whites too, who are marginalized and exploited in a plantation economy.

Yerby thus pits his reformed, democratic American hero against the aristocratic Creoles—including his son—who want to protect their culture and class privilege, in total disregard for the good of America and the "common man." Yerby's readers, in 1946, had just lived through national demands for "patriotic dedication to unity and suppression of one's class [and ethnic] dissatisfactions" (Erenberg and Hirsch 2); in their eyes, Etienne's and the other Creole's selfish anti-American attitude would appear not only short-sighted, but treasonous. Notably, accusations of treason were leveled against *Gone with the Wind* by leftists such as the CPUSA and the International Labor Defense leader William L. Patterson, who argued that *Gone with the Wind* "is propaganda, pure propaganda, crude propaganda. It is anti-Negro propaganda of the most vicious character. It is un-American propaganda. It is subversive" (15). Thus Yerby's effort to unite his American readers against the Creoles can be seen as a critique of *Gone with the Wind* in particular, and a revision of the southern historical romance in general: the Creoles are the threat to the nation's future, not African Americans.

Earlier, Yerby connected Harrow—the class and mastery it represented—with the creation of the son, the completion of Stephen's masculine American fantasy. With the onset of the Civil War, however, Stephen becomes fully aware that Harrow is at the heart of the national conflict: "A house divided against itself cannot stand. . . . [T]hree million blacks sweating in the sun . . . and John Brown out of his grave and marching. . . . They hanged him but he is not dead . . . you cannot kill an idea. *And because of that idea Harrow must perish, its Negroes gone, the slave cabins tenantless, the fields parched and weed ruined, the house itself burnt*" (484; emphasis added). Harrow was of course built on slave labor, and Etienne was raised on its fruits. Stephen's elite, racist, masculine ideal breaks down over the course of the novel until, finally, during the war, both Harrow and "its son," Etienne, are nearly destroyed—Etienne returns from the war bitter, ragged, and maimed.

Stephen's acceptance that Harrow must be destroyed precisely because of the exploitation it represents (both in stolen labor and wealth) is in glaring contrast to Mitchell's romanticization of Tara's origins, in which she disavows the expropriated labor and suffering on which it is founded. The narrator asserts that Gerald had built Tara himself, "had done it all, little, hard-headed, blustering Gerald." This remark follows, with no sense of irony or self-awareness, Scarlett's casual admission a few sentences earlier that Tara "was built by slave labor" (45). Moreover, Mitchell intends the reader to admire Scarlett's ruthless efforts to preserve Tara no matter how much additional suffering that preservation entails: 'Yes, Tara was worth fighting for. . . . She would hold Tara, if she had to break the back of every person on it" (362).

Gone with the Wind, like other southern historical romances, actively cultivates nostalgia for the "old days," encouraging the reader to feel regret, loss, and even anger at the passing of the Old South. Yerby interrupts these affects, mobilized in the name of white-supremacist, regional identification, and offers national feelings in their place. *The Foxes of Harrow* suggests that the destruction of the Old South is necessary for the fulfillment of the American ideal—true democracy, without regard to race, ethnicity, or class. Through this shift in focus, Yerby successfully fulfills his readers' expectations, without appealing to their racism and without overt protest. He provides the tale of action, love, and loss his audience looks for in the genre, while also affirming their patriotic faith that America is truly exceptional.

Moreover, Yerby replaces the genre's racialized construction of gender with a national one. If Stephen is to be a man, he must be an American. And insofar as manhood is predicated upon racial and class oppression, it is un-American. For Yerby, the reformed Stephen represents a heroic American ideal. Yerby, however, had no faith that this ideal would be realized anytime soon in America, which is why he used the money he made from the novel to leave America and live out his days in Europe.[20] As his short stories from this era repeatedly suggest, it was impossible in America to be black and to be a "man," which for Yerby typically means having sufficient patriarchal authority to safeguard one's private life. As a black writer, one who wanted a large audience, and a living from his writing, he opted to project "the problem" into the distant past and to symbolically resolve it through the conscience of a romantic white protagonist who, through his suffering, develops ethically and eventually commits himself to the ideals of liberal nationalism. This asked much less of a mainstream American reading public than asking them to think and feel with angry and injured black protagonists whose suffering generates only despair, and whose claims on manhood and full enfranchisement required social transformation *in the present*. Accordingly, Yerby chose to mute his social critique and *exhort* rather than *demand* that America live up to its own ideals.

* * *

Thus far I have discussed how once Yerby decided that he would not get a hearing in midcentury America protesting racial discrimination, he turned to the popular genre of southern historical romance, balancing his audience's rejection of protest with his own rejection of white supremacy. But mainstream resistance to African American authors openly expressing their resentment of racism in fiction has a deeper, more complex effect in Yerby's writing than a simple change of subject matter and perspective.

Critics such as Malcolm Cowley and Robert Bone who dismiss Yerby's romances as simple, cynical commercialism underestimate his self-conscious appropriation of the genre. Notwithstanding Yerby's revision of the southern historical romance's racist ideology, however, Blyden Jackson's impression that Yerby retells "the Golden Legend . . . not from the side of his mouth" is still fairly accurate ("Full Circle" 34). What Jackson is identifying is both the absence of overt protest *and* the generally sympathetic treatment of white slaveholders such as Stephen Fox. Yerby wants his readers to admire Stephen, and the grounds of that admiration are revealing.

As my earlier discussion suggests, Yerby leaves no doubt in his reader's mind that Stephen is a "man's man." The first time the reader encounters him he is being put off a riverboat for cheating at cards. The captain looks on in admiration and remarks, "A black-hearted scoundrel—but still . . ." The second officer finishes his sentence, "'But still a man . . . very much a man'" (3). Countless other characters echo this sentiment at different points in the novel, as Stephen's virility remains unblemished, even in his ultimate defeat. As one reviewer noted, Stephen Fox "can only be described as a reincarnation, in one body, of Lucifer, D'Artagnan, Frank Merriwell, and Superman. There is nothing he cannot do, no man he cannot best, no woman he cannot have" (*Saturday Review of Literature*, February 23, 1946).

Admittedly, Yerby's depiction of Stephen's hypermasculinity could be said to merely conform to the well-established formula of a romance novel hero. Indeed, Yerby says he purposely met this generic expectation "to eliminate as far as was humanly possible, the chances of [*Foxes*] failing" ("How and Why I Write" 145). Yerby insisted throughout his career that his decision to switch from protest fiction to popular fiction entailed a sacrifice of his personal interests for those of his audience. I would like to argue, however, that his choice of the southern historical romance allowed him to express a deep longing—the longing for unqualified masculinity.

I would now like to return to Yerby's assertion that the first ingredient of successful romance writing is the "picaresque protagonist." Yerby's rationale for this dictum is suggestive. The romance novel hero must be a "dominant male," he says, because "American women find that after having had their mothers and grandmothers convert the United States into a matriarchy with their ardent feminism, and reduce the bearded patriarch that grandfather was into the pink and paunchy Caspar Milquetoast of today, the average American female reader subconsciously enjoys reading about a male who can get up on his hind legs and roar. They will deny this statement, hotly. Nevertheless, it is so" ("How and Why I Write" 147).[21] Yerby's belief that American women had "convert[ed] the United States into a matriarchy" reflects the feelings of many men in his era who were forced to confront gradual but widespread changes in gender roles. World War II exerted as destabilizing (and, for some men, frightening) an influence on the position of women in American society as it did on the position of African Americans. Significant numbers of women became, for a time, the heads of household and the breadwinners; these economic shifts precipitated challenges to other patriarchal restrictions as well. The historian Elaine Tyler May points out that in addition to new job opportunities, the war expanded female intellectual and sexual autonomy, and thus produced a whole new set of anxieties after the war (Erenberg and Hirsch 128–43).

Less than six months after VJ day, Yerby published *Foxes*, a novel whose symbolic center is the home. The world of Harrow appealed to Yerby's readers (most of whom were middle-class white women) in part because of its remoteness—in time, place, luxury, and social stability.[22] In 1946, suburban America was busy putting its house back in order, settling in after years of straitened depression and wartime disruption. The antebellum plantation society found in *Foxes* was, by contrast, affluent and structured. Slavery's gender and racial hierarchies were so rigid that it was known by many as "the patriarchal institution." The historian Eugene Genovese has argued that "the justification of black slavery derived from the general justification of slavery, regardless of race, as ordained by God, and slavery and all class stratification derived from the prior divine command that women submit to men—racial subordination derived from class subordination, which derived from gender subordination" (127). While more recent readers may question the accuracy of Genovese's claim, his reading aligns with the nineteenth-century proslavery advocate George Fitzhugh's reading of the social order: "[S]lave society . . . is a series of subordinations. . . . [F]athers, masters, husbands, wives, children, and slaves, not being equals, rivals, competitors and antagonists, best promote each other's selfish interests when they do most for those above or beneath them" ("Southern Thought" 291). Fitzhugh and others described the plantation household as a perfect manifestation of the ideal Victorian social structure. The (white) man's secure position of authority in his triple role as father-master-husband created the stability needed, presumably, to ensure harmony and benefit for all.

In slavery, wealthy white men were "lords and masters" of the home in a way they weren't in the era of Rosie the Riveter.[23] Yerby resented the developing empowerment of women, as is readily apparent in his remarks on American gender relations: "Men and women today in all races, all climates, are bitter antagonists.... You have American women, who own the goddamn earth, demanding liberty from their husbands, and their men are the most downtrodden, debased, and enslaved men on the face of God's earth, where the women wear the pants in the world's greatest matriarchy" (J. Hill, "Interview" 214–15).[24] While Yerby could smugly assert that his female readers "subconsciously enjoyed" reading about "dominant" men, given his own feelings about castrating American women, it's clear that he did too.

Thus the southern historical romance offered Yerby more than a wide audience; Old South legend provided Yerby's sense of embattled masculinity an unexpected avenue of expression and identification, despite being the very source of his racial oppression. Yerby grew up in a segregated South dedicated to "keeping blacks in their place." Ironically, this popular form offers Yerby access to a fantasy of unquestioned male domination. We can detect in Yerby's complaint about America's "downtrodden, debased, and enslaved men" a barely submerged longing for the seemingly unimpeached authority of the plantation lords he took as his subject.

Evidence of this attitude appears again and again in *Foxes*. At one point in the novel, Odalie moves out of Harrow because Stephen refuses to send away a friend of his who has been raping his female slaves; Stephen remains steadfast in his decision because, he says, "my dogs, my horses, my blacks—and my women—obey me.... She will come back. I shan't lift a finger" (215). Of course, Odalie does come back, chastened and repentant. Stephen is perfectly aware of his position at the top of the plantation chain of power, articulating almost verbatim the words of George Fitzhugh.[25] This scene bears a striking resemblance to, and yet stands in stark contrast to, an early scene in *Gone with the Wind*, where Ellen O'Hara demands that Gerald fire Jonas Wilkerson, the overseer, for impregnating the "poor white" Emmie Slattery out of wedlock. Unlike Stephen, Gerald immediately obeys his wife's order to punish the sexual transgression. Mitchell makes clear in this and other scenes that Ellen is the true head of household, just as Scarlett rules Tara after Ellen's death.[26]

As tempting as it may have been to subvert Mitchell's matriarchy by reconstituting masculine domestic authority, it is impossible for Yerby to wholly identify with a white plantation lord. Yerby's desire for uncompromised masculinity springs in part from his experience of racial oppression at the hands of white men. Unlike Yerby's protest stories, there are no angry and openly rebellious black men in *Foxes* (a narrative replete with violent and rebellious white male characters). Despite Yerby's willingness to accommodate his audience's racist anxieties, however, Yerby clearly resents this literary stricture. In *Foxes*, the resentment that Yerby voiced directly in his early protest fiction becomes muted and displaced; it surfaces throughout the text in varied and seemingly contradictory ways. Because the rebellious black male is suppressed, he becomes an absent presence in *Foxes*.

The traces of Yerby's censored anger are most clearly evident in the threat of slave insurrection that appears throughout the text. Many white characters in *Foxes* openly express their fear of slave insurrection, a fear in keeping with the novel's historical setting. In addition to the minor slave revolts that occurred with some regularity in all slaveholding territory, Toussaint L'Ouverture, followed by Jean-Jacques Dessalines, led a revolution in Haiti (1791–1803) that terrified slaveholders throughout the Western Hemisphere, and especially those in the Louisiana Territory. More than ten thousand whites, slaves, and free people of color from Saint Domingue fled to New Orleans, prompting action in local government against what one civic official described as "the evils to be apprehended from the improper introduction of slaves and other people of Color from the Islands." They feared that "a Spirit of Revolt and Mutyny has crept in amongst Them" and that they could foment a large-scale insurrection in America as well.[27]

Yerby highlights this aspect of his historical background repeatedly, introducing the subject a mere ten pages into the narrative. Shortly after Stephen hitches a ride on a boat transporting pigs to New Orleans, the captain points out an oak where the first of twenty-three blacks was hanged for insurrection. The captain recalls, "They tried to mutiny, the murderin' black devils." Yerby refers to this particular insurrection several more times in the narrative, as the rebellion's leader is the grandfather of the central black character, Little Inch, who appears later.[28] The threat of mutiny comes up again at a slave auction where the auctioneer has trouble selling a group of slaves from Saint Domingue. One buyer in the crowd explains the hesitation by stating, "They've seen other Nigras kill white men and maybe they've kilt some theyself" (79). A Creole friend of Stephen expresses the fear explicitly: "Have you ever thought, Stephen, how readily the same thing could happen here? We're outnumbered by our blacks almost as much as they were. A few fire brands, eloquent of tongue, a few bold blacks, and the whole mass of African brutes could sweep over us like a tide" (62). Stephen's response is telling: "From all I've heard," he says, "your Caribbean black is a different breed of dog from ours. They are very cold and long of head, capable of thought. I've even heard them called intelligent. What American black can entertain a thought for half an hour without falling asleep?"

The invidious distinction that Yerby draws between the "bold," "intelligent," and rebellious "Caribbean black" and the lazy, contented "American black" appears several times in the text. At another point, Stephen makes a similar comment on the superior intelligence and courage of Caribbean blacks: "We did not make the same error as the French did in Haiti and Saint Domingue of attempting to enslave those intelligent ones. We chose our Negroes more wisely" (337). It would seem that Yerby is being ironic here, but he reproduces the same anti-African (North) American sentiment in an interview. When speaking of the slave trade, Yerby makes the fairly oversimplified claim that African slaves from warlike tribes (e.g., the Dahomey and Ashanti) successfully rebelled against their masters (Yerby offers L'Ouverture, Jean Jacques Dessalines, and Henri Christophe, as well as the Ashanti in Brazil as proof of his thesis); those Africans from tribes that were "accustomed" to slavery in Africa easily adjusted to slavery in the New World. He asserts that these more docile tribes ended up in America and thus contributed to the success of slavery here. Black Americans are descendants of slaves, he suggests; black South Americans, as in the following example, are descendants of warriors: "The difference between [Africans in] North America and South America is that in North America they had slaves and in South America they had men.... How long could the Civil War have gone on if our ancestors had done what they damn well ought to have done [i.e., rise up when the Confederate soldiers went away to war].... To be a fifth column behind the Confederate forces should have been absolutely irresistible. They didn't need weapons; all they needed was a torch" (227).[29] Yerby's assertion of the difference between "slaves" and "men" illustrates his tendency to criticize black *men* in particular when discussing American slavery. This contempt for the cowardice of American black men manifests in *Foxes* as well. In keeping with the restrictions of his genre, Yerby includes very few explicit critiques of slavery in the narrative; the few places where he does openly criticize slavery, however, he invokes the same "slave" versus "man" dichotomy that he used in the foregoing interview.

It is telling and, at first glance, surprising that the characters who draw the slave/man contrast are black women. Yerby feels able to grant his black female characters a greater range of expression, though their observations about the difference between slaves and men becomes rather problematic in light of Yerby's feelings about strong women. The most openly rebellious black character in the text is La Belle Sauvage, a "wild" female slave "straight out of Africa" (138). Stephen purchases her as a wife for his docile and loyal field hand Achille. La Belle Sauvage rejects him and calls him a "slave Nigra": "You no man ... my tribe man no make slave. Warrior him die, but him no make slave. Even woman no make slave—die first, killee self first" (167). She does eventually kill herself, after she is thwarted in her effort to kill her newborn to prevent him from living as a slave.

The child is given to his grandmother, Caleen, who is also a rebellious character (she is a *mamaloi*—a voodoo priestess—Yerby's revision of Mitchell's ever-faithful Mammy). When Caleen is first given the child, she says to herself, with "veiled and crafty" eyes, that he will take after his grandfather who was hanged for leading an insurrection, rather than his docile father: "Never such a one will he be like Achille, but a man, him. His body will they enslave, yes, but never his mind and his heart. . . . *A man, him*. A warrior, yes!" (206; emphasis added).

The most impassioned speech against slavery comes from Stephen's octoroon mistress, Desiree. When Stephen asks her why she chose to be the mistress of a white man instead of marrying a black man, she says: "They are not men. You do not permit them to be. When they rise up and attempt manhood, you shoot them down like dogs and exhibit their bodies in Jackson Square—like Bras Coupe, remember. To live at all they have to fawn and bow, and permit you the liberty of their homes and the favors of their daughters. I am a woman, monsieur; I can only love a man—not a thing!" (273). For Desiree, slavery and racism strip black men of their essential humanity—make them "dogs" and "things"—and render them unlovable. Desiree embodies Yerby's desire (the desire for unqualified manhood), and like Desiree, Yerby "can only love a man—not a thing!" In *Foxes*, Yerby's only explicit indictment of slavery is that it emasculates black men. Of all the atrocities committed in slavery, (including the destruction of families, torture, rape, and murder), this is the one to which Yerby repeatedly returns.

On the one hand, Yerby's capacity to voice his "protest" more freely through his female characters than his male characters speaks to the aforementioned prescriptions against representing black masculinity. On the other hand, in light of Yerby's anxiety about "castrating women," it seems that Yerby is projecting his own doubts about black male potency onto black women. The alleged failure of manhood in black men articulated by these women conveys a masked aggression against black men that consistently reflects the feelings Yerby himself expressed on this subject; black men, especially Americans, were too weak to resist enslavement, and thus partly to blame for their condition.[30]

Not surprisingly, the black male characters in *Foxes* all bear the stamp of Yerby's ambivalence. One character is Aupre, the brother of Stephen's mistress, Desiree. He is light-skinned enough to pass and lives as a successful playwright in France. An overrefined, at times even effete, intellectual, he suffers a vicious beating at the hands of Etienne's slaves (Aupre bested Etienne in a duel while they were in France, and Etienne exacts retribution after discovering that Aupre is an octoroon).[31] Another black male character is Achille, the father of Little Inch, and the son of Caleen and "Big Inch," the aforementioned insurrectionist. Stephen describes Achille as "a giant of a black, intelligent and capable of carrying out the most exacting task without supervision.... [T]here was no trace of rebelliousness in [him]" (143–44). Good-natured, smart, and loyal, Achille essentially has the personality of a good dog; his only act of violence is when he rapes La Belle Sauvage. Although he is descended from what Yerby considers the more warlike and rebellious Haitian Africans, it may be that Achille's docility, loyalty, and complacency about his servitude are what Yerby considers the "Achilles' heel" of black men.

Achille's son, Little Inch, is the central black male character. He is raised by his grandmother, Caleen, who teaches him not only to read, but also to "outwit his enemies as she had for so many years outwitted them. In seeming surrender, he must conquer" (213)—this last phrase could be said to express Yerby's strategic rewriting of the genre's racist investments. Yerby's treatment of Little Inch often recalls Frederick Douglass, though with some important differences. Yerby alludes to the famous scene in Douglass's 1845 *Narrative* when Hugh Auld forbids Douglass to read by saying: "It would forever unfit him to be a slave.... As to himself, it could do him no good, but a great deal of harm. It would make him discontented and unhappy" (49). When Stephen catches Little Inch teaching himself to read, Stephen says that he may continue, but only with books Stephen selects: "There are many things which are no good for ye to read—'twill cause only trouble and confusion in your mind" (243). Inch learns to write well, and, like Douglass, when he escapes he writes his own pass and flees by water. When in the North, Little Inch is taken in by abolitionists who say they want to use him on the abolitionist circuit as another Douglass. Yerby seals the comparison by arranging for Inch to actually meet Frederick Douglass, who befriends the fugitive Inch briefly until he is recaptured.[32]

There is one crucial difference in their lives, however. Inch never experiences Douglass's self-transformation from "slave to man" by thrashing a white man. Unlike Douglass, Inch never emancipates himself "in spirit" through defeating his own Covey. Inch commits only one act of violence, and it is *against a black man*. During his escape, Inch steals clothes from a slave on another plantation; before knocking him unconscious, Inch thinks to himself that it is men like him—ones who are, in Inch's estimation, "serene with contentment" (415)—that cause insurrections to fail. Outside of this brief episode, Inch is strictly an intellectual who fights for his freedom through flight.

Yerby does give Inch a suggestive symbolic victory after the end of the Civil War. At the novel's end, Etienne retrieves Stephen from a prisoner-of-war camp, and it is Inch, now commissioner of police in New Orleans, who *frees* Stephen. Inch asks Etienne and Stephen to stay for dinner before leaving the camp, and then serves the meal using china from Harrow; this "redistribution of wealth" undercuts the Lost Cause cliché, perpetuated by Mitchell and others, where loyal slaves protect the "family" wealth by hiding the silver from the Yankees.[33] The climax of this scene occurs, however, when Inch introduces his new wife and stepson—Desiree, Stephen's former mistress, and the son Stephen fathered. Desiree has had sex with all three men present. She clearly represents an overinvested link in the struggle for power between these men. Inch's reclamation of the black woman and the black son from his former white masters is inextricably linked to his new *public* authority—now that he is a citizen and, in that fleeting Reconstruction moment, is imbued with the power of the state, he also can lay claim to a *private* life, one in which he is a traditional patriarch with access to domestic and erotic privilege. Desiree loves Inch, presumably, because he is a man, and no longer a slave, or what she earlier called a "thing." The reader is left to speculate on her reasoning, however, because she says nothing in the scene beyond politely greeting Stephen and Etienne, and she does not appear again in the narrative. Desiree's function at this moment is wholly symbolic, as the sexual foundation of masculine authority. Her status as a sexual cipher is highlighted when Inch's eyes come to rest "blankly on Desiree as though she were not there."

Paradoxically, this scene highlights the fact that the southern historical romance's attention to the causes, meanings, and effects of the Civil War actually allows Yerby a space to represent black men momentarily empowered—unlike his protest stories. In Yerby's rendition, the reader sees the profound structural transformation necessary for black manhood and democratic equality. It allows him to affirm the nation's democratic values and to represent the nation mobilized in the name of racial justice. The import of this dramatic reversal of fortunes is quickly qualified, though, as Inch admits that "This [empowerment of blacks during Reconstruction] came too soon. We weren't ready. White men will rule the South again . . . perhaps for always." Once again, Yerby defuses moments of black male protest and rebellion into either veiled resentment or placid resignation.

Yerby's attitude toward black men in *Foxes*, which oscillates between loathing and restrained sympathy, permeates the work generally. One scene more than any other expresses the depths of Yerby's ambivalence. As Etienne returns from the war, he suddenly remembers his participation in the infamous battle and massacre at Fort Pillow, which took place near Memphis on April 12, 1864. Although the details of the event are disputed, Etienne's memories adhere fairly closely to most historical accounts. Brigadier General Nathan Bedford Forrest (who would later go on to found the KKK) demanded that the Union soldiers unconditionally surrender, and, when they refused, he launched an assault that quickly routed the troops. Most accounts agree that upon discovering that two hundred of the six hundred Union soldiers were black, the Confederates set about slaughtering the soldiers, targeting the black ones, even after they had surrendered.[34] This passage stands out in the novel for many reasons: not only is it the most violent in the text, it is also the only moment when Yerby represents overt violence against black men. The absence of violence against black men in *Foxes* is another of Yerby's fundamental departures from the southern historical romance's racial structure; Dixon, Page, and Mitchell all use lynchings as a means of restoring social order. Scenes of lynching were also a staple of racial protest fiction, a classification that Yerby was studiously avoiding. However, the brutal suppression of African American men returns with a vengeance in this brief scene.

One Confederate soldier bashes a black soldier's head into a pulp with his gun, while another Confederate bayonets a black soldier, "the gutspike going in just above the navel ripping sidewise, so that the Negro's guts tumbled out in pinkgray sausage rolls" (521). Narrated as a reverie, the scene has a grotesque, dreamlike quality that Yerby intensifies by feminizing the most violent Confederate: "There was another boy, with the face of a girl and long lashes that swept his cheeks when his lids drooped," with footwork "like a ballet dancer." This "girlish youth," who was "almost dainty," impales one African American through his back as he attempts to run away. The bayonet pins the black soldier to the ground, and when he tries to rise he enacts a "macabre sort of calisthenics . . . slid[ing] his body up and down the blade."

Throughout the scene, Yerby repeatedly draws the reader's attention to images of violent penetration. The last penetration—the fleeing soldier who is impaled from behind and then moves "up and down" the blade—evokes sexual violation, especially sodomy. This "shameful," radically uncavalier valence gestures toward what is closer to the surface: the grossly unheroic—and hence unmanly—nature of the massacre. Yerby's attention to the soldier's girlishness further emphasizes the unmanliness of the Confederates. Yerby strips away the usual consolidating, self-affirming, masculinized glory of battle. In this scene, the murder of black men explicitly symbolizes the weakness, both physical and moral, of white supremacists; Etienne, who participates in the killing, vomits at the horror of the scene. The reader can derive no purging satisfaction from this scene, no false security that killing black men restores order. Here white-supremacist violence is feminized, cowardly, and dishonorable.

But if the white men are disgraced in this scene, so are the black men. Etienne's memory begins after his men have routed the black troops: "It had been very easy—that fight. There were only six hundred men in the outworks and old Nat had driven them back into the fort within an hour" (520). After pointing out how poorly these black men performed in battle, Yerby shows them getting penetrated, symbolically "fucked" by the Confederates—passive and feminized by association. Yerby shows no black soldier fighting, only a "little, emaciated, yellowish Negro" running away. When seen in light of the earlier attacks on black manhood, this scene embodies the most intense expression of Yerby's veiled aggression and contempt for the weakness of black men; the graphic detail of the slaughter suggests the depth of his shame at their—or rather, his—impotence. But it also suggests, obliquely, an additional point of identification with the white slaveholders who are attacking the black men.

At every turn, *The Foxes of Harrow* is an intensely ambivalent text. It expresses both a muted resentment of slavery and a muted admiration and longing for the power of the white men who rule. It voices respect, *sotto voce*, for those black men who rose in insurrection—men who never actually appear in the text, but hover at its margins as anxiety-producing memories—and shame that black men were unable to overthrow their oppressors. Though masked and in certain respects transposed, *Foxes* nevertheless conveys the very same structures of affect, especially regarding black men, that we encounter in his protest stories.

* * *

By the time Yerby published *Foxes* in 1946, *Gone with the Wind*, both novel and film, had long transcended its status as a regional narrative and had become wholly absorbed into the mainstream American imagination. Linda Williams rightly argues that *Gone with the Wind* "universalized for all white Americans the romance of Southern history as the American story of nation-making at the same time that it constructed an entirely new kind of American hero in the selfish-headstrong-greedy Scarlett" (194). Mitchell's narrative was quickly woven into the fabric of American identity, despite the fact that her work, unlike Yerby's, never expresses any love for or loyalty to America itself. Quite the opposite. *Gone with the Wind* is replete with scenes of federal troops committing depredations and with indignant cries against the "unjust" implementation of federal laws; Scarlett's famous rallying cry, "I'll never be hungry again," is preceded by a previous declaration that she repeats throughout the work, "as God is my witness, the Yankees aren't going to lick me" (357). Moreover, although Scarlett's gender-bending displays of "gumption" contribute to the sense that she is a *"new* kind of American hero," her identity is nevertheless based in no small part on perpetuating the Old South's white-supremacist social structure. Mitchell encapsulates the entire novel's racist ethos when she writes of Scarlett that "all her nerves hummed with hate" (447). *Gone with the Wind* is anti-Union and antiblack from beginning to end, and thus, according to Yerby's narrative, deeply anti-American. Yerby wanted to tell a story of the Old South that was less racially coercive and more sympathetic—one that reminded his readers that the region held the seeds of democratic promise, of hope for "the people." However, as we have seen, Yerby's harnessing of the national imaginary in order to reframe and reroute the racist and regionalist investments of southern historical romance is also driven by a contemporary masculinist project, in which his sympathy for the plantation lord is in the service of restoring a thoroughly patriarchal notion of privacy. Yerby's longing for this privileged access to privacy says as much about his unresolved feelings about race as it does about gender. Contrary to Blyden Jackson's belief that Yerby's representation of the Old South suggests that "what happened ... is no longer a life-and-death issue to the Negro," *Foxes* makes clear that, at least for Yerby, what Jackson calls "the great passion" was far from being "spent." As I have tried to show, Yerby's sympathetic portrait of Stephen Fox cannot be separated from the pain that Yerby felt about black male emasculation. And even though *Foxes* is not a "protest" novel, it is still fundamentally structured by "the Negro problem," underscoring how far Yerby was from being liberated from the "shackles of race." In *Foxes*, sympathy is no less symptom than solution.

5 / Talk about the South: Unspeakable Things Unspoken in Zora Neale Hurston's *Seraph on the Suwanee*

In 1975, Alice Walker launched one of the greatest revivals in modern American literary history with her *Ms.* magazine essay "In Search of Zora Neale Hurston." The extraordinary range of Hurston's achievements, which include groundbreaking novels, autobiography, short fiction, drama, political and cultural essays, reportage, folklore, and ethnography, has garnered her an audience, both critical and popular, that continues to grow unabated. Hurston's status as the great literary foremother of contemporary African American women writers stems principally from her work in the 1920s and 1930s, and especially her masterpiece, *Their Eyes Were Watching God* (1937). *Their Eyes*' protofeminist sensibility, its sensitive exploration of the intricacies of working-class, southern black community, and its brilliant demonstration of the expressive potential of black vernacular speech in novelistic discourse have made it a signal text in the creation of an African American literary tradition, as well as required reading in countless American studies, women's studies, and American literature courses.[1] *Seraph on the Suwanee* (1948), Hurston's fourth and last published novel, has received a far chillier response, and was until recently often condemned or dismissed out of hand. Although it initially garnered favorable reviews, particularly from the white press, *Seraph* has tended to baffle and disturb even Hurston's most devoted readers. The critic Mary Helen Washington, for example, dismisses *Seraph* as "an awkward and contrived novel, as vacuous as a soap opera" (*Invented Lives* 21), and Bernard Bell expels it from his influential study on the African American novel because "[it] is neither comic, nor folkloristic, nor about blacks" (128). *Seraph*'s most damning critique, however, comes from Hurston's first great champion, Alice Walker. She describes Hurston's later work as "reactionary, static, shockingly misguided and timid" and adds that this is "especially true of *Seraph on the Suwanee*, which is not even about black people, which is no crime, but *is* about white people for whom it is impossible to care, which is" (xvi).

The critic Carla Kaplan admits that "it is hard to understand *why* Hurston would have written it":

> Why, for example, would she go from depicting the black community she knew so well, portrayed so lovingly, and criticized so handily to a story about Southern crackers and their difficult rise to financial success? Why would she go from using rape as a central metaphor for exploitation in *Their Eyes* to a story in which rape is merely misunderstanding: a "pain remorseless sweet" and a "memory inexpressibly sweet"? Why does she paint a positive and comic image of the very "pet negro system"—"every Southern white man has his pet Negro"—which she decried elsewhere as a "residue of feudalism"? (443)

These difficult questions deserve our attention, I believe, because they speak to issues that were very much on Hurston's mind late in her career, and, more importantly, their answers yield valuable insights on her notoriously complex attitudes toward such issues as southern race relations, gender, and literary protest. In recent years, several scholars have taken up this enigmatic work, and the emerging consensus is that Hurston is enacting an elaborate joke on the text's literary subjects—poor white southerners—and on her readers, especially around issues of race and gender.[2] After all, the final revelation of the protagonist, Arvay Henson, is that "her job was mothering. What more could any woman want and need?" (*Seraph* 351). Given Hurston's lifetime of stalwart independence, how could she *not* be joking? But this critical focus on the joke as a narrative theme and rhetorical strategy tends to produce what I term a hermeneutics of disavowal—a mode of inquiry that downplays the frequently disturbing manifest content of *Seraph* as a purely ironic and subversive performance or "mask" that is then separated from the "true" meaning and investments of the text, which presumably are to be found somewhere sub rosa. Attention to masking, rhetorical indirection, and what Henry Louis Gates refers to as "double-voiced discourse"[3] are of course central to understanding Hurston's work, but this approach can also have the unfortunate effect of implying that Hurston's appropriation of whiteness in *Seraph* is wholly parodic and therefore bears little relation to her personal and political beliefs. Close attention to the way race operates in the novel's affective economy belies the tidiness of this division between public performance and private belief.

I contend that, as much as we might prefer otherwise, Hurston was in many respects very much in earnest when she wrote *Seraph*. The novel was to be, in her own words, a "true picture of the South" (Carla Kaplan 561), one aimed at a popular audience, and especially designed to rebut what she considered distorted images of the region offered by southern conservatives and northern liberals.[4] Hurston's attempt to render a light, comedic, and romantic "song of the South" ultimately fails, however, for precisely the reason given by Alice Walker—the narrative is populated by highly unsympathetic white characters, ones about whom it is "impossible" to care. And this includes the protagonist, Arvay Henson, despite her redemption at the novel's ending. *Seraph* is populated by "crackers," Hurston's term, whom she represents with an unsettling contempt. I argue that Hurston's attempt to produce an *affirmative* narrative of the New South is unintentionally thwarted by her brutal treatment of the crackers, as they obliquely give expression to a powerful though heretofore unrecognized rage that pulses through the novel. The novel "fails" (in its efforts to be quaint, charming, and romantic) because it is unable to mediate between two competing forms of affect—the first conveying a deep-seated longing for interracial harmony and progress in the South, and the other revealing an unacknowledged undercurrent of fury at the dim possibility of this vision ever being materialized. The incommensurability of these forms of affect is precisely what makes *Seraph* such a fascinating novel, one worthy of our attention not only because it has much to teach us about the late phase of Hurston's career, but also because of what it reveals about her long-standing hostility to racial protest, and more generally the ways in which race, region, class, gender, and genre determine the form and effects of sympathy.

I frame my inquiry into Hurston's text and its negotiation of the post–World War II color line with a set of questions posed by Toni Morrison. In 1989, Morrison urged students of American literature to reexamine "the American canon . . . for the 'unspeakable things unspoken'; for the ways in which the presence of Afro-Americans has shaped the choices, the language, the structure—the meaning of so much American literature" ("Unspeakable Things" 23). For Morrison, the "spectacularly interesting question is, 'What intellectual feats had to be performed by the author or his critic to erase me from a society seething with my presence, and what effect has that performance had on the work?'" In this and her 1992 follow-up collection of essays, *Playing in the Dark*, Morrison rereads white-authored canonical American texts with an eye toward the myriad ways in which the authors fundamentally rely on an "Africanist" presence, however muted and repressed, as a ground of otherness that *produces* a putatively coherent, though ultimately anxious, sense of whiteness. Morrison's primary concern in these essays is not with black-authored texts, yet in an aside she poses a question that is particularly germane for a reconsideration of *Seraph*: "[W]hat happens to the writerly imagination of a black author who is at some level *always* conscious of representing one's own race to, or in spite of, a race of readers that understands itself to be 'universal' or race-free?" (xii; emphasis in original). Given *Seraph*'s focus on white characters, we can take Morrison's query one step further and ask, What happens to the writerly imagination of a black author when she represents *whiteness* to a white reading audience that understands itself to be "universal" or race-free? What does whiteness open up discursively in this work, and what does it foreclose? How does the text's Africanist presence, both the seen and the unseen, inform, stabilize, and disrupt Hurston's treatment of whiteness? What are the unspeakable things unspoken?

To account fully for Hurston's treatment of race (and identity more generally) in this work, we must first locate the text within its specific social and historical context. Despite the axiomatic quality of this approach to reading the function of identity within a literary text, no critics of *Seraph* have properly situated the work and its treatment of identity within the moment of its production. This dehistoricization has contributed to the work's tendency to baffle its modern readers. The critical emphasis on Hurston's deployments of subtle masks and jokes has also obscured the degree to which the text is in many respects actively engaged in national debates raging around the South immediately following the Second World War.[5] The South was undergoing convulsive changes after the war as the rapid growth of agribusiness, industrialism, consumerism, and urbanization transformed every level of southern society. Easily the most threatening change, however, was the birth of the civil rights movement, which was set in motion by wartime political gains. Galvanized by a series of legislative victories, such as the defeat of the all-white primary and the poll tax, by increasing political organization and activism, and by the liberating experience of overseas military service, African Americans in the North and South intensified their struggle for freedom. Racist whites responded to these signs of black political insurgency with the greatest outburst of mob violence and lynchings since the end of World War I.[6] These conflicts received both national and international coverage, and thus became an increasing source of embarrassment and concern to the United States as it vied for allies during the early years of the Cold War. The South, once again, became the nation's great "problem" to be solved.[7] Thus, we may need to tweak Morrison's query one last time and ask, What happens to the writerly imagination of a southern black author when she is representing the South to a nation in certain respects quite literally at war with itself over the status of the "Africanist" presence in the American body politic?

It is against this backdrop of racial violence and intense public scrutiny that Hurston dedicated herself to rendering her "true picture of the South" (Carla Kaplan 561). She rightly recognized that the United States, and especially the North, often unfairly and inaccurately laid the responsibility for the "race problem" solely at the feet of the South. Accordingly, she intended *Seraph* to be a redemptive and revealing treatment of the region in all its complexity, a perspective that included white southerners like Jim Meserve, the protagonist's husband, whom Hurston described in a letter to her editor Burroughs Mitchell as "a member of that liberal class which has always existed in the South in a minority, who believed in the benefits of the Union and advancement" (561). "In truth," she continues, "the South presents a very confusing picture. Virginius Dabney and Bilbo side by side. High-mindedness and savagery side by side.... I want the book to look like the people it is written about."[8] She also insisted on representations of African Americans that did not reproduce what she considered the usual "oversimplifications": "[The Negro] is either pictured by the conservatives as happy, picking his banjo, or by the so-called liberals as low, miserable and crying. The Negro's life is neither of these. Rather, it is in-between and above and below these pictures. That is what I intend to put in my new book" (Hemenway 299).[9] It seems less than clear how far Hurston departed from the conservative stereotype of African Americans, a point I will take up in more detail below, but there are certainly no "low, miserable and crying" African Americans in *Seraph*.

Hurston's long-standing refusal to "protest" is by now quite familiar, appearing most famously in her 1928 essay "How It Feels to Be Colored Me," where she declared: "I am not tragically colored. There is no great sorrow dammed up in my soul, nor lurking behind my eyes.... I do not belong to the sobbing school of Negrohood" (827). Hurston was equally averse to leftist and liberal attacks on the South's oppressive social structure, believing that literary representations of racial oppression constituted another form of minstrelsy and were little more than thinly veiled communist propaganda.[10] In her 1938 review of Richard Wright's *Uncle Tom's Children*, generally presumed to be at least partly an act of retaliation against Wright's critical review of *Their Eyes* the year before, she wrote: "[T]he reader sees the picture of the South that the communists have been passing around of late. A dismal, hopeless section ruled by brutish hatred and nothing else. Mr. Wright's author's solution, is the solution of the PARTY—state responsibility for everything and individual responsibility for nothing, not even feeding one's self. And march!" ("Stories of Conflict" *Folklore* 913). She adds that "his stories are so grim that the Dismal Swamp of race hatred must be where they live. Not one act of understanding and sympathy comes to pass in the entire work" (912).[11]

Hurston's vision of the South in *Seraph*, in contrast, is structured around moments of interracial "understanding and sympathy." Unlike the gothic vision of southern racial terror and entrapment depicted in Wright's *Uncle Tom's Children*, and then again in *Black Boy* (1945), Hurston's narrative bears more than a passing resemblance to a plantation romance, though one updated for and set in the New South. Her unlikely appropriation of the plantation romance allows her, paradoxically, to imagine an alternative world of interracial possibility, and thereby provides a fictive reconciliation of the pervasive and intractable social conflicts of the postwar South. The text's connections to this historically racist literary tradition are not immediately apparent because of the narrative's setting in the early twentieth-century New South and its attention to the lives of poor whites. Rather, *Seraph* bears a homologous relationship to the plantation romance, wherein Arvay's husband, Jim Meserve, represents the all-powerful southern white man as head of household who protects and provides for his wife, children, and African American labor force. The extended "interracial family" (an especially potent fantasy fueled by race conflict in the New South) lives on the Meserve estate and repays the father-husband-master's protection and generosity with undying loyalty and love.

This unlikely racial pastoral speaks directly to the New South's identity crisis during a time of radical social and political change, a struggle that often crystallized in debates about the South's relationship to tradition and modernity. Hurston breaks from the tendency of white southern apologists, especially the Agrarians, to fetishize the Old South and its traditions as a site of *antimodernity*, a place of psychic refuge from the loss and alienation embodied in the onslaught of industrialization and increasing urbanization.[12] *Seraph*, on the other hand, enthusiastically praises the positive changes that Hurston sees taking place in the region, the "progress" and "development" brought on by new industry, commerce, and science. Yet her text also celebrates the South's difference from the rest of the nation in racialized terms that are readily recognizable in Old South social structure. What Hurston preserves from conservative narratives of the Old South is the fantasy of innocent black-white relations; these loving relationships are the positive source of the South's difference.

Hurston's pastoral is fraught with conflict, though. The "crackers" in the novel, represented primarily by Arvay and her family, consistently stand in the way of the New South's emergence as the Promised Land. The crackers are primitive—ignorant, bigoted, lazy, fearful of change, and occasionally savage. Thus far critics have overlooked how Hurston allegorizes her sense of the South's contemporary struggles through her representation of Jim and Arvay's relationship—"high-mindedness and savagery side by side." Jim must struggle throughout the novel to overcome Arvay's backwardness so that his family, which stands in for the region, will prosper. The poor whites function in the narrative as scapegoats for the South's ills, thereby effectively creating an avenue for Hurston to voice a critique of the region's problems without alienating her mainstream white audience and without "go[ing] to the mourners bench" (Carla Kaplan 482)—in other words, without protesting.[13] Poor whites as a subject of fiction, social commentary, and historical inquiry were in fact experiencing something of a vogue during and after the Depression; best-selling southern authors Marjorie Kinnan Rawlings (a Floridian and personal friend of Hurston), Erskine Caldwell, and the historian W. J. Cash all took on poor whites during these years.[14] These and other writers of the period frequently depicted poor whites via stereotypes usually assigned to African Americans, that is, as either quaintly innocent or savagely primitive. Hurston draws on these familiar stereotypes of the poor white as a ready means to communicate with her postwar audience in much the same way that white writers after Reconstruction had achieved a symbolic national reunion through proliferating demeaning images of African Americans.

But scapegoating crackers is a double-edged sword for Hurston, for while the poor white allows her to render a critique of southern backwardness, her strategy of representational displacement—projecting negative African American stereotypes and experiences onto poor whites—actually stages, indirectly, what she most wanted to disavow: black abjection. Hurston depicts the world of the crackers as marked by crushing poverty, ignorance, rape, lynching, and an enduring plantation social structure; she even goes so far as to draw on eugenicist ideas about inferior, animal-like, and unsocializable "kinds" of people.[15] In other words, Hurston indirectly voices what she refused to say about the oppression of African Americans, however unintentionally and, arguably, unconsciously: the crackers end up as surrogates, figures that simultaneously obscure and reveal the seething racial conflicts of the postwar South. What is completely absent from the text—overtly racialized violence, Jim Crow, sharecropping, chain gangs, the KKK—reappears in altered form and in affect, an affect that overpowers the manifest discourse of the work. Hurston's "unspeakable" rage at the condition of African Americans becomes legible in the narrative through her vicious treatment of the poor white characters. It is this suppressed rage and contemptuous rendering of the poor whites that makes these characters, in the words of Alice Walker, "impossible" to care about.[16] Hurston's plantation romance, upon closer inspection, begins to evince surprising affective affinities with Wright's gothic nightmare. Finally, it is not only racial violence that is absent from Hurston's "true picture of the South"; also missing are ambitious, educated, and accomplished African Americans—in other words, anyone remotely resembling Hurston herself. Hurston's sense that she had to erase herself from her southern pastoral constitutes the most powerful and tragic illustration of the repressed Africanist presence in *Seraph*—Zora Neale Hurston is the unspeakable thing unspoken.

* * *

Seraph on the Suwanee centers on the life of Arvay Henson, a poor, uneducated, and extremely insecure Florida "cracker". The novel begins in rural Florida just after the turn of the twentieth century, when Arvay, who has declared her intent to become a missionary, is being courted by the handsome newcomer Jim Meserve. Although Jim is poor, he is no ordinary "cracker"—he is charismatic, ambitious, and his "ancestors had held plantations upon the Alabama River before the war" (7). Their courtship is difficult, mainly because Arvay's fear of rejection leads her to repeatedly withdraw into a self-protective shell. Jim then decides to take the situation in hand by raping her and then carrying her off to the courthouse to elope. Hurston intends this "rape-seduction" scene to be comic, for when Arvay objects mildly to having been raped, Jim replies: "You sure was, and the job was done up brown. . . . Sure you was raped, and that ain't all. You're going to keep on getting raped" (57). Despite how offensive and disturbing this scenario is to contemporary readers, Hurston never leaves any doubt that Jim loves Arvay and their children; he devotes his life to caring for his family, and providing for all their needs. Even so, Arvay's insecurity persists, and after twenty years of struggle, Jim leaves out of frustration, telling her to come to him once she has made up her mind to stop "loving like a coward." Arvay decides to go back home to her "kind," but finds her family has only grown more poor and malevolent with time. Only then does she fully realize the fate from which Jim has saved her. During her efforts to win Jim back, she realizes that though Jim acts like an "overpowering general," on the inside he is just like a little baby, hungering for her "hovering." In the novel's climax, Arvay realizes that "[h]er job was mothering. What more could any woman want and need? . . . Jim was hers and it was her privilege to serve him" (351).

* * *

On one level, *Seraph* is the story of the Meserve family's ascent from poverty to prosperity. The family's progress is also mirrored in the region's transformation from a stagnated backwater to an affluent emblem of the New South. Hurston imbues Jim Meserve with the attributes essential to the New South's success. He is smart, ambitious, and interested in building the future, rather than glorifying the ideals of the past.[17] Jim declares that "[w]hile my old man was sitting around reading and taking notes trying to trace up who did what in the Civil War, and my two brothers were posing around waiting for the good old times that they had heard went on before the War to come back again, I shucked out to get in touch with the New South" (203). Hurston's quick dismissal of Jim's backward-looking family, who never appear in the text, allows her to marginalize representationally what was in fact the predominant white attitude toward southern identity and politics at this moment.

The year of *Seraph*'s publication, 1948, was also the year when the belligerently segregationist "Dixiecrat" Party emerged (with the late Strom Thurmond as its presidential candidate) to protest the national Democratic Party's consideration of a civil rights plank in the party platform for the upcoming elections. All but the most liberal southerners of this moment were, like Jim's father and brothers, looking to the past for their models of race and class politics. Despite benefiting from forward-looking New Deal policies and prolabor, pro-union activism from such organization as the CIO, most southern whites distrusted these organizations, believing that they represented communist influence and portended additional northern and federal domination (Daniel 13). If inclusive labor activism cultivated suspicion and resentment among most whites, civil rights activism incited murderous rage. White southerners could not ignore the sporadic yet undeniable signs that the days of "separate but equal" were coming to an end. World War II precipitated a wide range of dramatic social, economic, political, and technological changes. In addition to the mechanization of agriculture and the massive out-migration of black and white populations in search of better employment (as well as increased social opportunity for the black population), the war also increased black self-assertion and violent white reaction. In the South alone, the war years witnessed "six civilian riots, more than twenty military riots and mutinies, and between forty and seventy-five lynchings" (Daniel 11). If white supremacists tended to "win" these battles, they were losing ground, albeit unevenly, on numerous other key fronts. In the 1944 case of *Smith v. Allwright*, the Supreme Court struck down the all-white primary, while the NAACP set about expanding its southern membership rolls, branches, and African American voter registration, which went from 200,000 registered black voters in 1940 to 600,000 in 1946, a 200 percent increase in just six years (Sullivan 141).[18] Though what has come to be known as the civil rights era would not fully emerge for several more years, black and white southerners alike sensed that a new day in race relations had arrived.

Of course, *Seraph* is set in the first three decades of the century, not the years following World War II. Nevertheless, the particular historical pressures of the postwar moment are everywhere evident in the text. Hurston engages contemporary struggles around the changing status of the color line most pointedly through her treatment of Jim and Arvay's relationship to the black community. As other critics have noted, when Jim Meserve sets out to get in touch with the New South, he ultimately succeeds by getting in touch with the knowledge, goodwill, and hard labor of African Americans. After Jim and Arvay marry, they move to Citrabelle, an agricultural area dominated by citrus farming. Jim, who knows nothing about this trade, decides to go to "the jooks and gathering places in Colored Town" for information—"since they were the ones who did all the manual work, they were the ones who actually knew how things were done" (74). Jim establishes himself, and quickly repays his black laborers by making them "the highest paid men in that part of the state" (75). After Jim buys a piece of property from a "Cracker ... [who] was too damned lazy and trifling" (78) to take care of it himself, Jim uses his connections to "the underground system in Colored Town that the Whites did not know about" (82) to get his house built quickly and cheaply. Jim's crew felt that he was "a perfect gentleman, and they were only too glad to oblige him" (82). The narrator tells us that Arvay "had no understanding to what extent *she* was benefiting from the good will that Jim had been building up ever since he had come to town.... Jim was getting the benefit of every doubt [from local blacks], and the doubts were numerous" (83; emphasis added). Here and elsewhere in the text Hurston makes a point of describing the interracial local economy's harmonious system of exchange, even as she chooses to ignore the fact that based on knowledge, experience, and ability, Jim should be working for a black foreman, rather than stepping right into the role of "boss man." Gone are any traces of labor conflict in the narrative, much less any references to the commonplace but less idyllic labor practices of sharecropping, tenant farming, and peonage, as well as the widespread vagrancy laws that often forced blacks into chain-gang labor.[19]

Even Hurston's worker's paradise has its limits, however. Though Jim may be generous toward his black workers, there is never any question that he and his labor force are social equals. Jim's relationship to his workers is explicitly paternal, and Hurston drives this point home when she describes Joe Kelsey, Jim's favorite black employee, as his "Pet Negro." Hurston explains that "[e]very Southern white man has his pet Negro. His Negro is always fine, honest, faithful to him unto death, and most remarkable. He never lies, and in fact can do no wrong. [Even if the pet commits a crime,] [i]f the white patron has his way, the pet will never serve a day in jail for it. The utmost of his influence will be invoked to balk the law. Turn go *his* Negro from that jail!" (61). Although this passage seems clearly intended to amuse, Hurston's language, nevertheless, clearly evokes a white man's "ownership" of a black man.

This evocation of the "peculiar institution" is reinforced when Joe Kelsey and his family move into a home that Jim builds on his estate. Joe's children work the groves, while Joe runs Jim's whiskey still, one of his many acts of loyalty: "Joe had been careful to protect Jim [from the law], capable, and ever so honest and faithful. Joe had run the risk of the chain-gang being faithful to him" (117). As discussed in the previous chapter, the historian Grace Hale has argued that this ideal of racial harmony and mutual dependence, a staple of the many forms of plantation pastorals produced in the decades following Reconstruction, was an essential characteristic of the plantation romance. With the rise of the New South, many southern authors (Thomas Dixon, Thomas Nelson Page, and Margaret Mitchell, to name only a few of the best-known novelists) justified the need for segregation in the present by describing a prelapsarian social order that existed "before the war." Plantation life was imagined in terms of an idealized "interracial family"; this allegedly harmonious and "racially innocent" world was destroyed forever by the Yankees and later by the "New Negroes," with their political, social, and economic aspirations.[20] Hurston conjures the lost interracial family again, however, in her New South idyll. When Arvay's son Kenny moves to New York to pursue a career as a musician, Joe is sent up to look after him. Hurston tells us that "Arvay was comforted to think that 'Uncle Joe' would be there with Kenny" because Joe is "one in the family." Joe assures Arvay that "it'll be just like you was there. . . . We Meserves'll look after one another" (252). Joe's son Jeff reiterates this familial sentiment later, when he comments, "us Meserves don't mistrust one another" (313).

Jim cares for and relies on "his" pet Negroes, and they in turn devote their lives to "doing" for him, his family, and his property. There are no uppity New Negroes or angry "Bad Niggers" to be vilified in favor of the faithful "old darky."[21] Hurston's romance suggests that we need not look to "those old plantation days" for "racial innocence"; rather, the past lives on in the present, which has been improved by the New South's "progress." Relatedly, because of the "freedom" on the Meserve "plantation," Hurston can easily avoid addressing such topics as the brutal enforcement of segregation and Klan terror.

One way to understand Hurston's fantastically positive vision of the South is to see it as a kind of utopian aspiration. As Richard Dyer has argued in reference to the utopian impulse of the musical, certain forms of entertainment offer "the image of "something better" to escape into, or something we want deeply that our day-to-day lives don't provide. Alternatives, hopes, wishes—these are the stuff of utopia, the sense that things could be better, that something other than what is can be imagined and maybe realized" (222). Dyer explains that the utopianism of popular forms of entertainment should be understood in terms of *sensibility* rather than in terms of social structure, where a wish-fulfilling narrative offers ephemeral, imaginative solutions to very real lacks and needs. Hurston, similarly, preferred to dwell on and accentuate the South's possibilities—especially as evinced in individual, interpersonal moments of sympathy—rather than what was true more generally, particularly in terms of race relations.

Thus far I have argued that Hurston's New South racial pastoral reproduces many elements of white southern segregationist ideology, but it also has an illuminating antecedent in a black segregationist. Booker T.

Washington expressed his vision of the New South most memorably in his (in)famous Atlanta Exposition Address, where he implores white southerners to "Cast down your bucket where you are":

> Cast it down among the eight millions of Negroes whose habits you know, whose fidelity and love you have tested in days when to have proved treacherous meant the ruin of your firesides. Cast down your bucket among these people who have, without strikes and labour wars, tilled your fields, cleared your forests, built your railroads and cities, and brought forth treasures from the bowels of the earth, and helped make possible this magnificent representation of the progress of the South.... While doing this, you can be sure *in the future, as in the past*, that you and your families will be surrounded by the *most patient, faithful, law-abiding, and unresentful people* that the world has seen. As we have *proved our loyalty to you in the past*, in nursing your children, watching by the sickbed of your mothers and fathers, and often following them with tear-dimmed eyes to their graves, *so in the future, in our humble way*, we shall stand by you with a devotion that no foreigner can approach, ready to lay down our lives, if need be, in defence of yours, interlacing our industrial, commercial, civil, and religious life with yours in a way that shall make the interests of both races one. (147–48; emphasis added)

Indeed, as we have just seen, when Jim was struggling to establish himself in Citrabelle, he "cast down his bucket" among African Americans, and prospers enormously. Both Washington and Hurston promise a white audience symbolic continuity with an earlier racial order by invoking "the *same* Negroes who have proved [their] loyalty to you in the past" as key to the prosperity of the New South. Hurston's "old" Negroes are the same "patient, faithful, law-abiding, and unresentful people" who populate Washington's narrative of racial harmony and reconciliation.[22]

Houston Baker argues that Washington ascended to his status as "Master of Tuskegee Plantation" by working "within the framing mind of the South to produce not a utopia of black modernism at Tuskegee, but a retrograde and imperialist plantation. This plantation was brokerage ground for Booker T.'s own personal power, wealth, and influence over national 'Negro affairs'" (*Turning South Again* 64). Washington claimed a "mission from God" to discipline (and, consequently, to immobilize) the "black-South body" (97). In *Up from Slavery*—written, ostensibly, to raise money for the Tuskegee Institute—Washington describes the "black country districts" he intends to uplift and civilize with his vocational education. According to Baker, *Up from Slavery* "articulates a picture of abjection, misdirection, hygienic incompetence, corrosive diet, spendthrift ignorance, sexual explicitness, inept manners, abhorrent one-room shanties" (78). The purpose of this damning representation of the black masses is to displace Washington's own "lack" as a figure of authority: "Washington scapegoats and imperializes the black masses in order to wear the master's weeds"—that is, Washington symbolically incarcerates the black masses on a "modern" New South plantation as a way to achieve a modicum of his own "black public-sphere mobility" (66).

Washington's rhetorical strategies in addressing a conservative white audience shed light on the peculiar racial and class inflections of value in Hurston's own project. *Seraph* begins just after the turn of the century, when the vast majority of blacks were still living in the South, and doing the most degrading work for the lowest pay.[23] Many African Americans were—as sharecroppers, day laborers, convict laborers—still in slavery-like conditions, still effectively working as field hands on plantations. As I will demonstrate, Hurston displaces the "lack" that she sees among African Americans in the Deep South by displacing the ignorance and abjection that Washington locates in the black masses onto the poor whites; African Americans in Hurston's tale are the gainfully employed, contented, and invaluable labor force of the Meserve plantation (though they remain static and immobilized—socially, politically, economically).[24] Jim succeeds not only by depending on happy and loyal African Americans, but also by transcending the fear and ignorance of the poor whites (represented primarily by Arvay and her family); Arvay and her "kind"—a term that Hurston employs repeatedly—embody the "backwardness" that ostensibly prevents the South from entering modernity. In other words, Hurston scapegoats the "crackers" as the cause of the South's intractable social ills, a move that allows her to address social problems in the South without overt recourse to the oppression of African Americans, what she would consider "self-pity." Instead of the black masses, it is the poor whites that need to be educated, uplifted, purified, civilized, and incorporated into the discourses of middle-class American modernity.

* * *

Whereas Jim represents Hurston's New South ideal—he is irreverent, strong, ambitious, smart, generous, and fearless—Arvay and her "kind" represent his antithesis: they are fearful, racist, selfish, treacherous, cruel, and, above all, ignorant. In the opening pages, we learn that in addition to the "primitive forests" and the beautiful Suwanee, "there was ignorance and poverty, and the ever-present hook worm.... Few were concerned with the past.... Few knew and nobody cared that the Hidalgos under De Sota had moved westward along this very route" (2). It is important to note that Hurston was far from alone in her condescending and frequently contemptuous presentation of poor whites as the "dead weight" of the South. The New South narratives by the historians W. J. Cash and C. Vann Woodward essentially figured poor whites in the same terms, while the authors Erskine Caldwell and William Faulkner, to take only two of the best-known examples, produced ultimately cruel and mocking portraits of Depression-era poor whites, in which they represented not only the most degraded and depraved of the South's social classes, but in those rare instances when they reached the middle class, as do certain branches of Faulkner's Snopes clan, they end up exhibiting the North's worst excesses of philistinism and avarice. We can account for the increased presence of poor whites in historical and literary discourse during the middle decades of the century by considering that thousands, eventually millions, of erstwhile farmers flooded southern cities and towns in search of work after being displaced by technological and scientific advances in agriculture. Pete Daniel points out that by World War II, local newspapers and commentators observed with distaste, condescension, and even horror the habits of the migrant workers who now began to jostle the middle class on the streets and in businesses, and to encroach on neighborhoods to which they formerly had little access (17).

This perception of general southern poor-white squalor and benightedness is made manifest in Arvay and her family, whose ignorance is frequently shocking, on occasion amusing, and at times appalling. Literally almost every thought Arvay has until the novel's end is wrong. The text is replete with phrases such as "Arvay had no idea about anything," or "Arvay had acted dumb," or Arvay "put the worst interpretation on it." At times Arvay's ignorance is intended to be funny, as when she complains about the higher standard of living in Citrabelle: "Heaven wasn't going to be any refreshment to folks if they got along with no more trouble than this.... It was the duty of man to suffer in this world, and these people round down here in south Florida were plainly shirking their duty.... There just didn't seem to Arvay to be any kind of honest work that kept folks bowed down from can't-see-in-the-morning till can't-see-at-night" (73). Arvay clings to her warped and stunted worldview as a kind of self-defense, particularly when she wants to defend her impoverished origins. After one of Arvay and Jim's many arguments, Hurston tells us that "Arvay scorned off learning as a source of evil knowledge and thought fondly of ignorance as the foundation of good-heartedness and honesty. Peace, contentment and virtue hung like a rainbow over turpentine shacks and shanties" (272).

Arvay's ignorance quickly loses its charm, however, and she soon seems less quaintly strange than downright unlikable. One way that Hurston brings this about is by repeatedly drawing our attention to the fact that Arvay, constantly in a state of compensatory self-absorption, never inquires about or acknowledges the many sacrifices that Jim makes for her and her family: "She knew nothing of his twisting and turning and conniving to make life pleasant for her sake.... [S]he never asked anything" (80). Jim seeks Arvay's approval by taking on ever-larger projects, intended to provide for her comfort, but she acts "listless" and "uninterested." Jim eventually accuses her of being "unthankful and unknowing like a hog under a acorn tree... never looking up to see where the acorns are coming from" (262). Hurston takes special pains to remind the reader that Arvay never credits the extent to which her own escape from poverty is directly underwritten by the kindness and hard work of the African Americans upon whom Jim relies—from the development of Jim's citrus farm, to the whiskey still run by Joe, to the materials and the labor for the construction of the house in which she lives. On the contrary, Jim's reliance on Joe exacerbates Arvay's insecurity: "You come from some big high muck-de-mucks, and we ain't nothing but piney-woods Crackers and poor white trash. Even niggers is better than we is, according to your kind. Joe Kelsey's word stands higher than mine any old day. You can say it don't, but actions speak louder than words. You give him more credit for sense than you do me" (126). The reader has no choice but to agree with her assessment. Arvay's insecurity about Joe eventually leads to the only strife in the Meserve "interracial family," where Arvay treats Joe so rudely that he eventually moves away.

Jim must repeatedly override Arvay's irrationality, especially her fear of change, if they are to make their way in life and avoid ending up like Arvay's family and the other crackers in Sawley—poor, ignorant, and mean. For example, when Jim proudly tells Arvay that he intends to buy a piece of swampland so that he can one day develop it, Arvay responds fearfully: "I don't want no parts of that awful place. It's dark and haunted-looking and too big and strong to overcome. It's frightening! Like some big old varmint or something to eat you up" (80). Jim does buy the land, and his son-in-law clears the land to make an upscale new residential development. The narrator tells us: "As Jim had predicted, *modern machinery and methods* had cleared that swamp in an amazingly short time.... The swamp monster retreated before the magic of man" (195; emphasis added). Soon the engineers bring the "comforts of civilization" to the area (e.g., sewers, water mains, electric lines, and a highway), and right away, "the right people bought sites in the new development.... [It] exerted a tremendous effect on Citrabelle and the surrounding country. It came along and stratified the town. The original line of the swamp gave accent like a railroad track. Those who belonged moved west" (196–97).

Jim's entrepreneurial vision literally transforms the local region; it brings modernity to the area and a new (white!) middle and upper class (i.e., "the right people"). Jim and Arvay can easily watch the "change" from their front porch because the highway "began no more than a hundred feet from her front gate."[25] In most romanticized visions of southern life, change is to be resisted, especially the destruction of the agrarian way of life. But as Jim observes, "this place is worth a whole lot more than it used to be on account that development." The significance of the New South's arrival seems lost on Arvay, prompting Jim to remark, "You don't seem to realize how big this development is and what a change it has made in things around here." Of course, Jim is right: the effect of this kind of modernizing "development" on the South was so profound that it came to be known as "the bulldozer revolution."

When Arvay returns to Sawley for a visit, she discovers that her hometown is being modernized as well, including a new highway, new grocery stores and hotels, new forms of industry, and new agricultural methods. A taxi driver tells Arvay, "Since the Old Gentleman died and Young Brad Cary took hold of things, some good changes have been made, but a lot of these old fogies and dumb peckerwoods don't like it" (274). Arvay "took sides with the peckerwoods in a timid way" and points out wistfully that "in the good old days, the folks in Sawley was good and kind and neighborly." But the taxi driver rejects her nostalgia: "I ain't seen no more goodness and kindheartedness here than nowhere else. Such another back-biting and carrying on you never seen. They hate like sin to *take a forward step. Just like they was took out of their cradles, they'll be screwed down in their coffins*" (274; emphasis added). In other words, "crackers" are incapable of change, afraid of "development," and outside of the march of progress.[26]

One of the most common ways that Arvay and the other "crackers" rationalize their inability to "take a forward step" is through a self-serving and misguided use of Christianity. When we first meet Arvay, she has "turned her back on the world" to become a missionary, and Hurston wryly points out that neither Arvay nor any of the other crackers recognize the social implications of taking "the Word to the heathens." When Arvay declares her intent to become a missionary, "[t]here had been nothing about the heathens of China, India, and Africa wallowing around on the heavenly chairs, nor ankling up and down the gold streets. None of [the congregation] could have imagined such a thing.... It was too much, and nobody tried to imagine any such thing. [The heathen] ought to consider himself pretty lucky to get saved from Hell. What became of him after that was [just not] talked about" (5). Jim sees through her missionary fervor, and once Jim and Arvay "elope" (i.e., after he rapes her and then takes her to the courthouse), Jim announces: "No more missionarying around for you. You done caught your heathen, baby" (57). Heathen though Jim may be, Hurston makes it clear that it is Jim who has "caught" Arvay, and that he is doing the saving in this relationship.[27]

This fact belatedly becomes clear to Arvay as well when she returns to her now decaying and rat-infested childhood home; she asks herself, "[W]ould she have ever *escaped* from this ugly and lonesome place if Jim had not come along and *just seized upon her* and *carried her off to the light*? She doubted it" (134; emphasis added). The violent, coercive nature of Arvay's redemption—both in the original rape scene and in the language of the preceding passage—warrants pausing over, especially given that Arvay elsewhere refers to feeling emotionally "enslaved" by Jim. Arvay complains, "I hope my child don't fall such a slave to nobody that they can just handle her anyway they will or may" (177). At one point Jim observes, "[A] woman knows who her master is all right, and she answers to his commands" (33). Later, after he has ripped Arvay's clothes off during a fight, Jim declares, "You're my damn property" (216). Though the language is disturbing, according to the logic of the narrative, Arvay's "enslavement" is in fact her good fortune.[28] Without Jim she would have been doomed along with her family to a "primitive" and wretched life— one completely lacking in what Hurston earlier in the narrative calls "the comforts of civilization" (196).

Here Hurston is inverting the typical Western logic and practice of "modern" Christian missionarism. The missionaries save the "primitive heathens" who would otherwise be damned to Hell because they live outside of Christianity—usually figured as the spiritual means to "enlightenment" and "civilization." In Hurston's narrative, Arvay and the other cracker Christians are the ones figured as "primitives"—they are ignorant, backward, ruled by self-destructive "traditions," and outside of modern time. As the taxi driver from Sawley observed, "Just like they was took out of their cradles, they'll be screwed down in their coffins." They never develop intellectually or materially and will be left behind by "progress." Jim is figured as a "heathen" missionary who comes from afar, bursts into Arvay's benighted Christian world, and "seizes" her and "carries her off" to the "light" of the New South. Hurston reverses the logical trajectory of the Atlantic slave trade, where the blond, blue-eyed Arvay is forcibly taken from her primitive home, made a "slave," and brought to "civilization" for her own good.[29] This figuring of the crackers as "slaves" of ignorance and backwardness, the "kind" of people who need to be saved by New South progress, recalls clearly Booker T. Washington's desire to save the now symbolically enslaved black masses through the "gospel of Progress."

But Hurston's provocative signification on the South's oppressive history is complicated by the logic of her racial coding—that is, crackers substituted for African Americans—which reveals much more of her sense of pain and outrage at the causes of African American abjection than she intends. For Hurston, "progress" is always the responsibility of the individual, though what's in the individual is mysteriously enshrined in the "flesh." After Arvay wins Jim back, she reflects: "All that had happened to her, good and bad, was a part of her own self and had come out of her. Within her own flesh were many mysteries. She lifted her left hand before her eyes and studied it in every detail with wonder. With wonder and deep awe like Moses before his burning bush. What all, Arvay asked of herself, was buried and hidden in human flesh? If you could just know, it would be all the religion that anybody needed. And what was in you was bound to come out and stand" (349–50). On the surface, this passage reinforces, in quasi-mystical language, Hurston's greatest theme: individuals are solely responsible for their own fate and should neither rely on God for assistance nor blame their own failures in life on racism or economic exploitation. Yet her repeated references to the flesh also connote other unspoken issues. Throughout *Seraph*, Hurston connects what "kind" of person someone is to his or her flesh. When Arvay returns to her childhood home for a visit some years after she has moved away with Jim, she is appalled at the appearance of her sister Larraine's family: "*Common in the flesh and common in what they had on*. . . . Arvay was not sure that she would like to own them in Citrabelle. . . . So common-cladded, *and their poor looking skins, and unbred feet and legs, and the whole make of them.* She was indeed glad that Jim was not standing beside her now and seeing her folks as she saw them" (133; emphasis added). In this scene, we learn that the Henson family is in desperate straits because Carl, Larraine's husband, is unemployed and refuses to look for work. Consequently, "rats, roaches, and flies were simply taking the place" (132–33). The appearance of Arvay's family, especially their "common flesh," reflects their lowly character.

Hurston repeats these impressions later in the narrative when Arvay returns home again after she has been telegrammed that her mother is ill. When walking up to the house, she observes that Larraine is a "ton of coarse looking flesh sitting on the dilapidated old steps in a faded cheap cotton dress and dirty white cotton stockings." Arvay also thinks to herself that Larraine's children are "mule-faced and ugly enough. . . . [E]ven in a croker-sack, Angeline [Arvay's daughter] would look like their mistress" (275–76). In this episode, Arvay discovers that her mother, Maria Henson, terminally ill, has been holding out for a month to see Arvay once more before she dies. Larraine and Carl purposefully have not told Arvay about her mother's illness because they want to take over the house and its meager possessions after she dies. They wait until it is too late for Maria to recover before they send for Arvay, knowing that Arvay would try to get Maria medical attention. After Maria dies, effectively because of Carl and Larraine's neglect, Carl refuses (without being asked) to help pay for Maria's funeral expenses, and when Arvay is in town buying groceries for Larraine's family, she comes home to find the house, which Maria willed to Arvay, stripped literally to its foundation. The point of this episode, as with Arvay's first visit home, is to enlighten Arvay and the reader to the fact that Jim has saved her from being just like Larraine and her family—not merely poor and stupid, but lazy and immoral.[30]

Hurston connects individual fate and the flesh in an even more pronounced way with Arvay's first son, Earl, who is both mentally handicapped and physically deformed. Not surprisingly, he looks nothing like Jim, and clearly takes after one of Arvay's relatives "who was sort of queer in his head" (68). Earl, when upset, makes "inhuman screams" and "animal howls . . . [which had] nothing human in them" (100). When a Portuguese family with two daughters moves onto the Meserve estate, Earl becomes even more bestial, "whining and whimpering and making growly noises in his throat" (123); when Arvay tries to restrain him, he bites her. Arvay tries to blame Earl's actions on the "furriners'" scent, but Jim replies: "Something about one or the other of those girls has woke up something in the boy.... *It's been there all along. You see the boy can't control himself*" (125; emphasis added). Jim wants to have Earl put away—both for his own safety and the safety of those around him—but yields to Arvay's wishes to let him stay. Before long, Earl sexually assaults one of the Portuguese girls—the girl is found with her skirt pulled up to her waist and a bite-mark on her thigh. Earl then flees into the swamp; a lynch mob quickly gathers but then relents out of respect for Jim. The "posse" tries unsuccessfully to recapture Earl safely, and Jim is forced to kill Earl in self-defense.

At the end of the novel, Arvay reflects on Earl as a biological emblem of her destiny: "Earl was in her and had to come out some way or another.... Yes, *Earl had been bred in her before she was even born, but his birth had purged her flesh*. He was born first. It was meant to be that way. Somebody had to pay off the debt so that the rest of the pages could be clean.... She had been purged out, and the way was cleared for better things.... Then it was like the Resurrection. *The good that was in her flesh had taken form*. Angeline, female beauty, had come out of her, and Kenny, as handsome a boy as you would find anywhere" (350; emphasis added). The language of this passage carries unmistakable eugenicist overtones. As Chuck Jackson has observed, Earl is clearly what early twentieth-century eugenicists would have described as a "cacogenic" child (642, 647). Unlike the "good and beautiful" Angeline and Kenny, who are consistently associated with Jim, over and against Arvay, Earl literally embodies the degeneracy that was "bred" into Arvay's flesh, a "weak-strain" passed on from Arvay's "kind" that was destined to express itself. Despite the care and attention that Jim and Arvay offer Earl, he is unsocializable, animal-like, and a sexual threat to "white" women.[31] Hence Hurston deploys not only widely known eugenicist discourse but also, intentionally or otherwise, the racialized myth of the black rapist and the racialized ritual of lynching, an act intended theoretically to counteract the black threat against white women. But as Hurston was well aware, lynching as southern racial ritual had little to do with protecting white women and much to do with immobilizing African Americans, socially, politically, and economically.

The effect of Hurston's curious reiteration of the meaning of the flesh is that the reader becomes aware of what Hurston has desperately disavowed and repressed throughout the narrative. It is a thrice-told tale that the South was founded on a social hierarchy based on the flesh, what Houston Baker calls "an *epidermalization* of oppression. Skin color—in combination with facial features and hair texture—became Southern grounds for maintenance of the ideological and economic project of White Supremacy.... It was more literal than metaphorical... therefore, to agree with scholars and writers who assert that 'slavery' indeed continued 'after the war.' And the mark of Reconstruction's innovative mechanisms of White Supremacy remained skin color, *blackness*" (*Turning South Again* 43). In other words, *despite* (and to some degree, *because of*) Hurston's recalcitrant insistence on absolute individual responsibility, *Seraph* is nevertheless replete with images and expressions that *remind* us that, yes, one's flesh has a profound influence on one's fate. Hurston's emphasis on the meaning of the flesh casts her impish reproduction of an idealized New South plantation into a new light. Claudia Tate's keen analysis of the "discourses of unconscious desire" in African American novels is helpful here.

> These discourses allow the author to express unacknowledged and socially censored wishes by inscribing them in the novel's rhetorical features.... We can ... understand unconscious discourses as compromise formations "between the wish to communicate and the wish to conceal, whereas the wish to conceal, not to know, is the more conscious" (Hook, Psychoanalysis 121). The language of the text performs this paradoxical mediation of speaking and muting, disclosing and masking, in much the same way that hysterical symptoms conspicuously stage the hidden obsession of the neurotic subject. (179)

Hurston's life experiences and knowledge of southern race relations most certainly impressed upon her the reality of slavery's persistence in the New South—at least in terms of social organization, attitudes, and ritualized behaviors. Virtually all of her public remarks on southern race relations in the last decades of her life, including *Seraph*, seemed to express a "wish to conceal" these facts.[32] Hurston attempts to "master" this legacy by "restaging" it in *Seraph*, as though she could, through idealized fantasy, contain and control (even profit on) its far-reaching effects on her life, the life of all African Americans, and the life of the nation. As I have suggested, Hurston reconciles, consciously or otherwise, all that she knows about the South's oppression of African Americans by displacing it onto the backs, or more precisely, in the flesh of the crackers. But as we have seen, Hurston's racial idyll, her southern romance, is poisoned by what she unconsciously "wishes to communicate"—rage and contempt. In a 1943 letter to the African American journalist Claude Barnett, Hurston divulged a rare glimpse of the outrage that I believe both structures and destabilizes *Seraph*: "[T]he iron has entered my soul. Since my god of tolerance has forsaken me, I am ready for anything to overthrow Anglo-Saxon supremacy, however desperate. I have become what I never wished to be, a good hater. I no longer even value my life if by losing it, I can do something to destroy this Anglo-Saxon monstrosity" (Carla Kaplan 14). It is precisely this deep fund of emotion that sabotages her efforts to work within and control the (white) mind of the South.

* * *

I have argued that the desire to understand Hurston's *Seraph* as an entirely tongue-in-cheek racial masquerade or subversive critique prevents us from detecting what this work reveals about Hurston's deeply conflicted attitudes toward the region, toward southern whites, and especially toward the condition of African Americans in the South. *Seraph* holds a special place in Hurston's oeuvre because it complicates in productive ways the already complex narratives about Hurston's contribution to American, African American, and southern literary history, and especially her attitude toward literary protest and leftist critique. I've suggested that Hurston's "true picture of the New South" attempts to evade protest by celebrating the region's "progress" and "development"—catchphrases for a range of technological, commercial, and economic transformations that somehow manage to allow for the persistence of idealized Old South race relations. And here is the crux of the problem, a problem that in many ways is classically southern. For all the hope invested in "development," the South wanted to avoid being wholly assimilated into the North's consumerist, capitalist system; in other words, the South wanted to retain some sense of regional "difference." This difference coalesced principally around an idealization of the past and in remaining in certain respects precisely antimodern, a contradictory rhetorical posture that makes it impossible to talk about "progress" in a straight way. "Crackers," here and elsewhere, have carried the blame for the South's failure to modernize and the burden of this rhetorical contradiction. In *Seraph*, Hurston symbolically resolves these contradictions through interracial sympathy and Arvay's "uplift." Along the way, however, the rage and sorrow that Hurston disavowed her entire career comes flooding out.

The conflicted quality of this text is even more readily legible with reference to the tragic conditions of Hurston's final years. No matter how many times Hurston rejected social factors as determining forces in the lives of individuals, we are left with the fact that she could not earn a living, despite her extraordinary learning and talent. Because of her "flesh," her final years are destitute. In the end, Hurston could not give up the one thing that she had left—her fierce pride. Even to her dying days, when she was sick, without family, rejected by the literary establishment, and penniless, Hurston considered self-pity the greatest sin. In a letter to a friend she declares: "I say to hell with it! My back is broad. Let me, personally and privately, be responsible for my survival or failure to survive in this man's world. . . . I want no double-standard of measurement. . . . I am a conscious being, all the plaints and pleas of the pressure groups inside and outside the race, to the contrary" (Carla Kaplan 504). For Hurston to have consciously and directly attacked racial and economic oppression in the South would have constituted the loss of her ego's only remaining shield. Nevertheless, her last published novel is so laced with "unspeakable" venom and fury that it thwarts its own objectives. *Seraph on the Suwanee* ultimately fails in its efforts to sustain its own utopian vision of a New South prospering through interracial sympathy. But given the elemental conflict between Hurston's lived experience and her belligerent idea of self-reliance and racial privacy, how could it have turned out any other way? *Seraph*'s failure seems inevitable, given that Hurston reproduces a mind—the mind of the South—that tries desperately to repress not only what Hurston knows, but even her very existence.

6 / The Unfinished Project of Western Modernity: *Savage Holiday*, Moral Slaves, and the Problem of Freedom in Cold War America

> *I'm a rootless man, but I'm neither psychologically distraught nor in any wise particularly disturbed by it. Personally, I do not hanker after, and seem not to need, as many emotional attachments, sustaining roots, or idealistic allegiances as most people. I declare unabashedly that I like and even cherish a state of abandonment, of aloneness; it does not bother me; indeed, to me it seems the natural, inevitable condition of man, and I welcome it. I can make myself at home almost anywhere on this earth and can, if I've a mind to and when I'm attracted to a landscape or a mood of life, easily sink myself into the most alien and widely differing environments.*
>
> —RICHARD WRIGHT, *White Man, Listen!*

Richard Wright was, at the start of the post–World War II era, unquestionably the world's most influential and revered, even if controversial, black author. His work was widely discussed at home and abroad, translated into many languages, and selling well enough to provide a comfortable life for him and his family. He was also arguably the writer who sought authorial racial privacy more fervently than any other in this study. Whereas the young careers of Willard Motley and Frank Yerby suggested new possibilities for commercial success and subject matter among black writers, Wright's demonstrated new possibilities for literary and cultural authority. As we have seen, several writers turned to the white-life novel at least partly in response to the immense shadow that he cast on the literary landscape. Nevertheless, the narrow terms of Wright's authority, as a "Negro writer" of protest fiction, increasingly felt like a trap, the antithesis of the freedom that Wright sought politically, intellectually, and culturally. By 1957, Wright would assert: "I have no religion in the formal sense of the word. . . . I have no race except that which is forced upon me. I have no country except that to which I'm obliged to belong. I have no traditions. I'm free. I have only the future"

(*Pagan Spain* 21). Before Wright could declare this state of radical self-determination—this state of privacy—he and his family had to permanently resettle in Europe. Wright left the United States in 1947 for Paris and, according to his biographer, Michel Fabre, he was soon living the life of a "Parisian intellectual," exchanging ideas with such French luminaries as Jean-Paul Sartre and Simone de Beauvoir, as well as Léopold Sédar Senghor, Aimé Césaire, and C.L.R. James, leading thinkers and artists in a vibrant black expatriate colony. Not only did Wright find France a more congenial country (he remarked that there was "more freedom in one square block of Paris than there is in the entire United States of America" (Rowley 398), his move also fueled his ongoing struggle for intellectual emancipation. In a 1955 letter to his former *Harper's* editor, Ed Aswell, he observed: "When I got off the ship in Le Havre [France] in 1946, I shed a burden of racial tension that I had never wanted to carry. Now, freed of this (which most people assume was the only thing a black writer could write out of, that is racial fears and feelings), I've let what would normally come to the fore in me become my main preoccupation. That preoccupation is: the individual and his society. . . . [It] cuts across racial, class, sexual, religious, and political questions."[1] Wright told the novelist William Gardner Smith in an interview that "My break from the U.S. was more than a geographical change. It was a break with my former attitudes as a Negro and a Communist—an attempt to think over and re-define my attitudes and my thinking. I was trying to grapple with the big problem—the meaning of western civilization as a whole and the relation of Negroes and other minority groups to it" (Fabre 366).

The rise of the Cold War made Wright's "break" even more imperative. He described the precariousness of his position in a letter to his longtime agent Paul Reynolds:

> I know that to talk about the Negro problem in this Cold War situation is difficult. If somebody in Russia tells the truth about what he feels, the communists say he is helping the United States, and, if in the United States somebody tells, say, how a black man feels, he can be said to be trying to help Russia. The artist today works in an impossible atmosphere; there is no call for truth-telling. . . . All of this makes it hard for a writer. I have grown to feel that I would rather not write about Negroes anymore; I've grown to feel that nobody, not even Negroes, wants to listen anymore. Yet, I'm convinced that I'm telling some important truths. What does one do in a situation like that? Frequently, of late, I've

been casting around in my mind the possibility of dropping writing about Negroes entirely. Yet that too represents a problem. (March 2, 1959; qtd. in Fabre 485)

Wright wanted to tell the truth about the modern West, but the truth was neither limited to the Negro problem nor assimilatable to Cold War propaganda, either U.S. or Soviet. He was a nonaligned Western thinker who claimed a vast critical horizon.

One of the ways that Wright attempted to secure his discursive freedom was, for the duration of one novel, "dropping writing about Negroes entirely."[2] Wright's third novel, *Savage Holiday* (1954), turns away from the systemic racism and black domestic pathology that marked *Native Son* and *Black Boy* to investigate the private life of a white insurance executive, Erskine Fowler. Here there are no African Americans traumatized by white-supremacist terror, only a white man suffering from the psychological scars of maternal abandonment. As I argue below, Fowler appears to be the ideal subject of hegemonic privacy—he is a wealthy white man, a prominent member of his church, as well as a Mason and Rotarian. Nevertheless, he is terrified of privacy—literally and figuratively—and is thus properly understood as a figure of psychological, social, and political *privation*; he is radically dependent on external authority, and his lack of true self-consciousness, an authentic self-relation, renders him incapable of self-governance. He is what Wright considered a "moral slave," one unable to endure what I call "existential privacy," the condition of absolute autonomy that Wright ascribes to himself in the epigraph to this chapter. Thus we can see Wright attempting to generate authorial racial privacy by decentering the legacy of slavery and highlighting white, rather than black, privation. Wright interrogates the content of hegemonic privacy, including received ideas around religion, work, and "the family," as a way to take on "the big problems" facing Western civilization: the deep ideological structures that continue to produce Western savagery.

Wright's intellectual and thematic shift, while personally liberating, was not warmly received. Despite how productive this period of his career was—he published three novels, three book-length travel narratives, a collection of essays, and many short stories, essays, and reviews—his reputation began to wane.[3] His current status as a major American writer still rests overwhelmingly on the works he published before leaving the United States. As Paul Gilroy notes, the critical consensus was that "as far as his art was concerned, the move to Europe was disastrous" (156). Critics claimed that his work suffered because he lost touch with his wellspring of inspiration, working-class urban and southern black American experience. This loss was exacerbated by Wright's immersion in European philosophical modes of thought, such as existentialism, and a perception that his new work relied too heavily on psychiatric and psychoanalytic discourses (156). Gilroy rightly points out the problematic quasi- or even explicitly essentialist suppositions that have driven many of these evaluations of his early and later career, in particular the implied demand that he always adhere to his imposed status as representative voice of a presumably monolithic black America. More recently, several critics, Gilroy among them, have set about reconsidering Wright's later work. Gilroy's chapter on Wright in *The Black Atlantic* offers an early but representative illustration. He approaches Wright's fiction and nonfiction as "an extended exercise in intercultural hermeneutics which has important effects upon Wright's theories about 'race,' modernity, identity, and their interrelation" (150). "Perhaps more than any other writer," Gilroy concludes, "[Wright] showed how modernity was both the period and the region in which black politics grew" (186). En route to this conclusion, Gilroy draws on several of Wright's nonfiction works, and all of Wright's full-length texts from this era, especially the fiction, with the notable exception of *Savage Holiday*, which garners only a few passing references and no analysis. Despite the avowedly anti-essentialist nature of his project, Gilroy's notable neglect of Wright's white-life novel implicitly functions to reinscribe Wright's status as a "*black* intellectual" whose true and legitimate subject is a racially delimited notion of "black politics" and culture.

Gilroy is far from alone in this omission. Wright's later works are increasingly generating serious critical reconsideration, but nearly always to the exclusion of *Savage Holiday*. Of the many works in Wright's extensive fictional oeuvre, *Savage Holiday* is arguably the least promising candidate for recovery. Not only does it leave aside his socially prescribed area of expertise, the explication of modern black politics and subjectivity, but for many it reads like a thinly fictionalized psychological case study, one burdened by heavy-handed applications of warmed-over Freudian analyses and poisoned by a misogynistic investment in oedipal complexes. Until very recently, most critics attended to Wright's psychoanalytic argument, with little or no reference to the function of "race" or modernity in the narrative.[4] I am particularly sympathetic to Gilroy's approach, both his attention to Wright's analyses of race and modernity, and Wright's preoccupation with an "insider-outsider duality." I contend, however, that *Savage Holiday* should neither be ignored nor read in isolation. Instead, it should be considered both in dialogue with his larger philosophical and political concerns at this moment, as I've already suggested, as well as in relation to *The Outsider*, which appeared only one year earlier. By using *The Outsider* as a hermeneutic, we can see *Savage Holiday* as much more than a psychoanalytic potboiler, and instead as an existentialist "family romance" in which Wright emplots the contradictions of Western modernity. Wright's narrative meditation on the problem of freedom in Western modernity suggests that such signs of normative white heteropatriarchal authority as the corporation, Christianity, and the heteropatriarchal family are *not* evidence of virtue and rationality entitling one to the authority associated with what I call hegemonic privacy. Rather, they are disciplinary and alienating sources of privation. According to Wright, Western modernity radically undermined what he called the "beautiful mythologies" that had previously shaped and ordered existence, especially religion and its authoritative institutions and dogma; these challenges left Westerners feeling "psychologically naked" ("Tradition and Industrialization" 710). But rather than "cherish[ing this state] of abandonment, of aloneness," as Wright claims that *he* does, he argues that many Westerners cling to atavistic and compensatory "substitutes," such as racism, work, and the church (*White Man, Listen!* 647). This fearful avoidance of existential self-creation in favor of inauthentic identities has the effect of estranging Westerners not only from themselves, but also from others, whom they try to dominate in an effort to manage their own existential crises. Hence hegemonic privacy is not true privacy, given that it depends on the authority of tradition and the subjugation of others. Existential privacy, in contrast, depends upon nothing more than the authority of the self. It allows for communion with others, but does not depend on their subordination.

 In both *The Outsider* and *Savage Holiday*, Wright deploys psychological and existentialist discourses to enact a social and cultural critique that moves well beyond his moment's perception of black critical agency. Psychology and existentialism enable him to present an anti-essentialist notion of racial difference: Blacks and whites are "different" only to the extent that they are the product of different historical forces and socially imposed conditions; underneath these surface differences, however, black and white Americans are the same because both are products of Western modernity—a position that Wright had been arguing in one form or another since his days in the Communist Party. His audience, nevertheless, persisted in reading his work as being exclusively concerned with "the Negro." Consequently, in *The Outsider* and *Savage Holiday*, Wright presents "Western Man" rather than "the Negro" as his explicit subject. He attempts to plumb the depths of Western Man's "heart" and "mind" in order to determine what leads "men" to hate, dominate, and kill, thereby making racism (and sexism) particular effects of these deeper, more fundamental conflicts. Wright bridges the distance between these general, abstract concerns and his characters' personalities and motivations by drawing on contemporary anxieties about masculine failure and bad mothering. Both *The Outsider* and *Savage Holiday* have protagonists whose "criminal" feelings and actions originate with their mothers—Damon is "criminalized" by his mother's oppressive and invasive moralism (he describes her as "ravaging" him emotionally) and Fowler by his mother's neglect and immoral behavior. Thus while Wright reproduces certain timeworn misogynistic attitudes, attention to his use of what was known as "momism" allows us to better appreciate the strategies he developed in his search for an alternative, anti-essentialist mode of representation and thought. More broadly, however, we can see that Wright's focus on discourses of imperiled domesticity plainly echoes his fellow white-life novelists' critical turn toward private white spaces in crisis.

* * *

The story of *Savage Holiday* runs as follows: forty-three-year-old white insurance executive Erskine Fowler is forced to retire after thirty years of faithful service to make room for his boss's son, a recent Harvard grad. The morning after his retirement party, he gets out of his bath to try to quickly retrieve the Sunday newspaper. He steps out of his apartment, naked and dripping wet, and is then locked out when the wind blows the door shut behind him. He panics, runs to the roof of the building to enter his apartment via the fire escape, but in the process frightens a young boy, Tony, who is playing on the roof. Tony believes that Fowler is after him, and in his attempt to flee falls off the ten-story building to his death. Fowler immediately tries to displace his feelings of guilt onto the boy's mother, Mabel, whom he feels is the one truly responsible for the boy's death because she has habitually neglected her child while working late nights in a bar and engaging in "immoral" behavior. During the next two days, Fowler obsessively pursues Mabel, even offering to marry her, which he imagines will bring her under his control and assuage his sense of guilt and loneliness. She briefly considers his offer, primarily because she has little money and no close family or friends, but then thinks better of it. He flies into a jealous rage, and then kills her by stabbing her repeatedly in the stomach with a butcher knife. Immediately afterward, he realizes that he has just acted out a repressed, guilt-ridden childhood fantasy of killing his own mother who neglected him, as Mabel neglected Tony, while giving her attentions to men. Fowler promptly goes to the police and turns himself in. When questioned by the police, he offers no explanation of his motives, thinking to himself: "How could he ever explain that a daydream buried under the rigorous fiats of duty had been called forth from its thirty-six-year-old grave . . . a guilty dream which he had wanted to disown and forget, but which he had had to reenact in order to make its memory and reality clear to him!" (220).

Wright had originally intended to include *Savage Holiday* as part of a larger, three-part work called "Celebration." Wright drafted but was not able to generate interest for the latter two sections—one was called "Strange Daughter" and the other "When the World Was Red." "Strange Daughter" was about a psychologically and sexually repressed young white woman who is eventually killed by her Nigerian lover when he discovers that she is pregnant, and thus threatens to violate his religious taboo against reincarnating his ancestors outside of the religious bloodline. "When the World Was Red" describes the fateful, historic encounter between Montezuma and Cortez, which Wright frames primarily as a clash between religions. As is evident from these summaries, these works are related to *Savage Holiday* thematically in their emphasis on the repressive effects of religion within society.

Of interest for this study, however, is the way that Wright intended to link all three works. Wright proposed a device that he called an "impersonal mood" that, "rendered in a kind of free verse prose, says yes to all forms of experience which seek an outlet when environment balks it. Such a mood would be amoral in its appeal. . . . This mood would champion no social or political or religious doctrine." Specifically, the section preceding *Savage Holiday* would include "nature in its outlook" and man would be seen as "a strange part of nature." This natural perspective would, Wright believed, highlight "the weight of society, [and thus] its moral claims would be thrown into relief"; this contrast would thereby "automatically" criticize the claims of the novel, "but not from any ideological point of view." The first section of the impersonal mood would be from an "organic," vegetative perspective, before moving into "a description of an eagle killing a lamb, and then a lion mating in a zoo. . . . I had hoped to shed criticism upon how such men lived their lives; the comment would have been implicit in the context."⁵ Wright's recourse to natural, ostensibly objective, perspectives and analogies in his "mood" should be seen as a bid for racial privacy; he was clearly hoping to preemptively frame *Savage Holiday* outside of the overdetermined racial and Cold War ideological contexts that stifled him as a citizen and an artist. Wright expresses his desire that *Savage Holiday* enjoy the benefits of racial privacy directly in a letter to his agent, Paul Reynolds. *Savage Holiday* "deals with just folks, white folks. Don't know if Harper will like my switching or not. But, as you can see, there was no sense in making this a Negro story. The story is mainly psychological. It will speak for itself. It's either good or very bad; I don't know which. I was of a mind to say to try to publish this under another name. What I am worried about is that people will read this in a light of saying that this is a Negro writing about whites. Which is true. But they might read it with more a desire to try to find fault than just to be moved by or interested in the story" (Fabre 379).

Although Wright hoped that *Savage Holiday* would have a different reception than that of his previous works, its plot is in many respects quite similar to his earlier corpus. It includes the recurring features of an angry, alienated, and isolated male protagonist, painful scenes of dysfunctional family life, brutal violence, and an "accidental death" followed by flight and eventual capture. But unlike most of his other texts, all but one of the characters is white; there are virtually no references to race; and all of the action takes place in entirely white environments—a middle-class apartment building and a Baptist church.⁶

Savage Holiday was the only one of Wright's novels to appear initially in paperback. Wright claimed that after the manuscript was rejected by *Harper's*, he attempted to "bypass the publishers and go directly to the reading public.... Avon published the book and there was not a single word about it in any American newspaper. Just absolute silence, not even an echo."⁷ The Dutch translation of the novel did receive at least one positive review, and Michel Fabre reports that the French press took the work fairly seriously.⁸ Wright made very few public remarks on the novel, likely because it generated no interest. The few comments that are available were translated from two French radio interviews, and are worth quoting at length. Wright summed up his objective in writing *Savage Holiday* as follows: "In this novel, I have attempted to deal with what I consider as the most important problem white people have to face: their moral dilemma. This is why I have chosen this white New Yorker as a protagonist" (*Conversations with Richard Wright* 167). He says that he named the work *Savage Holiday* because my character, Erskine Fowler, discovers that being free and wealthy (for he has enough money) at his age does not at all represent the kind of wonderful opportunity most people would wish. The very fact that he feels he is free, free from any compelling obligation, is for him the most terrifying thing that ever befell him. He proves unable to take advantage of his freedom, to even simply bear it, because he is inhabited by a sense of guilt which makes him unhappy and pushes him to the final catastrophe. Until then he had been capable of forgetting, we can even say repressing, his feeling of guilt through his acquisition of material wealth. And now he finds himself suddenly deprived of his job and work. (167–68)

He continues, "What matters is his fear of assuming the responsibilities entailed by his new kind of life, a holiday, i.e., a life deprived of the props and supports of a daily task to perform. His dilemma brings him to be responsible for two deaths—he is accidentally responsible for the death of his female neighbor's son, and he deliberately murders her some time later" (168). Taken by themselves, these explanations offer fairly little clarification of what he considers "the most important problem white people have to face." At best this provides a highly oblique analysis of what we typically think of when analyzing American whiteness. He does make one comment, however, that makes the connection more clear:

It is true that in my early work I was almost wholly concerned with the reactions of Negroes to the white environment that pressed in upon them. Having left America and having been living for some time in France, I have become concerned about the historical roots and the emotional problems of Western whites which make them aggressive toward colored peoples. You can see from this that my travels into the Argentine, into Africa and Asia even have an autobiographical inspiration. I was looking for explanations of the psychological reactions of whites. In my novel *The Outsider*, the hero of which was a Negro, I had already abandoned the black hero proper. That novel is anchored mainly in reflection and is concerned with problems that would beset anyone, black or white. (167)

Given that *Savage Holiday* is conspicuously devoid of white people acting "aggressive toward colored peoples," the novel does not readily make clear how it advances his efforts to illuminate whites' attitudes toward, and treatment of, racial minorities. The connection between these ideas becomes much more clear when *Savage Holiday* is read with recourse to other works by Wright, especially *The Outsider*—the text that he mentions when responding to a query about what he was attempting to achieve in *Savage Holiday*.

The Outsider is a tale about Cross Damon, an embittered, bookish African American postal worker deeply frustrated with his job and personal relationships—including those with his wife and children, his mistress, and his mother. By chance he is mistaken for dead after a subway accident, so he seizes this opportunity to start his life over again. Damon has always felt like an "outsider," but he takes this state of mind to a new level by repudiating all of his former relationships and obligations. In his mind, he is now outside his family, his race, and even outside "civilization," especially its social and moral responsibilities. His sense of moral freedom, combined with his desire to conceal his past, leads him to lie incessantly and commit innumerable crimes, including three murders. One of the men he kills is a communist leader, and Damon is eventually shot and killed by party agents.

Wright's configuration of Cross Damon's personality and motives is the first clue we have to grasping the racial, moral, and political critique of *Savage Holiday*. As mentioned in chapter 1, as early as *Black Boy*—that is, at the peak of Wright's popular and critical acclaim—he felt that dominant-culture notions about the meaning of blackness, particularly those in the publishing industry, were far too narrow to adequately capture the full range of black subjectivity. He responds in his next published novel by offering Cross Damon, who, according to the original dust-jacket copy, is "an American Negro who can't be encompassed by the stereotyped patterns used by both bigots and liberals to explain the Negro." Wright told *Jet Magazine* ahead of *The Outsider*'s publication that Damon's "psychological problems will make those of Bigger Thomas (hero of Native Son) look like nothing" ("New Richard Wright Novel" 41). Both of these comments indicate Wright's attempts to carve out a new space of discursive authority, and the novel is even more direct. Wright depicts Damon in a manner that insistently defies commonplace notions regarding "the black hero." The narrator tells us that

> Cross's opportunistic rejection of his former life had been spurred by his shame at what a paltry man he had made of himself.... His consciousness of the color of his skin had played no role in it. Militating against racial consciousness in him were the general circumstances of his upbringing which had shielded him from the more barbaric forms of white racism; also the insistent claims of his own

inner life had made him too concerned with himself to cast his lot
wholeheartedly with Negroes in terms of racial struggle.... What
really obsessed him was his nonidentity, which negated his ability
to relate himself to others. (194–95)

In short, in addition to Damon's being highly contemplative, his psyche has suffered no significant racial injury; he is unconcerned with racial struggle, and is "obsessed" not with what it means to be "a black man in a white man's world," but rather with a sense that he has no identity at all, racial or otherwise. He is not a figure of black privation: one encompassed by his biology, incapable of self-consciousness, and externally determined—if anything, his interiority occludes the social.

The preceding passage is only one of many moments in which the narrator intrudes to remind the reader that Damon is not "the black hero proper," as though Wright assumes that his audience will be unwilling, or possibly incapable, of believing that Damon could have any motivations, perspectives, attitudes, or desires that were not fundamentally racial. "There was no racial tone to his reactions," the narrator tells us; "he was just a man, *any* man who had had an opportunity to flee and had seized upon it" (109; emphasis in original). Later in the novel the narrator observes that "he knew that deep in the hearts of many of those millions was the same desire.... It was not because he was Negro that he had found his obligations intolerable; it was because there resided in his heart a sharp sense of freedom that had somehow escaped being dulled by intimidating conditions" (503). One of Damon's many ethical dilemmas is when Eva, a naïve racial liberal, falls in love with him because she imagines him a racially persecuted black man; he wonders, "[C]ould he allow her to love him for his color when being a Negro was the least important thing in his life?" (385). These remarks are all attempts by Wright to forestall racially reductive readings of his protagonist, and by extension his novel, which considers (alongside racial concerns) such "universal" subjects as whether "man's heart, his spirit, is the deadliest thing in creation" (171). These comments are attempts, then, to generate at least a modicum of authorial racial privacy with a mainstream reading audience that, despite its ideological diversity, shared a propensity to deal in stereotypes when it came to "the Negro." Both *The Outsider* and *Savage Holiday* refuse the racial liberal reader's desire for suffering black objects, while also rejecting the white-supremacist reader's skepticism about a black subject's capacity for philosophical inquiry and, finally, the Myrdallian reader's supposition that all African Americans think about is "the Negro problem."

Wright counters his readers' will to racial reduction by positing the notion of "psychological men," those both cursed and blessed with a "double vision" that allows them to see that they are "both *inside* and *outside* our culture at the same time" and thus forced to live with a "dreadful objectivity" (163–64).[9] As a "psychological man," Damon grasps that he is not essentially a "Negro," but rather the product of Western modernity. As his white alter ego and fellow outsider Detective Houston observes, African Americans "are going to inherit the problems that we have, but with a difference. . . . Every emotional and cultural convulsion that ever shook the heart and soul of Western man will shake them. Negroes will develop unique and specially defined psychological types. They will become psychological men, like the Jews. . . . They will not only be Americans or Negroes; they will be centers of *knowing*, so to speak" (163–64). Although it is the combination of his blackness and his philosophical inclinations that make Damon an "outsider," there are many of his "kind," including many "Jews," and all others who "are so placed in life by accident of race or birth or chance that what they see is terrifying" (169)—to wit, those whose outsider-ness enables them to recognize that "maybe man is nothing in particular" and that "maybe the whole effort of man on earth to build a civilization is simply man's frantic attempt to hide himself from himself," especially from the awareness that "[m]an may be just anything at all" (171).

Wright is, of course, not the first to introduce these ideas. These ruminations are clearly indebted to, among others, Du Bois's notion of "double-consciousness" as well as Freud's *Civilization and Its Discontents*, the insights of which had by this time been fully incorporated into the repertoire of Western intellectual discourse. What is important to notice is how Wright is using "psychology" as an antiracist hermeneutic, one that enables a powerful identificatory mobility and capacity for signification that extends far beyond what is typically allowed to "blackness" as a discursive category. As a psychological man, he is able to see that "man" may be nothing or anything, which indicates that man is *not* essentially racial. Here Wright is plainly employing Sartre's foundational existentialist proclamation that "existence precedes essence." Although one always acts within a specific set of limits, human beings are ultimately "condemned to be free" and thus faced with the "despair" and "anguish" of being personally responsible for acting without any external guarantees (Cotkin 171). Damon is contemplating existential dread when he asks, "May not human life on this earth be a kind of frozen fear of man at what he could possibly be? And every move he makes, couldn't these moves be just to hide this awful fact?" (172). This universal condition, however, has clear implications for interrogating modern racial ideologies. Black men, like all other men, could be *anything* (good or ill), and those things that restrict modern social relations, *including Jim Crow*, are attempts to repress and deny "this awful fact."

In one of the most stunning moments of cross-racial identification in the work, after Damon has been taken in by the police as a suspect for the killings he committed earlier, he imagines that the "general public [might feel] so revolted that they would want to drag him into some dirty alley and take his life and be done with it." But rather than hating this imagined lynch mob, he *identifies* with them: "He understood that reaction and feared it; it was the same cold fury he had felt against Herndon and Gil and Hilton. . . . Should such now fall to him, *he would be watching his own compulsions in reverse!*" (503; emphasis added). The marauding vigilante mobs of *Native Son*, which Wright figured in Bigger's mind as implacable, natural forces (recall the blizzard that covers Chicago in whiteness as Bigger is being hunted down in a citywide manhunt) are transformed in *The Outsider* into mirror images of Damon's own personality—a kind of sinister "community of feeling." And in case the reader overlooks this comparison and its implications, Houston restates it explicitly: "Today the *compulsive* acts of the lynching mobs have become enthroned in each individual heart. Every man now acts as a criminal, a policeman, a judge, and an executioner" (564; emphasis added). Every person, regardless of race, has the potential to murder unless she is able to keep that "compulsion" or "impulse" in check—blacks share this capacity with whites because they share the same conditioning forces of Western modernity. Although these are negative examples, demonstrating the capacity for senseless destruction, the inverse is also true—"man," as his own ultimate "law giver," also can be fundamentally creative and a force for good in society. For example, Damon and Houston are both "impulsive criminals," but Houston can "curb his desires" because he chose to become a detective as a sort of psychic safety valve. As a detective, he can "protect himself against himself by hunting down other criminals! [He has] balanced his emotional drives! He could experience vicariously all the destructive furies of the murderer, the thief, the sadist, without being held to accountability" (174).

In contrast to outsiders such as Damon and Houston, those who recognize that Western man's "heart, his spirit, is the deadliest thing in creation"—are the *insiders*, the Erskine Fowlers of the world who are profoundly dangerous because they lack true self-consciousness and are thus unaware of their own capacity for destructiveness. One year after *The Outsider* appears, Wright redeploys his thesis on the heart and spirit of Western man, but this time his test case is the corporate executive, a commonplace figure of normative white masculine authority in midcentury America. Despite the differences in the protagonists' racial identity and personality, *Savage Holiday*'s moral and psychological arguments are essentially the same as those of *The Outsider*, though rendered with a focus on the insider. Fowler is described as "a six-foot, hulking, heavy, muscular man with a Lincoln-like, quiet, stolid face.... His facial features seemed hewn firm and whole from some endurable substance; his eyes were steady; he was the kind of man to whom one intuitively and readily rendered a certain degree of instant deference ... with no hint in his attitude of apology for himself or his existence, confidant of his inalienable right to confront you and demand his modest due of respect" (*Savage Holiday* 14). Fowler at first appears to conform perfectly to the ideal of WASP manhood and the Protestant work ethic. He has earned respect and financial independence from having worked tirelessly as a "faithful steward" of Longevity Life Insurance (14).[10] As "the superintendent of the Mount Ararat Baptist Sunday School," he is also a man of standing in the religious community" (121). But these markers of virtue soon prove to be symptoms of weakness after Fowler loses what Wright describes in the aforementioned interview as "the props and supports of a daily task to perform."

Fowler and Damon are each other's negative image; despite their surface differences, they share a surprising number of similarities, and their juxtaposition affords important insights into the other's character. The most important point of overlap is that they are both what the social science discourse of the day would have described as "victims of bad mothering." As mentioned in the earlier analysis of Petry's *Country Place*, bad mothers could damage their sons either by "maternal overprotection" or "maternal rejection." Ruth Feldstein has shown that "all forms of maternal pathology caused one of two basic problems: sons who were either insufficiently aggressive, inhibited, and sexually passive and repressed; or sons who were too aggressive, insufficiently cooperative, and violent" (60). Damon is nothing if not "too aggressive, insufficiently cooperative, and violent." He is a self-described "impulsive criminal" who after abandoning the "responsibilities and obligations" of his earlier life launches into what amounts to a killing spree, murdering three people in just over a few months. Damon believes that it was his mother who "had taught him to feel what he was now feeling. He was at this moment living out the sense of life that she had conferred upon him, a sense of life which, in the end, he had accepted as his own. *It had been her moral strictures... that had made him a criminal in a deeper sense than Houston's questions so far could admit"* (512; emphasis added). Damon has suffered from what a contemporary psychologist might have described as "mother domination." Fowler, on the other hand, has been a victim of "maternal rejection." He, like Tony (the boy who falls to his death), was mocked by other children for his mother's sexual libertinism—*"all the boys had said that his mother was bad"*—and he recalls being angry at his mother *"for having gone off and left that night when he'd been ill"* (216, 220; emphasis in original). When she "abandons" him, he has a fantasy that *"he had taken a dirty brick bat and had beaten the doll's head in, had crushed it and had told Gladys: 'There's my mamma. . . . I killed her; I killed her 'cause she's a bad woman'"* (216; emphasis in original). He then fantasizes that his mother had said, *"Look in the mirror and see how bad you are!"* Damon, too, imagines that he has killed his mother: "[H]is mother had been dead for him for years, and that was why he had been able to reflect on her so coldly and analytically while she had been living." When Houston tells Damon that his mother has died, the detective even claims that "[i]t is believed that she died of shock, the shock of what you had done to her" (511). But Damon's mother's literal death seems less significant to Houston than Damon's lack of visible reaction: "Last night you stood there in my office and *committed the greatest and last crime of all.* You didn't bat an eye when I told you that your mother was dead. . . . *Boy, you killed your mother long, long ago. You must have known your mother well, understood her both emotionally and intellectually*; and when one can see and weigh one's mother like that, well, she's dead to one" (562; emphasis added). In stark contrast to Damon, Fowler responds to his dead (symbolically killed) bad mother by becoming a case study in what would have been considered excessive male passivity and sexual repression. He is a middle-aged bachelor with no sexual experience, and he has spent his entire life utterly dependent on the authority of others. He cloaks his gynophobia in moral righteousness, which takes its sanction from religious dicta.

Fowler's religiosity is part of what Wright earlier described as his "moral problem"; it is another sign of his disturbed self-relation and psychic dependency, that is, another symptom of his privation. Early drafts of the novel spend much more time detailing Fowler's religious commitments, including extensive scenes in which he interacts with his Aunt Tillie, the highly religious woman who raised him. It is her idea that he start going to church, a proposition that he eagerly embraces because it allows him to avoid spending time at home alone, to avoid privacy, on the one day a week in which his mind is not preoccupied with work. Wright in fact considered naming the novel "Sunday Sickness," "Everyday as Sunday," and "Seven Sundays a Week," among other titles.[11] Echoes of this emphasis remain in the published title's reference to a "holiday," the modern version of the "holy day." Wright underscores how religion serves a primarily compensatory, rather than moral or spiritual, function in Fowler's life when he goes to church on the morning of Tony's death. As soon as he arrives, he feels "contented. He was *home*" (85; emphasis in original). He introduces the morning's topic, "GOD'S ETERNAL FAMILY," which is taken from Matthew 12: 46–50 (85; capitalization in original). During his sermon, Fowler speaks passionately about how Jesus implored his listeners to follow his example in "den[ying] His mother and His brothers" in favor of "God's universal family." "What terrible words! But what *saving* words!" (88; emphasis in original). Christianity allows Fowler to avoid the terrors of his own "home," "saving" him from becoming fully conscious of his feelings about his biological mother. It operates simultaneously as a mechanism for repressing the maternal and as a means of preserving the security offered by the idea of the family—an idea which Damon believes that he, as an outsider, is beyond. Accordingly, Christianity is a symptom of willful alienation, not Western enlightenment; it prevents an authentic self-relation.

More than a key to his psychic configuration and existential crisis, Fowler's religiosity is central to Wright's larger critique of Western modernity.[12] Once again, *The Outsider* makes explicit what remains primarily implicit in the final, published version of *Savage Holiday*. Just prior to meeting Detective Houston, Damon encounters a priest, whom he resents because he believes that the "priest was secure and walked the earth with a divine mandate.... Cross ... regarded him as a kind of dressed up savage intimidated by totems and taboos that differed in kind but not in degree from those of the most primitive of peoples" (156). Wright continues what is implicitly racialized language by observing, the "*real slaves* of the twentieth century are not those sharecroppers who wince at the stinging swish of a riding boss's whip; the slaves of today are those who are congenitally afraid of the new and the untried, who fall on their knees and break into a deep sweat when confronted with the horrible truth of the uncertain and enigmatic nature of life" (484; emphasis added). Fowler, who lectures his neighbor Mabel that she should go to church because "one learns to live by following moral laws," is undoubtedly an emotionally "primitive," "dressed up savage"—when he is cast out of the insurance business and is literally and figuratively stripped of his three-piece suit, he becomes a murderous, "naked savage" running amok through civilization. Even more striking is the way in which Wright signifies on the concept of the slave, which he extracts from its racial history for redeployment in his existentialist, antiracist critique. Katherine Adams has shown that American slavery was once justified through assertions of "black privation . . . where it was argued that Africans lacked the self-awareness that makes one fully human and capable of self-possession, and were naturally dependent upon control by others" (18–19). Wright dispenses with biological determinism and argues that the "real slaves of the twentieth century" are figures of spiritual, moral, and emotional lack. The "slaves of today" are those who cannot face the unguaranteed existence of disenchanted modernity; they shun freedom and the creative possibilities of existential privacy, relying instead on the safety of external authority and established traditions. Wright's striking redefinition of slavery—in which he decouples race and freedom in Western modernity—underwrites his efforts to break the chains that bind him as an artist to "the Negro problem." That is, it is an assertion of his authorial racial privacy. Wright as an artist is asserting his right to explore "the new and untried."

Wright contends that modern slaves have responded to the decline of religious authority in the West, and their consequent "psychological nakedness," by turning to any number of religious substitutes—including racism, imperial conquest, and even the obsessive pursuit of wealth through work, which Wright says in America is "a kind of religion" (Kinnamon and Fabre, *Conversations* 168).[13] The religious function of work is especially clear in a passage removed from the published version of the novel, in which Fowler's boss declared, "Let no Doubting Thomas persuade you that the Cathedral of 20th century business is not man's tried and tested school for ferreting out life's knotty meanings and secrets!"[14] For Fowler, work has served largely the same purpose as religion: "Work had not only given Erskine his livelihood and conferred upon him the approval of his fellowmen; but, above all, *it made him stranger to a part of himself that he feared and wanted never to know*. At some point in his childhood he had assumed toward himself the role of a policeman . . . locked himself up in a prison cage of toil" (33). In addition to producing his self-alienation, it has also, like religion, functioned as a substitute family. The book opens with Fowler's retirement party, one that he is participating in against his will, during which the president asserts correctly, "Brothers and sisters, just think—Erskine Fowler looked upon Longevity Life as his family!" (12). This domestic sentiment is repeated several times during the scene, an association that reinforces the depth of the company's betrayal. "For twenty years he had *worshipped* these men," the narrator tells us, "and now they were hating him" (27; emphasis added). Notably, the president identifies himself as "head of this family," and concludes his speech by "clap[ping] Fowler in a fatherly way on the back, pronouncing: God bless and keep you, Erskine!" (14).

This familial "abandonment" (26) strikes at the core of Fowler's psychic defenses, threatening to open repressed primal wounds. He immediately feels a "subtle sense of terror, potent, but vague, seep[ing] into his soul" (32). He also feels "repelled ... [by a] haunting sense of not quite being his own master." Within a day of this betrayal and the death of his neighbor's son, Fowler hits upon the idea of marrying Tony's mother, Mabel, as a way to contain his guilt and recuperate his lost self-mastery. Due to his dysfunctional relationship with his mother, he has never had an intimate relationship with a woman, but as he faces being engulfed by privacy, the prospect of domestic authority offers him a glimmer of hope: "His lips parted as the idea swam luminously in his consciousness. She'd obey him! She was simple; and above all, he'd be the boss; he'd dominate her completely" (134). If he can privatize Mable, then he can begin to reconstitute the hegemonic privacy threatened by his job loss. Mable resists, and he condemns her viciously, "his hate breaking forth in a torrent of words to *lash* at her, to humble her, to break her down so that *he could love her, master her*, have his say-so about her" (199; emphasis added). For a moment Mabel, in a state of desperation, considers his offer. She pleads, "Erskine, teach me how to live, won't you? ... I'm through; I'm licked ... You'll teach me, tell me what's right?" (208). She quickly reconsiders, though, recognizing that to allow herself to be incorporated into his private life, through his offer of marriage and material comfort, would turn her into Fowler's moral slave. After she refuses what to her would be akin to a social death, Fowler kills her in an all-white kitchen: "[S]he flicked on the light and stood nude amid the white refrigerator, the white gas stove, the gleaming sink, the white topped table" (214). Wright implies here that the postwar consumerist ideal of "female freedom" allegedly available in modern housewifery was little more than "white slavery."[15]

Thus, although Wright repeatedly employs midcentury social science discourse about the dangers of bad mothering, his narrative refuses the patriarchal nuclear family and domestic arrangements as a viable resolution to Fowler's existential crisis. Instead, after killing Mable, Fowler immediately turns himself in to the police, bringing to fruition his lifelong habit of self-policing (33). After being cast *outside* into a world of personal freedom and responsibility, he succeeds in less than two days in getting himself back "inside" what Wright at the end of his career termed "the law of the father."[16] As a prisoner, he is happily relieved of the self-reliance demanded by existential privacy. He eagerly submits to being privatized by the state, which removes his capacity for autonomy: the narrator tells us that "Erskine was a model prisoner, [and] had adjusted himself with amazing swiftness to prison routine, was aiding in the prison chapel, and was doing religious work among the inmates."[17]

Fowler is what Wright elsewhere describes as one of "the emotionally thin-skinned [who] cannot imagine, even in the middle of our twentieth century, a world without external emotional props to keep them buttressed to a stance of constant meaning and justification, *a world filled with overpowering mother and father and child images to anchor them in emotional security, to keep a sense of the warm, intimate, sustaining influence of family alive*" ("Tradition and Industrialization" 710; emphasis added). Cross Damon appears to eschew such familial security, but in fact Wright incorporates an idealized, alternative "family," one predicated on a kind of fraternal interracial intimacy—that is, a nonhierarchical form of interracial sympathy, understood as a "conformity of feelings, inclinations, or temperament" (*OED*). Detective Houston, whom Damon already has suspected of "sympathizing with him" (565), visits Damon in the hospital when he is dying. Houston asks Damon, "with the voice of a brother asking an urgent, confidential question," what he wants Houston to tell others: "to make a bridge from man to man. . . . Men hate themselves and it makes them hate others. . . . We must find some way of being good to ourselves. . . . Man is all we've got. I wish I could ask men to meet themselves. . . . We're strangers to ourselves. . . . I've lived alone, but I'm everywhere. . . . The myth men are going. . . . The real men, the last men are coming. Somebody must prepare the way for them . . . Tell the world what they are like. . . . We are here already, if others but had the courage to see us" (584, 585).

In the end, though Damon is "beyond the family" (562), he and Houston are "brothers." Race doesn't interfere with their familial bond because they are psychologically related as outsiders and, underneath it all, as Western men. But this vision of family is not sentimentalized. For example, race doesn't prevent Damon and Fowler, and even Bigger, from belonging to the same "family" of Western modernity that produces the lynch mob. Despite the many differences in social circumstances and local environmental forces, they are Western men, and thus share a capacity for compulsive violence. To a certain extent, Wright had been promulgating this position since he discovered that "Bigger Thomas was not black all the time; he was white, too, and there were literally millions of him, everywhere.... [A]s a writer, I was fascinated by the similarity of the emotional tensions of Bigger in America and Bigger in Nazi Germany and Bigger in old Russia. All Bigger Thomases, white and black, felt tense, afraid, nervous, hysterical, and restless" ("How Bigger Was Born" 518).

The Outsider, Savage Holiday, and even *Native Son* are thus about much more than "whiteness" or "blackness." They all convey Wright's belief that to solve "the big problems" of Western civilization, we must first abandon the "primitive" Western tendency toward racial, gender, and religious chauvinism in favor of sympathetic psychological fraternity—fraternity made possible by the tradition-smashing conditions of Western modernity. Modernity's capacity for generating what Wright describes as chronic and critical skepticism, while challenging and threatening, is also a conduit for making "a bridge from man to man," a metaphor of egalitarian sociability that allows for existential privacy. "In spite of myself," Wright says, "my imagination is constantly *leaping ahead* and trying to reshape the world I see ... toward a form in which all men could share my creative restlessness" (705; emphasis added). Modernity unleashes "creative restlessness," allowing one to move beyond such Western "traditions" as Christianity, Jim Crow, and imperialism, irrational systems designed to fix (racialized) bodies, and inauthentic identities, in the past. But as *Savage Holiday* makes clear, these traditions keep white men trapped in the past as well. Despite the self-congratulatory claims of midcentury white liberal nationalists, these works make clear that "white racial prejudice" was not the only "backward custom" of an otherwise perfect and rational American democracy; rather, it was but one of many symptoms of persistent Western "savagery." The West faces a problem more subtle and radical than "the Negro problem"; the West's greatest problem is that it is not Western enough. Perhaps more than any other writer in this study, Wright showed how modernity was much more than the "period and the region in which black politics grew," as Gilroy puts it, but was the period and region in which existential privacy was possible.

Conclusion

Abandoning the Black Hero has investigated the question of why and to what effect did nearly every significant black novelist of the mid-twentieth century "abandon the black hero" in favor of white protagonists, if only momentarily. I have argued that the authors' sympathetic treatment of their white protagonists indicates neither a disavowal of blackness, nor a naïve assimilationist desire, but a bid for authorial racial privacy in a public sphere structured by the color line. Many black writers resented that "Negro literature" had become synonymous with racial protest, to the exclusion of other experiences, interests, and perspectives. The writers under study here experienced this delimited space of enunciation as yet another incarnation of Jim Crow, remanding black writers to the margins of public discourse as suffering, injured others. In response, the white-life authors refashioned themselves as *subjects*, rather than *objects*, of sympathy, a shift that opened up greater aesthetic freedom as well as new horizons of moral and critical authority.

The authors' sympathetic treatment of their white subjects in no way required them to forego critical engagement, however. These works are not "passing." In every case, they unsettle hegemonic understandings of whiteness in general, and white heteropatriarchy in particular, to show how the normative ideals that underwrite white manhood, and white privacy more generally, also injure whites themselves. In a powerful discursive inversion, the authors depict whites, rather than blacks, as bound, even enslaved and imprisoned, by mainstream ideals and traditions. The white-life novels suggest that it could be otherwise; they hold out the possibility that the "father's house," the archetypal scene of hegemonic privacy and the "law of the father," could in fact become a space of social transformation.

This trope is a reminder that the white-life novel's concerns frequently overlap with the concerns of novels centered on black life. For example, the one major black writer of this moment who did not author a white-life novel, Ralph Ellison, also drew on sympathy and privacy in his efforts to evade the restrictions inherent in the label "Negro writer." *Invisible Man* concludes with his narrator's query, "[W]ho knows, but that, on the lower frequencies, I speak for you?" (581). This sympathetic gesture challenges his white reader to do much more than feel his pain; the narrator dares his reader to recognize that they are coinheritors of the same national principles, the same national icons ("Ford, Edison, and Franklin" [7]), even the same Western traditions—recall that in the prologue the narrator descends "like Dante" into Louis Armstrong's music, and then hears "an old woman singing a spiritual as full of Weltschmerz as flamenco" (9).

Before the narrator can create this border-crossing, cosmopolitan enunciative space, however, with its concomitant epistemological and moral authority, the narrator had to first locate a space of racial privacy. He makes a "room of his own," as it were, out of a "hole in the ground" (6). He is initially chased into the hole by racist white vigilantes, but he then claims it as a surrogate domestic space. It is in this "shut-off and forgotten" basement in a whites-only building—located, not coincidentally, in a "border area" near, rather than in, Harlem—that he is able to withdraw from public life and for the first time develop an authentic self-relation. When he aspired to public life as a race man, his relation to himself had been distorted by his willingness to assume hegemonic versions of blackness—as an entertainer, as a conservative and then communist Booker T. Washington, and even as a "big black bruiser" (522). Once he withdraws from the external determination of racialized publicity, he develops the self-confidence and ingenuity to "solve the problem" (7)—if not the Negro problem, at least that of achieving true self-consciousness and intellectual autonomy. The space of privacy, however, is strikingly dreamlike, at times almost hallucinatory. Not only is the prologue marked by references to nightmare visions and "the spell of the reefer," but the narrator also claims to have wired his room with 1,369 light bulbs (8). "When I finish all four walls," he says, "then I'll start on the floor" (7). The surreality of his hole underscores how elusive, nearly impossible, privacy is for an African American in the mid-twentieth century.

Even so, Ellison and his white-life novel contemporaries "speak for you" by speaking from within, producing works that both "denounce and defend" (580) not only America's, but the West's, political, social, and cultural order. Moreover, as Ellison redresses violated black privacy through invoking shared national horizons, the white-life novelists produce privacy by recalling and then reimagining the ideals of white authority (domestic, regional, and national) that occlude black privacy in the first place.

The black American author's quest for racial privacy did not end in the mid-twentieth century, however. One of the larger goals of this study is to help readers recognize how the concerns and strategies of the postwar white-life novel are manifest throughout African American literary history, including our current moment. I conclude with a brief discussion of a recent work that approaches racial privacy by directly engaging with Ellison's analysis of the effects of public exposure—Percival Everett's *Erasure* (2001). The manner in which Everett reworks key themes from *Invisible Man* reveals how the conflicts around privacy and publicity endure, though in altered forms, for a post–civil rights and post–Black Aesthetic generation.

Everett's *Erasure* describes the experience of a black man plunged into racialized publicity, though with strikingly different results. From the opening lines of *Erasure*, the protagonist, Thelonious "Monk" Ellison, expresses a desire for privacy and an apprehension about exposure: "My journal is a private affair, but as I cannot know the time of my coming death, and since I am not disposed, however unfortunately, to the serious consideration of self-termination, I am afraid that others will see these pages" (1). As these lines and the book's title indicate, suicide is a central theme of *Erasure*. However, in contrast to the Invisible Man, Monk Ellison plunges into, rather than outside of, hegemonic concepts of blackness. Although he says he is *not* disposed to self-termination, by choosing to cynically participate in racialized mass publicity, he erases himself not just as an author, but as an individual. In the end, his formerly authentic self-relation is replaced by a relation to commodified, hegemonic blackness, a relation that destroys what little racial privacy he once had.

The ways in which racialized publicity injure Monk Ellison plainly echo the experiences of the Invisible Man, and Everett reinforces these parallels with repeated allusions to Ellison's novel. For this study, I am less concerned with teasing out the many moments of intertextuality between these works, and more concerned with the ways in which

Erasure portrays the baleful effects of African American literature *as a discourse*—one that imperils authorial racial privacy by functioning as an incitement to racial discourse. *Erasure* expresses these concerns in a manner strikingly similar to black authors and critics from the mid-twentieth century—even going so far as incorporating within the narrative a transparent rewriting of *Native Son*, the text (dis)credited with the ascendancy of racial protest as racial pathology. Fittingly, Monk Ellison titles his "realistic" portrayal of black life *My Pafology* (later renamed *Fuck*), and it operates in the life and career of its author in a manner akin to the way *Native Son* was seen to operate in the lives and careers of mid-twentieth-century black writers. *My Pafology*'s extraordinary popularity propels the protagonist's loss of authorial racial privacy; it causes him, in the words of Richard Wright, to become "regarded fatally as a Negro writer."

The majority of Monk Ellison's oeuvre parallels the white-life novel in that it falls beyond the recognizable limits of African American literature. Critics and editors regularly bring this apparent shortcoming to his attention.[1] One reviewer comments about a recent work that, although it is technically accomplished, "*one is lost to understand what this reworking of Aeschylus'* The Persians *has to do with the African American experience*" (2; emphasis in original). Monk previously had written one novel that addressed racial conflict—his one self-described "realistic" novel—which he says sold well and received good reviews. However, he adds flatly, "I hated writing the novel. I hated reading the novel. I hated thinking about the novel" (61). Monk identifies himself early on in the novel as someone who "hardly ever think[s] about race. Those times when I did think about it a lot I did so because of my guilt for not thinking about it. I don't believe in race" (2). He acknowledges that racism exists, and that it can at times have life-threatening consequences, "but that's just the way it is." In other words, that's just "reality." According to reviewers of his work, though, an African American writer unconcerned with the "Negro problem" is "unrealistic" and uninteresting.

What Monk does believe in is the value of art, and the integrity of those committed to it beyond commercial concerns. This is the privacy that matters to him. Art is inseparable from his sense of self, and it is his most vital source of self-expression and subject formation. One of the means by which he introduces these concerns is through a series of dialogues woven throughout the narrative proper; they are set off by italics, and appear to be ideas penned down in Monk's journal as reflections on his own aesthetic and personal struggles. Most of the dialogues take place between European visual artists (Ernst Barlach and Paul Klee, Ernst Kirchner and Max Klinger, for example), though a few take place between Adolph Hitler and Dietrich Eckhart, a German author and Nazi propagandist. The majority of the conversations address the Nazi persecution of artists whose thinking and art were considered "degenerate" (49). Monk confesses that he had to "admit to a profound fascination with Hitler's relationship to art and how he so reminded me of so many of the artistic purists I had come to know" (39). Monk depicts the Nazis' commitment to pure blood (39) as expressed through a desire for pure art—or rather, a desire for art that will aesthetically manifest the superiority of pure Aryan blood.

The Nazi's violent suppression of impure art gets refracted in surprising ways in the main narrative. The resistant artists seem like the obvious point of identification for Monk, but a complex, though indirect, identification with the Nazis surfaces as well, particularly in Monk's reactions to the blockbuster success of *We's Lives in Da Ghetto*, a novel by an African American author, Juanita Mae Jenkins. Its plot is both clichéd and ridiculous, a hodgepodge of stereotypes about black urban life, and the prose is marked by flagrantly imprecise renderings of African American vernacular English—as evidenced in the book's title. Aside from being a best seller and netting $3 million for movie rights, the novel also garners reviews from highbrow periodicals that hail it as "a masterpiece of African American literature." While all of these facts appall Monk, what most disturbs him is the public perception that Jenkins's work is a "true" or "real" representation of African American life. Monk asks, "[W]hy did Juanita Mae Jenkins send me running for the toilet? I imagine it was because Tom Clancy was not trying to sell his book to me by suggesting that the crew of his high-tech submarine was a representation of his race (*however fitting a metaphor*). Nor was his publisher marketing it in that way. If you didn't like Clancy's white people, you could go out and read about some others" (214; emphasis in original). While Monk was coolly philosophical about the existence of racists who would like to do him—and other African Americans—harm, he is shaken to the core of his being by Jenkins's success because her success affects him personally; its representation of black life facilitates racist entailments on his authorial privacy. Although he is relatively successful—he is a full professor at a prestigious university—his career has nevertheless been hampered because he is a black author who doesn't write "African American literature," which in the narrative is synonymous with work that depicts black life as defined by violence, ignorance, poverty, and familial dysfunction.

In the moment of furious inspiration immediately preceding the writing of *My Pafology*, which was precipitated by "star[ing] at Juanita Mae Jenkins's face on *Time* magazine," he begins "screaming inside, complaining that I didn't sound like that, that my mother didn't sound like that, that my father didn't sound like that and I imagined myself sitting on a park bench counting the knives in my switchblade collection and a man came up to me and he asked me what I was doing and my mouth opened and I couldn't help what came out, 'Why fo you be axin?'" (61–62).

Here and throughout *Erasure*, mass-mediated notions of African American literature, and Jenkins's work in particular, abject Monk, eliciting nausea and pain that "started in my feet and coursed through my legs, up my spine and into my brain." The public desire for literary depictions of black pathology deeply injures him and robs him of his self-possession; he imagines losing control of his own voice, and begins speaking instead in the voice of hegemonic blackness. His loss of voice plainly foreshadows his complete loss of self that occurs with the success of *My Pafology*. Monk's outraged private denunciation of *We's Lives* echoes that of the Nazi outrage against degenerate, impure art. Everett twists the knife by having Monk finally succeed commercially by producing a novel that conforms to what amounts to a Nazi perspective on black life. He reinforces this association with the following exchange between D. W. Griffith, the director of *The Birth of a Nation,* and Richard Wright. Griffith tells Wright, "I like your book very much" and Wright replies with ambiguous politeness, "thank you" (193).

Monk has Wright in mind when he begins writing *My Pafology*. He recalls "passages of *Native Son* and *The Color Purple* and *Amos 'n' Andy*," a juxtapositioning that renders the former two works, considered by many as "classics" of modern African America literature, equivalent to acts of minstrelsy. Notably, he writes the work in his father's office, and on his "father's old manual typewriter. . . . a book on which I knew I could never put my name" (61–62). The insistent connection to his father resonates on multiple levels. We know that his father committed suicide, and we come to learn that his father had an extramarital affair that produced an "illegitimate" child, the existence of which he kept hidden from the world. Thus the novel that he writes as a parody of "African American literature" can be seen as an illegitimate child and, indirectly, as a form of suicide—an act of self-erasure.

The work begins to disrupt his sense of self after it receives a reception identical to that of Jenkins's work—in terms of money, publicity, and prestige as a work of racial realism—and he chooses *not* to publicly repudiate the work. After being offered huge sums of money, he even agrees to go on television as the pseudonymous Stagg R. Leigh, whom he presents as a thuggish ex-convict recently out of prison. He initially believes that he can cynically manipulate the public in the spirit of Ellison's Rinehart. His rude behavior both frightens and pleases his public because it conforms to their idea of the surly black criminal: "There he was for public scrutiny and the public was loving him" (248). After "Stagg" meets with the movie producer Wiley Morgenstein to discuss film rights for the book, Monk's editor tells him that Morgenstein is "in love with you. He's scared to death of you, but he said, '*That fuckin' guy's da real thing*.'" Monk quips in return, "He's right" (222).

Allusions to Paul Laurence Dunbar and James Weldon Johnson in the narrative suggest that Monk can be seen as "wearing the mask" or as "passing," but as the Invisible Man discovers when he takes on the persona of Rinehart, the ethical distance between one's masquerade and one's true self quickly collapses. Unlike the Invisible Man, who terminates the charade and retreats into privacy, the increasingly emotionally unstable Monk stays in character to such an extent that he accepts the National Book Award on national television as Stagg R. Leigh. Monk is thereby framed publicly as a black criminal just as Van Go Jenkins is in the climax of *My Pafology*. It seems that the prestige of the National Book Award pushes Monk over the edge, given that it is supposed to recognize the highest achievements in fiction. But by accepting the award as Stagg, and, once again, choosing not to denounce the work, he has aided in his own erasure—in what he considers his social death—by validating works like *My Pafology* as accomplished examples of African American literature.

Given *Erasure*'s overtly critical attitude toward works like *Native Son*—works that depict the inevitable fall of the black protagonist due to the overwhelming forces of racism—Monk Ellison's dissolution must give the reader pause. He appears to have been reduced by hegemonic racial publicity to black privation. Is the reader to assume that Monk's demise represents the "hard, gritty truth" of racism that he had naively denied (2)? If so, how can this be reconciled with the novel's extremely skeptical treatment of narratives that appear to exploit black characters stripped of their consciousness and political will? Is this ending a trap? Is it bait cast by Everett, who conspicuously incorporates a trout-fishing motif in *Erasure*, including references to "canny" and "wary" brown trout (58)? Is Everett the canny brown trout, or is he the fisherman deploying racial bait to catch those readers who picked up the novel unself-consciously looking for "African American literature"? Recall that Everett, like Monk Ellison, has written numerous novels, most of which do not conform to commonplace notions of African American literature (see, for example, *Glyph* [1999]), but *Erasure*, like *My Pafology*, and before that, *Second Failure*, has outsold them all. *Erasure* even mirrors *My Pafology* in that it has been optioned for a movie (reportedly to be directed by Angela Bassett). Consider also the appearance of Percival Everett as a character in his later novel *I Am Not Sidney Poitier* (2009), in which he states directly that he didn't like *Erasure*, adding, "I didn't like writing it, and I didn't like it when I was done with it" (226). This phrasing is strikingly similar to the language that Monk uses when talking about *Second Failure*, his "realistic" novel about race. These issues cannot easily be resolved, and that may be his point. *Erasure* insistently prompts the reader to question not merely the content of African American literature, but the implications of the deep-seated, often unconscious pleasures sought within works that are placed within this categorization. Everett even depicts Monk "contemplating the notion of a public and its relationship to the health of art" (144).

As these works and the postwar white-life novels make clear, African American literary production far exceeds what the public often expects—and sometimes what it desires—from African American literature, much less Negro literature. Works like *Erasure* elicit discomfiting questions—to what extent do we, as critics, readers, and authors—as the reading public satirized by Everett—continue to frame Monk Ellison as Stagg R. Leigh? To what extent do we still regard Richard Wright, author of both *Native Son* and *Savage Holiday*, "fatally as a Negro writer"?

It is of course ironic that it was necessary to group these works according to the authors' racial identity before I could recognize the manner in which they were struggling to resist Jim Crow infringements on their authorial privacy. I had to violate their racial privacy to identify their efforts to protect their racial privacy. But not all intrusions against privacy are equal, and the intent of this study has been to highlight what comes into focus when black writers decenter black life as the principal object of inquiry. Not surprisingly, a great many things emerge—frequently overlooked themes, genres, intellectual orientations, as well as modes of thought and representation. No less important, however, is what the study of these works brings to our attention about our own critical habits. As I've suggested, the imperative that African American literary studies maintain a position of critical exteriority to whiteness—a position of noncomplicity with whiteness as white supremacy—has the unintended consequence of reproducing certain intellectual limitations that the white-life novels were at such pains to transcend.[2] Thus one of the benefits of attending to sympathy and privacy in these midcentury works is that it enables us to better perceive representational strategies and themes that have been obscured by interpretive practices predicated on an identificatory refusal of whiteness.[3] Instead, we can see the white-life novel enacting identificational mobility in the service of aesthetic freedom. Attention to sympathy and racial privacy *throughout* the tradition can help us recognize the ways that current sociopolitical desires can at times produce a needlessly prescriptive notion of African American literature and literary history. Sympathy and privacy as concepts thus may help us to *recover* the black hero as well.

Notes

Introduction

1. Other than "Health Card," which appeared in *Harper's* and won Yerby the 1945 O. Henry Award for new short fiction, nearly all of Yerby's short stories were published in Popular Front magazines, including *Tomorrow*, Jack Conroy's *New Anvil*, and Louis Adamic's *Common Ground*. I discuss Yerby's relation to the Popular Front in chapters 1 and 4.

2. I borrow the phrase "white-life novel" from Robert Fikes Jr., "Escaping the Literary Ghetto: African American Authors of White Life Novels, 1946-1994" and "The Persistent Allure of Universality: African American Authors of White Life Novels, 1890-1945." Although Fikes provides a very useful overview of the texts, his essays are primarily descriptive, not analytic. He makes no attempt to investigate how different authors were engaging with the idea of whiteness as a social and political category.

3. Several other white-life novels were published during the ten-year period under examination here. Motley published a sequel to *Knock, Let No Man Write My Epitaph* (1958), as well as *We Fished All Night* (1951). Yerby published a novel almost every year for the next twenty years. All but three of his thirty-three novels have white protagonists. William Gardner Smith published *Anger at Innocence* in 1950. Considerations of time and space led me to limit my selections. I left out Smith's work because it is a minor novel by a minor writer that neither sold well nor received significant critical attention. It is worth mentioning that its focus on white psychological and domestic crises fits the pattern displayed by other novels in this study. The only significant black writer who did not write a white-life novel is Ralph Ellison, who of course published only one novel during his lifetime. He did, however, write a short story with a white protagonist called "A Party Down at the Square," which features the reactions of a white boy who witnesses a lynching; it was not published during his lifetime, but appears in the posthumous collection *Flying Home and Other Stories* (1996). The editor John Callahan estimates that the story was written during the 1930s or 1940s,

which would locate it during the era of Ellison's more formal associations with the radical Left. The story's antilynching critique and valorization of interracial sympathy would certainly be in keeping with contemporary Popular Front sensibilities. It is also worth noting, though, that Ellison's unfinished second novel, published initially as *Juneteenth* (1999), features a phenotypically white central character, Adam Sunraider, whose racial origins are never determined.

4. Lawrence P. Jackson's *The Indignant Generation: A Narrative History of African American Writers and Critics, 1934–1960* provides a valuable and engaging overview of this era. The scope and objective of his study leads him to provide limited discussion of the works collectively, and very little (or in some cases, no) analysis of the works individually. Another notable work addressing this moment (but that does not address the white-life novel directly) is Bill V. Mullen's *Popular Fronts: Chicago and African American Cultural Politics, 1935–46*.

5. See Gates, *The Signifying Monkey*; and Gates, "Talking Black: Critical Signs of the Times."

6. Regarding the "urge to whiteness," see Hughes, "The Negro Artist and the Racial Mountain." Paralleling this judgment, recent work focused on recuperating the history of the Left from decades of Cold War opprobrium has tended to point to the immediate postwar years as lamentable for the dissolution of radical energies. At first glance, the white-life novel could be (mis)taken as symptom of this trend. Bill Mullen's study of the Negro Popular Front in Chicago argues that "Chicago almost immediately became a site symbolic of the *impossibility* of sustained progressive or radical black cultural work, and a home to a new black bourgeoisie endowed and entitled by postwar prosperity to make over the streets in Bronzeville. The subsequent exodus and internal silencing of dissenting voices led to a diminishing of black radical intellectualism with Chicago parallel to that nationally" (184). He cites authors such as Wright and Motley as part of the exodus and silencing. From this vantage point, not only do the white-life novels appear to represent a racial defection, but also a broader political and class-based apostasy confluent with the rise of a reformist and relatively quietist black bourgeoisie.

7. Certainly one of the most dogmatic and critical assessments of the idea of the white-life novel comes from Molefi Kete Asante, who argues:

> There are two types of texts produced by individuals who have been removed or have removed themselves from terms of blackness: the decapitated text and the lynched text. A text which is decapitated exists without cultural presence in the historical experiences of the creator; a lynched text is one that has been strung up with the tropes and figures of the dominating culture. African American authors who have tried to "shed their race" have been known to produce both types of texts. The decapitated text is the contribution of the author who writes with no discernible African cultural element; the aim appears to be to distance herself or himself from the African cultural self. Among the best practitioners of this genre of writing is the author Frank Yerby. His contributions to literature have been made as a part of the European and white experience in the West. Although he responded to criticism long enough to write the *Dahomeans* [sic], he remained fundamentally committed to a style of writing which placed him outside of his own historical experiences. Thus, his

African voice remains essentially silent. Yerby is the kind of author one reads and says, if you do not know, that this must be a white writer. Even my white students are surprised to discover that the author of some of the finest Southern plantation novels is an African American. While he became relatively successful in a commercial sense in this vein of writing, Frank Yerby has no clear literary tradition and adds to no new school of aesthetics. He produces decapitated texts with no guiding heads and no sense of soul.

8. While I argue that the white-life novel "frees" the authors to enter certain *public* forms of debate, I also, following Claudia Tate, attend to the manner in which whiteness enables the articulation of other private, socially unsanctioned, and frequently disavowed forms of desire. Cultural formations such as the novel often function as vehicles for personal fantasy, ones that facilitate the expression of desires that may exceed the limits of social acceptability—impossible desires, so to speak. Here attention to the nature of cross-racial performance in these works becomes especially important; careful scrutinization of these representations of whiteness helps make legible the powerful though obscure and deeply vexed *identifications* that underwrite these texts.

9. See, for example, Amelia E. Johnson, *Clarence and Corinne* (1890); Paul Lawrence Dunbar, *The Uncalled* (1898) and *The Love of Landry* (1900); Charles Waddell Chesnutt, *The Colonel's Dream* (1904); and William Attaway *Let Me Breathe Thunder* (1939).

10. Ellison originally wrote his essay "Twentieth Century Fiction and the Black Mask of Humanity" in 1946; it was reprinted in *Shadow and Act* (1964). The pagination refers to the Modern Library Edition of *The Collected Essays of Ralph Ellison*.

11. I discuss this essay at length in chapter 1. In a letter to a friend, Hurston likened white liberal discourses about African Americans to the exclusionary logics of segregation: "[F]ixing us in a type and place is a sort of intellectual Jim Crow and is just as insulting as the physical aspects. In fact, it helps to bolster the physical aspects when our 'friends' defend us so disastrously" ("To Burton Rascoe" 503).

12. Castiglia, "Abolition's Racial Interiors and the Making of White Civic Depth," 34. See also his *Interior States*, esp. chap. 3.

13. I borrow the phrase "critical exteriority" from Robyn Wiegman, "The Ends of New Americanism."

14. In chapter 1, I provide a brief overview of the various political, economic, and social forces shaping the dramatic expansion of "whiteness" in the first half of the twentieth century.

15. I adapt this Foucauldian phrase from Roderick A. Ferguson, *Aberrations in Black*, especially chap. 2.

16. These notions of privacy clearly overlap, and they also do not include the full scope of subjects implied by the term "privacy." I do not attempt in this study to provide an exhaustive or essential definition of "privacy." The literature on "privacy" is vast, and the one thing on which all agree is the near impossibility of establishing conclusively the meaning and content of "privacy." I concur with the legal scholar Daniel Solove, who argues that privacy always has been and will remain contextual and historically specific. Thus, a more productive way to approach privacy is to focus on those *activities that privacy protects*, including authorial autonomy, but also extending

beyond it to encompass protection from intrusion in matters considered essential to autonomous and dignified selfhood—this typically includes noninterference around the family and home (which of course connotes matters of sexuality and intimacy), freedom of political and religious association, the right to pursue educational and economic opportunity, informational privacy, etc. (see Solove, *Understanding Privacy*). My thinking on privacy has also been influenced by Katherine Adams, *Owning Up*. I discuss race and privacy in greater detail in chapter 2. For an interesting discussion of race and privacy in the context of American law and visual culture, see Eden Osucha, "The Whiteness of Privacy." On race, privacy, property, and the law in the context of nineteenth-century African American literature, see Jon-Christian Suggs, *Whispered Consolations*, esp. chap. 4.

17. I do not mean to overstate the extent to which the denial of privacy stood as a specific, explicit goal of the Jim Crow regime; it is one aspect of the diminishment of the civic worth of black citizens. When I talk about the denial of privacy for African Americans, I am speaking metaphorically about a denial of political, social, intellectual, and cultural autonomy.

18. Despite these avowed ideological justifications, it must be recognized that Jim Crow received a powerful impetus from an ongoing investment in exploiting African American labor—both in the agricultural sector in the South, and in the manufacturing and service sectors in the North. The violations of black *political*, *familial*, and *social* privacy were a tool and correlate of the need to violate black *economic* privacy. I am indebted to Kenneth Warren for this clarification. Also, although I discuss the coconstitutive relationship between white privacy and black privacy throughout the book, I discuss it at length in chapter 2 with particular reference to Petry's early short fiction.

19. The issue was entitled *The Negro in Literature: The Current Scene*, and is reprinted in full in Trudier Harris, *Afro-American Writers 1940–1955*. It is worth noting that the issue excluded the best-known black communist critics, such as Eugene Holmes, Eugene Gordon, Doxey Wilkerson, and Lloyd Brown (not to mention Richard Wright, who by this point had publicly renounced all ties with the Communist Party). Lloyd Brown critiqued the symposium, though, in his two-part essay "Which Way for the Negro Writer?"

20. West published a work on the black middle class entitled *The Living Is Easy* (1948).

21. It should be noted here that Redding is not *recommending* that black writers avoid writing about black people. He goes on to encourage black writers to exploit the "mine of creative material [offered by the "Negro's special race-experience" which is] no longer *artificially bounded* by fear and shame, [and] is full of lessons and of truth for the whole world" (305; emphasis added).

22. As I discuss in chapter 4, Frank Yerby was singled out more than any other white-life novelist for this kind of praise, most likely because his "success" with the subject of slavery implied an unprecedented mastering of its painful legacy.

23. Blyden Jackson offered a corrective to what he considered Brown's misreading of the contributors: "They did not decry the Negro writer choosing a Negro theme. They were merely mindful of the number of Negroes who had chosen Negro themes not because they were artists but because they were Negroes" ("Faith without Works" 386).

24. Arthur Davis attributes the appearance of white-life novels to the successes of the civil rights movement and laments that "when the enemy capitulated [to the inevitability of integration], he shattered our most fruitful literary tradition. The possibility of imminent integration has tended to destroy the protest element in Negro writing" (142). The effect, he says, "is obvious here"—a body of work marked by "a spiritual numbness" (144).

25. See *Blues, Ideology, and Afro-American Literature*. Baker's formulation has been critiqued for its exclusiveness by scholars such as Ann DuCille, who argues in *The Coupling Convention* that the "blues matrix's" privileging of the cultural production of southern, rural, poor African Americans leaves out a significant number of black communities and perspectives, including those of northern, urban, middle-class women.

26. For a provocative discussion of the role of racial authenticity in the construction of black critical discourse, see J. Martin Favor, *Authentic Blackness*.

27. There are far too many important works to offer a comprehensive list here, but a few representative examples include Blount and Cunningham, *Representing Black Men*; Wall, *Changing Our Own Words*; Johnson and Henderson, *Black Queer Studies*; and Gates, *Tradition and the Black Atlantic*.

28. Gene Andrew Jarrett's *Deans and Truants: Race and Realism in African American Literature* stands as an important exception to this generalization. Jarrett has introduced a very suggestive notion of "racial realism" as his critical phrase for the quasi-essentialist suppositions that have governed much African American canon formation—the expectation that black literature must bear a realist, or mimetic, relation to blackness. Jarrett effectively demonstrates how exclusive and misleading this lens can be. Unlike the current study, Jarrett prefers a longer view, stretching from the nineteenth century to Toni Morrison, and he spends only one chapter on a postwar white-life novel and author, Frank Yerby's *The Foxes of Harrow*. He dedicates a chapter to Richard Wright as a "New Negro Radical" committed to racial realism, but he addresses neither Wright's own stated resistance to this paradigm nor his white-life novel, *Savage Holiday*. See also Jarrett's anthology *African American Literature Beyond Race*.

29. Critical whiteness studies is by now a well-established, though far from uncontested, field. Inherently interdisciplinary, it is also widely represented in a range of traditional disciplines, especially sociology, history, anthropology, and literary studies, and in such interdisciplinary fields as cultural studies, gender and sexuality studies, race and ethnic studies, and class and labor studies. Matt Wray has recently defined "*white* as a *social* category, not a *racial* category," not to deny its racial meanings, but rather to highlight that "the social domination that *whiteness* enables is of many different forms and relies on many different kinds of social difference" (10, 11; emphasis in original). Wray stresses that whiteness is best seen as a "flexible set of social and symbolic boundaries that give shape, meaning, and power to the social category white"; this perspective helps one stay attuned to "the historical processes and social agents that generate symbolic boundaries and grant them social power" (11).

30. Mia Bay also published a work in 2000 with a near identical title, *The White Image in the Black Mind: African American Ideas about White People, 1830–1925*. The scope of Bay's illuminating study ends twenty years prior to the works under discussion here.

31. Although I take issue with the previously cited examples for the narrowness

of their depiction of black treatments of whiteness, this study has clearly benefited enormously from the work taking place under the rubric of critical whiteness studies. As the following chapters demonstrate, my understanding of race in mid-twentieth-century America is fundamentally indebted to such scholars as David Roediger, Matthew Frye Jacobson, and Grace Elizabeth Hale, and my analysis of such phenomena as cross-racial identification is obviously informed by the work of Eric Lott (to name only two instances, *Love and Theft* and "White Like Me"), and to a lesser extent, Toni Morrison's *Playing in the Dark*.

32. A classic instance of this usage is Adam Smith's *The Theory of Moral Sentiments*.

33. The literature on this aspect of sympathy is enormous. Examples from the American context that have influenced my thinking include Castiglia, "Abolition's Racial Interiors"; Barnes, *States of Sympathy*; and Berlant, "Poor Eliza."

1 / "I'm Regarded Fatally as a Negro Writer"

1. Sterling Brown, "The Negro Author and His Publisher."

2. I address this topic at length, with particular reference to *The Outsider* and *Savage Holiday*, in chapter 6.

3. Overstreet was an internationally renowned philosopher and adult-education advocate.

4. Other critics have treated these critiques in an *ad hominem* fashion, in which Hurston's dissent could be dismissed as resentment of Wright's success and his critiques of her novels, and, as Howe suggested, Baldwin and Ellison could be seen as not only caught up in an oedipal struggle with Wright, but also overly indebted to an elitist, bourgeois, vital center-liberal (read white) humanism. Similarly, Wright himself (who steadfastly refused to give publishers additional incarnations of *Native Son* and *Black Boy*) could be and has been chided for being too enamored with Continental (read white) philosophy, and thus having fallen away from his authentic and legitimate racial roots.

5. See Matthew Frye Jacobson, *Whiteness of a Different Color*; Roediger, *The Wages of Whiteness*; Gary Gerstle, *American Crucible*; Matthew Pratt Guterl, *The Color of Race in America*; Noel Ignatiev, *How the Irish Became White*; and Thomas Guglielmo, *White on Arrival*.

6. See Jacobson, *Whiteness of a Different Color*, 39–135. Reynolds Scott-Childress points out that "experts" on race in 1888 estimated that there existed between two and sixty-three races. In 1924, the Supreme Court observed in the process of adjudicating a naturalization case that there were between four and twenty-nine. The lower estimates constitute what Scott-Childress refers to as "color races" and the higher numbers "nation races," the largest number of which hailed from Europe.

7. David Roediger argues that in the final analysis the New Deal's and the CIO's antiracist rhetoric and policies overwhelmingly benefited the European "nation races." Although African Americans and other people of color did benefit from certain progressive policies and sentiments, overall the New Deal and industrial unionism played a significant role in creating the conditions for new immigrant unity with native-born whites, a unity clearly structured by the racist exclusions of people of color. As Roediger makes clear, these institutions raised the stakes for claiming whiteness, and in the process ensured that whites, now including "provisionally white" new immigrants, would violently defend their privileges—symbolic and material (*Working toward Whiteness* 230).

8. It is worth noting that social science scholars such as Franz Boas and his students had been arguing for the primacy of environment and culture in understanding race since at least the beginning of the century.

9. See Lawrence Jackson, *Indignant Generation*, 97–100.

10. In terms of the Popular Front and literary culture, see Michael Denning, *The Cultural Front*; Alan Wald, *Exiles from a Future Time*, and *Writing from the Left*; and Barbara Foley, *Radical Representations*; for specific attention to the Old Left and African American literary culture, see Bill Mullen, *Popular Fronts*; William Maxwell, *New Negro, Old Left*; James Smethurst *The New Red Negro*; and Barbara Foley, *Wrestling with the Left: The Making of Ralph Ellison's Invisible Man*.

11. I use the phrase "European domestic fascism" to invoke a link, noted by such postwar intellectuals as Arendt, Césaire, and Sartre, between the racist policies and practices being enacted in Europe with those that had long been enacted overseas as part of colonial and imperial projects.

12. See Mullen, *Popular Fronts*; and Maxwell, *New Negro, Old Left*, esp. chaps. 2 and 3.

13. Baldwin gave his impressions of the *People's Voice* in his 1948 *Commentary* essay "The Harlem Ghetto," which was collected in *Notes of a Native Son*.

> The *Amsterdam [Star-News]* has been rivaled, in recent years, by the *People's Voice*, a journal, modeled on *PM* and referred to as *PV*. *PV* is not so wildly sensational a paper as the *Amsterdam*, though its coverage is much the same (the news coverage of the Negro press is naturally pretty limited). *PV*'s politics are less murky, to the left of center . . . and its tone, since its inception, has been ever more hopelessly militant, full of warnings, appeals, and open letters to the government—which, to no one's surprise, are not answered—and the same rather pathetic preoccupation with prominent Negroes and what they are doing. Columns signed by Lena Horne and Paul Robeson appeared in *PV* until several weeks ago, when both severed their connections with the paper. Miss Horne's column made her sound like an embittered Eleanor Roosevelt, and the only column of Robeson's I have read was concerned with the current witch hunt in Hollywood, discussing the kind of movies under attack and Hollywood's traditional treatment of Negroes. (*Notes* 60–61)

14. Seaver also published Ellison and Gwendolyn Brooks in *Cross-Section*, alongside Norman Mailer and Arthur Miller, among others (Denning 225). Lawrence Jackson described *Cross-Section* as "an obvious product linked to the 1930s, the League of American Writers, and the Communist Party" (*The Indignant Generation* 179).

15. It is difficult to properly gauge Himes's attitude toward these activities; his recollections suggest at times opportunism rather than serious engagement.

16. "He Seen It in the Stars"; "Let Me at the Enemy—an' George Brown"; "My But the Rats Are Terrible"; "A Penny for Your Thoughts" (1944); "Make with the Shape"; "A Night of New Roses" (1945); "One More Way to Die" (1946).

17. "Motley the Marxist: Red, Black and Gay," paper presented in the "Willard Motley Reconsidered" panel, American Studies Association, Hartford, CT, October 16, 2003.

18. Mullen argues that, in the short term, *Native Son* influenced *white* literary treatments of American race relations more so than African American authors' treatment of the subject.

19. Alain Locke, who was in the audience when Hughes delivered the speech, and whose observations were included in *Fighting Words*, also invoked the discourse of democratic interracialism:

> And here is where this question of our front for democracy takes on, I think, a special significance: that we, so to speak, soldiers on this particular cultural front, have a duty of very bravely raising our arms against the stereotypes, of being extremely objective, and of doing a work that can only be done in close collaboration between the white and the Negro artist. As I see it, the white writer has at least the advantage of objectivity, for of course he can release himself to face the facts; and the Negro writer has the advantage of psychological intimacy, even though it has certain dangers of too zealous partisanship. (*Fighting Words* 76–77)

See also Ellison, "Richard Wright."

20. Baldwin describes his "devastating" tenure working as a messenger for *PM* in similar language: "If the black newspapers had considered me absolutely beyond redemption, *PM* was determined to save me: I cannot tell which attitude caused me the more bitter anguish" (*The Price of the Ticket* xiii). Both here and in the above quotation, white liberal sympathy causes Baldwin "pain" and "anguish" because his subjectivity is supplanted with a projected image of injured otherness.

21. Hereafter cited as *AAD*. Nikhil Pal Singh points out that after the appearance of the encyclopedic *AAD*, which was nearly 1,500 pages long, funding sources for the study of African American life and culture that departed from Myrdal's conclusions were "exhausted." *AAD* stood as the preeminent conceptualization, and thus "people were only interested in outcome studies framed around the teleological supposition that racial discrimination was declining and that this could then be measured" (*Black Is a Country* 261 n. 39).

22. Myrdal qualifies this observation with the following remark: "We do not imply that white American culture is 'higher' than other cultures in an absolute sense. The notion popularized by anthropologists that *all* cultures may be good under the different conditions to which they are adaptations, and that no derogatory association should *a priori* be attached to primitive cultures, is a wholesome antidote to arrogant and erroneous ideas closely bound up with white people's false racial beliefs and their justification of caste. But it does not gainsay our assumption that *here, in America*, American culture is 'highest' in the pragmatic sense that adherence to it is practical for any individual or group which is not strong enough to change it" (929; emphasis in original). The force of this qualification is undermined, however, by the fact that, aside from Myrdal's critique of the persistence of white racism in America, he consistently affirms white cultural norms as national and even universal norms, ones that black Americans, and indeed the whole world, should strive to emulate. Moreover, as Ralph Ellison points out in his review of *AAD* (written in 1944, but published in his 1964 collection of essays, *Shadow and Act*), not only does Myrdal here and elsewhere presume that Negro culture is not American, but that "Negroes should desire nothing better than what whites consider highest. But in the 'pragmatic sense' lynching and Hollywood, fadism [sic] and radio advertising are products of the 'higher' culture, and the Negro might ask, 'Why, if my culture is pathological, must I exchange it for these?'" (*Collected Essays* 339). As

I will show, the white-life novels challenge these national norms, particularly the oppressive effects of white heteropatriarchy.

23. The early sociological works of W.E.B. Du Bois represent a powerful exception to this tendency. See, for example, *The Philadelphia Negro* (1899) and *The Souls of Black Folk* (1903).

24. These liberal social scientists achieved some degree of success, at least in the courtroom. As Scott has shown, although there was little scientific evidence to offer in the way of objectively proving that segregated schools were inherently unequal, social scientists were virtually unanimous in their belief that enforced segregation had detrimental psychological effects on black children, even if the children had access to equal facilities. Consequently those arguing to overturn *Plessy v. Ferguson* were able to marshal several members of the social science community as expert witnesses, whereas segregationists had virtually no scientific experts to defend their position.

25. See Scott 102; Singh 145; and Ferguson 88.

26. The danger was not in admitting differences in culture, behavior, or achievement between the two races, but in "inferring that observed differences were innate and a part of nature" (*AAD* 1:148). However, by this point in time, sociologists had "discarded the idea that black people were biologically inferior, but despite the arguments of anthropologists, they retained an image of them as culturally inferior" (McKee 6).

27. Singh, *Black Is a Country* 142–62.

28. To be fair, Myrdal points out that non-U.S. citizens sense the same sort of "queerness" when they look at white attempts to assess democracy, in which "the subject of the Negro is a void or is taken care of by some awkward, mostly un-informed and helpless, excuses" (784). However, he again undermines the persuasiveness of his qualification by reasserting derogatory black difference: "The tragedy of caste is that it does not spare the integrity of the soul of either the Negro or the white man." Does this mean it would be something less than tragic if it affected only the "soul of the Negro"? Moreover, Myrdal asserts that "the difference in degree of distortion of worldview is just as great as the difference in size between the American Negro community and the rest of the world" (784).

29. Ellison queries dubiously, in response to this depiction of black thought, "But can a people ... live and develop for over three hundred years simply by *reacting*?" (*Collected Essays* 339).

30. Hurston's image of black emptiness and "nonexistence" clearly chimes with Ellison's metaphor of black social absence, "invisibility," which appeared two years later in *Invisible Man*.

31. She likens this belief to the "extravagant" belief that the "Chinese have bizarre genitals"—a reference that indirectly evokes white obsession with black sexual difference, which Hurston, in typical form, avoids.

32. In "Desegregating the 1950s: The Case of Frank London Brown," Mary Helen Washington reads Gibson's essay, and this passage in particular, quite differently. She describes Gibson as a "conservative" whose essay is "virulently anti-black" (21). She highlights Gibson's rejection of blackness as an "iron curtain" to argue that "while Gibson means to imply that blackness is a constriction, he inadvertently describes its power: blackness is inherently oppositional. Using the rhetoric of the cold war, Gibson equates blackness with communism, as powerful in its opposition to the United Sates

as to the Soviet Union. To be black in cold war America is to be both subversive and dangerous" (22).

33. For an illuminating and detailed discussion of Ellison's critique of sociological thought on black culture, see Kenneth Warren, *So Black and Blue*.

34. Gibson's essay, which was originally published in the *Kenyon Review* in 1951, was reprinted in 1953 along with a reprinting of "Everybody's Protest Novel" in *Perspectives USA*, also an anti-Stalinist journal, though this one was intended to win hearts and minds in Europe. The issue editor, Lionel Trilling, grouped the two essays under the fairly ironic heading "Two Protests against Protest."

35. Geraldine Murphy offers an extensive and subtle reading of the gender and sexual politics of Baldwin's early essays, in which she illuminates the manner in which Baldwin draws on (but also revises to accommodate his subjectivity as a black gay man) the anti-Stalinist liberal tendency to feminize progressive-left thinking as soft and naïve, over against the rigorous and clear-eyed New Critical celebration of the irony and complexity of the social world ("Subversive Anti-Stalinism: Race and Sexuality in the Early Essays of James Baldwin").

I believe Murphy's framing can be applied in certain respects to figures like Ellison and Gibson (minus issues of sexuality), in that these thinkers appropriated anti-Stalinist liberal thinking while also orienting it toward their specific racial concerns. As my foregoing discussion suggests, anti-Stalinist liberal rhetoric appealed to writers like Baldwin, Gibson, and Ellison because its insistence on complexity defied what they considered the demeaning and simplistic portraits of blackness produced by the social sciences. To be sure, Baldwin and Ellison were invested in distancing themselves from their earlier connections to the Left, but it is also true that the rhetoric of "universalism" and "humanism" offered a language for a kind of heroic resistance. It was at once a means of refusing narrow and racially disparaging formulae of the social sciences, while also tapping into a global progressive discourse. The universalist rhetoric of "Man" was the same language deployed by the United Nations, for example, in its antifascist and anticolonial pronouncements. For many contemporary black writers, it is a rhetoric of emancipation, an aspiration for denied rights. For discussions of Ellison's complex relationship to anti-Stalinist, liberal nationalist ideology, see Lawrence Jackson, *Ralph Ellison*, and *The Indignant Generation*; Arnold Rampersad, *Ralph Ellison*; and Barbara Foley, *Wrestling with the Left*.

36. I use the masculine pronoun here not only because Baldwin was singling out Wright for his faith in sociology, but also because a significant majority of protest writers were male. Moreover, it seems clear that Baldwin is put off by the Popular Front both because of its depictions of the Negro problem, but also because of its heteronormative, masculinist investments. Around this time he also wrote several reviews of novels where he criticized their treatments of same-sexuality, particularly their reliance on antigay, pathologizing discourses of sociology and psychoanalysis. See, for example, "Preservation of Innocence," which was originally published in *Zero* in summer 1949; citations in this study are from the reprinted version in *Collected Essays*.

2 / The Home and the Street

1. Ervin and Holladay, *The Critical Response to Ann Petry*. Alex Lubin's *Revising the Blueprint* revises this particular "blueprint," however, with three essays out of seven that deal extensively with *Country Place* (including an earlier version of this chapter).

For two other suggestive essays on *Country Place*, see especially Bernard, "Raceless Writing and Difference"; and Dubek, "White Family Values." Both Bernard and Dubek foreground Petry's subtle critique of white racial attitudes, though Bernard is more focused on aligning Petry's novel with the history of black canonization and Dubek's analysis attends to Petry's engagement with contemporary gender constructions. Neither work compares *Country Place* to her other works in this period or addresses questions of sympathy and privacy. Moreover, I depart from Dubek in her insistence that the entire novel must be read as a projection of Doc Fraser's consciousness.

2. Several critics, such as Philip Butcher, Robert Bone, and Arthur Davis, among others, have referred to *Country Place* as "raceless," "assimilationist," and "integrationist."

3. My thinking has also been influenced by Katherine Adams, *Owning Up*. For an excellent overview of privacy in the context of U.S. law and policy, see Daniel Solove, *Understanding Privacy*.

4. In her classic study of black women's labor, *Labor of Love, Labor of Sorrow*, Jacqueline Jones writes that "by 1944 black women constituted 60 percent of all private household workers (up 13 percent over the figure for 1940), reflecting white women's hasty flight from service as soon as the Great Depression ended" (237). This statistic points to the fact that white women dominated the ranks of clerical positions, and that black women, far more than black men and white women, were excluded from nearly all war-boom jobs. Moreover, Roderick Ferguson has shown that "with African American women dominating the ranks of prostitution in cities like New York and Chicago, and because of the already existent discourse of black women's sexual appetites, urban black womanhood became synonymous with prostitution" (42).

5. Lauren Berlant has analyzed how women from Harriet Jacobs to Anita Hill have felt compelled to publicly address the nation in the hopes of persuading the state to take an active interest in protecting the private lives of all black women, to remedy the fact that "coerced sexualization has been a constitutive relay between national experience and particular bodies," in this case, "the public history of African American women" (245). This history has driven some women to acts of "diva citizenship" where they feel they have no choice but to act on behalf of other black women and break the "sanitizing silences of sexual privacy in order to create national publics trained to think, and thus to think differently, about the corporeal conditions of citizenship" (239). These women strive to expose how the nation's rhetoric of abstract formal equivalency obscures the degree to which the white male citizen's "domestic and erotic privilege" is underwritten by sexually denigrated black female (minority) embodiedness.

6. Lubin, along with David Roediger, George Lipsitz, and others, shows how these conditions were also underwritten by decades of national/federal intervention on behalf of whites, including racially structured access to housing, loans, forms of relief, and employment during and after the New Deal and World War II. I discuss these issues at some length in chapter 1 (see Roediger, *Working toward Whiteness*; and Lipsitz, *The Possessive Investment in Whiteness*). The most influential discussions of the "domestic imperative" come from Elaine Tyler May, *Homeward Bound*; and Joann Meyerowitz, *Not June Cleaver*.

7. See Cheryl Greenberg, *Or Does It Explode?*; and Nat Brandt, *Harlem at War*.

8. Accounts of the riots from historians, sociologists, and writers, including Ellison and Baldwin, point to the presence of people from all classes on the streets that night,

not just hoodlums. Baldwin writes in his autobiographical essay "Notes of a Native Son": "[T]hat summer I saw the strangest combinations ... something heavy in their stance seemed to indicate that they had all, incredibly, seen a common vision, and on each face there seemed to be the same strange, bitter shadow" (*Notes of a Native Son* 100).

9. See Ferguson, *Aberrations in Black*; Kevin Mumford, *Interzones*; and Daryl Michael Scott, *Contempt and Pity*.

10. As Michael Warner puts in *Publics and Counterpublics*: "[I]n the classical conception [of privacy] as [Hannah Arendt] interprets it, the private is almost entirely without value, even without content. That, she emphasizes, is the point: the private is privative, a negative category, a state in which one is deprived of context for realizing oneself through action and in free interaction with others. *The most private person is the slave*. The life of the polis is opposed to all that is one's own (idion)—hence a merely private or idiosyncratic person would be an idiot" (297; emphasis added).

11. In *Blackness and Value*, Lindon Barrett argues that the chronological complexity of *The Street* is an indication that "the street seemingly possesses no future" and that Lutie is trapped in a "progression of equally oppressive present moments" (103).

12. "Bereave" derives etymologically from the Old English term *berēafian*, which means "to rob."

13. The employee who causes the snafu, "Harvard medical student Stuart Reynolds," spends time comparing the bones of the two women because "he was making a private study of bone structure in the Caucasian female as against the bone structure in the female of the darker race, and Louella Brown was an unexpected research plum" (167). Reynolds, like Peabody, exploits Louella Brown's body, appropriating her as an object of racial science in his "private study." The political and "scientific" implications of his discovery are entirely ignored, however; she gains her final resting place in the center of white privilege because of her haunting, not because the public recognizes the bogusness of racial science.

14. Berlant argues that "in the fantasy world of national culture, citizens aspire to dead identities—constitutional personhood in its public sphere abstraction and supra historicity, reproductive heterosexuality in the zone of privacy. Identities not live, or in play, but dead, frozen, fixed, or at rest" (60).

15. See the *New York Times*, *New Masses*, etc. Despite these negative reviews, the author Laura Hobson wrote a favorable blurb for the publishers, and the Petry Papers at Boston University include several enthusiastic fan letters for *Country Place*, with more than one preferring it to *The Street*. She also received positive letters from her former writing teacher, Mable Louise Robinson, and one from Carl Van Vechten.

16. David Littlejohn faults what he considers Petry's sensationalism as well, but argues that her extraordinary capacity for sympathy with her characters redeems this flaw (see the epigraph to this chapter). He observes that she has "an uncomfortable tendency to contrive sordid plots. ... She seems to require a 'shocking' chain of scandalous doings. ... So wise is her writing, though, so real are her characters, so total is her sympathy, that one can often accept the faintly cheap horrors and contrivances" (155).

17. See Clark, "A Distaff Dream Deferred?"

18. Based on working notes transcribed by Elisabeth Petry, Petry's first written notes on the novel were "Why not write a love story—not a usual one—but one about

a middle-aged man and woman. One very old, one middle-aged, one young—and how can they be tied together—that none of the three of them wanted to live." She then considers having the novel divided into three books, one focused on Johnnie Roane, Mrs. Gramby, and "middle-aged Frank" [Ed Barrell]. "There has to be a link between them, a relationship, something that ties them all together, links them up—did they know each other—was there a reason why they died at the same time—were they afraid—did they know about it beforehand—in *The Bridge of San Luis Rey* [Pulitzer Prize–winning novel by Thornton Wilder (1927); adapted in 1929 and 1944 as a film] the only relationship was that they all happened to be on the bridge when it collapsed and each one had reached some impasse, was about to be faced with some awful embarrassment. In view of the fact that the these people can't be linked by a bridge or a common disaster, What will the link be [sic]. Each one groped for something that life denied him and in the determination, the seeking after found only disillusion." These notes are in the possession of Elisabeth Petry.

19. Petry figures the effects of the hurricane in a manner highly reminiscent of the effects of World War II—this is not surprising, given that Petry originally considered structuring her novel around the war rather than a hurricane ("Notes for *Country Place*"). The hurricane, like the war, is an overwhelming, violent, disruptive, and terrifying crisis that brings out both the worst and the best in people, self-serving violence as well as selfless acts of heroism. The hurricane disrupts social order, throws the future into uncertainty, and even challenges the townspeople's faith in God. During the storm, a tree falls across the door of the congregational church (147).

20. See especially Herman, *The Romance of American Psychology*, for a discussion of the ascendance of psychological discourse into mainstream social and political commentary in the postwar period.

21. I discuss the presence and effects of this discourse in Wright's *Savage Holiday* in chapter 6.

22. Mearns might take some consolation in the fact that he is not alone—the masculinity of nearly every man in the text is compromised in some fashion, either sexually, emotionally, physically, or some combination of all three. The Weasel, for example, is described as a "rat-faced little man," with "small hands" and "humped over shoulders" (19, 7, 16). His grotesque, animal-like appearance and sneaking, scandal-loving demeanor are repeatedly associated with filth and perversion. The reader learns that The Weasel impregnated a mentally handicapped fifteen-year-old state ward. She was at least a foot and a half taller than him, and when he bought her sodas at the drugstore "she made a loud sucking noise as she pulled the soda up through the straw. The sound seemed to delight him" (139). "Perhaps he had the normal male sexual urge caged inside his abnormal, wizened body," Doc speculates, again donning his hat as drugstore psychoanalyst; "Perhaps he set about the conquest of a large female as a kind of *perverted compensation* for his own smallness" (138; emphasis added). The Weasel is both morally and physically unfit, unhealthy.

The Weasel most admires Ed Barrell, the wife-seducing local car salesman and mechanic, whose carriage expresses a "kind of male powerfulness" (15). Doc says that Ed reeked of gasoline, cheap cigars, and "the sour smell of lechery" (100). Ed's potency is hollow, though. He is an immoral figure who dies because he has a "bad heart"—literally (he dies of a heart attack) and figuratively. His incessant pursuit of other men's wives is depicted as a compulsion: "It was kind of like a disease with him" (258).

Johnnie seems the most whole as a man (he is healthy and doesn't appear to be saddled by any perversions), but his mother too is described as somewhat smothering, and the effect seems to be that he is "passive" in his relationship with Gloria, given that he consistently sacrificed his desires to accommodate hers, that is until he discovers the affair. It is notable that when he comes home full of hopeful illusions about his future with Glory, he occupies a room with Glory in his parents' house. In the end, though, he sets out on his own for the big city to pursue his dreams of becoming a painter.

23. See Lipsitz, *The Possessive Investment in Whiteness*; Roediger, *Working toward Whiteness*; and Ferguson, *Aberrations in Black*.

24. Her pain leads her to both envy and sympathetically identify with two young and healthy, yet suffering, men: "Yes, she thought, I would rather be any of them, the young lawyer [Rosenberg] or that other young man, that young Johnnie Roane, who has a harlot of a wife" (88).

25. For all of *Country Place*'s differences from *The Street*, and its naturalist ethos of environmental influence, this phrasing echoes a key passage from *The Street* in which the narrator states of Lutie Johnson, "All those years she'd been heading straight as an arrow for that street *or some other street just like it*" (426; emphasis added). In *Country Place*, Petry allows for human agency to alter, at least in this town, the effect of environment (specifically, Lennox's quiet yet persistent history of ethnic and religious discrimination).

26. Petry's resolution also revises contemporary family discourse in another important way: Her new American domestic arrangement does *not* seamlessly conform to the established ideologies of the healthy black family; liberal social science analyses of the black family all presumed that the problem in the black family was that white racism kept black men from gainful employment, which forced black women to be the breadwinners, and thus also in charge of the household. Along with this economic dependence developed sexual independence. These circumstances produced what were known as black matriarchies, which further lowered black male self-esteem. Accordingly, a healthy black family required the reinscription of the black woman under the sign of black male authority.

3 / White Masks and Queer Prisons

1. See, for example, Marlon Ross, "White Fantasies of Desire."

2. See David Riesman, *The Lonely Crowd*. Women were considered "naturally" other-directed, and hence too much other-direction among women was not a problem that required a solution. On the contrary, the problem most in need of correction among women was increasing female independence.

3. Cuordileone, chap. 3.

4. Alan Wald, "Motley the Marxist: Red, Black, and Gay," paper presented at American Studies Association, Hartford CT, October 2003.

5. See also Himes's interview by John A. Williams, "My Man Himes: An Interview with Chester Himes," in *Conversations with Chester Himes*, in which Williams

declares (approvingly) that Himes is the "most masculine writer" in the African American literary tradition (29–82).

6. As Regina Kunzel has argued, historians of same-sexuality have largely ignored prison sex because of its associations with criminality and sexual violence—prisoners are "bad" subjects not well suited to the project of refuting dominant-culture antigay prejudices. This attitude, of course, reflects a similar discomfort on the part of scholars of African American literary history, then and to some extent now, who are not eager to highlight "deviance" among blacks any more than the dominant culture already does.

7. See, for example, Nugent, "Smoke, Lillies, Jade"; Thurman, *Infants of the Spring*; Larsen, *Passing*; Fisher, *The Walls of Jericho*; and McKay, *Home to Harlem*.

8. See Carby, "Policing the Black Woman's Body" 747; Ferguson, *Aberrations in Black* 1–53; and Scott, *Contempt and Pity* 1–70.

9. See Ross, *Manning the Race*, chaps. 6 and 7.

10. The Cold War linking of communism with perceived crises of gender and sexuality has been addressed by a number of scholars, most recently David K. Johnson, *The Lavender Scare*. See also Lee Edelman, "Tea Rooms and Sympathy"; Robert J. Corber, *Homosexuality in Cold War America*; Michael Rogin, "Kiss Me Deadly"; D'Emilio and Freedman, *Intimate Matters*; and Jeffrey Escoffier, *American Homo*.

11. Halperin identifies the three additional categories as effeminacy, pederasty or "active" sodomy, and passivity or inversion (92). I include definitions of these categories as I make reference to them in my discussion.

12. One of the problems that readers have with the text then and now is its moments of intense sentimentality. But rather than reading this affect as stylistic failure, it is useful to consider D. A. Miller's contention in *A Place for Us* that sentimentality in certain contexts can be read as a crucial mode of pre-Stonewall (pre–Gay Pride) queer affect. The sentimentality of early Broadway musicals, for example, even though it occurs within heterosexual scenarios, facilitated the expression of non-normative longings that were otherwise unrepresentable, and had no permissible outlet.

13. Himes to Van Vechten, "Letters from Blacks" Folder, Van Vechten Papers, James Weldon Johnson Collection, Beinecke Library, Yale University.

14. An online search of the MLA bibliography in January 2012, with the term "Chester Himes" yielded 195 hits; the addition of the phrases "Cast the First Stone" or "Yesterday Will Make You Cry" reduced the hits to one.

15. Ross, "White Fantasies of Desire." For a thoughtful and substantive review of *Yesterday Will Make You Cry*, one that directly addresses same-sexuality, see Stephen Murray's "Afraid of Their Own Thoughts: Chester Himes' Homophobia/Prison Novel—A Review," www.toxicuniverse.com/review.php?rid=10004117. See also Gregory Woods's enthusiastic but brief appraisal in *A History of Gay Literature*.

16. In the same 10 June 1946 letter to Carl Van Vechten quoted previously, Himes expresses discomfort about what he perceived to be the feminizing qualities of his skin after seeing a photograph taken of him by Van Vechten: "Thanks for your letter and the photographs which were very fine indeed. However, there is a smoothness in the facial lines which I do not quite like. I would like for all the blemishes, marks, scars and lines of the face to show, even at the risk of appearing like a thug." Detectable here are lingering traces of what Siobhan Somerville identifies as the early twentieth-century association of the mulatto (Himes was light-skinned) and the gender

invert (see *Queering the Color Line*, chaps. 3 and 4). With this in mind, we could read Himes's desire for his "blemishes, marks, scars and lines" to be more plainly visible, and thus to risk appearing like a "thug," as a simultaneous desire to better approximate a stereotypical notion of hard, hypermasculine "blackness," and thus to appear less "effeminate."

17. It may also be that Himes's Cold War editors were the ones abjected by Dido's happy queerness—he "disorients" them as the sexual "criminal with a good conscience" (see Kristeva, *Powers of Horror*).

18. One could argue that the truth of Foucault's assertion is borne out by the reaction among antigay activists and politicians to the Supreme Court's striking down of antisodomy laws, which immediately led to the proposal of state and federal constitutional amendments to ban gay marriage.

19. The novel went through several manuscript versions. In a letter to Carl Van Vechten, who persuaded Himes to donate his papers to Yale, Himes explained that the first version, called "Day after Day" was written about 1936–37; the next version "The Way It Was," in 1939–40; and the version called "Black Sheep," in the winter of 1949 (Margolies and Fabre 184).

20. See Somerville, *Queering the Color Line*; and Ross, *Manning the Race*.

21. Letter dated 19 October 1952, Yale Collection, qtd. in Sallis, *Chester Himes, A Life*, 110.

22. Himes to Van Vechten, dated 18 February 1947; Himes to Motley, dated 8 August 1947, "Letters from Blacks" Folder, Van Vechten Papers, James Weldon Johnson Collection, Beinecke Library, Yale University.

23. My attention to the productive effects of intercultural encounter has been influenced by Susan Stanford Friedman, *Mappings*.

24. Willard Motley Papers, Special Collections, Northern Illinois University. A list of the contents of his papers are online at www.ulib.niu.edu/rbsc/motley.htm.

25. See Klinkowitz and Wood, "The Making and Unmaking."

26. Motley based Nick in part on a teen he knew from the streets of Chicago's red-light district; in an unpublished work called "The Beautiful Boy" he described Nick's prototype as follows: "From the firm straightness of his legs to the broad hardness of his shoulders to the princely cut of his head he was a statue of beauty—alive—breathing—looking out beyond lashes as heavily silky as a girl's with soft blue eyes" (Nick's eyes would eventually be brown) (Willard Motley Papers, Northern Illinois University).

27. Motley phrased it this way in an article by Horace Cayton for the *Pittsburgh Courier*: "I wanted the book to go on its own legs—a first novel by an unknown writer. Had the reading public known that I was colored some people would have bought the book and praised it because I am a Negro. I wanted to know if the book was good or bad on its merits alone." This statement evades the fact that some readers wouldn't have bought the book in the first place if they knew in advance that its author was black. Motley also adds that "German-Americans don't write only about Germans. Nor do Scotch, Irish, Italian writers describe only their group. People, it seems to me, define down into much-alike characters regardless of race or color, depending upon their economic, social, and psychological status" (Cayton, "Literary Expansion"). Implicit here is that Motley is claiming the same racial privacy and prerogatives available to these "white" authors.

28. I employ the idea of "the state" in the broadest sense, including what Althusser refers to as the "repressive state apparatus" (i.e., the police, the prison system, the

courts) as well as various "ideological state apparatuses," such as the church and the education system (see Althusser).

29. It seems worth noting that if Motley's sole objective in moving into the slum was to study the underclass, he could have certainly moved into the burgeoning black ghetto. However, poor black neighborhoods were profoundly segregated: the historian Arnold Hirsch tells us that by 1940, when Motley moved into the slum, half of all black neighborhoods were 100 percent black. Hence Motley's experiences in an all-black neighborhood wouldn't provide him the evidence necessary to make his central antiracist claim, that "people were just people." Had he lived in a black ghetto, rather than a multiethnic slum, he would not have been able to produce his integrated "ghetto pastoral."

30. Years later, the queer authors John Rechy (*City of Night* 1963) and Hubert Selby Jr. (*Last Exit to Brooklyn* 1964) would follow Motley's example by writing queer works in the naturalist idiom.

31. See *Black Queer Studies*, which includes several essays that address this issue. See especially Marlon Ross, "Beyond the Closet as Raceless Paradigm" (161–89) for an analysis of the racial unconscious informing some of the work of Sedgwick and Foucault. See also Jose Estaban Munoz, *Disidentifications*.

32. See esp. Henderson, "James Baldwin's *Giovanni's Room*: Expatriation, 'Racial Drag,' and Homosexual Panic," *Black Queer Studies*; and Holland, "(Pro)creating Imaginative Spaces."

33. Baldwin's habitual focus on "boys" and "men," and his failure to at least acknowledge the particular conditions and stakes of moving from being a "girl" to a "woman," plainly illustrate Baldwin's own gender biases, which have been noted by several feminist critics (see, for example, Cora Kaplan, "A *Cavern Opened* in My Mind").

34. Ehrenreich 14–28; Cuordileone 146. Note that in "Many Thousands Gone," Baldwin declares that "Aunt Jemima and Uncle Tom are dead, their places taken by a group of *amazingly well-adjusted* young men and women, almost as dark, but ferociously literate, well-dressed and scrubbed, who are never laughed at, who are never likely ever to set foot in a cotton or tobacco field or in any but the most modern of kitchens" (27; emphasis added). In the face of ubiquitous hostility and uncertainty, the new generation of black Americans stakes its claim in the American Dream, which as Baldwin personally knows, demands enormous courage, and, implicitly, a kind of maturity that is demonstrated by knowing how to survive and succeed under such adverse conditions.

35. Definition of "communion" from the *American Heritage Dictionary* (3rd ed.).

36. Baldwin also singles out "isolation" as a violence-inducing American condition in "Many Thousands Gone": "Bigger has *no discernible relationship to himself, to his own life, to his own people, nor to any other people*—in this respect, perhaps, he is most American.... What [*Native Son*] reflects—and at no point interprets—is the *isolation* of the Negro within his own group and the resulting fury of impatient scorn" (34, 35; emphasis added). Bigger's isolation is an index of his privation—in Baldwin's reading, he utterly lacks any self-relation, which is directly connected to his lack of relation to others. Isolation obviously stands in direct opposition to communion, and again evokes the notion of spiritual loss: "A man who isolates himself seeks his own desire; He rages against all wise judgment (Proverbs 18:1, *NKJV*)."

37. Baldwin offers a clear indication of what Hella offers David in "The Male Prison," his review of Andre Gide's *Madeleine*. Gide's wife, Madeleine, "kept open for him a kind of door of hope, of possibility, the possibility of entering into communion with another sex" (235). She was the "string connecting him to heaven.... She was his Heaven who would forgive him for his Hell and help him to endure it. As indeed she was and, in the strangest way possible, did—by allowing him to feel guilty about her instead of the boys on the *Piazza d'Espagne*" (233, 234).

38. I take up this concept in more detail in chapter 2 with reference to Ann Petry's *Country Place*.

4 / Sympathy for the Master

1. In 1982, Yerby estimated that *Foxes* sold 10–12 million copies, including international sales. This number is probably exaggerated, since its domestic sales were less than 3 million in 1976 (see Hackett and Burke, *80 Years of Best Sellers*). Considering that Yerby was among the top-selling authors in Europe in the decades following World War II, it is safe to say that the total sales figure for *Foxes* is considerably higher than 3 million, and that it is one of the all-time best-selling novels by an African American. Yerby wrote thirty-three historical romances—all but three centered on the adventures of white protagonists—with total sales exceeding 55 million copies. Though he was the first black author to become a millionaire from his pen, and the best-selling author in African American literary history, Frank Yerby is now virtually unknown.

2. See Darwin T. Turner, "Frank Yerby as Debunker"; and James Hill, "The Anti-Heroic Hero." William Hill, in line with other Yerby apologists, suggests that we "[look] beneath the romantic veneer of swashbuckling and sex in the novels ... [to discover] the manner in which Yerby slyly punctures the myths of Southern culture and aristocratic pretensions" (5). Hill argues that "Yerby merely abandons *overt* protest, adopting a dual level of writing: he paints a thick screen of love and lust, violence and blood, to please a larger number of readers on one level, and *sub rosa*, writes a message of protest that undercuts the foundations of the romantic world he builds" (41).

William Hill is implying that the surface of Yerby's fiction is only a "screen," or what he calls elsewhere a "magnolia mask," and hence does not contain the "true" meaning of the text, which is to be found somewhere "sub rosa." This approach attempts to exonerate Yerby from writing mere popular romance, but it also suggests that popular fiction, understood as simple entertainment, is somehow without substance, an ephemeral and self-indulgent pleasure rather than an enduring and socially valuable form of knowledge. I want to argue against the easy division of the text's meaning into two discrete levels: an inconsequential, diversionary, decorative surface over a substantive depth. Instead, my reading focuses on the dynamic tension between the "surface" and the "depth," and the meaning it produces.

3. Gene Jarrett presents Yerby as refusing demands for racial realism in favor of an emphasis on American cultural nationality. Although my reading does address Yerby's use of nationalist rhetoric, I spend more time exploring the interrelationship between genre, gender, race, and nation, including Yerby's own vexed personal investment in the southern historical romance. It should be noted that Jarrett takes issue with the use of the term "white-life novel":

These scholarly characterizations uncritically equate the ostensible absence of blacks in literature with the presence of whites. They also associate this absence with the code words that have historically denoted black ideological affiliation with self-serving and racist white political interests. The terminology says more about its users than it does about the literature itself; it raises more problems than it solves. Certain literary examples can reveal the conceptual limitations of this terminology. Frank Yerby's first published novel, *The Foxes of Harrow*, focuses not merely on a white man but on an Irishman trying to secure cultural citizenship in antebellum Louisiana. (9)

While whiteness was certainly much more fluid in antebellum Louisiana, *Foxes* is clearly critically engaged with the construction not just of whiteness, but of southern whiteness and its particular instantiation of white heteropatriarchy through the southern historical romance. "Anomalous," one of Jarrett's terms for nonracial realist works, is too imprecise to be helpful in categorizing Yerby's novel. As I argue, *Foxes* is a self-conscious intervention in mid-twentieth-century discourses regarding the ethnic, historical, regional, and cultural sources of modern white American manhood.

4. See Lott, *Love and Theft*.

5. The League superseded the more revolutionary John Reed Clubs after the Communist Party withdrew its support in 1935. Michael Denning has shown that they continued many of the John Reed Clubs' activities, including sponsoring lectures, radio broadcasts, and writing schools, activities that he contends "organiz[ed] the infrastructure of the cultural front" (224).

6. There is no extant copy of this novel; Yerby claims to have burnt it in frustration.

7. Harlan Hatcher estimates that between 1936 and 1937 nearly twenty historical novels treating the Civil War had been published, and around the same number were anticipated for the following year (781).

8. Bill Mullen has pointed out that "1939 was frequently evoked in the [*Chicago Defender*'s] pages not as the year of the Stalin-Hitler pact that signaled the 'official' end of the party's Popular Front period, but of *Gone With the Wind*" (4). He suggests that *Gone with the Wind* had a galvanizing effect on Popular Front organizing, as the *Defender*, along with the Communist Party and Chicago's organized Left, led boycotts of the film. "From 1939 to 1945, the film in fact became in the newspaper's pages a *synecdoche for the world war itself*: a sign of both political and cultural 'imperialism' abroad and a more ominous enemy within U.S. borders—namely the alliance between white capital ('powerful financial groups') in Hollywood, and the culture industry" (4; emphasis in original).

9. See James L. Hill, "An Interview." As critics such as Turner and Hill have pointed out, though Yerby later publicly disdained the label "protest writer," all of his works, including *Foxes*, are full of social critique.

10. Of course, Mitchell revises many conventions of the plantation romance, especially those around gender and the class background of the planter class. Her work refuses then-popular ahistorical fantasies of a plantation society populated by noble and genteel planters whose mansions were graced by elegant and retiring mistresses, virtuous queens of domesticity (see Grace Hale, *Making Whiteness*). Linda Williams points out that "[t]he deeper appeal of [*Gone with the Wind*] lay in its portrayal of a rebellious father-identified Irish girl who flouted all tradition"

(194). Mitchell's text also accepts, with great bitterness, that the Old South is dead, and that the only reasonable course of action under the circumstances is to establish a means to succeed in the New South. Nevertheless, Mitchell's investment in the racism that undergirds the southern historical romance is unambiguous; though she accepts the end of slavery, she insists that the New South must be no less racially stratified. Her representation of Reconstruction, for example, is intended to valorize the rise of the Ku Klux Klan.

11. See Kristeva 4.

12. At this point in time, the only African American novel with a black male protagonist to reach a wide audience, *Native Son*, was centered around an *antihero*—Bigger Thomas. More than two decades after publishing *Foxes* and several other southern historical romances, Yerby eventually published three novels with black protagonists—*Speak Now* (1969), *The Dahomean* (1971), and *A Darkness at Ingraham's Crest* (1979). While these novels, especially the latter two, received largely positive reviews, they also sold poorly in comparison to his early southern romances.

13. Yerby's narrative of disaffiliation from the Popular Front and protest of course perfectly echoes the "hard" masculinist ethos of the Cold War. Arthur Schlesinger Jr., along with other centrist liberals and conservatives, stigmatized radical protest as soft, sentimental, and naïve; he described the vestiges of radicalism as "Doughface progressivism . . . kept alive by main force in the face of all the lessons of modern history. . . . Politics becomes, not a means of getting things done, but an outlet for private grievances and frustrations" (159). See esp. Cuordileone, *Manhood*.

14. He claimed in an interview that he wrote his early novels with the "middle-class housewife mentality in mind. . . . I know that type of woman very well, because I receive thousands of letters from them. Usually letters that make my flesh crawl, praising ideas that were not even in the book but which they read into it out of their own frustrations." These readers, he believes, "are seeking to escape from the humdrumness of existence. It's escape fiction—which has its place because, after all, life is pretty rough. Let people escape once in a while" (Fuller 192). The implicit misogyny and revulsion in this remark appears elsewhere in Yerby's comments and has a direct bearing on my reading of *Foxes*' gendered, racialized anxieties. Yerby seems especially disturbed at his success in speaking to the "middleclass housewife mentality," as though he is implicated in satisfying their imaginative desire. By speaking to their private desires so effectively, Yerby fears that he has been incorporated into this female reading public, and so the popular romance edges threateningly toward gender dissonance, a disavowed literary transvestism.

15. Carter G. Woodson, known by many as "the father of black history," was also pleased with Yerby's historical fidelity; in his review, he declared *Foxes* "one of the truly historical novels of our time. It is an all but perfect portrayal of New Orleans, of Louisiana, and incidentally of the Southwest from the close of the first quarter of the Nineteenth Century to the Civil War" (353).

16. Similarly, Thomas Nelson Page, in *Red Rock: A Chronicle of Reconstruction* (1898), sets out to describe how southerners overcame "the greatest humiliation of modern times: their slaves were over them—they re-conquered their section and preserved the civilization of the Anglo-Saxon" (viii).

17. Stephen Fox's status as Irish immigrant turned patriotic American also fits well with the era's unprecedented rise in European naturalization. The historian Reed

Ueda has pointed out that "[n]aturalization reached its most active point in American history and served as a mechanism for European immigrants to secure their legal status and political identity. For them World War II brought the culmination of the tradition of patriotic naturalization" (213).

18. See also my discussion of this topic in Ann Petry's "In Darkness and Confusion," in chapter 2.

19. Here Yerby may well be drawing on George Washington Cable's *The Grandissimes* (1880). Cable also dramatizes the Creole-American conflict, but, unlike Yerby, he explicitly critiques slavery and the color caste system. Of course, Cable's avowed purpose was to speak to the "conscience of the South," while Yerby's was to entertain. This difference in intention may also account for why "free men of color" are so central to Cable's tale, and why they are nearly absent in Yerby's except for Stephen's octoroon mistress, Desiree. Though she suffers because of discrimination, Yerby focuses primarily on her sexual allure and dedication to Stephen.

20. Yerby gave the following explanation in a 1966 interview for his departure from America: "To put it as an oversimplification, I just don't have time to waste on such non-sensical questions as casing a joint, or this or that restaurant, to find out whether I will go in there and sit for three hours before some stupid ass of a waitress comes to spill a glass of water down my neck.... I just don't have the time. It's ridiculous. I should, if I were a combative, courageous-type militant who would put himself at the forefront of the Movement and go out and get himself shot in the belly a couple of times to advance things. So, I'm a coward. Let's face it" (Fuller 188).

21. Yerby uses very similar language in a later novel to describe the oppression of black men. In *A Woman Called Fancy* (1951), a sympathetic white character observes: "I've known black boys who were in the first rank intellectually, which makes life damned miserable for them, the poor bastards.... What do you think it does to a bright boy to know it would cost him his life if he ever *reared up on his haunches and acted like a man?*" (280–81; emphasis added). The reappearance of this expression points to the connection that I detect in Yerby's embattled sense of manhood and his turn to popular fiction. Though he would likely deny this assertion "hotly," Yerby's fantasy world is surprisingly similar to that of his readers—particularly his female readers whom he repeatedly denigrates.

22. This may be the element of "relevance" that John Fiske, in"Popular Discrimination," argues is crucial for the success of popular cultural texts.

23. Immediately following the end of the war there was enormous pressure for women to leave the workforce and return their "place" in the home as wives and mothers. According to May, the urgency behind this cultural dictum derived both from women's social advances, and because many men felt, ironically, unmanned in suburban America—presumably due to the loss of frontiers, opportunities to prove themselves in traditionally "masculine" ways, and the spirit-sapping demands of corporate conformity. Though many white women were reinscripted into a domestic narrative, their gains were by no means wholly reversed; the developing feminist movement was simply driven underground during this period, before erupting full force in the 1960s.

24. Yerby's hostility toward "matriarchs" reflects, and may even partly stem from, the widespread belief in postwar social science literature that black men were emasculated as much by dominating black *women* as by white men (see Scott).

25. Later in the novel, Yerby includes a reference to Fitzhugh's *Cannibals All or*

Slaves without Masters, adding to the likelihood that Stephen's use of this patriarchal rhetoric was not coincidental.

26. Stephen and Gerald represent the greatest parallel among characters in Yerby's and Mitchell's texts—Stephen and Gerald both emigrated to America penniless and in flight from governmental persecution in the Old World. They both won their land and first valet by gambling and an ability to hold their liquor, and then through hard work (and slave labor!) they built prosperous plantations. Both men existed on the fringe of plantation society but nevertheless defied the odds by marrying a cold, beautiful belle from an aristocratic New Orleans family.

27. Kastor 62–65.

28. Although it remains unspecified, Yerby may be referring to the 1795 Pointe Coupee Conspiracy, where a number of enslaved Haitian Africans were executed after having been accused of conspiring to mutiny; historical accounts suggest that they were inspired by the Haitian Revolution.

29. He also remarks that "one of the things I am proudest of about my ancestors is that one night on the island of Haiti, when my ancestors left, you could read a newspaper from one end of the island to the other by the light of the burning plantations. . . . They defeated Napoleon; they beat the pure piss out of him" (J. Hill, "Interview" 226–27). This suggests yet another point of ambivalence for Yerby, as he identifies with both the rebellious Haitians and the submissive Africans in North America.

30. Yerby's use of black women to voice protest at first glance seems to valorize the strength of black women, but it is worth noting that both La Belle Sauvage and Desiree are raped. After La Belle Sauvage insults Achille, he thinks: "She had no right to say that, her. She had no right to make him feel like a dog or a horse or any owned thing. Yet he must have her" (127). He then takes her into his cabin and rapes her. After Achille thus symbolically establishes his manhood by "breaking her spirit," the two begin their relationship. Desiree is raped by Etienne after she refuses his advances and says he compares poorly to his father. At first glance, it appears that Yerby intends for the reader to admire these women, but they are both punished after speaking against (black) men. The threat of sharp-tongued, insolent women appears earlier in the novel in an exchange between Stephen and Achille: "Ye're a confirmed woman hater, aren't ye, Achille? I can't say that I blame ye." Achille responds with a smile: "They talks too much, the wimmins. . . . Always they have the big mouth, yes!" (144). The threat of women with "big mouths" has a clear analogue in the mid-1940s also.

31. After he is beaten and left in the muddy streets of New Orleans, he says to himself, "I am a playwright,' he wept. 'I belong to the *Académie!* My works are produced at the *Comédie Française*. I am a writer and an artist and a genius. A genius, I tell you, a genius!' . . . [T]here was no other sound in the street but the rasping of his breath, the beating of his heart, and the racking sound of his sobs" (271). This character seems modeled on Victor Séjour, the New Orleans–born author of the first known work of "African American fiction"—"Le Mulâtre" (*The Mulatto*) (1837). Séjour, like Aupre, was a celebrated playwright who had been educated in France.

32. The events of Inch's recapture, however, are—as Carter G. Woodson notes in his review—modeled on another fugitive slave: "the abolition story of Anthony Burns from which it is taken almost verbatim" (354).

33. Yerby also radically rewrites another staple of the southern historical romance in this scene, the happy reunion of master and ever-loyal former slave. As Hale and

others have noted, when all else is lost for Scarlett, Mammy is "the last link with the old days" (*Gone with the Wind* 862); Mammy is equal with her former masters only in her contempt for the "trashy free issue niggers." No honorable, intelligent, and independent African Americans such as Inch are allowed to enter Mitchell's narrative.

34. See, for example, Ward, *River Run Red*.

5 / Talk about the South

1. One notable challenge to the rationales and motives behind Hurston's celebrated status is Hazel Carby's "The Politics of Fiction, Anthropology, and the Folk: Zora Neale Hurston."

2. See, for example, Ducille, *The Coupling Convention*; Meisenhelder, *Hitting a Straight Lick*; Claudia Tate, *Psychoanalysis and Black Novels*; and John Lowe, *Jump at the Sun*. Tate's work is especially astute in illuminating the degree to which aspects of Hurston's own personal insecurities and familial conflicts are inscribed in Arvay. Lowe's exhaustive analysis is particularly useful in demonstrating how Jim's capacity to joke renders him a quite sympathetic figure, despite his domineering behavior. He also does a good job detailing how *Seraph* "constitutes Hurston's love song to Florida" (261). I agree with this assessment, but locate her "love song" and her treatment of the "crackers" in larger political debates.

3. See *The Signifying Monkey* 110–13.

4. The best evidence that Hurston intended to reach a mainstream audience was her effort, ultimately unsuccessful, to interest a Hollywood studio in her novel (Carby, Foreword x).

5. Lowe connects many of *Seraph*'s details to information Hurston gathered while working for the Florida Federal Writers' Project, as part of that which she contributed to *The Florida Negro* and *The Florida Guide* (works not published in her lifetime). He does not, however, consider *Seraph* in light of contemporary national and regional social conflict.

6. For a cultural history of these dramatic regional transformations see Daniel, *Lost Revolutions*. For a political history of this era, see Sullivan, *Days of Hope*. For a focus on civil rights activism in Florida, see Ortiz, *Emancipation Betrayed*. For civil rights activism generally, see Payne and Green, *Time Longer Than Rope* (see chaps. 7 and 13 for civil rights activism in Florida).

7. For a provocative discussion of the civil rights struggle, its relationship to the Cold War, and its legacy for the contemporary "culture wars," see Singh, "Culture/Wars."

8. Dabney was a relatively liberal journalist and historian at the University of Virginia; Theodore Bilbo was a notoriously racist, prosegregationist, and anti–New Deal senator from Mississippi.

9. In the previous letter to Burroughs Mitchell, Hurston writes: "Nor is that trite picture of the noble and freedom-loving Negro true. There were thousands and thousands of free Negroes in the South before the War, and many of them held slaves, and fought like tigers in the Confederate armies to maintain slavery. Some didnt [sic] own any, but fought for the South anyway. I am not one of those sentimentalist [sic] who love to take sides whether my stand is valid or not" (Carla Kaplan 561).

10. See my discussion of Hurston's "What White Publishers Won't Print" in chapter 1. Hurston wrote to a friend that Bucklin Moon's *Darker Brother* "gives a falsely

morbid picture of Negro life. If his picture is true, how does he account for the thousands on thousands of wealthy, educated Negroes? ... [T]hat awful picture does Negroes in general more harm than good. One might reason, 'if the body of Negrodom is that weak and shiftless and criminal, no need to bother one's head about them'" (Hurston to Edwin Osgood Grover, November 7, 1943, qtd. in Carla Kaplan 496).

11. There are in fact numerous acts of interracial sympathy in the collection; see, for example, "Fire and Cloud," and especially "Bright and Morning Star," which was added in an edition after the one that Hurston reviewed. Hurston's language is somewhat prophetic, though; in *Black Boy*, published seven years later, Wright did describe his desire to escape "that southern swamp of despair and violence" (414).

12. For a good overview of the Fugitives and their reactionary agrarian philosophy, see Michael Kreyling, *Inventing Southern Literature*, esp. chap. 1.

13. Hurston elaborates her refusal to participate in literary protest in a 1943 letter to the poet Countee Cullen: "Why don't I put something about lynchings in my books? As if all the world did not know about Negroes being lynched! My stand is this: either we must do something about it that the white man will understand and respect, or shut up. No whiner ever got any respect or relief. If some of us must die for human justice, then let us die. For my own part, this poor body of mine is not so precious that I would not be willing to give it up for a good cause. But my own self-respect refuses to let me go to the mourners bench. Our position is like a man sitting on a tack and crying that it hurts, when all he needs to do is to get up off it" (Carla Kaplan 482; emphasis in original).

14. See, for example, Rawlings's *The Yearling* (1938) and *Cross-Creek* (1942), Caldwell's *Tobacco Road* (1932; paperback, 1947), and W. J. Cash's *The Mind of the South* (1941). These authors, of course, represent only a small selection of the most famous examples. Moreover, a 1950 article in *Phylon* entitled "'Cracker Culture': A Preliminary Definition," by Mozell C. Hill and Bevode C. McCall, reveals that not only had several authors written "cracker" novels around this time, but that two of them even used "Suwanee" in their titles: Cecile Marie Matschat, *Suwanee River, a Strange Green Land* (1938), and B. F. Borchardt and E. Sears, *Suwanee Valley* (1940). It should be noted that there were also well-known works that tried to produce dignified portraits of poor white southerners, such as James Agee's *Let Us Now Praise Famous Men* (1941) and John Steinbeck's classic *Grapes of Wrath* (1939).

15. For a provocative reading of Hurston's use of eugenicist discourse in *Seraph*, see Chuck Jackson, "Waste and Whiteness: Zora Neale Hurston and the Politics of Eugenics."

16. Hurston's deeply ambivalent representation of poor white southerners has a great deal of precedent. For useful analyses of the variously progressive and reactionary treatments of poor whites, see esp. Wray and Newitz, *White Trash*; and Hartigan, *Odd Tribes*. Wray's *Not Quite White* analyzes the history of "white trash" in America from the eighteenth century to the eugenics movements of the early twentieth century. One of his central concerns is to discuss the kind of "boundary work" being done by various groups over time in their depictions of and interventions in the lives of "white trash." My essay considers the kind of boundary work "crackers" perform in Hurston's midcentury plantation pastoral. Her vision of interracial harmony requires that she also identify *difference within* whiteness. For detailed overviews of poor whites in southern literature, see Carr, *A Question of Class*; and Cook, *From Tobacco Road*.

17. DuCille and Meisenhelder have argued that we should take Hurston's highly favorable treatment of Jim as purely ironic. This understanding of Jim is the key to understanding *Seraph* as, in Meisenhelder's reading, Hurston's "most subversive attack on the values of what she called 'Anglo-Saxon' civilization. In *Seraph on the Suwanee*, she exposes the foundation of that culture as one resting on oppression of white women, exploitation of people of color, and domination of Nature. To make this critique (and still get the book published), she presents it from behind the trickster's mask of praise, subtly developing her themes through a complex set of symbols developed in other works" (95–96). Meisenhelder elaborates her argument primarily by comparing *Seraph* with *Their Eyes*. In particular, she argues that we can best appreciate Hurston's critique by noting that Arvay's relationship with Jim bears striking similarities to Janie's oppressive relationship with Jody, and striking dissimilarities to "the vigor and equality" (96) of her relationship with Teacake. The main problem with this reading is that Jim is less like Jody and more like Teacake than the comparison implies. If Hurston intends the work to be wholly subversive, how do we account for the fact that Jim embodies a range of qualities that Hurston repeatedly extols in other contexts? In her biographical entry for *Twentieth Century Authors*, she declares: "I love courage in every form. I worship strength. I dislike insincerity, and most particularly when it vaunts itself to cover up cowardice" (695). Jim represents, in general terms, a rugged, southern type of frontier individualism that Hurston admired. In particular, I believe Jim constitutes a fond tribute to the "one person who pleased me always. That was the robust, grey-haired, white man who had helped me get into the world." This man, whom we learn about in her autobiography, is never given a proper name (see *Folklore* 585–88). According to Hurston, he happened to be passing by when Hurston's mother was giving birth, and then "grannied her into existence." He took an active interest in her well-being until he died, when she was ten. "The hard-riding, hard-drinking, hard-cussing, but very successful man was thrown from his horse and died.... He was an accumulating man, a good provider, paid his debts and told the truth.... He was supposed to be so tough, it was said that once he was struck by lightning and was not even knocked off his feet, but that lightning went off through the woods limping. Nobody found any fault with a man like that in a country where personal strength and courage were the highest virtues. People were supposed to take care of themselves without whining" (587–88). This could easily serve as a description of Jim. In fact, Jim even uses the lightning tale when courting Arvay. He tells the incredulous Arvay that "it's a habit of mine ... when I catch a streak of lightning aiming at me, to stand in my tracks and slap it right back where it come from." When one bolt manages to strike him, however, he says: "I wasn't hurt at all, but that sneaking bolt of lightning was done up pretty bad. Yes, Ma'am! Last I seen of it, it was going off through the woods a'limping" (27). My more fundamental disagreement with Meisenhelder's use of *Their Eyes* as a key to *Seraph* derives from the fact that Arvay does not come across as a victim of oppression the way Janie does because she is fundamentally *unlike* Janie (aside from having a spiritual connection to a fruit-bearing tree) and, for that matter, most middle-class white women, who constituted the majority of Hurston's audience. Arvay is extraordinarily unsympathetic (in ways that I detail below), which is why Jim's aggressive, dominating behavior toward her lacks the pathos of Jody's cruelty toward Janie. Janie's vision of herself and the world elicits our sympathy and

admiration; Arvay's perspective is consistently bigoted, ignorant, and self-defeating, which thwarts the reader's capacity to easily identify with her struggles.

18. The NAACP expanded its branches in South Carolina, for example, from eight in 1939, with 800 members, to forty in 1945, with 10,639 members (Sullivan 141).

19. See Ayers, *The Promise of the New South*.

20. See Hale, *Making Whiteness*.

21. The Negroes are not "spoiled" when they pick up a bit of money either. Jim rewards Joe amply for running the still, and we learn that "*Under Jim's pressure*, Joe had put some of his likker money into two lots in Colored Town." After Joe moves away from the Meserve estate, he immediately begins "cutting the tom-fool": "He had the shell of a six-room house thrown up on his lots and moved into the unfinished structure. *That was as far as the house ever got.* Joe bought himself a car and announced that he had got to be people in Citrabelle. Doing things on a high-toned scale. Heavy-set Daddy. If a woman asked him for a nickel, he gave her a ten-dollar bill" (117; emphasis added). Joe later tells an elaborate yarn about how he has lost all of his money because he has no business sense. In other words, as soon as Joe gets out from under the watchful eye of Jim (the beneficent white father-master), he squanders his money like an irresponsible child. Joe's personality and behavior echo all too clearly the bigoted Reconstruction myth that blacks were not only happy, but better off on the plantation, where they can be looked after.

22. Another key parallel between these visions, which I will address in detail below, is a celebration of and faith in "progress." Here Hurston's text breaks from Old South mythology; in lieu of fantasies about an imagined edenic past, one outside of modern progress and time, Hurston's racial pastoral is located firmly in time, and it moves steadily forward with the march of progress.

23. In 1900, over 90 percent of American blacks resided in the South: "The failure of the tremendous expansion of American industry to change materially the essentially peasant and domestic status of most Negroes is evident from the fact that in 1890, 88% and in 1900, 86.7% of all Negroes were still employed in the least remunerative and least dignified occupations" (Logan qtd. in Baker, *Turning South Again* 81).

24. In an extensive and avowedly psychoanalytic review of Baker's *Turning South Again* and *Public Spheres, African American Writing, and Black Fathers and Sons in America* (2001), Anne Goodwyn Jones has argued that Baker's effort to turn south again in a revisionist mode "seems to mean, intellectually as well as personally, a reversion to the past" that "continue[s] to silence black women," despite a significant body of well-known black feminist critique of his work's masculinist tendencies (144, 168). While I certainly do not endorse the erasure of black feminist critique, I do find Baker's analysis of Washington's rhetorical strategies useful, in large part because it helps to illuminate precisely Hurston's own self-erasure, at least in terms of representation, in *Seraph*.

25. Roads are often figured as symbols of personal growth and possibility in Hurston's work. See, for example, "Drenched in Light," "How It Feels to Be Colored Me," and *Their Eyes Were Watching God*, where Isis, Hurston, and Janie, respectively, stand at the roadside, dreaming of new worlds and awaiting opportunity.

26. Arvay's desire to return to the "good old days" would certainly have been rare among poor whites, as the shift from farms to cities often brought about improved

living conditions and quality of life, including "hourly wages, decent housing, better schools, [and] adequate medical care" (Daniel 20).

27. When Jim tells Arvay that he intends to marry her, she thinks to herself that "this was like coming through religion.... Put your whole faith in the mercy of God and believe. Eternal life, Heaven, and its immortal glory were yours if you would only believe. The hold-back was that it was not all that easy to believe. Now was she to believe that this very pretty man clothed in all the joys of Heaven and earth was for *her?*" (26).The preceding passage contains the first of many instances in which Jim is compared with God; Arvay believes that Jim has "everything in the world at his command" (26). Later in the novel, the narrator tells us Arvay's belief that "[w]hat God neglected, Jim Meserve took care of. Between the two, God and Jim, all things came to pass" (152). "Yes, Jim Meserve in his flesh was really there at the table with her. This was a miracle right out of the Bible. For some reason, still and as yet not revealed to Arvay, this miracle of a man had married her" (168). Jim is the Word made flesh.

28. Jim believes that he "serves" Arvay as well. He claims that when you are in love, "You just got to go on serving 'em all your born days" (176); Arvay admits that Jim "had told her time and again that *she owned him* through and through" (177; emphasis added). But the feeling of mutual bondage, mutual dependence—of the master being "owned" by the slave—is, in addition to being a familiar notion from Hegel's description of the master/slave dialectic, a commonplace conceit of the southern "interracial family" that sentimentalizes and masks gross power inequity.

29. In terms of Christian typology, Sawley (standing in for the Old South) represents Canaan, unredeemed under bondage to the law of sin and death. But Jim Meserve carries Arvay into the New Dispensation. The Meserve plantation is the New Canaan, the updated and purified Promised Land.

30. The supposition that crackers are "bad" people—in this case, morally—is also a long-standing stereotype. Wray found that "In every period I examined, in every stereotypical representation I analyzed, and in virtually every historical document I read, strong claims were made about the moral unworthiness of poor whites" (19).

31. Interestingly, Hurston acknowledges that the Portuguese were newcomers to whiteness, but seems to imply that to deny them that status, as Arvay does, is backward: "Jim had said they were white folks, but the man turned out to be a Portuguese, and his name was Corregio. That made them foreigners, and no foreigners were ever quite white to Arvay. Real white people talked English and without any funny sounds to it. The fact that his wife was a Georgia-born girl that he had married up around Savannah did not help the case one bit, so far as Arvay could see. The woman had gone back on her kind and fallen from grace" (120).

32. Consider the following diatribe against black protest writing that Hurston wrote in 1938 for the Florida Federal Writers' Project. She argues that when a Negro writer wants to "sing a song to the morning," he doesn't because "his background thrusts itself between his lips and the star and he mutters, 'Ought I not to be singing of our sorrows? That is what is expected of me and I shall be considered forgetful of our past and present. If I do not some will even call me a coward. The one subject for a Negro is the Race and its sufferings and so the song of the morning must be choked back. *I will write of a lynching instead.*' So the same old theme, the same old phrases get done again to the detriment of art" ("Art and Such" 908; emphasis added).

6 / The Unfinished Project of Western Modernity

1. Wright visited Paris before moving there with his family in 1947 (Wright to Ed Aswell, 21 August 1955, Box 31, File 2, Michel Fabre Papers, Emory University.

2. Wright's travelogue *Pagan Spain* (1957) might be seen as the one full-length nonfiction work in which he did this as well.

3. Novels: *The Outsider* (1953), *Savage Holiday* (1954), and *The Long Dream*, (1958); travel narratives: *Black Power* (1954), *The Color Curtain* (1956), and *Pagan Spain* (1957); essay collection: *White Man Listen!* (1957); posthumously published collection of short stories: *Eight Men* (1961).

4. In Tate's *Psychoanalysis and Black Novels*, she focuses on how *Savage Holiday* inscribes matricidal desire that recurs in Wright's work. Knadler's *The Fugitive Race* considers how Wright undermines the authority of the "organization man" by having his identity shattered by queer panic. JanMohamed reads *Savage Holiday* as "entirely overtaken with the effectivity of death in the primal scene and the subsequent production of matricidal and infanticidal desires" (37). Two other interesting studies of *Savage Holiday* that attend to whiteness are Lale Demirturk's "Mapping the Terrain of Whiteness" and Dubek's "'Til Death Do Us Part." Dubek's reading is the closest to my own; she offers an illuminating analysis of Wright's work as a critique of postwar domestic narratives. My work departs from these latter readings principally through my focus on privacy and *Savage Holiday*'s connection to *The Outsider*.

5. Wright to Ed Aswell, 21 August 1955, Box 31, File 2, Michel Fabre Papers, Emory University.

6. When Erskine is climbing into his apartment, Mabel had caught a glimpse of his feet, though at this point she doesn't know what has happened and thinks nothing of it. After she finds out about Tony's death, she mentions what she saw to a neighbor, who thinks she is making the story up to cover up her immoral behavior. The neighbor remarks: "[T]hese loose women . . . When somebody catches em with a man, they start yelling rape! It's a wonder she didn't say it was a nigger she saw" (109). Dubek argues that "the neighbor's response reveals the intersecting and hierarchical nature of the social construction of race, gender, class, and sexuality in America" (606). Even so, this remark is not commented upon by the narrator or the other characters, and the specter of the black male rapist, ever-present in the Wright's earlier works, never appears again. In fact, black male characters may be seen as conspicuously absent in the novel. Fowler does have a "colored" maid, Minnie, but she appears only briefly in the novel, and offers to cook a meal for the grieving Mabel. Dubek claims that "Minnie links the two households, suggesting at once the necessity and erasure of black identity/labor to the creation and continued health of the white family/nation" (609). I am less persuaded by this reading in light of how minor her role is. Wright does have a few other published fictional works with mostly white characters: his short story, "Big Black Good Man," and "Man, God Ain't Like That," both of which appear in his collection *Eight Men*. Unlike *Savage Holiday*, both of these stories take white supremacy as an explicit theme.

7. Wright to Ed Aswell, 21 August 1955, Box 31, File 2, Michel Fabre Papers, Emory University.

8. *Unfinished Quest* 381. Margrit de Sabloniere translated the work into Dutch, and

it was published by Sijthoff in Leiden, the Netherlands (see "Barbaarse Sabbath," Box 61, Folder 718, Richard Wright Papers, Beinecke Library, Yale University).

9. This double vision is highly reminiscent of how Wright describes his own perspective on Western society: "Being a Negro living in a white Western Christian society, I've never been allowed to blend, in a natural and healthy manner, with the culture and civilization of the West. This contradiction of being both Western and a man of color creates a psychological distance, so to speak, between me and my environment.... [T]hough Western, I'm inevitably critical of the West. Indeed, a vital element of my Western-ness resides in this chronically skeptical, this irredeemably critical, outlook. I'm restless" ("Tradition and Industrialization" 705).

10. When Fowler is forced into retirement, the company president declares, "Well done, thou faithful steward of our trust." The phrasing echoes the lines from Matthew 25:23, "Well done, good and faithful servant," which reinforces Fowler's position as a "moral slave."

11. Box 59, Folder 698, Richard Wright Papers, Beinecke Library, Yale University.

12. Gerald Early's afterword to the 1994 reissue of *Savage Holiday* also notes the significance of religion to the novel and Wright's postwar career (229).

13. Modern racism is "another kind of religion, a religion of the materially dispossessed, of the culturally disinherited.... I know instinctively that this clinging to, and defense of, racism by Western whites are born of their *psychological nakedness*, of their having, through historical accident, partially thrown off the mystic cauls of Asia and Africa that once too blinded and dazed them" (705; emphasis added). Wright almost entirely brackets the issue of white racism in *Savage Holiday*, but Fowler plainly embodies an instance of "psychological nakedness" among modern white Westerners.

14. Box 59, Folder 701, Richard Wright Papers, Beinecke Library, Yale University.

15. See Dubek, "'Til Death Do Us Part," for an extended discussion of Mabel within the context of what she calls the postwar cult of domesticity (606–10).

16. I discuss parallels between the protagonists and plots of *Savage Holiday* and *A Father's Law* in "A Queer Finale."

17. Box 59, Folder 700, Richard Wright Papers, Beinecke Library, Yale University.

Conclusion

1. Hereafter I refer to Monk Ellison as Monk in order to distinguish him from Ralph Ellison.

2. Warren explores a comparable issue at length in *What Was African American Literature?*; he questions whether the unself-conscious categorization of literature by contemporary black writers as "African American literature" allows Jim Crow notions of racial difference to persist in the guise of progressive politics.

3. Robyn Wiegman introduces the notions of critical exteriority, noncomplicity, and identificatory refusal in her essay "The Ends of New Americanism."

Works Cited

Adams, Katherine. *Owning Up: Privacy, Property, and Belonging in U.S. Women's Life Writing, 1840–1890*. Oxford: Oxford UP, 2009.
Agee, James. *Let Us Now Praise Famous Men: Three Tenant Families*. Boston: Houghton Mifflin, 1941.
Althusser, Louis. "Ideology and Ideological State Apparatuses." *Norton Anthology of Theory and Criticism*. Ed. Vincent B Leitch. New York: Norton, 2001. 1483–508.
Asante, Molefi Kete. "Locating a Text: Implications of Afrocentric Theory." www.ipoaa.com/afrocentric_theory.htm.
Attaway, William. *Let Me Breathe Thunder*. New York: Doubleday, Doran, 1939.
Ayers, Edward. *The Promise of the New South: Life after Reconstruction*. New York: Oxford UP, 1992.
Baker, Houston. *Blues, Ideology, and Afro-American Literature: A Vernacular Theory*. Chicago: U of Chicago P, 1984.
———. *Critical Memory: Public Spheres, African American Writing, and Black Fathers and Sons in America*. Athens: U of Georgia P, 2001.
———. *Turning South Again: Re-thinking Modernism/Re-reading Booker T.* Durham, NC: Duke UP, 2001.
Baldwin, James. *Collected Essays*. New York: Library of America, 1998.
———. "Disturber of the Peace: James Baldwin—An Interview." *Conversations with James Baldwin*. Ed. Fred L. Standley and Louis H. Pratt. Jackson: UP of Mississippi, 1989. 64–82.
———. "Everybody's Protest Novel." *Notes of a Native Son*. Boston: Beacon, 1955. 13-23.
———. *Giovanni's Room*. New York: Dial, 1956.

———. "'Go the Way Your Blood Beats': An Interview with James Baldwin." By Richard Goldstein. *James Baldwin: The Legacy.* Ed. Quincy Troupe. New York: Touchstone, 1989. 173–85.

———. "An Interview with James Baldwin on Henry James." By David Adams Leeming. *The Henry James Review* 8.1 (1986): 47–56.

———. "The Male Prison." *Collected Essays.* New York: Library of America, 1998. 231–35.

———. "Many Thousands Gone." *Notes of a Native Son.* Boston: Beacon, 1955. 24–45.

———. *Nobody Knows My Name: More Notes of a Native Son.* New York: Dial, 1961.

———. *Notes of a Native Son.* Boston: Beacon, 1955.

———. *The Price of the Ticket: Collected Non-fiction, 1948–1985.* New York: St. Martin's, 1985.

Balibar, Etienne. "Is There a Neo-Racism?" *Race, Nation, and Class.* Ed. Balibar and E. Wallerstein. New York: Verso, 1991. 17–28.

Barnes, Elizabeth. *States of Sympathy: Seduction and Democracy in the American Novel.* New York: Columbia UP, 1997.

Barrett, Lindon. *Blackness and Value: Seeing Double.* Cambridge: Cambridge UP, 1999.

Bay, Mia. *The White Image in the Black Mind: African American Ideas about White People, 1830–1925.* New York: Oxford UP, 2000.

Bell, Bernard. *The Afro-American Novel and Its Tradition.* Amherst: U of Massachusetts P, 1987.

Berlant, Lauren. "Poor Eliza." *American Literature* 70.3 (1998): 635–68.

———. *The Queen of America Goes to Washington City: Essays on Sex and Citizenship.* Durham: Duke UP, 1997.

Berlant, Lauren, and Michael Warner. "Sex in Public." *Critical Inquiry* 24.2 (Winter 1998): 547–66. Reprinted in *Intimacy.* Ed. Lauren Berlant. Chicago: U of Chicago P, 2000.

Bernard, Emily. "Raceless Writing and Difference: Ann Petry's *Country Place* and the African American Canon." *Studies in American Fiction* 33.1 (Spring 2005): 87–117.

Blount, Marcellus, and George P. Cunningham, eds. *Representing Black Men.* New York: Routledge, 1996.

Bone, Robert A. *The Negro Novel in America.* 1958. Rev. ed. New Haven: Yale UP, 1964.

Bontemps, Arna. "From Lad of Ireland to Bayou Grandee." *Chicago Sun Book Week* February 10, 1946: 1.

Borchardt, B. F., and E. Sears. *Suwannee Valley.* New York: Harbinger House, 1940.

Brandt, Nat. *Harlem at War: The Black Experience in World War II.* Syracuse, NY: Syracuse UP, 1996.

Brown, Lloyd. "Which Way for the Negro Writer?" *Masses & Mainstream* 4.3 (March 1951): 53–63.

———. "Which Way for the Negro Writer? II." *Masses & Mainstream* 4.4 (April 1951): 50–59.

Brown, Sterling A. "The Negro Author and His Publisher." *Quarterly Review of Higher Education among Negroes* 9.3 (July 1941): 140–46.

Burnett, W. R. "Hopeless Waiting." Rev. of *Cast the First Stone* by Chester Himes. *Saturday Review* 17 January 1953: 15.

Burns, Ben. "Off the Book Shelf." Rev. *The Foxes of Harrow*. *Chicago Defender*. 2 February 1946: 15.

Butcher, Philip. "Our Raceless Writers." *Opportunity* 26 (Summer 1948): 114–15.

Cable, George Washington. *The Grandissimes: A Story of Creole Life*. New York: Scribner's, 1880.

Caldwell, Erskine. *Tobacco Road*. 1932. New York: Scribner's Sons, 1947.

Carby, Hazel V. Foreword. *Seraph on the Suwanee*. By Zora Neale Hurston. New York: HarperPerennial, 1991. vii–xviii.

———. "Policing the Black Woman's Body in an Urban Context." *Critical Inquiry* 18 (Summer 1992): 738–55.

———. "The Politics of Fiction, Anthropology, and the Folk: Zora Neale Hurston." *New Essays on Their Eyes Watching God*. Ed. Michael Awkward. Cambridge: Cambridge UP, 1990. 71–93.

Carr, Duane. *A Question of Class: The Redneck Stereotype in Southern Fiction*. Bowling Green, OH: Bowling Green State U Popular Press, 1996.

Carter, Michael. "Meet Frank 'Foxes of Harrow' Yerby." *Afro American* 2 March 1946: 14.

Cash, W. J. *The Mind of the South*. New York: Knopf, 1941.

Castiglia, Christopher. "Abolition's Racial Interiors and the Making of White Civic Depth." *American Literary History* 14.1 (2002): 32–59.

———. *Interior States: Institutional Consciousness and the Inner Life of Democracy in the Antebellum United States*. Durham, NC: Duke UP, 2008.

Cayton, Horace. "The Known City." *New Republic* 12 May 1947: 30–31.

———. "Literary Expansion: Another Best-Seller by a Negro Is Not of the Negro or His Environs." *Pittsburgh Courier* 24 May 1947: 7.

———. *Long Old Road: An Autobiography*. New York: Trident Press, 1965.

Certeau, Michel de. *The Practice of Everyday Life*. Trans. Steven Randall. Berkeley: U of California P, 1984.

Charles, John C. "A Queer Finale: Sympathy and Privacy in Wright's *A Father's Law*." *Richard Wright: New Readings in the 21st Century*. Ed. Alice Mikal Craven and William E. Dow. New York: Palgrave, 2010.

Chauncey, George. *Gay New York: Gender, Urban Culture, and the Making of the Gay Male World, 1890–1940*. New York: Basic, 1994.

Chesnutt, Charles W. *The Colonel's Dream*. 1905. Miami: Mnemosyne, 1969.

Clark, Keith. "A Distaff Dream Deferred? Ann Petry and the Art of Subversion." *African American Review* 26.3 (1992): 495–505.
Cook, Sylvia Jenkins. *From Tobacco Road to Route 66: The Southern Poor White in Fiction.* Chapel Hill: U of North Carolina P, 1976.
Corber, Robert J. *Homosexuality in Cold War America: Resistance and the Crisis of Masculinity.* Durham, NC: Duke UP, 1997.
Cotkin, George. *Existential America.* Baltimore: Johns Hopkins UP, 2003.
Cuordileone, K. A. *Manhood and American Political Culture in the Cold War.* New York: Routledge, 2005.
Daniel, Pete. *Lost Revolutions: The South in the 1950s.* Chapel Hill: U of North Carolina P, 2000.
Davis, Arthur P. *From the Dark Tower: Afro-American Writers 1900 to 1960.* Washington, DC: Howard UP, 1974.
Davis, Jane. *The White Image in the Black Mind: A Study of African American Literature.* Westport, CT: Greenwood, 2000.
Delany, Samuel. *Times Square Red, Times Square Blue.* New York: New York UP, 1999.
Demirturk, Lale. "Mapping the Terrain of Whiteness: Richard Wright's *Savage Holiday*" *Melus* 24.1 (1999): 129–40.
Denning, Michael. *The Cultural Front: The Laboring of American Culture in the Twentieth Century.* London: Verso, 1998.
D'Emilio, John, and Estelle B. Freedman, eds. *Intimate Matters: A History of Sexuality in America.* 2nd ed. Chicago: U of Chicago P, 1997.
Donaldson, Susan, and Anne Goodwyn Jones. "Haunted Bodies: Rethinking the South through Gender." *Haunted Bodies: Gender and Southern Texts.* Ed. Jones and Donaldson. Charlottesville: U of Virginia P, 1997. 1–19.
Douglass, Frederick. *Narrative of the Life of Frederick Douglass, An American Slave, Written by Himself.* 1845. New York: Signet, 1968.
Drexel, Allen. "Before Paris Burned: Race, Class, and Male Homosexuality on the Chicago South Side, 1935–1960." *Creating a Place for Ourselves: Lesbian, Gay, and Bisexual Community Histories.* Ed. Brett Beemyn. New York: Routledge, 1997.
Dubek, Laura. "'Til Death Do Us Part: White Male Rage in Richard Wright's *Savage Holiday*." *Mississippi Quarterly* 61.4 (Fall 2008): 593–613.
———. "White Family Values in Ann Petry's *Country Place*." *Melus* 29.2 (Summer 2004): 55–76.
Du Bois, W.E.B. *The Philadelphia Negro: A Social Study.* Boston: Ginn, 1899.
———. *The Souls of Black Folk.* Chicago: McClurg, 1903.
Ducille, Ann. *The Coupling Convention: Sex, Text, and Tradition in Black Women's Fiction.* New York: Oxford UP, 1993.
Dunbar, Paul Lawrence. *The Love of Landry.* New York: Dodd, Mead, 1900.
———. *The Uncalled.* New York: Dodd, Mead, 1898.

Dyer, Richard. "Entertainment and Utopia." *Movies and Methods: An Anthology.* Vol. 2. Ed. B. Nichols. Berkeley: U of California P, 1994. 220–32.
Early, Gerald. Afterword. *Savage Holiday.* By Richard Wright. Jackson: UP of Mississippi, 1994. 223–35.
Edelman, Lee. "Tea Rooms and Sympathy; or, The Epistemology of the Water Closet." *The Lesbian and Gay Studies Reader.* Ed. Henry Abelove, Michèle Aina Barale, and David M. Halperin. New York: Routledge, 1993. 553–74.
Ehrenreich, Barbara. *Hearts of Men: American Dreams and the Flight from Commitment.* New York: Anchor, 1987.
Ellison, Ralph. *Flying Home and Other Stories.* Ed. John F. Callahan. New York: Random House, 1996.
———. *Invisible Man.* New York: Random House, 1952.
———. *Juneteenth.* Ed. John F. Callahan. New York: Random House, 1999.
———. "Richard Wright and Recent Negro Fiction." *Direction* (Summer 1941): 12–13.
———. "Twentieth-Century Fiction and the Black Mask of Humanity." *The Collected Essays of Ralph Ellison.* Ed. John F. Callahan. New York: Random House, 1995.
———. "The World and the Jug." *The Collected Essays of Ralph Ellison.* Ed. John F. Callahan. New York: Random House, 1995.
Erenberg, Lewis, and Susan Hirsch, eds. *The War in American Culture: Society and Consciousness during World War II.* Chicago: U of Chicago P, 1996.
Ervin, Hazel Arnett. *Ann Petry: A Bio-Bibliography.* New York: G. K. Hall, 1993.
Ervin, Hazel, and Hilary Holladay, eds. *The Critical Response to Ann Petry.* Westport, CT: Praeger, 2005.
Escoffier, Jeffrey. *American Homo: Community and Perversity.* Berkeley: U of California P, 1998.
Everett, Percival. *Erasure.* New York: Hyperion, 2001.
———. *Glyph.* Saint Paul, MN: Graywolf, 1999.
———. *I Am Not Sidney Poitier.* Saint Paul, MN: Graywolf, 2009.
Fabre, Michel. *The Unfinished Quest of Richard Wright.* 2nd ed. Trans. Isabel Barzun. Urbana: U of Illinois P, 1993.
Fabre, Michel, and Robert E. Skinner, eds. *Conversations with Chester Himes.* Jackson: UP of Mississippi, 1995.
Favor, Martin. *Authentic Blackness: The Folk in the New Negro Renaissance.* Durham, NC: Duke UP, 1999.
Feldstein, Ruth. *Motherhood in Black and White: Race and Sex in American Liberalism, 1930–1965.* Ithaca, NY: Cornell UP, 2000.
Ferguson, Roderick A. *Aberrations in Black: Toward a Queer of Color Critique.* Minneapolis: U of Minnesota P, 2004.
Fikes, Robert, Jr. "Escaping the Literary Ghetto: African American Authors of

White Life Novels, 1946–1994." *Western Journal of Black Studies* 19.2 (1995): 105–12.

———. "The Persistent Allure of Universality: African American Authors of White Life Novels, 1890-1945." *Western Journal of Black Studies* 20.4 (1996): 221–26.

Fisher, Rudolph. *The Walls of Jericho*. 1928. Ann Arbor: U of Michigan P, 1994.

Fiske, John. "Popular Discrimination." *Modernity and Mass Culture*. Ed. James Naremore and Patrick Bratlinger. Bloomington: Indiana UP, 1991. 103–16.

Fitzhugh, George. *Cannibals All or Slaves without Masters*. Richmond: A. Morris, 1857.

———. "Southern Thought." *The Ideology of Slavery: Proslavery Thought in the Antebellum South, 1830–1860*. Ed. Drew Gilpin Faust. Baton Rouge: Louisiana State UP, 1981.

Fleming, Robert. *Willard Motley*. Boston: Twayne, 1978.

Foley, Barbara. *Radical Representations: Politics and Form in U.S. Proletarian Fiction, 1929–1941*. Durham, NC: Duke UP, 1993.

———. *Wrestling with the Left: The Making of Ralph Ellison's Invisible Man*. Durham, NC: Duke UP, 2010.

Foucault, Michel. "Friendship as a Way of Life." *Ethics*. Ed. Paul Rabinow. Vol. 1 of *Michel Foucault: The Essential Works*. London: Penguin, 1997.

———. *The History of Sexuality*. Trans. Robert Hurley. New York: Pantheon, 1978.

Franklin, H. Bruce. *Prison Literature in America: The Victim as Criminal and Artist*. Expanded ed. New York: Oxford UP, 1989.

Friedman, Susan Stanford. *Mappings: Feminism and the Cultural Geographies of Encounter*. Princeton, NJ: Princeton UP, 1998.

Fuller, Hoyt. "Famous Writer Faces a Challenge." *Ebony* June 1966: 188–94.

Garcia, Jay. "Psychology Comes to Harlem: Race, Intellectuals, and Culture in the Mid-Twentieth Century U.S." Diss. Yale U, 2003.

Gates, Henry Louis, Jr. "Canon-Formation, Literary History, and the Afro-American Tradition: From the Seen to the Told." *Afro-American Literary Study in the 1990s*. Ed. Houston A. Baker Jr. and Patricia Redmond. U of Chicago P, 1989. 14–39.

———. *The Signifying Monkey: A Theory of African American Literary Criticism*. New York: Oxford UP, 1988.

———. "Talking Black: Critical Signs of the Times." *The Norton Anthology of Theory and Criticism*. Ed. Vincent B. Leitch. New York: Norton, 2001. 2424–31.

———. *Tradition and the Black Atlantic: Critical Theory in the African Diaspora*. New York: Basic Civitas, 2010.

Gayle, Addison. "The Black Aesthetic." *The Norton Anthology of African American Literature*. 2nd ed. Ed. Henry Louis Gates and Nellie McKay. New York: Norton, 2004. 1912–18.

Genovese, Eugene D. "Toward a Kinder and Gentler America: The Southern

Lady in the Greening of the Politics of the Old South." *In Joy and in Sorrow: Women, Family, and Marriage in the Victorian South, 1830–1900*. Ed. Carol Bleser. New York: Oxford UP, 1991. 125–34.

Gerstle, Gary. *American Crucible: Race and Nation in the Twentieth Century*. Princeton, NJ: Princeton UP, 2001.

Gibson, Richard. "The Color of Experience." *Nation* February 7, 1959: 123.

———. "A No to Nothing." *Kenyon Review* 13 (1951): 252–55.

Gilroy, Paul. *The Black Atlantic: Modernity and Double Consciousness*. Cambridge: Harvard UP, 1993.

Gloster, Hugh M. "The Significance of Frank Yerby." *Crisis* 5.1 (January 1948): 12–13.

Greenberg, Cheryl. *Or Does It Explode? Black Harlem and the Great Depression*. New York: Oxford UP, 1991.

Guglielmo, Thomas. *White on Arrival: Italians, Race, Color, and Power in Chicago, 1890–1945*. New York: Oxford UP, 2003.

Guterl, Matthew Pratt. *The Color of Race in America, 1900–1940*. Cambridge: Harvard UP, 2001.

Hackett, Alice Payne, and James Henry Burke, eds. *80 Years of Best Sellers: 1895–1975*. New York: Bowker, 1976.

Hale, Grace. *Making Whiteness: The Culture of Segregation in the South, 1890–1940*. New York: Pantheon, 1998.

Halperin, David M. "How to Do the History of Male Homosexuality." *GLQ: A Journal of Lesbian and Gay Studies* 6.1 (2000): 87–123.

"Harlem: Post-Mortem." *Washington Post* 8 August 1943: B6.

Harper, Phillip Brian. *Private Affairs: Critical Ventures in the Culture of Social Relations*. New York: New York UP, 1999.

Harris, Cheryl I. "Whiteness as Property." *Harvard Law Review*. 106.8 (1993): 1707–91.

Harris, Trudier, ed. *Afro-American Writers 1940–1955*. Vol. 76 of *Dictionary of Literary Biography*. Detroit: Gale Research, 1988.

Hartigan, John, Jr. *Odd Tribes: Toward A Cultural Analysis of White People*. Durham, NC: Duke UP 2005.

Hatcher, Harlan. "The New Vogue of Historical Fiction." *English Journal* 26.10 (December 1937): 775–84.

Hemenway, Robert. *Zora Neale Hurston: A Literary Biography*. Urbana: U of Illinois P, 1980.

Henderson, Mae G. "James Baldwin's *Giovanni's Room*: Expatriation, 'Racial Drag,' and Homosexual Panic." *Black Queer Studies: A Critical Anthology*. Ed. E. Patrick Johnson and Mae G. Henderson. Durham, NC: Duke UP, 2005.

Herman, Ellen. *The Romance of American Psychology: Political Culture in the Age of Experts*. Berkeley: U of California P, 1995.

Hill, James. "The Anti-Heroic Hero in Frank Yerby's Historical Novels." *Perspectives of Black Popular Culture. Ed. Harry B. Shaw. Bowling Green, OH: Bowling Green State UP, 1990. 144–54.

———. "An Interview with Frank Garvin Yerby." Resources for American Literary Study 21.2 (1995): 206–39.

Hill, Mozell C., and Bevode C. McCall. "'Cracker Culture': A Preliminary Definition." Phylon 11.3 (third quarter 1950): 223–31.

Hill, William. "Behind the Magnolia Mask: The Fiction of Frank Yerby." Master's thesis, Auburn U, 1968.

Himes, Chester. Cast the First Stone. New York: Chatham, 1952.

———. My Life of Absurdity: The Autobiography of Chester Himes. Vol. 2. 1976. New York: Paragon, 1990.

———. The Quality of Hurt: The Autobiography of Chester Himes. Vol. 1. 1972. New York: Paragon, 1990.

———. Yesterday Will Make You Cry. New York: Norton, 1998.

Hirsch, Arnold. Making the Second Ghetto: Race and Housing in Chicago, 1940–1960. Chicago: U of Chicago P, 1998.

Holladay, Hilary. Ann Petry. New York: Twayne, 1996.

Holland, Sharon Patricia. "(Pro)creating Imaginative Spaces and Other Queer Acts: Randall Keenan's A Visitation of Spirits and Its Revival of James Baldwin's Absent Black Gay Man in Giovanni's Room." James Baldwin Now. Ed. Dwight McBride. New York: New York UP, 1999. 265–88.

Hook, R. H. "Psychoanalysis, Unconscious Phantasy and Interpretation." Anthropology and Psychoanalysis: An Encounter through Culture. Ed. Suzette Heald and Ariane Deluz. New York: Routledge, 1994. 114–30.

hooks, bell. "Representing Whiteness in the Black Imagination." Cultural Studies. Ed. Lawrence Grossberg et al. London: Routledge, 1992. 338–42.

Howe, Irving. "Black Boys and Native Sons." A World More Attractive. New York: Horizon, 1963.

Hughes, Langston. "The Negro Artist and the Racial Mountain." Voices from the Harlem Renaissance. Ed. Nathan Irvin Huggins. New York: Oxford UP, 1976. 305–9.

Hurston, Zora Neale. "Art and Such." Folklore, Memoirs, and Other Writings. New York: Library of America, 1995. 905–11.

———. Folklore, Memoirs, and Other Writings. New York: Library of America, 1995.

———. "How It Feels to Be Colored Me." Folklore, Memoirs, and Other Writings. New York: Library of America, 1995. 826–29.

———. Seraph on the Suwanee. 1948. New York: HarperPerennial, 1991.

———. "Stories of Conflict." Folklore, Memoirs, and Other Writings. New York: Library of America, 1995. 912–13.

———. Their Eyes Were Watching God. New York: Lippincott. 1937.

———. "To Burroughs Mitchell." October 2, 1947. Zora Neale Hurston: A Life in Letters. Ed. Carla Kaplan. New York: Doubleday, 2002. 557–61.

———. "To Burton Rascoe." September 8, 1944. *Zora Neale Hurston: A Life in Letters*. Ed. Carla Kaplan. New York: Doubleday, 2002. 502–4.

———. "To Countee Cullen." March 5, 1943. *Zora Neale Hurston: A Life in Letters*. Ed. Carla Kaplan. New York: Doubleday, 2002. 480–82.

———. "To Edwin Osgood Grover." November 7, 1943. *Zora Neale Hurston: A Life in Letters*. Ed. Carla Kaplan. New York: Doubleday, 2002. 495–97.

———. "What White Publishers Won't Print." 1950. *The Norton Anthology of Theory and Criticism*. Ed. Vincent Leitch. New York: Norton, 2001. 1159–62.

"Hurston, Zora Neale." *Twentieth Century Authors: A Biographical Dictionary of Modern Literature*. Ed. Stanley J. Kunitz and Howard Haycraft. New York: Wilson, 1942. 694–95.

Ignatiev, Noel. *How the Irish Became White*. New York: Routledge, 1995.

Jackson, Blyden. "Faith without Works in Negro Literature." *Phylon* 12.4 (4th quarter 1951): 378–88.

———. "Full Circle." *Phylon* 9.1 (1946): 30–35.

Jackson, Chuck. "Waste and Whiteness: Zora Neale Hurston and the Politics of Eugenics." *African American Review* 34.4 (Winter 2000): 639–60.

Jackson, Lawrence. "The Birth of the Critic: The Literary Friendship of Ralph Ellison and Richard Wright." *American Literature* 72.2 (2000): 321–55.

———. *The Indignant Generation: A Narrative History of African American Writers and Critics, 1934–1960*. Princeton, NJ: Princeton UP, 2010.

———. *Ralph Ellison: Emergence of Genius*. New York: Wiley and Sons, 2002.

Jacobson, Matthew Frye. *Whiteness of a Different Color: European Immigrants and the Alchemy of Race*. Cambridge: Harvard UP, 1998.

JanMohamed, Abdul. *The Death-Bound-Subject: Richard Wright's Archaeology of Death*. Durham: Duke UP, 2005.

Jarrett, Gene Andrew (ed). *African American Literature Beyond Race: An Alternative Reader*. New York: New York UP, 2006.

———. *Deans and Truants: Race and Realism in African American Literature*. Philadelphia: U of Pennsylvania P, 2006.

Jarrett, Thomas D. "Recent Fiction by Negroes." *College English* 16.2 (November 1954): 85–91.

Jenkins, Candice M. *Private Lives, Proper Relations: Regulating Black Intimacy*. Minneapolis: U of Minnesota P, 2007.

Johnson, Amelia E. *Clarence and Corrine; or, God's Way*. Ed. Henry Louis Gates Jr. New York: Oxford UP, 1988.

Johnson, David K. *The Lavender Scare: The Cold War Persecution of Gays and Lesbians in the Federal Government*. Chicago: U of Chicago P, 2004.

Johnson, E. Patrick, and Mae G. Henderson, eds. *Black Queer Studies: A Critical Anthology*. Durham, NC: Duke UP, 2005.

Jones, Anne Goodwyn. "Houston Baker and the South: More Tight Spots." *Southern Literary Journal* 36.2 (Spring 2004): 145–70.

Jones, Jacqueline. *Labor of Love, Labor of Sorrow: Black Women, Work, and the Family from Slavery to the Present*. New York: Basic, 1985.
Kaplan, Carla. *Zora Neale Hurston: A Life in Letters*. New York: Doubleday, 2002.
Kaplan, Cora. "'A *Cavern Opened* in My Mind': The Poetics of Homosexuality and the Politics of Masculinity in James Baldwin." *Representing Black Men*. Ed. Marcellus Blount and George P. Cunningham. New York: Routledge, 1996. 27–54.
Kastor, Peter. *The Nation's Crucible: The Louisiana Purchase and the Creation of America*. New Haven: Yale UP, 2004.
King, Richard H. *Race, Culture, and the Intellectuals, 1940–1970*. Baltimore: Johns Hopkins UP, 2004.
Kinnamon, Kenneth, and Michel Fabre, eds. *Conversations with Richard Wright*. Jackson: UP of Mississippi, 1993.
Klinkowitz, Jerome, and Karen Wood, "The Making and Unmaking of *Knock on Any Door*." *Proof* 3 (1973): 121–37.
Knadler, Stephen P. *The Fugitive Race: Minority Writers Resisting Whiteness*. Jackson: UP of Mississippi, 2002.
Kreyling, Michael. *Inventing Southern Literature*. Jackson: UP of Mississippi, 1998.
Kristeva, Julia. *Powers of Horror: An Essay on Abjection*. Trans. Leon S. Roudiez. New York: Columbia UP, 1982.
Kunzel, Regina. "Situating Sex: Prison Sexual Culture in the Mid-Twentieth-Century United States." *GLQ: A Journal of Lesbian and Gay Studies* 8.3 (2002): 253–70.
Larsen, Nella. *"Quicksand" and "Passing."* Ed. Deborah E. McDowell. 1928, 1929. New Brunswick, NJ: Rutgers UP, 1986.
Leeming, David. *James Baldwin: A Biography*. New York: Knopf, 1994.
Lipsitz, George. *The Possessive Investment in Whiteness: How White People Profit from Identity Politics*. Philadelphia: Temple UP, 1998.
Littlejohn, David. *Black on White: A Critical Survey of Writing by American Negroes*. New York: Grossman, 1966.
Locke, Alain. "The New Negro." *The New Negro*. Ed. Locke. 1925. New York: Atheneum, 1968.
Logan, Rayford. *The Betrayal of the Negro: From Rutherford B. Hayes to Woodrow Wilson*. New York: Da Capo, 1997.
Lott, Eric. *Love and Theft: Blackface Minstrelsy and the American Working Class*. New York: Oxford UP, 1993.
———. "White Like Me: Racial Cross-Dressing and the Construction of American Whiteness." *Cultures of United States Imperialism*. Ed. Amy Kaplan and Donald E. Pease. Durham, NC: Duke UP, 1993. 474–95.
"Louisiana before the War." *Christian Science Monitor* 16 February 1946: 14.
Lowe, John. *Jump at the Sun: Zora Neale Hurston's Cosmic Comedy*. Urbana: U of Illinois P, 1994.

Lubin, Alex. *Revising the Blueprint: Ann Petry and the Literary Left*. Jackson: UP of Mississippi, 2007.
Margolies, Edward, and Michel Fabre. *The Several Lives of Chester Himes*. Jackson: UP of Mississippi, 1997.
Match, Richard. "The Vulpine Master of Harrow." *New York Times*, February 10, 1946: 8.
Matschat, Cecile Hulse. *Suwannee River, a Strange Green Land*. New York: Farrar and Rinehart, 1938.
Maxwell, William. *New Negro, Old Left: African American Writing and Communism between the Wars*. New York: Columbia UP, 1993.
May, Elaine Tyler. *Homeward Bound: American Families in the Cold War Era*. New York: Basic, 1988.
McBride, Dwight. *Why I Hate Abercrombie & Fitch: Essays on Race and Sexuality*. New York: New York UP, 2005.
McKay, Claude. *Home to Harlem*. 1928. Boston: Northeastern UP, 1987.
McKee, James B. *Sociology and the Race Problem: The Failure of a Perspective*. Champaign: U of Illinois P, 1993.
Meisenhelder, Susan Edwards. *Hitting a Straight Lick with a Crooked Stick: Race and Gender in the Works of Zora Neale Hurston*. Tuscaloosa: U of Alabama P, 1999.
Meyerowitz, Joann, ed. *Not June Cleaver: Women and Gender in Postwar America, 1945–1960*. Philadelphia: Temple UP, 1994.
Miller, D. A. *Place for Us: Essay on the Broadway Musical*. Cambridge: Harvard UP, 1998.
Milliken, Stephen F. *Chester Himes: A Critical Appraisal*. Columbia: U of Missouri P, 1976.
Mitchell, Margaret. *Gone with the Wind*. 1936. New York: Pocket Book, 1969.
Morrison, Toni. *Playing in the Dark: Whiteness in the Literary Imagination*. New York: Random House, 1992.
———. "Unspeakable Things Unspoken: The Afro-American Presence in American Literature." *Criticism and the Color Line: Desegregating Literary Studies*. Ed. Henry Wonham. New Brunswick, NJ: Rutgers UP, 1996.
Morton, Frederic. Rev. of *Cast the First Stone*. *New York Herald Tribune Review of Books* 10 January 1954: 6.
Motley, Willard. *Knock on Any Door*. New York: Appleton, Century, Crofts, 1947.
———. *Let No Man Write My Epitaph*. New York: Random House, 1958.
———. *We Fished All Night*. New York: Appleton, Century, Crofts, 1951.
Mullen, Bill V. *Popular Fronts: Chicago and African American Cultural Politics, 1935–46*. Urbana: U of Illinois P, 1999.
Muller, Gilbert H. *Chester Himes*. Boston: Twayne, 1989.
Mumford, Kevin J. *Interzones: Black/White Sex Districts in Chicago and New York in the Early Twentieth Century*. New York: Columbia UP, 1997.

Munoz, Jose Estaban. *Disidentifications: Queers of Color and the Performance of Politics*. Minneapolis: U of Minnesota P, 1999.

Murphy, Geraldine. "Subversive Anti-Stalinism: Race and Sexuality in the Early Essays of James Baldwin." *ELH* 63.4 (1996): 1021–46.

Myrdal, Gunnar. *An American Dilemma: The Negro Problem and American Democracy*. New York: Harper and Brothers, 1944. Cited as *AAD*.

The Negro in Literature: The Current Scene. Spec. issue of *Phylon* 2 (fourth quarter 1950). Reprinted in *Afro American Writers, 1940–1955*. Ed. Trudier Harris. Vol. 76 of *Dictionary of Literary Biography*. Detroit: Gale Research, 1988.

"New Richard Wright Novel Out in February." *Jet Magazine* 11 December 1952: 41.

Nugent, Richard Bruce. "Smoke, Lillies, and Jade." *Fire!!* 1.1 (1926): 33–39.

Ortiz, Paul. *Emancipation Betrayed: The Hidden History of Black Organizing and White Violence in Florida from Reconstruction to the Bloody Election of 1920*. Berkeley: U of California P, 2005.

Osucha, Eden. "The Whiteness of Privacy: Race, Media, Law." *Camera Obscura: A Journal of Feminism, Culture, and Media Studies* 24.1 70 (2009): 67–107.

Overstreet, Harry Allen. "The Negro Writer as Spokesman." *Saturday Review of Literature* September 2, 1944: 5–6.

Page, Thomas Nelson. *Red Rock: A Chronicle of Reconstruction*. New York: Scribner's, 1898.

Patterson, William L. "Gone with the Wind." *Chicago Defender* 6 January 1940: 15.

Payne, Charles M., and Adam Green, eds. *Time Longer Than Rope: A Century of African American Activism: 1850–1950*. New York: New York UP, 2003.

Petry, Ann. *Country Place*. Boston: Houghton Mifflin, 1947.

———. "The Great Secret." *Writer* July 1948: 215–17.

———. *Miss Muriel and Other Stories*. 1971. New York: Houghton Mifflin, 1999.

———. *The Street*. Boston: Houghton Mifflin, 1946.

———. "Working Notes for *Country Place*." Manuscript. N.d.

Petry, Elisabeth. *At Home Inside: A Daughter's Tribute to Ann Petry*. Jackson: UP of Mississippi, 2009.

Pettigrew, Thomas. *The Sociology of Race Relations: Reflection and Reform*. New York: Simon and Schuster, 1980.

Posnock, Ross. *Color and Culture: Black Writers and the Making of the Modern Intellectual*. Cambridge: Harvard UP, 1998.

"Race Bias Denied as Rioting Factor." *New York Times* 3 August 1943, sec. 1: 11.

Rai, Amit S. *Rule of Sympathy: Sentiment, Race, and Power, 1750–1850*. New York: Palgrave, 2002.

Rampersad, Arnold. *Ralph Ellison: A Biography*. New York: Knopf, 2007.

Rawlings, Majorie Kinnan. *Cross Creek*. New York: Scribner's, 1942.

———. *The Yearling*. New York: Scribner's, 1938.

Rechy, John. *City of Night*. New York: Grove, 1963.

Redding, J. Saunders. "The Fall and Rise of Negro Literature." *Negro Digest* (September 1949): 41–49.

———. "The Negro Author: His Publisher, His Public and His Purse." *Publisher's Weekly* 24 March 1945: 1284–88.

Rieger, Christopher. "The Working-Class Pastoral of Zora Neal Hurston's *Seraph on the Suwanee*." *Mississippi Quarterly* 56.1 (Winter 2002–3): 105–24.

Riesman, David. *The Lonely Crowd: A Study of the Changing American Character.* New Haven: Yale UP, 1950.

Roediger, David R. *Black on White: Black Writers on What It Means to Be White.* New York: Schocken, 1998.

———. *The Wages of Whiteness: Race and the Making of the American Working Class.* London: Verso, 1991.

———. *Working toward Whiteness: How America's Immigrants Become White: The Strange Journey from Ellis Island to the Suburbs.* New York: Basic, 2005.

Rogin, Michael. "Kiss Me Deadly: Communism, Motherhood, and Cold War Movies." *Representations* 6 (1984): 1–36.

Ross, Marlon. "Beyond the Closet as Raceless Paradigm." *Black Queer Studies: A Critical Anthology.* Ed. E. Patrick Johnson and Mae G. Henderson. Durham, NC: Duke UP, 2005. 161–89.

———. *Manning the Race: Reforming Black Men in the Jim Crow Era.* New York: New York UP, 2004.

———. "White Fantasies of Desire: Baldwin and the Racial Identities of Sexuality." *James Baldwin Now.* Ed. Dwight McBride. New York: New York UP, 1999. 13–55.

Rothman, Nathan L. "In Technicolor." Rev. of *The Foxes of Harrow. Saturday Review of Literature* 23 February 1946: 38.

Rowley, Hazel. *Richard Wright: The Life and Times.* New York: Holt, 2001.

Sallis, James. *Chester Himes: A Life.* New York: Walker, 2000.

Schlesinger, Arthur, Jr. *The Vital Center: The Politics of Freedom.* Boston: Houghton Mifflin, 1949.

Scott, Daryl Michael. *Contempt and Pity: Social Policy and the Image of the Damaged Black Psyche, 1880–1996.* Chapel Hill: U of North Carolina P, 1997.

Scott-Childress, Reynolds. "Race, Nation, and the Rhetoric of Color: Locating Japan and China, 1870–1907." *Race and the Production of Modern American Nationalism.* Ed. Scott-Childress. New York: Routledge, 1999.

Séjour, Victor. "The Mulatto." Trans. Philip Barnard. *The Norton Anthology of African American Literature.* 2nd ed. Ed. Henry Louis Gates Jr. and Nellie Y. McKay. New York: Norton, 2004: 353–65. Trans. of "Le Mulâtre." *La Revue des Colonies* 3 (1837): 376–92.

Selby, Hubert, Jr. *Last Exit to Brooklyn.* New York: Grove, 1964.

Singh, Nikhil Pal. *Black Is a Country: Race and the Unfinished Struggle for Democracy.* Cambridge: Harvard UP, 2005.

———. "Culture/Wars: Recoding Empire in an Age of Democracy." *American Quarterly* 50.3 (1998): 471–522.
Smethurst, James. *The New Red Negro: The Literary Left and African American Poetry, 1930–1946*. New York: Oxford UP, 1999.
Smith, Adam. *The Theory of Moral Sentiments*. 1759. London: A. Millar, 1761.
Smith, William Gardner. *Anger at Innocence*. Chatham, NJ: Chatham Bookseller, 1950.
Solove, Daniel. *Understanding Privacy*. Cambridge: Harvard UP, 2008.
Somerville, Siobhan. *Queering the Color Line: Race and the Invention of Homosexuality in American Culture*. Durham, NC: Duke UP, 2000.
Steinbeck, John. *Grapes of Wrath*. New York: Viking, 1939.
Stewart, Donald Ogden, ed. *Fighting Words*. New York: Harcourt Brace, 1940.
Stowe, Harriet Beecher. *Uncle Tom's Cabin or, Life among the Lowly*. 1852. New York: Penguin, 1981.
Suggs, Jon-Christian. *Whispered Consolations: Law and Narrative in African American Life*. Ann Arbor: U of Michigan P, 2000.
Sullivan, Patricia. *Days of Hope: Race and Democracy in the New Deal Era*. Chapel Hill: U of North Carolina P, 1996.
Tate, Claudia. *Psychoanalysis and Black Novels: Desire and the Protocols of Race*. Oxford: Oxford UP, 1998.
Taub, Richard. "An American Dilemma: The Negro Problem and Modern Democracy." *Africana: The Encyclopedia of the African and African American Experience*. Ed. Kwame Anthony Appiah and Henry Louis Gates Jr. New York: Basic Civitas, 1999. 89.
Taylor, Charles. *Modern Social Imaginaries*. Durham: Duke UP, 2004.
Thurman, Wallace. *Infants of the Spring*. Foreword by Amritjit Singh. 1932. Boston: Northeastern UP, 1992.
"Trouble in Harlem." Editorial. *Chicago Daily Tribune* 4 August 1943, sec. 1: 14.
Troupe, Quincy, ed. *James Baldwin: The Legacy*. New York: Touchstone, 1989.
Twentieth Century Authors: A Biographical Dictionary of Modern Literature. Ed. Stanley J. Kunitz and Howard Haycraft. New York: Wilson, 1942.
Turner, Darwin T. "Frank Yerby as Debunker." *Massachusetts Review* 9.3 (Summer 1968): 569–77.
Ueda, Reed. "The Changing Path to Citizenship: Ethnicity and Naturalization during World War II." *The War in American Culture: Society and Consciousness during World War II*. Ed. Lewis A. Erenberg and Susan E. Hirsch. Chicago: U of Chicago P, 1996. 202–16.
"Valentine Lays Rioting to Hoodlumism; Hears Rumors that Gangs Came from South." *New York Times* 3 August 1943, sec. 1: 11.
Vesala-Varttala, Tanja. *Sympathy and Joyce's Dubliners: Ethical Probing of Reading, Narrative, and Textuality*. Tampere, Finland: Tampere UP, 1999.

W.K.R. "Louisiana before the War." Rev. *The Foxes of Harrow*. *Christian Science Monitor* 16 February 1946: 14.
Wald, Alan. *Exiles from a Future Time: The Forging of the Mid-Twentieth-Century Literary Left*. Chapel Hill: U of North Carolina P, 2002.
———. *Writing from the Left: New Essays on Radical Culture and Politics*. New York: Verso, 1994.
Walker, Alice. "Zora Neale Hurston—A Cautionary Tale and Partisan View." *In Search of Our Mothers' Gardens*. New York: Harcourt, 1984. 83–92.
Wall, Cheryl A. ed. *Changing Our Own Words*. New Brunswick, NJ: Rutgers UP, 1989.
Ward, Andrew. *River Run Red: The Fort Pillow Massacre in the American Civil War*. New York: Viking, 2005.
Warner, Michael. *Publics and Counterpublics*. New York: Zone, 2002.
Warren, Kenneth. *So Black and Blue: Ralph Ellison and the Occasion of Criticism*. Chicago: U of Chicago P: 2003.
———. *What Was African American Literature?* Cambridge: Harvard UP, 2010.
Washington, Booker T. *Up from Slavery: Three Negro Classics*. New York: Avon, 1965.
Washington, Mary Helen. "Desegregating the 1950s: The Case of Frank London Brown." *Japanese Journal of American Studies* 10 (1999): 15–32.
———. *Invented Lives: Narratives of Black Women, 1860–1960*. Garden City, NY: Doubleday, 1987.
West, Dorothy. *The Living Is Easy*. 1948. New York: Feminist Press, 1996.
Wiegman, Robyn. "The Ends of New Americanism." *New Literary History* 42.3 (Summer 2011): 385–407.
Wilkerson, Doxy. "Negro Culture: Heritage and Weapon." *Masses & Mainstream* (August 1949): 3–24.
Williams, Linda. *Playing the Race Card: Melodramas of Black and White from Uncle Tom to O. J. Simpson*. Princeton, NJ: Princeton UP, 2001.
Wispé, Lauren. *The Psychology of Sympathy*. New York and London: Plenum Press, 1991.
Woods, Gregory. *A History of Gay Literature: The Male Tradition*. New Haven: Yale UP, 1999.
Woodson, Carter G. Rev. of *The Foxes of Harrow*. *Journal of Negro History* 31.3 (July 1946): 353–54.
Wray, Matt. *Not Quite White: White Trash and the Boundaries of Whiteness*. Durham, NC: Duke UP, 2006.
Wray, Matt, and AnnaLee Newitz, eds. *White Trash: Race and Class in America*. New York: Routledge, 1997.
Wright, Richard. *Black Boy (American Hunger): A Record of Childhood and Youth*. 1945. New York: Harper Perennial, 2006.
———. *Black Power. Three Books from Exile: "Black Power"; "The Color Curtain"; and "White Man, Listen!"* New York: Harper Collins, 2008.

———. *Eight Men*. 1961. New York: Harper Perennial, 1996.
———. "How Bigger Was Born." *Native Son*. 1940. New York: Harper Perennial, 2005.
———. *Native Son*. 1940. New York: Harper Perennial, 2005.
———. *The Outsider*. 1953. New York: Harper Perennial, 2008.
———. *Pagan Spain*. 1957. New York: Harper Perennial, 2008.
———. *Savage Holiday*. Ed. Gerald Early. 1954. Jackson: UP of Mississippi, 1994.
———. "Tradition and Industrialization." *Black Power: Three Books from Exile: "Black Power"; "The Color Curtain"; and "White Man, Listen!"* New York: Harper Collins, 2008. 699–728.
———. *White Man, Listen! Three Books from Exile: "Black Power"; "The Color Curtain"; and "White Man, Listen!"* New York: Harper Collins, 2008.
Yerby, Frank. *The Dahomean*. New York: Dial, 1971.
———. *A Darkness at Ingraham's Crest*. New York: Doubleday, 1979.
———. *The Foxes of Harrow*. New York: Dial, 1946.
———. "Health Card." *Harper's* May 1944: 548–53.
———. "The Homecoming." *Common Ground* 6 (Spring 1946): 41–47.
———. "How and Why I Write the Costume Novel." *Harper's* October 1959: 145–50.
———. "Roads Going Down." *Common Ground* 6 (Summer 1945): 67–72.
———. *Speak Now*. New York: Dial, 1969.
———. "White Magnolias." *Phylon* 5.4 (1944): 319–26.
———. *A Woman Called Fancy*. New York: Dial, 1951.

Index

Adamic, Louis, 36, 211n1
Adams, Katherine, 198, 214n16, 221n3
Althusser, Louis, 226n28
American Dilemma, An. See Myrdal, Gunnar
Anger at Innocence. See Smith, William Gardner
Arendt, Hannah, 222n10
Asante, Molefi Kete, 212n7
Aswell, Ed, 183, 237n1, 238n5, 238n7
Attaway, William, 4, 213n9

Baker, Houston, 15, 170–71, 178–79, 215n25, 236n23, 236n24
Baldwin, James, 2, 7–8, 13, 18, 19, 22, 25–26, 30, 38–39, 40, 44, 50–53, 86–87, 89, 91, 106, 114, 115–129, 216n4, 217n13, 218n20, 220n35, 220n36, 222n8, 227n33, 227n34, 227n36, 227n37; "Everybody's Protest Novel," 8, 50–52, 118, 120, 220n34; *Giovanni's Room*, 2, 19, 86–87, 90–91, 100, 106, 115–29; "Male Prison, The," 121–22, 227n37; *Notes of a Native Son*, 39, 217n13, 222n8; "Preservation of Innocence," 119–20, 121, 122–23, 220n36; *Price of the Ticket, The*, 218n20
Balibar, Etienne, 49
Barrett, Lindon, 55–56, 222n11
Beauvoir, Simone de, 183
Bell, Bernard, 56, 158–59

Berlant, Lauren, 57, 71, 72–73, 114, 125, 216n33, 221n5, 222n14
Bernard, Emily, 221n1
Black Boy. See Wright, Richard
blackness (*also* black abjection, black dysfunction, black familial disorganization, black pathology, black suffering, racial injury), 4, 8–10, 13–16, 20–21, 26–27, 39–42, 47–57, 74, 76, 90, 92, 110, 115, 118–19, 133–34, 136, 145, 164–65, 171, 176, 179, 184, 191–193, 201–7, 212n7, 215n26, 215n28, 219–20n32, 220n35, 226n16, 231n19, 237n32
Bogart, Humphrey, 2, 107
Bone, Robert, 14, 109, 146, 221n2
"Bones of Louella Brown, The." See Petry, Ann
Bontemps, Arna, 131
Brown, Lloyd, 13, 214n19, 214n23
Bunche, Ralph, 41
Butcher, Philip, 13–14, 221n2
Butler, Judith, 121

Carby, Hazel, 92, 225n8, 233n1, 233n4
Cast the First Stone. See Himes, Chester
Castiglia, Christopher 6, 38, 213n12, 216n33
Césaire, Aimé, 183, 217n11
Certeau, Michel de, 110, 112
Challenge, 36
Chauncey, George, 93–94

Chesnutt, Charles, 4, 22, 213n9
Christianity (*also* Jesus Christ, Christian), 42, 50, 83, 111, 175–76, 186, 197, 201, 237n29, 238n9. *See also* religion
civil rights movement, 10, 26, 30, 34, 161, 215n24, 231n20
Commentary, 39, 117, 217n13
Common Ground, 36, 133, 211n1
Conroy, Jack, 36, 211n1
Corber, Robert, 111, 119, 225n10
Country Place. See Petry, Ann
crackers, 2, 20–21, 48, 159–81 passim, 233n2 , 234n14, 234n16, 237n30. *See also* whiteness
Cullen, Countee, 234n13
Cuordileone, K. A., 88–89, 119, 121, 127–28, 224n3, 227n34, 230n13

Dahomean, The. See Yerby, Frank
Davis, Arthur, 14–15, 215n24, 221n2
Davis, Jane, 15–16
Delany, Samuel, 114
Denning, Michael, 33–35, 37, 111, 217n10, 217n14, 229n5
Dixon, Thomas, 134, 139, 154, 168
Douglass, Frederick, 113, 152–53
Dreiser, Theodore, 107
Dubek, Laura, 221n1, 238n4, 238n6, 239n15
Du Bois, W.E.B., 12, 44, 193, 219n23
Ducille, Ann, 215n25, 233n2, 234n17
Dunbar, Paul Lawrence, 4, 22, 208, 213n9

Ellison, Ralph, 4–5, 18, 23, 25, 40, 44, 49, 51, 203–4, 208, 211–12n3, 213n10, 216n4, 217n14, 218n19, 218n22, 219n29, 219n30, 220n33, 220n35, 221n8; *Flying Home and Other Stories*, 211n3; *Invisible Man*, 203–4, 208, 219n30; *Juneteenth*, 212n3; "A Party Down at the Square," 211n3; *Shadow and Act*, 213n10, 218n22
Erasure. See Everett, Percival
Ervin, Hazel, 56, 75, 220n1
Everett, Percival, 204–9; *Erasure*, 204–9; *Glyph*, 209; *I Am Not Sidney Poitier*, 209
"Everybody's Protest Novel." *See* Baldwin, James

fatherhood (*also* father), 50, 75, 82, 91, 129, 136, 142, 146–47, 149, 151–53, 163, 199–200, 203, 207, 229n10, 236n21. *See also* manhood
Feldstein, Ruth, 80–81, 195
Ferguson, Roderick, 9, 40–42, 51, 88, 114, 213n15, 219n25, 221n4, 222n9, 224n23, 225n8
Fikes, Jr. Robert, 211n2
Fisher, Rudolph, 91, 225n7
Flying Home and Other Stories. See Ellison, Ralph
Fort Pillow Massacre, 154–55
Foucault, Michel, 8, 17, 40, 51–52, 101, 104–5, 114, 226n18, 227n31
Foxes of Harrow, The. See Yerby, Frank
Franklin, H. Bruce, 96
Frazier, E. Franklin, 41, 92
Freud, Sigmund, 185, 193

Gates, Henry Louis, 2, 15, 159, 212n5, 215n27
gay, 2, 6, 86–129 passim, 217n17, 220n35, 220n36, 224n4, 225n6, 225n12, 225n15, 226n18. *See also* queer; heteronormative; straight
Gibson, Richard, 5, 18, 25, 40, 48–50, 51, 219n32, 220n34, 220n35
Giovanni's Room. See Baldwin, James
Gloster, Hugh, 12, 13, 131
Glyph. See Everett, Percival
Gone with the Wind. See Mitchell, Margaret
Gordon, Eugene, 214n19

Hale, Grace, 134, 168, 216n31, 229n10, 232n33, 236n20
Halperin, David, 95, 101, 225n11
Hammett, Dashiell, 36
Harper, Phillip Brian, 57–58, 115
Harper's Magazine, 133, 183, 189, 211n1
"Health Card." *See* Yerby, Frank
Henderson, Mae, 115, 215n27, 227n32
Heteronormative (*also* heterosexual, nonheteronormative, straight), 7, 9, 19, 42, 51, 62, 64, 88–94, 97, 100, 103, 106–7, 109–10, 114, 116, 120, 122, 124–25, 220n36, 222n14, 225n12, 229n3. *See also* homoraciality; gay; queer
Heteropatriarchy (*also* heteromasculinity, nonheteropatriarchal), 9–10, 20, 42, 54, 59, 82, 87–89, 91, 93, 106, 116–18, 120,

186, 202, 219n22. *See also* fatherhood; homoraciality; manhood
Hill, James, 131, 148, 228n2, 229n9, 232n29
Himes, Chester, 2, 12, 13, 19, 23, 36, 44, 48, 87, 89–90, 94–107, 114, 116, 217n15, 224n5, 225n13, 225n14, 225n15, 225n16, 226n17, 226n19, 226n21, 226n22; *Cast the First Stone* 2, 19, 87, 90, 91, 93–107, 109, 114, 116, 127, 129, 225n14; *If He Hollers Let Him Go,* 36; *Yesterday Will Make You Cry,* 90, 94–107
Holladay, Hilary, 56, 69, 76–77, 220n1
Holland, Sharon, 115, 227n32
Holmes, Eugene, 214n19
home (*also* domesticity, domestic space, domestic sphere, house), 6, 9–10, 12, 19–20, 27–28, 30, 34, 36, 40, 52, 54, 56–85 passim, 88, 93, 114–15, 121, 124–25, 133, 135–37, 139–40, 147–48, 153, 175–77, 184, 187, 197, 199, 203–4, 211n3, 214n16, 2221n5, 221n6, 224n26, 229n10, 231n23, 238n4, 239n15
"Homecoming, The." *See* Yerby, Frank
homoraciality, 87, 88, 111,117. *See also* heteronormative; heteropatriarchy
homosexuality (*also* homoerotic, queer), 19, 52, 86–129 passim, 225n10
"How and Why I Write the Costume Novel." *See* Yerby, Frank
"How It Feels To be Colored Me." *See* Hurston, Zora Neale
Howe, Irving, 22, 25, 49, 216n4
Hughes, Langston, 3, 11, 22, 31–32, 34, 37, 49, 212n6, 218n19
Hull-House Magazine, 36
Hurston, Zora Neale, 2, 5, 7, 13, 18, 20–21, 22, 24–26, 40, 44–48, 49, 51, 106, 158–81, 213n11, 216n4, 219n30, 219n31, 233n1, 233n2, 233n4, 233n5, 233n9, 233n10, 234n11, 234n13, 234n15, 234n16, 234–35n17, 236n22, 236n24, 236n25, 237n31, 237n32; "How It Feels To be Colored Me," 162, 236n25; *Seraph on the Suwanee,* 2, 20–21, 158–81 passim, 233n2, 233n5, 234n15, 235n17, 236n24; *Their Eyes Were Watching God,* 158, 159, 163, 235n17, 236n25; "What White Publishers Won't Print," 5, 44–48, 233n10

I Am Not Sidney Poitier. See Everett, Percival
incitement to racial discourse, 8, 40, 48, 52–53, 205
"In Darkness and Confusion." *See* Petry, Ann
International Literature, 35
Invisible Man. See Ellison, Ralph

Jackson, Blyden, 1, 12–13, 130, 146, 156–57, 214n23
Jackson, Chuck, 234n15
Jackson, Lawrence. 18, 23, 33, 212n4, 217n9, 217n14, 220n35
James, C.L.R., 183
Jarrett, Gene, 215n28, 228–29n3
Jarrett, Thomas, 131
Jenkins, Candice, 9
John Reed Club, The, 35, 229n5
Johnson, Amelia E., 4, 213n9
Johnson, Charles, 41, 47
Johnson, James Weldon, 208
Jones, Jacqueline, 221n4
Juneteenth. See Ellison, Ralph

Kaplan, Carla, 159
Knock on Any Door. See Motley, Willard
Kinsey, Alfred C., 93
Kristeva, Julia, 103, 136, 226n17, 230n11
Kunzel, Regina, 93–94, 225n6

Larsen, Nella, 91, 225n7
League of American Writers, 31, 35, 133, 217n14
Lee, Ulysses, 12
Left Front, 35
Let No Man Write My Epitaph. See Motley, Willard
Lipsitz, George (*also* possessive investment in whiteness), 7, 82, 114, 221n6, 224n23
Locke, Alain, 12, 39, 218n19
Lott, Eric, 133, 216n31, 229n4
Lowe, John, 233n2, 233n5
Lubin, Alex, 57, 58, 220n1, 221n6

"Male Prison, The." *See* Baldwin, James
male. *See* manhood
man. *See* manhood
manhood (*also* male, man, masculinity), 6, 20, 50, 80, 81–82, 88–157 passim, 187, 220n36, 230n13; American, 87, 88, 117,

119–20, 132, 138, 140–46; black, 14, 15, 20, 105, 106, 117–23, 132–33, 135–37, 141–45, 149–57, 168, 183, 192, 224n5, 226n16, 231n24, 232n30, 236n24, 238n6; Organization Man, 7, 21, 238n4; "patriarchal institution," 147; white, 6, 8, 10, 19–20, 68, 79, 82, 88–89, 97, 106, 114, 116, 117, 119–20, 123, 125, 130–57 passim, 163, 184, 195–201, 202, 223n22, 229n3, 231n24, 234n13, 237n31, 238n6
masculinity. *See* manhood
Maxwell, William, 34, 217n10, 217n12
May, Elaine Tyler, 147, 221n6
Meisenhelder, Susan, 233n2, 234–35n17
McBride, Dwight, 86–87
McKay, Claude, 34, 91, 225n7
Miller, D.A., 225n12
Milliken, Stephen F, 96–97
Mitchell, Burroughs, 162, 233n9
Mitchell, Margaret, 1, 20, 130, 132, 134, 139–42, 144, 148, 151, 153–54, 156, 168, 229–30n10, 232n26, 233n33; *Gone with the Wind*, 1, 20, 130, 131, 134, 144, 148, 156, 229n8, 229n10, 232n33
momism, 80
Moon, Bucklin, 4, 233n10
Morrison, Toni, 160–62, 215n28, 216n31
motherhood (*also* mother, mothering, mother domination), 57–59, 64, 67, 74, 77–82, 88, 118, 125–27, 136, 146, 151, 159, 177, 187–88, 191, 195–97, 199–200, 207, 224n22, 231n23. *See also* womanhood
Motley, Willard, 2, 7, 11, 12, 19, 26, 31, 36–38, 44, 87–92, 107–16, 182, 211n3, 212n6, 217n17, 224n4, 226n22, 226n24, 226n26, 226n27, 226n29, 227n30; *Knock on Any Door*, 2, 12, 19, 31, 87–92, 93, 107–16, 129, 221n3; *Let No Man Write My Epitaph*, 211n3; *We Fished All Night*, 211n3
Mullen, Bill, 29–30, 34–35, 36, 212n4, 212n6, 217n10, 217n12, 217n18, 229n8
Muller, Gilbert, 96–97
Mumford, Kevin, 112, 222n9
Murphy, Geraldine, 117–18, 220n35
Myrdal, Gunnar, 39, 40, 41–45, 47, 48, 54, 57, 84–85, 92, 192, 218n21, 218n22, 219n28; *American Dilemma, An (AAD)*, 39, 40, 41–45, 84–85, 92, 218n21, 218n22, 219n26

Narrows, The. See Petry, Ann
Native Son. See Wright, Richard
negro problem, the, 5, 7, 10, 14, 21, 23–25, 28, 37, 39–42, 44–52, 54, 57, 131, 145, 157, 162, 164, 171, 183–84, 190, 192, 198, 201, 203, 205, 220n36, 224n26
Negro Story, 36
negro writer (*also* negro literature and negro writing), 5, 8, 10, 11–13, 18, 21, 23–25, 31, 37, 39, 44, 46, 48, 49–50, 53, 76, 109, 131, 182, 189, 202, 203, 205, 209, 214n19, 214n23, 215n24, 218n19, 237n32
New Anvil, 36, 133, 211n1
New Challenge, 35
New Leader, 39, 117
New Masses, 35, 222n15
New Negro, The, 39
New South, the 2, 20–21, 131, 134, 160, 163–64, 166–72, 174, 176, 179–81, 230n10, 236n19
Notes of a Native Son. See Baldwin, James
Nugent, Bruce, 91, 225n7

O'Hara, Maureen, 1
Osucha, Eden, 214n16
Outsider, The. See Wright, Richard
Overstreet, Harry, 23–24, 49, 216n3

Page, Thomas Nelson, 134, 168, 230n16
Pagan Spain. See Wright, Richard
Partisan Review, 35, 39, 50, 117
"Party Down at the Square, A." *See* Ellison, Ralph
People's Voice, 35, 217n13
pet negro, 159, 168–69
Petry, Ann, 2, 7, 9, 11, 19, 23, 26, 31, 35–38, 55–85, 195, 214n18, 220–21n1, 222n15, 222n16, 222–23n18, 223n19, 224n25, 224n26, 228n38, 231n18; "Bones of Louella Brown, The," 19, 57, 59, 65–73, 74, 84, 85, 222n13; *Country Place* 2, 19, 56, 73–85, 195, 221n1, 222n15, 223n19, 225n25, 228n38; "In Darkness and Confusion," 19, 57, 59–65, 84, 85, 231n18; *Narrows, The*, 56; *Street, The*, 85
Pettigrew, Thomas, 41
Phylon, 11, 13, 32, 234n14
plantation romance. *See* southern historical romance

PM, 35, 217n13, 218n20
Popular Front, 18, 20, 26, 33–38, 52, 111, 114, 116–18, 132–33, 137–40, 143, 211n1, 212n3, 212n6, 217n10, 220n36, 229n8, 239n13
Posnock, Ross, 3
"Preservation of Innocence." *See* Baldwin, James
Price of the Ticket, The. *See* Baldwin, James
privacy (*also* private, private sphere), 8–10, 19, 21, 24–25, 38, 48–49, 51–54, 55–85, 87–89, 91, 102, 107–9, 112, 117, 121, 123–25, 129, 133, 136, 145, 153, 156, 160, 181, 182–84, 186–87, 189, 192, 197–201, 202–210, 213n8, 213–14n16, 214n17, 214n18, 221n1, 221n3, 221n5, 222n10, 222n13, 222n14, 226n27, 230n14, 238n4
protest (*also* protest fiction, protest literature, social realism), 1–2, 6–9, 13, 18–19, 21, 23, 25–26, 31, 36–40, 44, 48, 50–54, 56–57, 60, 63, 74, 76, 115–16, 118, 120, 130–34, 138, 141, 145–46, 149, 151, 154, 156–57, 159–160, 162, 164, 166, 180, 182, 202, 205, 215n24, 220n34, 220n36, 228n2, 229n9, 230n13, 230n13, 232n30, 234n13, 237n32
public (*also* publicity, publics, reading public), 6, 8, 10, 14, 19, 24, 26, 32–33, 35, 40, 46, 57–77 passim, 80, 85, 90, 91, 98, 100–3, 106, 110, 112, 114, 116–17, 125, 129, 145, 153, 160, 162, 171, 179, 189, 194, 202–9, passim, 213n8, 214n19, 221n5, 222n10, 222n13, 222n14, 226n27, 230n14, 236n24

queer, 2, 6, 9, 15, 19–20, 42, 81, 84, 86–129, 215n27, 225n12, 225n16, 226n17, 226n20, 227n30, 227n31, 227n32, 238n4, 239n16. *See also* gay; heteronormative

Rai, Amit, 17
Rascoe, Burton, 213n11
Redding, J. Saunders, 12, 32, 214n21
Reid-Pharr, Robert, 115
religion, 21, 37–38, 51, 80, 108, 111, 119, 134, 170, 176, 182–84, 186, 188, 195–201, passim, 214n16, 224n25, 237n27, 239n12, 239n13
Reynolds, Paul, 183, 189
Riesman, David, 88–89, 224n2

"Roads Going Down." *See* Yerby, Frank
Roediger, David, 15–16, 28, 38, 69–70, 216n31, 216n5
Roosevelt, Franklin Delanor, 12, 30, 34
Ross, Marlon, 86–7, 91–92, 100, 115, 117, 224n1, 225n9, 225n15, 226n20, 227n31

Sartre, Jean-Paul, 183, 193, 217n11
Saxton, Alexander, 36
Saturday Review of Literature, 23–24, 146
Savage Holiday. *See* Wright, Richard
Schlesinger, Arthur, 119, 127, 230n13
Scott, Daryl Michael, 41, 92, 219n24, 219n25, 222n9, 225n8, 231n24
Seaver, Edwin, 36, 217n14
Sedgwick, Eve Kosofsky, 87, 104, 114, 227n31
segregation, 4–6, 9–11, 28–30, 68, 105, 109–10, 113–14, 134–35, 148, 166, 169, 213n11, 219n24, 227n29, 233n8
Senghor, Léopold Sédar, 183
Seraph on the Suwanee. *See* Hurston, Zora Neale
Shadow and Act. *See* Ellison, Ralph
Singh, Nikhil Pal, 27–29, 43, 218n21, 219n25, 219n27, 233n7
slavery (*also* slave), 1, 6, 10–13, 17, 20–21, 41, 47–48, 50, 52, 63, 80, 102, 113, 130, 131–57, passim, 170–71, 175–76, 179, 182, 184, 197–99, 202, 214n22, 222n10, 230n10, 230n16, 231n19, 231n25, 232n26, 232n28, 232n32, 232n33, 233n9, 237n28, 239n10
Smith, William Gardner, 183, 211n3; *Anger at Innocence*, 211n3
social realism. *See* protest
social sciences (*also* psychology and sociology), 10, 26–27, 39–41, 44, 52, 57, 80, 88, 93, 186, 193, 195, 199, 215n29, 217n8, 219n24, 220n35, 220n36, 223n20, 224n26, 231n24
Solove, Daniel, 213–14n16, 221n3
Somerville, Siobhan, 225n16, 226n20
South, the (southern), 1–2, 20, 28, 32, 42–43, 62, 130–81 passim, 185, 213n7, 214n18, 215n25, 228–29n2, 229–30n10, 230n12, 230n16, 231n19, 232n33, 233n9, 234n11, 234n12, 234n14, 234n16, 234–35n17, 236n18, 236n19, 236n22, 236n23, 236n24, 237n28, 237n29

Southern historical romance (*also* plantation romance), 1–2, 20–21, 130–57, passim, 163, 165, 168–69, 179, 228n1, 228–29n3, 229–30n10, 230n12, 232n33
Suggs, Jon-Christian, 214n16
Street, The. *See* Petry, Ann
Stowe, Harriet Beecher, 50–51, 89, 118
sympathy, 2–3, 6–8, 16–21, 23–24, 37–38, 46–52, 54, 55–57, 60, 63–65, 67, 71, 74, 83–85, 89, 103–5, 110, 113, 123, 131–39, 146, 154, 156, 157, 160, 163, 169, 180, 181, 200–201, 202–3, 210, 212n3, 216n33, 218n20, 221n1, 222n16, 224n24, 233n2, 234n11, 235n17

Tate, Claudia, 3, 74, 179, 213n8, 233n2, 238n4
Their Eyes Were Watching God. *See* Hurston, Zora Neale
Thurman, Wallace, 91, 225n7
Tomorrow, 36, 133, 211n1
Toomer, Jean, 22
Turner, Darwin, 131, 228n2, 229n9

Uncle Tom's Children. *See* Wright, Richard

Vesala-Varttala, Tanja, 17

Wald, Alan, 36, 90, 217n10, 224n4
Walker, Alice, 158–59, 160, 165
Walker, Margaret, 12
Warner, Michael, 114, 222n10
Warren, Kenneth, 11, 131, 214n18, 220n33, 239n2
Washington, Booker T., 169–71, 176, 203, 236n24
Washington, Mary Helen, 158, 219n32
We Fished All Night. *See* Motley, Willard
West, Dorothy, 11, 35, 214n20
"What White Publishers Won't Print." *See* Hurston, Zora Neale
whiteness 3, 6–9, 14–16, 19, 21, 25–29, 40, 54, 59, 69–71, 82–85, 91, 93, 105, 109, 132, 142, 160–61, 190, 194, 201–2, 209–10, 211n2, 212n6, 213n8, 213n14, 214n16, 215n29, 216n31, 216n5, 216n6, 216n17, 221n6, 224n23, 229n3, 229n10, 234n15, 236n20, 237n31, 238n4. *See also* crackers; white American manhood; white liberal; white privacy; white supremacy

white liberal, 7, 18, 21, 39–40, 47, 49–54, 201, 213n11, 219n20
"White Magnolias." *See* Yerby, Frank
White Man, Listen! See Wright, Richard
white privacy, 9–10, 54, 89, 202, 214n18
white suffering, 6–7, 19–20, 76, 83, 110, 129, 145, 184, 224n24
white supremacy, 6, 8–10, 15–16, 65, 72, 131, 134, 136, 142, 145, 179, 238n6
Wiegman, Robyn, 213n13, 239n3
Wilkerson, Doxey, 214n19
Wispé, Lauren, 117
womanhood (*also* female, motherhood, woman), 79–81, 146, 166, 175, 231n23; black, 58, 65, 71, 136, 143, 153, 196, 199, 224n26, 231n23, 231n24, 232n30, 236n24; white, 137, 139–40, 147, 199, 230n14
World War II (*also* Second World War), 2, 4, 10, 12, 26–30, 34, 38, 70, 77, 80, 91–92, 132–33, 140, 147, 160–61, 167, 172, 182, 221n6, 223n19, 228n1, 231n17
Wright, Charles, 114
Wright, Richard, 1–2, 7, 9, 13, 21–25, 31, 36–38, 44, 49–50, 53–54, 75, 106–7, 118, 152, 163, 165, 182–201, 205, 207, 209, 212n6, 214n19, 215n28, 216n4, 218n19, 220n36, 223n21, 234n11, 237n1, 238n2, 238n4, 238n5, 238n6, 238n7, 238n8, 238n9, 239n11, 239n12, 239n13, 239n14, 239n17; *Black Boy*, 22, 163, 184, 191, 216n4, 234n11; *Native Son*, 7, 9, 22–23, 36, 39, 50, 53, 107, 184, 191, 194, 201, 205, 207–9, 216n4, 217n13, 217n18, 227n36, 230n12; *Outsider, The*, 21, 186–87, 190–97, 201, 216n2, 238n3, 238n4; *Pagan Spain*, 182–83, 238n2, 238n3; *Savage Holiday*, 2, 21, 182–201, passim, 209, 215n28, 216n2, 223n21, 238n3, 238n4, 238n6, 239n12, 239n13, 239n16; *Uncle Tom's Children*, 163; *White Man, Listen!*, 53, 182, 186
Wylie, Philip, 80

Yerby, Frank, 1–2, 11–12, 20, 26, 31, 36–38, 130–57, 182, 211n1, 211n3, 212–13n7, 214n22, 215n28, 228n1, 228n2, 228–29n3, 229n6, 229n9, 230n12, 230n13, 230n14, 230n15, 231n19, 231n20, 231n21, 231n24, 231n25, 232n26, 232n28, 232n29,

232n30, 232n33; "Health Card," 133, 137, 211n1; "Homecoming, The," 36, 135–36; "How and Why I Write the Costume Novel," 133–34, 137–38, 146–47; *Dahomean, The*, 212n7, 230n12; *Foxes of Harrow, The*, 1, 20, 31, 36, 130–57, passim, 215n28, 228n1, 229n3, 229n9, 230n12, 230n14, 230n15; "Roads Going Down," 36, 136; "White Magnolias," 137
Yesterday Will Make You Cry. See Himes, Chester

About the Author

John C. Charles is an assistant professor in English and Africana Studies at North Carolina State University in Raleigh.

www.ingramcontent.com/pod-product-compliance
Lightning Source LLC
Chambersburg PA
CBHW032003220426
43664CB00005B/118